JUSTIFICATION BY FAITH

SUPPLEMENTS TO
NOVUM TESTAMENTUM

VOLUME LXVIII

JUSTIFICATION BY FAITH

*The Origin and Development of
a Central Pauline Theme*

BY

MARK A. SEIFRID

E.J. BRILL
LEIDEN • NEW YORK • KÖLN
1992

The paper in this book meets the guidelines for permanence and durability of the Committee on Production Guidelines for Book Longevity of the Council on Library Resources.

Library of Congress Cataloging-in-Publication Data

Seifrid, Mark A.
 Justification by faith: the origin and development of a central
Pauline theme / by Mark A. Seifrid.
   p.   cm.—(Supplements to Novum Testamentum, ISSN 0167-9732;
v. 68)
 Includes bibliographical references and index.
 ISBN 9004095217 (alk. paper)
 1. Justification—Biblical teaching. 2. Bible. N.T. Epistles of
Paul—Criticism, interpretation, etc. I. Title. II. Series.
BS2655.J8S45   1992
234'.7'09015—dc20   91-41298
                                                              CIP

ISSN 0167-9732
ISBN 90 04 09521 7

Typeset by IMPRINT OXFORD

PRINTED IN THE NETHERLANDS

IN MEMORIAM

Arthur Martin Seifrid
1920-1961

TABLE OF CONTENTS

ACKNOWLEDGMENTS

I am indebted to a number of individuals and institutions for assistance I have received in carrying out this investigation. Early stages of the work were completed during a rewarding period of study in Tübingen, made possible by a grant from the *Deutscher Akademischer Austauschdienst*. Prof. Dr. Peter Stuhlmacher provided invaluable advice both during this visit, and in subsequent conversation. My wife and I remain grateful to Albrecht-Bengel-Haus, to its *Hausmutter*, Ingerose Finkbeiner, and to its Rektor, Dr. Gerhard Maier, not only for providing us with a place to stay, but also for the warm Christian fellowship and support which we found there. Prof. J. H. Charlesworth's insistence on close attention to early Jewish materials was of great help to me. I would be remiss if I did not express my appreciation to Don Carson, for his fine articulation of the Biblical tension between divine sovereignty and human responsibility, which has had a fundamental influence on my thinking. I am especially thankful to Prof. J. Christiaan Beker for his encouragement. In considerable measure, his approach to Paul has shaped this study.

ABBREVIATIONS

AGJU	Arbeiten zur Geschichte des antiken Judentums und des Urchristentums
ALGHJ	Arbeiten zur Literatur und Geschichte des hellenistischen Judentums
AnBib	Analecta Biblica
ANRW	*Aufstieg und Niedergang der römischen Welt*
ATANT	Abhandlungen zur Theologie des Alten und Neuen Testaments
AusBR	*Australian Biblical Review*
BDR	F. Blass, A. Debrunner, and F. Rehkopf, *Grammatik des neutestamentlichen Griechisch*
BETL	Bibliotheca ephemeridum theologicarum lovaniensium
BEvT	Beiträge zur evangelischen Theologie BHT Beiträge zur historischen Theologie
BJRL	*Bulletin of the John Rylands University Library of Manchester*
BJS	Brown Judaic Studies
BWANT	Beiträge zur Wissenschaft vom Alten und Neuen Testament
BZNW	Beihefte zur *Zeitschrift für die neutestamentliche Wissenschaft*
CahRB	Cahiers de la Revue Biblique
CBQ	*Catholic Biblical Quarterly*
CCWJCW	Cambridge Commentary on Writings of the Jewish and Christian World 200 BC to AD 200
CRINT	Compendia rerum iudaicarum ad novum testamentum
EKKNT	Evangelisch-katholischer Kommentar zum Neuen Testament
EvT	*Evangelische Theologie*
ExpT	*Expository Times*
FB	*Forschung zur Bibel*
FRLANT	Forschungen zur Religion und Literatur des Alten und Neuen Testaments
GTA	Göttinger Theologische Arbeiten

HDR	Harvard Dissertations in Religion
HNT	Handbuch zum Neuen Testament
HSS	Harvard Semitic Studies
HTKNT	Herders theologischer Kommentar zum Neuen Testament
HTR	*Harvard Theological Review*
ICC	International Critical Commentary
IEJ	*Israel Exploration Journal*
Int	*Interpretation*
JAAR	*Journal of the American Academy of Religion*
JBL	*Journal of Biblical Literature*
JJS	*Journal of Jewish Studies*
JSHRZ	Jüdische Schriften aus hellenistisch-römischer Zeit
JSJ	*Journal for the Study of Judaism in the Persian, Hellenistic and Roman Period*
JSNT	*Journal for the Study of the New Testament*
JSNTSup	*Journal for the Study of the New Testament* Supplement Series
JTS	*Journal of Theological Studies*
KEK	Kritisch-exegetischer Kommentar über das Neue Testament
KuD	*Kerygma und Dogma*
LEC	Library of Early Christianity
MTS	Marburger Theologische Studien
NIGTC	The New International Greek Testament Commentary
NovT	*Novum Testamentum*
NovTSup	*Novum Testamentum* Supplements
NTS	*New Testament Studies*
NTTS	New Testament Tools and Studies
OBO	Orbis biblicus et orientalis
PVTG	Pseudepigrapha Veteris Testamenti Graece
RB	*Revue Biblique*
RevQ	*Revue de Qumran*
RGG	*Religion in Geschichte und Gegenwart*
RHPR	*Revue d'histoire et de philosophie religieuses*
RNT	Regensburger Neues Testament
SANT	Studien zum Alten und Neuen Testament
SBLDS	Society of Biblical Literature Dissertation Series
SBLMS	Society of Biblical Literature Monograph Series
SBLSCS	Society of Biblical Literature Septuagint and Cognate Studies
SBT	Studies in Biblical Theology

SD	Studies and Documents
SHT	Studies in Historical Theology
SJLA	Studies in Judaism in Late Antiquity
SNT	Studien zum Neuen Testament
SNTSMS	Studiorum Novi Testamenti Societas Monograph Series
SR	*Studies in Religion/Sciences religieuses*
ST	*Studia Theologica*
STDJ	Studies on the Texts of the Desert of Judah
SUNT	Studien zur Umwelt des Neuen Testaments
TLZ	*Theologische Literaturzeitung*
TrinJ	*Trinity Journal*
TToday	*Theology Today*
TU	Texte und Untersuchungen
TZBas	*Theologische Zeitschrift*
USQR	*Union Seminary Quarterly Review*
UUÅ	*Uppsala Universitets Årsskrift*
WBC	Word Biblical Commentary
WdF	Wege der Forschung
WMANT	Wissenschaftliche Monographien zum Alten und Neuen Testament
WTJ	*Westminster Theological Journal*
WUNT	Wissenschaftliche Untersuchungen zum Neuen Testament
WW	*Word and World*
ZNW	*Zeitschrift für die neutestamentliche Wissenschaft*
ZThK	*Zeitschrift für Theologie und Kirche*

CHAPTER ONE

THE PLACE OF JUSTIFICATION BY FAITH
IN PAUL'S THOUGHT:
BASIC LINES OF INTERPRETATION

I. AN ORIENTATION TO THE PROBLEM AND
THE METHOD OF THIS STUDY

What role does 'justification by faith' play in Paul's thought? Does
it express the heart and essence of Paul's Gospel, as had been
assumed in Protestant scholarship from the time of the Reformers
well into the nineteenth century? Or is it a subsidiary concern,
formulated merely for the purpose of answering the charges of
Paul's adversaries? Historical research into Paul from the post-
Baur period until the present may be characterized by the various
answers given to these questions. Moreover, despite the advances
which the past 120 years have seen in the elucidation of Paul's
religious environment, scholars have not moved much closer to a
consensus on how 'justification by faith' is to be interpreted.

The current disagreement over the importance of this theme to
Paul stems in part from the tension between historical exegesis and
theological interpretation. Striving to be true to both concerns has
not proved easy, not only for those who have construed 'justification'
as the 'center' of Paul's thought, but also for those who minimize its
role. Twice in the modern era of research into Paul, in the work of
Baur and later in that of Bultmann, 'justification by faith' has been
accorded a central position in Paul's theology on the basis of an
overarching understanding of human existence. But Baur's idealistic conception of history as the progress of the collective human consciousness quickly fell away in the later nineteenth century, which
saw an increasing interest in the concrete reality of the Hellenistic
world as a basis for explaining Paul. And the post- Bultmannian era
has seen the rise of dissatisfaction with the limitations imposed by an
analysis of Pauline theology in terms of the self-understanding of the
individual. For most interpreters, the jagged edge of Paul's apocalyptic world-view, with its cosmic and universal dimension, is far too
prominent to allow an existential reading of Paul.

Yet the alternatives to Bultmann's interpretation of 'justification' which have been offered have failed to satisfy the demand for a reading of Paul which is both historically accurate and logically coherent. Although it commands a very large following, we shall see that Käsemann's line of thought—in which 'justification' is treated as the pinnacle of an apocalyptically-oriented theology—carries some serious flaws.[1] By positing a religio-historical background to Paul's understanding of justification (the apocalyptic motif of the 'righteousness of God'), Käsemann avoids the use of systematic abstractions for maintaining the centrality of the concept. Nevertheless, his attempt to gather the whole of Pauline theology under the umbrella of 'God's obedience-creating righteousness' glosses over some unexplained elements of Paul's thought.

Another difficulty inheres in the attempts of William Wrede, Albert Schweitzer, and E. P. Sanders to assert a 'participationistic' understanding of salvation as the central feature of Paul's theology. The formula of 'participation,' or 'being in Christ' as these scholars have presented it, cannot account for the paradox which exists between Paul's positive statements about salvation and the demands which he places alongside them. In so far as these scholars attempt to describe a theme which comprehends the whole of Paul's theology, they fail to reach their goal.

As these brief reflections indicate, the discussion concerning the place of 'justification by faith' in Paul's thought has been carried out largely in terms of a quest for a thematic 'center' from which the whole of Paul's theology may be deduced or explained. This statement applies not only to the various scholars named above, who have sought to show in one way or another that 'justification' or 'participation' ought to be regarded as the 'center' of Paul's thought. It also fits the various attempts to show that no coherent theological 'center' for Paul's thought may be found, and that instead Paul's 'experience of Christ' must serve as an interpretive *Mitte*.[2] Such attempts inevitably fall back on systematic and deductive analysis of Paul's thought in order to highlight its 'self-contradictory' elements.

Many scholars, especially in North America, have rightly called into question attempts, past and present, to demonstrate or contest

---

[1] See below, Section V and Chapter 2, Section II, Excursus.

[2] E.g. H. J. Holtzmann, *Lehrbuch der neutestamentlichen Theologie*, 2 vols. (Freiburg i. B.: J. C. B. Mohr [Paul Siebeck], 1897); G. A. Deissmann, *Paulus: Eine kultur und religionsgeschichtliche Skizze*[2] (Tübingen: J. C. B. Mohr [Paul Siebeck], 1925); or more recently, Heikki Räisänen, *Paul and the Law* (Philadelphia: Fortress, 1986).

the theological unity of Paul's thought which diminish the task of historical description. The letters of Paul which have been preserved are directed toward diverse and particular situations. They exhibit a wide range of subject matter and varying arguments. Explanatory connections between important topics are lacking on the whole: e.g. between forensic justification and final judgment, between participatory and juridical aspects of salvation, between salvation and ethics. Moreover, Paul's statements concerning crucial issues, e.g. the role of *Torah*, undergo significant shifts from letter to letter. As a result, when the formulation (or denial) of a theologically comprehensive 'center' is given priority over the historical task, theological concern tends to obscure the particular circumstances which occasioned and shaped Paul's arguments. In practice, the relationship between (historical) analysis and (theological) synthesis is necessarily reciprocal, since Paul perceived situations 'theologically.' But the aim of producing or disputing a theological summary must not ignore the historical dimension if it is to be true to the Paul who directed letters to specific situations. When Paul wrote, he regarded his arguments to be coherent for the purposes for which he intended them. Whether or not Paul *was* coherent is another matter. The interpreter has an obligation first to understand Paul and the aims of his arguments, before going on to pass judgment on how successful he was in carrying them out. To use J. Christiaan Beker's formulation, Paul was not a systematic theologian, but an interpreter of the Gospel and, one might add, an interpreter of the Scriptures which were his as a Jew.[3] He was not concerned nor did he have a need to draw up his beliefs in a tidy outline. Coupled with this observation is the fact that modern readers of Paul often do not participate in his presuppositions, and would encounter gaps in the pattern of his arguments, no matter how effective and coherent Paul might have been to his initial audiences. Thus a great amount of inductive work is necessary, and the acknowledgment of logical 'breaks' in the reconstruction of a coherent scheme of Paul's thought is inevitable.

If the preceding considerations are valid, an analysis of the role of 'justification' in Paul's thought should not be treated as a question of a theological 'center.' This assertion is not meant to deny the legitimacy of seeking a coherent structure to Paul's theology. It is rather intended to suggest that it is useful to suspend the quest for

---

[3] J. Christiaan Beker, 'Paul the Theologian: Major Motifs in Pauline Theology,' *Int* 43 (1989):353.

a theological 'center' in favor of determining how Paul came to contend for a justification by faith in Christ, and the manner in which his arguments involving this theme are employed.

The question of the origin of Paul's conception of 'justification' naturally leads to an examination of the nature of Paul's coming to faith in Christ. There is a widespread tendency in the current discussion to minimize the soteriological ramifications of the change in Paul's views in favor of its christological dimension. Paul, it is thought, came to believe in Jesus as Messiah—even as Savior of both Jew and Gentile—but did not substantially reflect on the relation of this affirmation to *Torah* until later conflicts with Judaizers arose. In large part, the present hesitancy to ascribe a soteriological element to Paul's adoption of faith in Christ stems from the work of E. P. Sanders. Sanders has demolished the illegitimate picture of 'life under the Law', one of uncertainty regarding a salvation obtained by merit, upon which the *Religionsgeschichtliche* portraits of Paul (and Liberal ones before them) rested. As a result, it seems that no soteriological category for understanding the transformation of Paul's thought remains. If Paul knew of God's grace and mercy prior to faith in Jesus as Messiah, what new idea, in terms of the dynamics of salvation, could his decision to believe have brought to him?

Nevertheless, a number of nagging issues bring into question the legitimacy of dismissing all soteriology from Paul's adoption of faith in Christ. In much the same manner as the *Religionsgeschichtliche* interpreters of Paul did, the effect of Paul's new belief on his earlier devotion to *Torah* has been frequently ignored in recent discussion. Yet Paul's change from persecutor to proclaimer of faith in Christ clearly involved a reordering of his understanding of *Torah*, and hence of his soteriology. For this reason alone it is legitimate to describe his coming to faith as a conversion.[4] Furthermore, while Sanders's widely-accepted critique of Protestant scholarship brings important criticisms to bear upon scholars of the late nineteenth and early twentieth centuries, it can be shown that he fundamentally misunderstands Bultmann's interpretation of Paul. As a result, important matters concerning Paul's pre- and postconversion understanding of salvation remain unaddressed. Moreover, we shall see in our discussion of Sanders's work, that an adequate description of Paul's conversion must give further attention to early Jewish sources in which apocalyptic eschatology is prominent. There are good reasons, then, for reexamining Paul's conversion and its relation to his understanding of 'justification.'

---

[4] See the discussion of this issue in Chapter 3, Section I.

The following survey of the interpreters of Paul who have set the stage for the present discussion of 'justification by faith' will highlight the need, both past and present, for an adequate treatment of Paul's conversion in its soteriological dimension. Chapters Two and Three represent a fresh attempt to reconstruct the meaning of Paul's conversion for his understanding of salvation.

In Chapter Four, we will develop another element of a historical description of 'justification,' an analysis of its function in Paul's letter to Rome. A distinction between Paul's 'thought,' i.e. the concepts and beliefs to which he himself adhered, and the arguments which he adopts only for the sake of his audience, has been repeatedly used as an interpretive tool. Yet little attention has been given to providing an appropriate criterion for distinguishing between Paul's beliefs and his *ad hominem* rhetoric. Frequently, and with some validity, it has been tacitly assumed that the origin of Paul's concept of 'justification,' may reveal its importance to him. Beyond this consideration, the guidelines which interpreters have offered generally derive from the order of Paul's arguments and the extent to which arguments on forensic justification show coherent connections to other aspects of his thought. It is doubtful however, that isolated and contingent arguments *alone* reveal Paul's convictions. It is better to proceed by reconstructing Paul's purpose in composing a letter, since his aim in writing represents his missionary concerns, and hence a point of reference from which to evaluate the importance which he attached to 'justification by faith.' Paul's letter to Rome is the natural focal point for such an investigation. Since it represents Paul's fullest and final expression of the theme of 'justification by faith,' it provides the boundary marker for the development of Paul's thought on the concept.

There is a further reason for giving attention to Romans. It is generally agreed that Paul's aim in Galatians is polemical. He seeks to defend the freedom of his Gentile converts from circumcision and adherence to the Law. It is difficult to discern whether such a battle-oriented statement on 'justification' was intended only for the purpose of refuting an adversary, or if it had wider significance for Paul. It is clear that 'justification' is a polemical teaching. The question is whether it is only this, and nothing more. An examination of Romans provides the opportunity to assess the significance which 'justification by faith' held for Paul at a mature stage of his thinking, and as we shall see in Chapter Four, apart from polemics.

The following survey of research, in addition to describing the role which important interpreters of Paul have assigned to 'justification by faith,' will serve two further purposes. First, we will examine the validity of alternatives to 'justification' as the 'center' of Paul's thought. The readings of Paul offered by Wrede, Schweitzer, and Sanders depict Paul's soteriology as based on *naturhaft* or participatory conceptions in a manner which excludes the possibility that forensic justification might be regarded as playing an important role in his theology. One of the appeals of such construals of Paul's thought is the logical link which, it is suggested, may be drawn between this understanding of Paul's soteriology and his ethics. We will examine this claim in the course of this chapter, giving particular attention to the well-known tension between the Pauline 'indicative' and 'imperative.'

Secondly, since Ernst Käsemann's entrance into the discussion of Pauline theology, the very nature of Paul's language regarding 'justification by faith' has been under debate. While Käsemann has made an important contribution in reasserting the inseparability of 'justification' and 'sanctification' for Paul, we shall see that for a variety of reasons it is best to regard these themes as *logically* and not *conceptually* inseparable for him. Consequently, we will direct our study toward defining the role a juridically conceived justification by faith has in Paul's thought. This is the issue which has been under contention in Protestant scholarship since the time of Baur.

II. PAUL AS AN INDEPENDENT THEOLOGIAN: WILLIAM WREDE

For a variety of reasons, William Wrede's *Paulus* (1904) provides an appropriate introduction to the present debate over the place of 'justification by faith' in Paul's thought. Like other adherents of the *Religionsgeschichtliche Schule* , Wrede bases his reconstruction of Paul on the premise that Paul's soteriology must be understood, according to the conceptions of Paul's day, in material terms. He also shares with other *religionsgeschichtliche* interpreters of Paul, such as Heitmüller and Bousset, a curious neglect of the effect of Paul's coming to faith on his commitment to *Torah*. He therefore provides a focal point for evaluating the earlier period of research.

Wrede also marks a new phase of the discussion. He decisively rejects the Liberal depreciation of Paul's speculative theology in favor of his religion: 'Seine Religion ist durchaus theologisch, seine Theologie ist seine Religion.'[5] Furthermore, in contrast to those who preceded him, Wrede asserts that the central element of

---

[5] William Wrede, 'Paulus,' in *Das Bild des Paulus in der neueren deutschen Forschung*, WdF 24, ed. K. H. Rengstorf (Darmstadt: Wissenschaftliche Buchgesellschaft, 1982), p. 42.

Paul's theology was not drawn from Paul's Hellenistic surroundings. Nor did it arise from apocalyptic Judaism, although from this source Paul received decisive formative influences. Rather, Paul is a starkly independent figure for Wrede, who by his own theological accomplishment made Christianity into an *Erlösungsreligion*.[6]

The resurrection of Paul's status as a theologian required that Wrede, unlike other interpreters of the *Religionsgeschichtliche Schule*, assess the place of 'justification' in Paul's theology. According to Wrede, 'justification' is Paul's *Kampfeslehre*, his polemical doctrine, composed for the purpose of refuting his opponents, but unimportant to his primary soteriology.

This proposal has set the terms for much of the current discussion. A review of Wrede's *Paulus* therefore supplies a chance to evaluate the viability of a position which continues in modified form to receive support.[7]

Although Wrede claims Paul as a theologian, he begins his description of Paul's theology with the qualification that:

> Niemals hat er ein System seiner Lehre entwickeln wollen, selbst im Römerbriefe nicht. Er schreibt immer als Missionar, Organisator und Volksredner, . . .[8]

Paul did not engage in deductive theological reasoning in the same manner as modern thinkers. His thought was determined rather by the casuistic methodology and allegorical *Schriftbeweise* of the Rabbinic schools.[9] Paul's lines of thought are therefore elastic, crossing and contradicting one another from letter to letter, and even from chapter to chapter. For Wrede, a certain portion of Paul's writings constitute the theology of another age, shaped by its peculiar patterns of thinking and practical concerns.

In Wrede's reading, the essence of Paul's theology, and thus of his soteriology, is the belief that the Son of God, a heavenly being, came to earth as a human and subsequently returned to heaven. This Son of God died as representative of the human *Gattung*, and

---

[6] Wrede, 'Paulus,' p. 69: Eine Erkenntnis allerersten Ranges aber war es, das Christentum als Religion mit eigenem Prinzipe d. h. als etwas völlig Neues zu erfassen.

[7] Important reviews of Wrede's work may be found in Albert Schweitzer, *Geschichte der Paulinischen Forschung von der Reformation bis auf die Gegenwart* (Tübingen: J. C. B. Mohr [Paul Siebeck], 1911), pp. 130–134; Rudolf Bultmann, 'Geschichte der Paulus-Forschung,' in *Das Paulusbild in der neueren deutschen Forschung*, WdF 24, ed. K. H. Rengstorf (Darmstadt: Wissenschaftliche Buchgesellschaft, 1982), pp. 324–326.

[8] Wrede, 'Paulus,' p. 41.

[9] Wrede, 'Paulus,' pp. 42–46.

with him died the whole of the race. The effects of Christ's death
are therefore actual. By this means humanity was delivered from
the 'flesh,' the material element of existence, and hence from
powers of this age: sin and death, angels and demons.

Paul makes no firm division between the ethical and the natural
or physical aspects of humanity. Redemption does not merely
bring ethical change, but an ontological change in human nature, from which ethical change results. The saving transformation
is 'real,' although the outward reality would become apparent only
at the imminent return of Christ.

While Paul's anticipation of the end was derived from Jewish
apocalyptic hopes, it was stripped of any vestiges of Jewish nationalism. Such hopes lie buried with the world of the 'flesh,' which
died with Christ.

Paul's thought furthermore, unlike that of Luther, is not based
on the individual, but on *Heilsgeschichte*, and particularly on the
turning point of the ages in the death and resurrection of Christ:

> Das Sterben mit Christus ist ein allgemeines Faktum, das sich an alle
> Gläubigen gleichmäßig vollzieht, kein mit besonderen Erfahrungen
> und Empfindungen verbundenes Erlebnis der einzelnen Seele.[10]

Faith, which appropriates this act of Christ, is simply obedient
acceptance of and agreement with the proclamation of this mo-
mentous event.[11]

As noted above, for Wrede, 'justification' is Paul's *Kampfeslehre*,
his polemical teaching, which he employs in defense of his more
basic ideas. The new religion of redemption had to be defended on
two fronts. On the one hand, the mission to the Gentiles had to be
kept free of the burden of Jewish practices. On the other, the
primacy of the Christian belief had to be secured over the whole
of Judaism. Paul's teaching on *Rechtfertigung* is nothing more than
the means of seeing that these two basic intentions are carried
out.[12]

Wrede therefore regards Paul's statements on 'justification' as
merely an outward form adopted for the purposes of arguing his
case:

> Gott rechtfertigt den Menschen 'umsonst,' aus 'Gnade.' Und dabei
> heißt 'rechtfertigen' nichts weiter, als daß er ihn von seiner Sünde

---

[10] Wrede, 'Paulus,' p. 62.
[11] Wrede, 'Paulus,' p. 61: 'Der Glaube ist ganz einfach gehorsame Annahme
und Bejahung der Predigt von der Erlösung. Die Überzeugung von ihrer Wahrheit stellt ohne weiteres jene mystische Verbindung mit Christus her, . . .'
[12] Wrede, 'Paulus,' p. 69

losspricht, ihm eben seine Gnade bedingungslos zuwendet, die sich der Glaube dann aneignet. D. h. der Ausdruck 'rechtfertigen' büßt seinen juristischen Sinn völlig ein, ja er schließt die juristische Vorstellung vom Verhältnis zwischen Mensch und Gott aus, oder er wird sachlich unpassend: der beste Beweiß, daß ihn Paulus nur um der jüdischen Lehre willen gewählt hat.[13]

Likewise, although Paul portrays the death of Christ in terms of Jewish sacrifice, this means only that it effects what the Jewish sacrifices were thought to effect, the forgiveness of sins.[14] Luther's question, of how the individual could know of forgiveness, is not Paul's question. Paul asks rather about the salvation of the whole of humanity and of the requirements for entrance into the Church.

Wrede explains the origin of Paul's religion of deliverance as arising from a combination of Paul's Jewish background and Paul's own creativity. The Hellenistic mystery religions suggested by Heitmüller find virtually no place in Wrede's reconstruction. Wrede likewise resists attempts to understand Paul solely against the backdrop of Judaism. Paul's theology is not merely the logical outworking of Paul's Jewish views under the influence of his conversion: Paul's references to his preconversion life reveal too little of the direction of Paul's thought at the time of his conversion to determine what the logical consequences of his conversion must have meant to him.[15] While his conversion may have facilitated the development of his Law-free Gospel, his mission among the Gentiles is the more likely cause for his having arrived at his understanding of *Rechtfertigung*. He may also have been influenced by the model of Hellenistic Jewish propaganda.[16]

Much of Wrede's resistance to deriving an interpretation of Paul on the basis of his Judaism is the result of Wrede's rejection of the Liberal portrait of Paul found in works such as that of Holtzmann: a Jewish Paul who agonized over his guilty conscience until at his conversion he came to the realization of divine grace. He rightly points out that there is no good evidence that Paul underwent such a struggle, 'Die Wahrheit ist: die Seelenkämpfe Luthers haben für dies Bild des Paulus Modell gestanden.'[17]

But this is not to say that Jewish ideas did not form a substantial part of Paul's thought according to Wrede. Paul must have believed in a heavenly being, a divine Christ, before he believed in

---

[13] Wrede 'Paulus,' p. 71.
[14] Wrede, 'Paulus,' pp. 72–3.
[15] Wrede, 'Paulus,' p. 79.
[16] Wrede, 'Paulus,' p. 37.
[17] Wrede, 'Paulus,' p. 79.

Jesus. And if this is so, these ideas must have been present in certain Jewish circles of which Paul was a part prior to his conversion:

> Soviel ist gewiß, jüdische Apokalypsen kennen wirklich einen Messias, der vor seinem Erscheinen bereits im Himmel lebt und erhabener ist als selbst die Engel.[18]

The life of the human Jesus became connected with this preconceived heavenly being in Paul's thought. The death and resurrection of Jesus were not the experiences of a mere human. In fact, these events supplied the solution to the puzzle of why this heavenly being became human. The incarnation took place for the salvation of the human race. Paul's doctrine of redemption was therefore formed out of the substance of his prior beliefs about the nature of the Messiah.[19] Paul had expected the Christ to conquer the evil powers of this world and to inaugurate a new Age. Upon his conversion, Paul came to view the death and resurrection of Jesus as the divinely determined means to this end. But the manner in which Paul came to this conviction is unknown: 'Wie er dazu kam, bleibe offen.'[20]

Despite the comprehensiveness of Wrede's theory, a number of significant problems arise upon review of his basic assumptions. Wrede rightly calls into question the image of a Luther-like Paul who struggled under the burden of the Law prior to his conversion. It is now widely acknowledged that such a view is not supported by Paul's letters nor by what Jewish sources themselves reveal about first-century Judaism. Wrede's approach to Paul marked an important shift away from the psychologizing portraits of Paul which dominated the research of the latter portion of the nineteenth century. But to dismiss such psychological images of Paul does not do away with the question of the effects of Paul's conversion on his earlier devotion to *Torah*. In his description of Paul's Jewish background, Wrede himself turns to Phil 3:5, 6, where Paul contends that he was blameless in his observance of *Torah*. Moreover, Jewish apocalypses in which the Messiah appears as a pre-existent supernatural being, especially 4 Ezra and 2 Baruch, urge observance of *Torah*. The hopes for salvation expressed in these apocalypses are centered on Israel, not the whole human race.[21]

---

[18] Wrede, 'Paulus,' p. 82.
[19] Wrede, 'Paulus,' p. 83.
[20] Wrede, 'Paulus,' p. 83.
[21] Alden Thompson, has argued that the author of 4 Ezra is concerned not only with the salvation of Israel, but also with that of the whole human race, *Responsibility for Evil in the Theodicy of IV Ezra*, SBLDS 29 (Missoula, Mont.: Scholars Press, 1977), pp. 156–241. But despite Ezra's questions about humanity

Assuming that Paul held such a belief prior to his conversion, Paul's belief in an exalted Messianic figure and his commitment to *Torah* would have been linked to one another.[22] How then did Paul's conversion drive them apart?

In another essay, Wrede contends that Paul's sole purpose in employing the theme of 'justification by faith' is to oppose the imposition of Jewish customs on Gentile converts. He thus interprets the expression 'works of the Law' as 'observance of Jewish ritual law,' exclusive of moral laws and virtues. While Paul's contrast between grace and merit might be explained as a result of reflection on his Pharisaic past or his conversion, 'his making faith into the opposite of works of the law could never be explained in this way.'[23]

This reduction of 'works of the Law' to Jewish customs is not at all convincing. Wrede's dichotomization of ritual and ethics runs against the grain of virtually all early Judaism, including the Hellenistic variety attested by Philo, since even for him ritual demands serve to teach ethical lessons.[24] The close connection between purity and transgression which appears in the Qumran materials is indicative of the essential unity of the issue in the minds of most first-century Jews.[25] Moreover, as Douglas Moo has observed, the expression 'works of the Law' never means anything more precise than 'works done in obedience to the Law.'[26] Wrede already had 4 Ezra available to him, where in an admittedly strict form of Judaism 'works' were accorded salvific value.[27] And it now appears that a fragment of a letter discovered in Cave 4 at Qumran

---

in the narrative, the basic stance of the work is centered on the salvation of those who display allegiance to *Torah*. Cf. Wolfgang Harnisch, *Verhängnis and Verheißung der Geschichte: Untersuchungen zum Zeit- und Geschichtsverständnis im 4.Buch Esra und in der syr. Baruchapokalypse*, FRLANT 97 (Göttingen: Vandenhoeck & Ruprecht, 1969), pp. 143–178.

[22] Furthermore, the Messiah appears in Jewish apocalypses as an exalted human, not as an immaterial angel, e.g. 1 Enoch 48; 4 Ezra 12, 13. Hence it is not clear that the problem of the Messiah becoming human would have provided the generative force to Paul's theology which Wrede assigns to it.

[23] William Wrede, 'The Task and Methods of "New Testament Theology"' in *The Nature of New Testament Theology* SBT Second Series 25, ed. and trans. Robert Morgan (Naperville, IL: Allenson, 1973), p. 100. = *Über Aufgabe und Methode der sogennanten neutestamentlichen Theologie* (Göttingen: Vandenhoeck & Ruprecht, 1897).

[24] See Philo's treatment of circumcision in *De Specialibus Legibus* 1.1–2.12.

[25] 1QS provides a clear example of this pattern of thought. See the discussion of 'Purity and Righteousness' in Chapter 2, Section II.E of this study.

[26] Douglas J. Moo, 'Law', 'Works of the Law,' and Legalism in Paul,' *WTJ* 45 (1983):73–100.

[27] See 4 Ezra 7:77 where Uriel tells Ezra, 'Etenim est tibi thesaurus operum repositus apud Altissimum.'

attests a connection between (anticipated) deeds of obedience ('works') and the attribution of righteousness by God: ‏ונחשבה‏ ‏לך לצדקה בעשׂוחך הישׁר והטוב לפנו‏.[28] It is therefore difficult to believe that no connection existed between Paul's postconversion conception of 'grace' and his earlier righteousness 'obtained through the Law.' Boasting in the Law, which expresses itself in a confidence in circumcision, includes a commitment to high moral standards.[29] The appeal to David as a witness to righteousness χωρὶς ἔργων in Rom 4:6-8, also presumes a broader conception of 'works' than 'mere' ritual practices, since here 'justification' is understood as the forgiveness of transgression. Nor is it possible to reduce the theme of 'justification by faith' to a mere opposite of 'works of the Law.' The phrase ἔργα νόμου does not appear in Phil 3 where the concept of a righteousness through Christ is contrasted with righteousness through the Law.

How is it then, that the heavenly Christ came to supplant the Law as the means to salvation? And how is it that the Jewish apocalypticism of Paul was stripped of its nationalistic hopes? Answers to such questions are crucial to Wrede's thesis, yet his brief essay offers no satisfactory answer to them. Because he cannot provide sufficient warrant for his selective use of Jewish apocalyptic writings, he ends up with a Paul who is not merely an independent theologian, but who is strangely detached from his environment. As Schweitzer comments:

> Also steht auch bei Wrede, wie bei Holsten und Holtzmann, die Lehre Pauli als eine isolierte Größe da, die weder Verbindung nach rückwärts noch Wirkung nach vorwärts aufweist.[30]

Further problems arise with Wrede's attempt to show that Paul worked from a theological center based on a realistic and material redemption. Wrede attempts to distance a portion of Paul's argumentation, his *Rechtfertigungslehre*, from Paul's own beliefs. Yet he supplies no corresponding criterion by which to judge when and where Paul's argument does reveal his thought.[31] This lack of an

---

[28] 4QMMT, line 7. See Elisha Qimron and John Strugnell, 'An Unpublished Halakhic Letter from Qumran,' *IEJ* 4 (1985):9–12. I am grateful to Prof. Dr. Peter Stuhlmacher for calling my attention to this manuscript and to the transliteration based on the photograph in the Qimron-Strugnell article.

[29] Rom 2:17–29.

[30] Schweitzer, *Paulinische Forschung*, p. 134.

[31] It is not clear, moreover, that Wrede is able to bridge the gap between Paul's theology and his religion by means of the notion of Paul as a 'folk theologian.' According to Wrede, 'Der einfache Satz: 'Jesus ist der Messias' mit seinem nächsten Folgerungen war alles; und er ist bereits der Keim eines Dogmas. Seine

appropriate means for establishing a realistic-material conception of redemption as the 'center' of Paul's theology creates difficulties which emerge in the concrete details of Wrede's work.

An important example serves to illustrate the problem: Paul's concept of righteousness as a present reality. In order to maintain his thesis that Paul is a theologian, Wrede must show that Paul's arguments regarding 'justification' cohere with the broader *Erlösungslehre* he proposes or that they result from the requirements of arguments with Judaizers. One would expect then, that unless the situation demanded it, Paul's usage of 'justification' would center on the coming of the future reality of righteousness.[32] However, as Wrede himself observes, Paul frequently writes of righteousness as a present reality or possession.[33] Wrede accounts for this aberration from his thesis by suggesting that Paul stressed the concept of a present righteousness only in order to oppose Jewish teaching, which conceived of eternal life as the result of a righteousness obtained on earth.[34] Yet Paul uses Abraham as a paradigm for believers (which certainly is not necessary for the argument of Wrede's Paul). And his references to present righteousness appear in contexts in which he does not combat Judaizers.[35] It is gratuitous then to locate Paul's 'true' position in a future hope of righteousness. Wrede's explanation appears all the more self- serving, since, according to his proposed 'center,' Paul simply could have argued (theologically!) that the need for a present righteousness obtained by obedience was superseded by the redemptive act of Christ, which guaranteed eternal life.

'Theologie' aber ist nur der entwickelte Keim. ('Paulus,' p. 42)' But given Wrede's admissions about the nature of Paul's writing, this claim becomes impossible to sustain. His Paul does not develop ideas in a theological manner, but works from inherited patterns of Biblical interpretation and *ad hominem* argumentative strategies. Wrede's statement that Paul's *Religion ist durchaus theologisch* is therefore highly misleading, since it passes over both the unconscious factors and the strategies of debate which Wrede sees at work in Paul's writing, factors which ultimately decide the structure and content of Paul's argumentation.

[32] It is to be remembered that in Wrede's reading of Paul, although the 'real' redemption has already occurred ideally ('Paulus,' p. 73), 'die äußerliche Verwirklichung bringt zuerst die Zukunft.' This includes righteousness: 'Auch die Gerechtigkeit, die der Mensch empfängt, wird daher erst in der Zukunft zur vollen Realität.'

[33] See Rom 1:17; 3:21, 24, 26; 4:1–11; 5: 1, 9, 17; 8:17; 9:30; 10:3, 10; 1 Cor 1:30; 2 Cor 3:9.

[34] Wrede, 'Paulus,' p. 73. Wrede's views undoubtedly stem from the Protestant emphasis on an uncertainty regarding salvation in early Judaism. He therefore construes Paul's references to a present righteousness as directed against legalism. But this position rests on a faulty understanding of early Judaism.

[35] Gal 3:6, Rom 4:3, 5, 9, 11; 8:10, 14:17; 1 Cor 1:30.

Therefore, while Wrede rightly rejects the notion that Paul's basic aim was to explicate his experience of new-found grace, he fails to establish his own thesis, that Paul's writings contain a consistent theological development of the idea of a 'realistic' redemption. No clear means are provided for distinguishing between Paul's 'thought' and the ideas he introduces only for the purposes of debate.

Despite the weaknesses of Wrede's portrait of Paul, his work retains considerable importance in its contribution to the discussion of Paul's theology. Unlike the interpreters who preceded him, Wrede was able to give a precise formulation to the role of 'justification' in Paul's thought: *Kampfeslehre*. Not only did the secondary status which Wrede assigned to this theme find an echo in Schweitzer's description of 'justification' as a *Nebenkrater*, but more recent investigators, especially Krister Stendahl, E. P. Sanders and Heikki Räisänen, have come to conclusions similar to that of Wrede regarding the role of 'justification' in Paul's writings. The issues raised by Wrede's *Paulus* therefore remain under discussion. Is it possible that Paul developed the idea of an opposition between faith and works in a situation independent of and detached from his own conversion? Is Paul's language concerning 'justification by faith' introduced for merely polemical purposes? These are the questions which Wrede's work leaves to modern interpreters of Paul.

III. PAUL AS A JEWISH APOCALYPTIC MYSTIC: ALBERT SCHWEITZER

In his provocative monograph, *Die Mystik des Apostels Paulus*, Albert Schweitzer returns to one of the weakest points of Wrede's thesis: a Paul inexplicably detached from his environment.[36] According to Schweitzer, Paul's soteriology, rather than being a product of

---

[36] Schweitzer's survey of Pauline research, in which the direction of his own interpretation was laid out, appeared in 1911, *Geschichte der Paulinische Forschung von der Reformation bis auf die Gegenwart* (Tübingen: J. C. B. Mohr [Paul Siebeck]). He developed his thesis in a monograph published almost twenty years later, *Die Mystik des Apostels Paulus* (Tübingen, J. C. B. Mohr [Paul Siebeck], 1930), his writing having been delayed by his service as a medical doctor in Lambaréné, French Equatorial Guinea. Cf. W. G. Kümmel, 'Albert Schweitzer als Paulusforscher,' in *Rechtfertigung: Festschrift für Ernst Käsemann*, ed. J. Friedrich, W. Pöhlmann, P. Stuhlmacher (Tübingen: J. C. B. Mohr [Paul Siebeck], 1976), pp. 269–289; 'Die 'konsequente Eschatologie' Albert Schweitzers im Urteil der Zeitgenossen,' in *Heilsgeschehen und Geschichte*, 2 vols., MTS 3, ed. E. Grässer, O. Merk, A. Fritz (Marburg: N. G. Elwert, 1965), 1:328–339; Westerholm, *Israel's Law*, pp. 23–32; Michel Bouttier, 'La Mystique de l'Apôtre Paul: Rétrospective et Prospective,' *RHPR* 56 (1976):54–67.

individual creativity, arises from Jewish 'eschatological mysticism.'

Schweitzer begins his portrait of Paul with convoluted apoca-lyptic expectations which he attributes to the *Schriftgelehrtentum* of Paul's day. The preconversion Paul anticipated two divine realms, first that of the Messiah within the natural order, followed by that of the eternal reign of God. Likewise, he expected two judgments, one by the Messiah, of the final generation of the human race, and one by God, of the whole of humanity at the close of the Messianic reign.

The unexpected resurrection of the Messiah led Paul to the conclusion that despite outward appearance, the powers of the Age to Come were at work in the world.[37] The first of two resur-rections of the dead already was taking place.[38] The period be-tween Jesus' resurrection and his return in glory was not a continuation of the natural world, but a *Zwischenzeit* in which the natural and the supernatural worlds commingle. Just as behind the curtains a stage is changed, so the supernatural is secretly at work in this world.[39] Those who have believed in the Messiah have, in a hidden manner, participated in his death and resurrection, and thus have already entered into the postresurrection existence.

This conception of existence in the Messianic reign decided the content of Paul's soteriology.[40] Since the elect belong to the super-natural world, the powers of this age, Sin, Death and the Law, have no real claim over them. They are 'in Christ,' i.e. the mystical body of Christ, '*eine naturhafte Größe*,'[41] to which they were joined in baptism.[42]

---

[37] While Paul originally imagined the scenario of final events in accord with scribal Judaism, after his conversion he adopted Jesus' conception of a super-natural existence in the Messianic kingdom (earlier he had thought of the Mes-sianic kingdom as purely of the natural order). Such a shift in Paul's thinking was due to his acceptance of Jesus as Messiah, *Mystik*, p. 96.

[38] The second resurrection would be that of all humanity at the close of the Messianic reign.

[39] Schweitzer, *Mystik*, p. 110.

[40] Schweitzer, *Mystik*, p. 111: 'Die fundamentale Bedeutung des Sterbens und Auferstehens Jesu besteht nach Paulus also darin, daß damit das Sterben und Auferstehen in der ganzen Leiblichkeit der zum messianischen Reich Erwählten in Gang gebracht wird.... Während das Sterben und Auferstehen an Jesu schon offenbar geworden ist, geht es an den Erwählten insgeheim, aber dennoch nicht weniger wirklich vor. Weil sie der Art ihrer Leiblichkeit nach mit Jesus Christus zusammengehören, werden sie durch seinen Tod und seine Auferstehung zu Wesen, die in Sterben und Auferstehen begriffen sind, wenn auch der Schein ihrer natürlichen Existenz noch erhalten bleibt.'

[41] Schweitzer, *Mystik*, p. 127.

[42] The celebration of the Lord's Supper likewise allows the elect to participate in the mystical Body of Christ, thus guaranteeing their share in the blessings of the coming Messianic kingdom. See Schweitzer, *Mystik*, pp. 260–264.

Paul's understanding of this existence 'in Christ' gives rise to his 'theory of the *status quo*.' If one enters into Christ, the conditions of one's prior state in the world become meaningless. Anyone who regards an alteration in the flesh as necessary to salvation reveals that he or she has not come to recognize existence in Christ. For this reason a Gentile who is circumcised forfeits his salvific union with Christ. Likewise, Jews must not refrain from the observation of *Torah*. Each is to remain in the state in which he or she was called.[43] Paul's firm commitment to this principle brought him into conflict with other Jewish Christians, particularly the Jerusalem apostles, who sought to impose circumcision on the Gentiles as a means of preserving the ceremonial purity of Jewish believers.[44]

In Schweitzer's judgment, the Law and 'eschatological mysticism' are incompatible.[45] A drive for an 'unmediated and absolute' ethic is inherent to apocalyptic thought. By implication, it seems, the Law was mediated and relative, and incompatible with *Eschatologie*. Otherworldly existence is irreconcilable with the Law, which is oriented toward life in this Age.[46]

To his credit, Schweitzer does not merely impose this dichotomy on Paul, but attempts—unsuccessfully—to provide a historical explanation. According to Schweitzer, Rom 7 shows that Paul knew from experience it was impossible to obtain righteousness from the Law.[47] This experience was not Paul's alone. The authors of 4 Ezra and 2 Baruch, despairing over the sinfulness of humanity, likewise fall back on the idea of the sin-forgiving grace of God in order to maintain a hope for salvation. Paul's understanding that the forgiveness of sins was an essential prerequisite to obtaining salvation, was common to the *Schriftgelehrtentum* of his day.[48] Nevertheless, despite his earlier feeling that the Law was insufficient for salvation, Paul did not come to view the Law and grace as incompatible until he arrived at his mystical conception of dying and rising with Christ. In Rom 7 Paul speaks from the later standpoint of the deliverance he had experienced in Christ. His preconversion struggle to obtain righteousness from the Law was probably not felt in the same measure as it appears there.[49]

---

[43] 1 Cor 7:20; Schweitzer, *Mystik*, pp. 191–200.

[44] Schweitzer, *Mystik*, pp. 193–195.

[45] Cf. Schweitzer, *Mystik*, p. 190: Paulus opfert das Gesetz der Eschatologie. Das Judentum gibt die Eschatologie auf und behält das Gesetz.

[46] Schweitzer, *Mystik*, p. 187.

[47] Schweitzer, *Mystik*, p. 209.

[48] Schweitzer, *Mystik*, p. 210–212.

[49] Schweitzer is concerned to deny the link between Paul's conversion and his soteriology, *Geschichte der Paulinischen Forschung*, pp. 82–83, 193. The shift in thinking

Schweitzer then, like Wrede before him, views righteousness by faith as a mere outgrowth of Paul's basic doctrine of redemption. He finds evidence for this in Galatians, where, he contends, Paul develops the doctrine of justification by faith by means of the *Mystik* of eschatological existence in Christ.[50] The topic of justification appears *only* where Paul engages in controversy over the role of the Law. Paul makes no reference to justification as the basis for the sacraments or for ethics. It would, in fact, be logically impossible to develop ethics out of such a doctrine. Nor are the other gifts of redemption, such as the gift of the Spirit and the hope of the resurrection, connected to the justification of the believer in Paul's letters. *Rechtfertigung* is an isolated idea, a mere restatement of the early Christian conception of the expiatory death of Jesus, which accomplished the forgiveness of prebaptismal sins.[51] Paul takes up the theme only in order to refute opponents who demanded that Gentiles keep the Law, making use of the expression 'righteousness by faith' merely because it was the only possible means of obtaining Scriptural warrant for his cause.[52] In contrast to the basic conception of Paul's soteriology:

> Die Lehre von der Gerechtigkeit aus dem Glauben ist also ein Nebenkrater, der sich im Hauptkrater der Erlösungsmystik des Seins in Christo bildet.[53]

Paul's ethic, according to Schweitzer, is a call to activate the new existence, *das Gestorben- und Auferstandensein mit Christo*. While believers are already fundamentally new creatures, they must consciously appropriate this new existence:

> Als vollendete Tatsache gilt dieser überirdische Zustand aber nur insoweit, als die Getauften sich dessen bewußt sein sollen, daß die Bedingtheiten des natürlichen Daseins für sie nicht mehr gelten, und sie ihnen also auch keine ihnen nicht mehr zukommende Bedeutung beilegen dürfen.[54]

---

did not take place at Paul's conversion, but it did occur no later than the end of his first missionary journey, since Paul reports in Galatians that he contended in Jerusalem for the freedom of Gentile converts from the Law. Schweitzer, *Mystik*, p. 219.

[50] Schweitzer, *Mystik*, pp. 204–207.

[51] Schweitzer, *Mystik*, p. 215.

[52] In this way Gen 15:6 and Hab 2:4 become susceptible to his purposes. Schweitzer, *Mystik*, pp. 202–204.

[53] Schweitzer, *Mystik*, p. 220.

[54] Schweitzer, *Mystik*, p. 292.

The believer is called, '*durch seinen Willen*' to allow the new principle of life to become a reality in thought and action.[55]

The union with Christ mediated through the sacraments is not indissoluble. Unworthy participation in the Lord's Supper may result in the loss of participation in the Messianic kingdom.[56] Some sins after baptism are atoned for by the suffering of the believer with Christ,[57] but since the union with Christ is of the natural order, it may be ruptured by other natural unions which are incompatible with it. Paul singles out three of these mortal sins: immorality (especially intercourse with a prostitute), circumcision after baptism, and participation in offerings to idols.[58] Such sins destroy the new existence in Christ, and with it the hope of life in the Messianic kingdom.

Here Schweitzer is forced into a self-contradictory position. Redemption and its effects are supposed to be purely of the natural order:

> In der Mystik des Seins in Christo besitzt er ja eine Vorstellung der Erlösung, aus der sich Ethik in unmittelbarer Weise als natürliche Funktion des Erlöstseins ergibt. In ihr ist logisch begründet, daß der Mensch vor dem Erlöstsein guter Werke nicht fähig war, nachher aber solche hervorbringen kann und muß, insofern als Christus sie in ihm wirkt.[59]

But if *das neue Lebensprinzip des Geistes* is actuated only by the will of the believer, it is difficult to see how it can be regarded as *natürlich*. One might well conceive of a progressive growth of the new existence within believers, but the possibility of characterizing it as 'natural' is forfeited when it is made dependent on its realization by the individual. This inconsistency is all the more evident in Schweitzer's insistence that believers might lose the new existence. If they are, '*grundsätzlich und wirklich . . . neue Kreatur(en),*' how can they do otherwise than manifest their new creation?[60]

This inconsistency is part of a broader weakness of Schweitzer's construal of Paul's theology: he cannot explain the relationship between the Pauline 'indicative' and 'imperative.'[61] If one has

---

[55] Schweitzer, *Mystik*, pp. 292–293.
[56] Schweitzer, *Mystik*, pp. 273–276.
[57] Schweitzer, *Mystik*, p. 146.
[58] Schweitzer, *Mystik*, pp. 129–130.
[59] Schweitzer, *Mystik*, p. 287. While Schweitzer uses the word '*natürlich*' somewhat ambiguously in this citation (it may mean either 'logical' or 'deriving from nature'), it is clear from his broader discussion that the idea of redemption as a natural phenomenon constitutes his basic thesis.
[60] Schweitzer, *Mystik*, pp. 292–293.
[61] On the history of this question see the summary by Georg Strecker, 'Indicative and Imperative According to Paul,' *AusBR* 35 (1987):60–72.

entered into an eschatological existence by virtue of a sacramental or naturally conceived union with the resurrected Messiah, the necessity for admonition of those who have entered that union very nearly vanishes. The previously established union either ought to produce inherent obedience, or to supply uninterrupted forgiveness of misdeeds, or some combination of the two, which would render the need for imperatives superfluous, *at least for an ethic like that of Paul, which is motivated by his soteriology.*[62]

Schweitzer appeals to the only possible explanation for the presence of imperatives. Failure to yield oneself to the new existence in the Lord results in a relapse into the old existence. The salvific union may be broken by disobedience.

However, it is questionable whether this conception of the salvific power of the exalted Messiah, which would amount to little more than an influence making salvation possible, corresponds in any way to Paul's dynamic conception of Christ's saving lordship,[63] or to Paul's certainty regarding the salvation of those 'in Christ.'[64] The texts which Schweitzer cites to support such a view fail to be convincing.[65] Most Pauline imperatives do not intimate

---

[62] Peter J. Tomson has sought to revive Schweitzer's interpretation of Paul's theology of the Law (i.e. that only Jewish Christians were required to keep all the commandments) and to couple it with the view of Stendahl, Davies, and others that Paul expected Gentiles to adhere to the Noachian commandments. Under this paradigm he finds *halakha* in Paul's letters. See his *Paul and the Jewish Law: Halakha in the Letters of the Apostle to the Gentiles*, CRINT 3.1 (Minneapolis: Fortress, 1990). The effort to uncover parallels between Paul's moral directives and early Jewish tradition is potentially significant, and may serve to further clarify Paul's ethic. W. D. Davies has already shown how fruitful a comparison of Paul with Rabbinic sources may be, *Paul and Rabbinic Judaism: Some Rabbinic Elements in Pauline Theology* (New York: Harper & Row, 1967). But Tomson misses the most basic element of Paul's thought by failing to notice that Paul bases his exhortation on his understanding of salvation. God's act in Christ is the lens through which Paul reads the Law, so that 'Christ,' not the Law and its associated *halakha*, is the controlling paradigm for appropriating 'Scripture' (e.g. 1 Cor 9:21, Gal 6:2).

[63] E.g. Rom 5:17–21, 8:2–11, 28–29; 1 Cor 15:20–28, 50–58; 2 Cor 2:14–16; Phil 2:9–11, 3:20, 21.

[64] E.g. Rom 6:23, 8:1, 2, 9–11, 38–39; 1 Cor 1:4–9, 30; 2 Cor 5:17–20; Phil 1:3–5.

[65] Rather than indicating that intercourse with a prostitute destroys union with Christ, Paul assumes quite the opposite: that such a liaison desecrates the simultaneously existing union with Christ (1 Cor 6:12–20). It is highly likely that Paul in this instance does not address a hypothetical situation, but deals with a habit current within the church at Corinth. Given that 1 Cor 6:12a and 6:13a represent slogans of the Corinthian community which Paul repeats for purposes of refutation, such a practice apparently existed and had been given theoretical underpinnings. Yet Paul presumes that a union with Christ still exists for the Christians with whom he carries out his dispute (e.g. 6:14, 15, 19, 20). The very inequality by which Paul characterizes the two relationships indicates that he regards the union with Christ not to be destroyed, but to be scandalized by intercourse with a prostitute: the one joined to a prostitute is one body with her, the one joined to the Lord is one spirit with him (6:16, 17). Paul goes on

that one might fall back into life apart from Christ.[66] Briefly stated, Schweitzer develops Paul's soteriology on a *mutable, material* basis. As a result, he cannot account for the nature of many of the Pauline imperatives, which presume an irrevocable offer of grace.

Other problems attend Schweitzer's work. His theory of the *status quo* brings him into an egregious error. The Law belongs to the natural world, which is dominated by angelic beings.[67] The

---

to assert that the spiritual union with the Lord carries with it God's claim on the whole of the individual, including the body. This prior claim of God on the body is not broken by fornication: the rhetorical question of 6:19 ἢ οὐκ οἴδατε ὅτι τὸ σῶμα ὑμῶν ναὸς τοῦ ἐν ὑμῖν ἁγίου πνεύματός ἐστιν is the explanation of Paul's assertion in 6:18 that ὁ δὲ πορνεύων εἰς τὸ ἴδιον σῶμα ἁμαρτάνει. The sin is the violation of God's right of ownership, an ownership which is not canceled by an immoral act. Paul's argument is directed against the failure to recognize the divine claim on the body inherent to union with the Lord, a theme which recurs in 1 Corinthians. Paul does not here contemplate the possibility of destroying a relationship with the Lord. His aim is to prevent the union of believers with Christ from being profaned, and to protect the Corinthians from the resulting divine punishment (cf. 1 Cor 10:1–11).

The same may be said for participation in offerings to idols (1 Cor 10:20–21). It is likely that some of the Corinthians were involved in such practices, since Paul must appeal to them for assent to his view (10:15). Yet Paul presumes that they share in the body and blood of Christ (10:16). His rhetorical question, 'Shall we provoke the Lord to jealousy?' presumes the Biblical concept of God's jealousy *for his own people* (see e.g. Exod 20:4–6, Psalm 77:58–64 [LXX]). As in the case of the visiting of prostitutes, Paul seeks to protect the Corinthians from God's angry zeal for his own possession.

Paul's attack on the acceptance of circumcision by Gentile believers provides the only real example of a religious practice which Paul regards as disruptive of union with Christ. Those who allow themselves to be circumcised have been severed from Christ, they have fallen from grace (Gal 5:4). But in this case, it is not a simple *naturhafte Verbundenheit* which is the basis for the opposition of Christ to the Law. For Paul the practice of Gentile circumcision indicated a commitment to the Law as the means of justification: κατηργήθητε ἀπὸ Χριστοῦ οἵτινες ἐν νόμῳ δικαιοῦσθε, τῆς χάριτος ἐξεπέσατε (Gal 5:4; cf. 4:21, see also 5:3; 2:4–6, 21). It is this principle which for Paul stands in opposition to righteousness given by faith in Christ (see e.g. Gal 2:5, 16–21; 3:11–14). Paul's antithesis between faith in Christ and keeping the Law as a means to salvation is therefore *metaphysical* not physical and *naturhaft*. Otherwise circumcision itself (i.e. even of Jews) would prohibit salvation. But for Paul, Jewish circumcision is an *adiaphoron* (Gal 5:6). Schweitzer attempts to overcome this difficulty by means of his theory of the *status quo*, but his arguments are not persuasive.

[66] Cf. Rudolf Bultmann, '*Das Problem der Ethik bei Paulus,*' in *Das Paulusbild in der neueren deutschen Forschung*, WdF 24, ed. K. H. Rengstorf (Darmstadt: Wissenschaftliche Buchgesellschaft, 1982), p. 182. Bultmann, arguing against the Pauline Sündlosigkeitstheorie of Paul Wernle, contends that Wernle's thesis commits its primary error by ignoring the eschatological character of justification, thus creating a logical contradiction between the indicative and the imperative: '. . . da doch Paulus den Imperativ gerade auf die *Tatsache* der Rechtfertigung gründet, den Imperativ aus dem Indikative *ableitet*. Weil der Christ durch die Rechtfertigung die Sünde los ist, soll er gegen die Sünde kämpfen: εἰ ζῶμεν πνεύματι, πνεύματι καί στοιχῶμεν.'

[67] Schweitzers *Mystik*, pp. 70–75, 185, 208–209. Cf. Gal 3:19–20; 4:3.

powers of the supernatural are at work in those who are in Christ so that the lordship of angels and of the Law no longer applies. But according to the theory of the *status quo* which Schweitzer attributes to Paul, believing Jews nevertheless must maintain the practices of the Law in order to be saved.[68] It is hard to discern what freedom from the Law could possibly mean in this case.[69] Moreover, contrary to Schweitzer's pleading, Paul did not consistently maintain *Torah*.[70]

The unresolved question of the criteria by which one is to distinguish between Paul's 'thought' and his 'argument,' which afflicted Wrede's sketch re-emerges with this odd and idiosyncratic Paul. Ironically, the greatest weakness of Schweitzer's reconstruction is his depiction of Paul as an isolated figure, who was unable to communicate with his contemporaries. Given that Paul arrived at his position through the restructuring of his conception of the events of the End, it seems inconceivable that he should not attempt to win others to his view by the very considerations which moved him. This objection to Schweitzer's portrait of Paul bears some weight, since Schweitzer attributes the notion that the Law would cease to function in the Messianic kingdom to the scribal Judaism of the first century.[71] If this tradition had been current in

---

[68] Schweitzer's theory of the Pauline *status quo* involves a number of exegetical difficulties. See *Mystik*, p. 193. Paul does permit the unmarried to marry (1 Cor 7:37, 39), thus allowing them to change their state. Moreover, it must be questioned whether one can disregard Paul's claim that he lived τοῖς ἀνόμοις ὡς ἄνομος (1 Cor 9:20, 21—the Corinthian church, being composed of Gentiles, ought to have had some means of assessing Paul's claim). It is possible to read 1 Cor 7:21 as a call for slaves to remain in slavery. But the context, in which servitude to Christ is commended, favors reading the verse as an encouragement for freedom, if obtainable (cf. 7:22, 23). And if this is so, the theory of the *status quo* has little exegetical support.

[69] Gal 5:1.

[70] See 1 Cor 9:21, Gal 4:12. Paul's entire ministry in which he was brought into regular contact with uncircumcised Gentiles would have made observance of purity and food-laws impossible.

[71] It is highly unlikely that first-century Judaism contemplated the abrogation (or alteration) of the Law in the Messianic Age. See on this topic, W. D. Davies, *Torah in the Messianic Age And/Or the Age to Come*, JBL Monograph Series VII (Philadelphia: Society of Biblical Literature, 1952); and especially Peter Schäfer, 'Die Tora der messianischen Zeit,' in *Studien zur Geschichte und Theologie des rabbinischen Judentums*, AGJU 15 (Leiden: E. J. Brill, 1978), pp. 198–213. Frank Thielman, *From Plight to Solution: A Jewish Framework for Understanding Paul's View of the Law in Galatians and Romans*, NovTSup 61 (Leiden: Brill, 1989), pp. 11–12, has chronicled the demise of attempts to interpret Paul on this basis. Schweitzer proceeds by way of *argumentum e silencio*. Since the Messianic Age would be supernatural, the Law logically would be void then. Because 4 Ezra and 2 Baruch say little regarding the Law in the Messianic Age, their silence is to be interpreted as assuming this position. Clearly, silence is a very weak argument in this instance. Schweitzer is forced to treat 4 Ezra 9::36, 37 arbitrarily. The text runs: 'Nos

Paul's day it is highly unlikely that he would not appeal to it in attempting to win his opponents over to his view.

Schweitzer's assumption that Paul's adversaries would not have listened to his logic, reducing Paul to proofs from Scripture, is therefore without basis in light of Schweitzer's own assessment of first-century Judaism.[72] All those who disagreed with Paul are prejudged as incapable of the reasoning which Paul possessed. And Paul is constrained to use arguments which do not go to the heart of the differences which lay between him and his opponents. This includes Paul's doctrine of the *status quo*, which finds articulation only in 1 Corinthians, never in polemics with Judaizing opponents. Thus one finds the ludicrous situation of Paul never employing in argument with his fellow Jewish Christians the considerations which he himself found convincing.

Moreover, in Schweitzer's reading, Paul's adoption of eschatological mysticism, whether at his conversion or later, would have made no difference to his basic soteriology. Both prior to and after his formulation of *Sein in Christo*, Paul hoped in the grace of God for forgiveness and salvation, like others in certain circles of first-century Judaism. By attaching this idea to Jesus' death, Paul merely gave it more precision. Hence neither Paul's conversion nor his taking up of his *Mystik* would have had any inherent soteriological value. His mysticism would have affected only his commitment to mission among the Gentiles. Even in this case, Paul's *Mystik* only would have added urgency or practical aid to a task in which Paul was already engaged.[73] One might have argued on the basis of Schweitzer's reconstruction that Paul developed his conception of *Sein in Christo* in opposition to *Torah* observance as the result of

---

quidem qui legem accepimus peccantes peribimus et cor nostrum quod suscepit eam, nam lex non perit sed permanet in suo honore.' The natural reading of the passage suggests that the Law is regarded as abiding permanently. Schweitzer must put forward the contorted suggestion that the Law will endure without being used in the Messianic age. Cf. also Hans-Joachim Schoeps, *Paulus: die Theologie des Apostels im Lichte der jüdischen Religionsgeschichte* (Tübingen: J. C. B. Mohr [Paul Siebeck], 1959), pp.177–183, who incorrectly argues that the Paul worked with an accepted notion of the end of Torah in the Messianic reign.

[72] E.g. Schweitzer, *Mystik*, p. 204: Man stelle sich die Lage vor, in der er sich mit seiner Lehre von der Freiheit vom Gesetz befindet! Wohl ergibt sie sich in zwingender Weise aus der eschatologischen Lehre von der Erlösung und aus der Mystik des Sterbens und Auferstehens mit Christo. Was nützt aber alle logische Richtigkeit, wenn die Gegner den Schriftbeweis für sich haben?

[73] According to Schweitzer, rather than requiring entrance into the nation of Israel as a prerequisite for salvation like other missionaries among the *Schriftgelehrtentum* or early Christians, upon adoption of his *Mystik* Paul viewed some among the Gentiles as having been directly elected by God for participation in the Messianic kingdom.

difficulty in proselytizing activity among Gentiles.[74] But Schweitzer proceeds in an entirely different direction. He contends that Paul's opposition to the Law is principial and not practical, that the freedom from the Law which Paul endorses flows entirely from his *Mystik*.

Despite the idiosyncrasy of Schweitzer's Paul, the advance which he represents should not be overlooked. In contrast to Wrede, for whom the question of the relationship of Paul's faith in Christ to his former pursuit of *Torah* remained unexplained, Schweitzer provides a theologically formulated answer. He is, in fact, the first major scholar since Baur to address this question in theological, rather than experiential terms. Vestiges of the older picture of an anxious existence under the Law remain (e.g. in Schweitzer's discussion of Rom 7), but Paul's break with *Torah* is now the result of strictly theological considerations.

Nevertheless, it is clear that Schweitzer remains trapped within the older understanding of legalistic Judaism offered by scholars such as Bousset, a view which already had begun to suffer challenges. Schweitzer cites 4 Ezra and 2 Baruch as examples of others of the *Schriftgelehrtentum* of the first century who despaired of righteousness through the Law and hoped in God's mercy. But contrary to Schweitzer's assumption, the authors of these two works reject the notion of mercy apart from the Law.[75] The opposition which he supposes to have existed between the Law and mercy in early Jewish thought is imposed on the texts not drawn from them.

This is all the more true for the dichotomy which Schweitzer draws between the Law and *Eschatologie*. It is unlikely in the extreme that a first-century Jew would have regarded the Law as only secondary and mediatory. The fundamental pattern of opposition between the Law and apocalyptic thought which Schweitzer derives by deductive means and uses to give weight to his thesis cannot be substantiated in first-century Judaism. Therefore, while Schweitzer's theological description of Paul's break with the Law represents an advance, he overlooks motifs which upon considera-

---

[74] The question of whether this is a likely scenario or not will be discussed later in this chapter. See the treatment of Francis Watson's thesis, Section VI.C.4.

[75] Both works are essentially an appeal for *Torah* observance in the post-70 CE period. Ezra's appeals for mercy on sinners (e.g. 8:30–36) go unanswered by the *angelus interpres*, Uriel. While neither of these figures is meant to represent heretical views, the authoritative message belongs to Uriel (e.g. 8:46–62). God, despite his strict justice, is regarded as merciful on his creation (e.g. 8:9–14). See 2 Bar 24:1, 2; 48:26–29 for a similar dual affirmation of justice springing from the Law and divine mercy. Cf. Harnisch, *Verhängnis und Verheißung der Geschichte*, pp. 142–178, and Chapter 2 of this study, especially the excursus on Bruce Longenecker's treatment of 4 Ezra.

tion of Paul's references to his preconversion life emerge as the probable effects of Paul's conversion on his earlier views.[76]

Schweitzer's general arguments against regarding the theme of 'justification by faith' as central to Paul's thought also fail to be convincing. While salvation-historical themes (which correspond to Schweitzer's 'eschatological mysticism') serve an important function in Galatians, the mere presence of this pattern of argumentation does not explain the opposition Paul sets up between the 'works of the Law' and the 'righteousness of faith.' Likewise, Schweitzer's claim that 'justification by faith' appears only in certain polemical contexts does not establish that it was of only relative importance to Paul. On the contrary, since Paul himself was Jewish, it is natural to suppose that arguments directed toward other Jewish Christians would bear some personal relevance for him. The fact that Paul generally does not develop his ethics directly from the idea of forensic justification says nothing of the importance of this theme. One might well construe Paul's ethics as being derived from other concerns central to Paul, or suppose that the relation between forensic justification and ethics is mediated by another set of ideas.[77]

Such objections to Schweitzer's view do not in themselves settle the question of whether or not 'justification by faith' should be regarded as a central element of Paul's thought, but Schweitzer's objections to the centrality of the theme of 'justification,' like the alternative position he presents, fail to be convincing.

In a sense, Schweitzer's work may be looked upon as the end of a long line of study beginning with Hermann Lüdemann, in which material or natural conceptions were presented as the fundamental elements of Paul's soteriology. Schweitzer differs considerably, of course, from Bousset and others who find the basis for Paul's soteriology in Hellenistic mysticism. In so far as he emphasizes Jewish apocalypticism as a determining element in Paul's thought, and introduces 4 Ezra and 2 Baruch as important background materials to the interpretation of Paul, he, like Wrede, represents an important advance over Bousset.[78] Yet it is not unfair to say that perhaps the most basic problem in Schweitzer's study is his failure to listen fully to his most important sources for apocalyptic Judaism, 4 Ezra and 2 Baruch. A series of Schweitzer's own deductive

---

[76] The nature of Paul's conversion, which is not at all limited to psychological questions, will form the substance of Chapters 2 and 3.

[77] E.g. the establishment of Christ's saving lordship, which Käsemann integrates into Paul's very conception of 'justification.'

[78] See W. D. Davies, *Paul and Rabbinic Judaism*, pp. vii–xv.

arguments are imposed on the materials, e.g. that the Law and God's mercy were placed in opposition to one another, and that the Law and the Messianic Age were regarded as antithetical. As a result, Schweitzer's *Paulus als Mystiker* differs very little from the cultic enthusiast of Hellenistic mysticism.

The explanation of Paul's soteriology as a *naturhaft* phenomenon therefore seemingly led into a dead end, since even the most viable background for establishing this thesis, apocalyptic Judaism, failed to produce a convincing description of Paul. In spite of this, Schweitzer's thesis, albeit in a highly modified form, has been taken up by E. P. Sanders, and has received fairly broad support in current scholarship. But this acceptance of some of Schweitzer's views did not take place until the apparently disparate elements of Paul's thought were brought together into a coherent image by the imposing work of Rudolf Bultmann.

IV. PAUL AS BELIEVER:
RUDOLF BULTMANN AND THE JUSTIFICATION OF THE INDIVIDUAL
AS THE CENTER OF PAUL'S THOUGHT

Rudolf Bultmann's distinctive contribution to the interpretation of Paul consists in his comprehensive synthesis of forensic and 'participationist' elements of Paul's thought. Not since Baur had a unified formulation of Pauline theology on such a grand scale been attempted.

The following discussion of Bultmann's work begins with articles published prior to his mature synthesis of Paul's thought. Such a review of Bultmann's early interpretation of Paul might seem to be an odd element to include within a survey of research. Yet a brief description of the transition which Bultmann underwent will bring to light a number of useful insights.

We shall see first of all, that the shift in Bultmann's thinking was not accomplished merely by his appropriation of existentialist language for the interpretation of Paul. Exegetical insights and interaction with the text of Paul's letters was clearly the driving force in this change. With Bultmann, then, one finds reason to ask if 'justification' might not play a larger role in Paul's thought than many current scholars are ready to allow. He, after all, began with a 'participationist' reading of Paul, and moved away from it.

Secondly, a review of Bultmann's early work is useful in assessing the validity of the rather harsh criticism which has been leveled against him by E. P. Sanders, who has accused Bultmann of misrepresenting early Judaism in the same manner as Wilhelm Bousset and other Protestant scholars before him. We shall see that the change in Bultmann's interpretation of Paul influenced the manner in which he construed Paul's relationship to Judaism, putting considerable distance between him and Bousset.

A. *Bultmann's Early Description of Pauline Soteriology*

While there is considerable conceptual continuity between Bultmann's early and later writings on Paul, in his earlier years Bultmann formulates his understanding of Paul in terms which reflect the *Religionsgeschichtliche Schule*.[79] Bultmann's earliest publication, a brief review of New Testament research, contains only a slight indication that Bultmann was inclined to allow a central role to the theme of 'justification.' He resists Wrede's thesis that *Rechtfertigung* is merely Paul's *Kampfeslehre*, yet he himself is unwilling to view it as a central feature of Pauline theology.[80] He acknowledges the importance of eschatology as a background to Paul's thought, but regards mysticism and religious experience to determine its basic content, including Paul's understanding of righteousness:

> Dennoch ist deutlich, daß Paulus mit diesem eschatologischen Begriff etwas ganz Anderes zum Ausdruck bringen will: das Erlebnis, in dem ihm die ganze Größe des sittlichen Gottes offenbar ward: Gott fordert so viel, daß kein Mensch sich der Erfüllung rühmen kann (es ist die Erkenntnis von der Unendlichkeit der Sittlichen Aufgabe), und Gott ist so groß in der Gnade, daß vor ihm kein Verdienst gilt, sondern nur ein Sichschickenlassen (es ist die Erkenntnis der Freiheit des sittlichen Handelns von religiösen Motiven, der Verzicht auf ein Handeln, das auf Gott gerichtet ist; freilich ruht das Interesse des Paulus auf der anderen Seite, auf der durch solche innere Stellung ermöglichten Beziehung zu Gott). Mit Eschatologie hat das nichts zu tun.[81]

The citation above displays not only the influence of the *Religionsgeschichtliche Schule*, but the Marburg Neo-Kantianism of the systematic theologian Wilhelm Herrmann.[82] One can perceive

---

[79] See W. G. Kümmel, 'Rudolf Bultmann als Paulusforscher,' in *Rudolf Bultmanns Werk und Wirkung*, pp. 174–193, ed. B. Jaspert (Darmstadt: Wissenschaftlichebuchgesellschaft, 1984) and Martin Evang, *Rudolf Bultmann in seiner Frühzeit*, BHT 74 (Tübingen: J. C. B. Mohr [Paul Siebeck], 1988), pp. 340–350.

[80] Rudolf Bultmann, 'Die neutestamentliche Forschung 1905–1907,' *Monatsschrift für Pastoraltheologie* 5 (1908–1909):124–132, 154–164.

[81] Rudolf Bultmann, 'Die Bedeutung der Eschatologie für die Religion des Neuen Testaments,' *ZThK* 27 (1917):85–86. See Martin Evang's important discussion of the significance of this article and Bultmann's later stress on eschatology in *Rudolf Bultmann in seiner Frühzeit*, pp. 264–276.

[82] Cf. Roger A. Johnson, *The Origins of Demythologizing: Philosophy and Historiography in the Theology of Rudolf Bultmann*, SHT 28 (Leiden: Brill, 1974), pp. 59–65.

already the basic lines of his later formulation of Paul's theology, but here Bultmann employs the category of experience to explicate Paul's language, as Herrmann himself did.

Bultmann's 1920 presentation 'Ethische und mystische Religion' to the gathering of the *Freunde der Christlichen Welt* represents a distancing of himself from Hermann with regard to the value of the historical Jesus for the Christian faith. A major thrust of the article is to underscore a difference between the ethical religion of Jesus (and the early Palestinian believers) and the mystical and cultic orientation of the Hellenistic community and Paul.[83] Paul is a Hellenistic Jew in whom no substantial influence of Palestinian Judaism can be traced.[84] He nevertheless stands between the early believers and the Hellenistic community as one in whom one finds a *eigenartige Verbindung von ethischer und mystischer Religion*.[85] The question of whether or not a higher unity linked the ethical and mystical themes is not within the scope of Bultmann's presentation.

Although the dichotomy which Bultmann here projects onto early Judaism, and continued to use throughout his career, now can be seen to be an oversimplification, it was of fundamental importance to his portrait of Paul. Under the influence of his teacher Heitmüller, Bultmann rejected the psychologizing readings of Rom 7 which had characterized Protestant scholarship from the later nineteenth century until his own day.[86] Rather than being a product of a guilt-stricken conscience, Paul's conversion was, 'the ecstatic experience of a Hellenistic Jew, which placed him under the power of the *Kyrioskult* of the Hellenistic community.'[87]

---

[83] Rudolf Bultmann, 'Ethische und mystische Religion im Urchristentum,' *Christliche Welt* 34 (1920):725–731, 738–743. Bultmann's theological stance retains the strong Marburg Neo- Kantian imprint which was to continue to shape his work. See Johnson's discussion of this article in *The Origins of Demythologizing*, pp. 62–65. Evang's detailed treatment of the same article is essential to a proper understanding of Bultmann's development, *Bultmann in seiner Frühzeit*, pp. 85–89, 290–332. The thesis which he develops, that Bultmann's adoption of existentialist categories represents his continuing reflection on problems of his early period, does not nullify the turning point in Bultmann's thought described below.

[84] Rudolf Bultmann, 'Ethische und mystische Religion im Urchristentum,' *Christliche Welt* 34 (1920):725–731, 738–743, esp. 727–728.

[85] Bultmann, 'Ethische und mystische Religion,' col. 730: 'Die Mystik reicht also in das Zentrum der paulinischen Frömmigkeit.'

[86] Bultmann, 'Ethische und mystische Religion,' 727–728. Cf. Wilhelm Heitmüller, 'Die Bekehrung des Paulus,' *ZThK* 27 (1917):136–153.

[87] Bultmann, 'Ethische und mystische Religion im Urchristentum,' col. 727–728: '. . . weder steht die Rechtfertigungslehre im Zentrum der paulinischen Anschauung, noch ist Röm. 7 eine Darstellung der inneren Entwicklung des Paulus, noch kann von einer bedeutsamen Einwirkung der palästinensischen Tradition auf Paulus die Rede sein. Somit erscheint die Bekehrung des Paulus in einem ganz neuem Licht; sie ist das ekstatische Erlebnis eines hellenistischen Juden, das ihn in den Bann des Kyrioskults der hellenistischen Gemeinde zog.'

The basic thought structure of Bultmann's later interpretation of Paul already is present in this essay, although the categories and language are remarkably different. In accord with Bultmann's later work, Paul is the prominent figure of early Christianity. While it is uncertain whether Jesus' preaching goes beyond a moralized conception of God, in Paul one finds a 'wonderful' expression of ethical religion, in which the self is directed to the reality of God and not merely to performance of moral demand.[88] Paul therefore stands out as the one figure in early Christianity in whom one finds God encountered as the 'Wholly Other,' and not merely as a projection of moralism.

Bultmann's 1922 review of the second edition of Barth's *Römerbrief* marks the transition point of his interpretation of Paul. Here Bultmann rejects mysticism and experience as the primary categories for the interpretation of Paul in favor of 'faith,' which he understands as obedient self- surrender in response to divine address.[89] *Rechtfertigung*, not mystic piety, now appears in Bultmann's assessment as a central feature of Paul's theology.

Bultmann firms up his new position exegetically in his 1924 article, 'Das Problem der Ethik bei Paulus.' The contrast with 'Ethische und mystische Religion' (1920) is remarkable. Both articles work with the same fundamental ideas. Yet the Pauline *Indikativ* in the later article is understood as *Rechtfertigung*, which has its basis in the judgment of God. No longer is the supernatural experience of the Spirit in Hellenistic mysticism the central feature of Paul's piety. Moreover, the ethical, Paul's *Imperativ*, is now rightly seen as deriving from the *Indikativ*, so that the two constitute a *echte Antinomie*, expressing a unified conception, not a contradiction.

The transition in Bultmann's interpretation of Paul was completed by his appropriation of existentialist language. Such terminology makes its appearance already in the 1922 review of Barth's *Römerbrief*. By the time Bultmann's 1930 article 'Paulus,' in the second edition of *RGG* appeared, this means of interpreting Paul was fully in place in his work.[90]

Nevertheless, it is clear that it was engagement with the Pauline materials themselves which induced Bultmann to allow a central

---

[88] Bultmann, 'Ethische und mystische Religion,' cols. 741–742.

[89] Rudolf Bultmann, 'Karl Barths 'Römerbrief' in zweiter Auflage,' *Christliche Welt* 36 (1922):320–323, 330–334, 358–361, 369–373, especially 358–361. Bultmann's comparison of Barth's language with the ideas of Herrmann gives a good indication of the path his own thought had travelled.

[90] See Johnson, *The Origins of Demythologizing*, pp. 175–202.

role to 'justification' in Paul's thought. The 1924 article, the fruit of a seminar on Paul in the *Wintersemester* 1923/1924, itself shows that it was Bultmann's continued wrestling with the primary sources which led him to the initial stage of his new understanding of Paul. Even Bultmann's early review of Barth's commentary, while essentially positive, reveals his disagreement with Barth, making it clear that he was rethinking his interpretation of Paul primarily in light of the text. Given that Bultmann had earlier interpreted Paul's thought as 'participatory' and experiential, his exegetically-prompted move away from this position warns against too-quickly dismissing forensic justification from a primary role in Paul's thought.

B. Bultmann's Mature Description of Pauline Soteriology

Bultmann's reformulation of the starting point of Paul's theology carried with it an array of significant results. With his new understanding of Paul's theology as an explication of believing existence, Bultmann could read Paul's theological discourse as refraining from all objectifying language about God.[91] Moreover, Bultmann could now view Paul's conversion and his later theological expression as conceptually coherent, so that in a manner much more satisfying than Wrede's sketch, Paul could be interpreted as a theologian. Furthermore, Bultmann brought back into focus the question of the change in Paul's understanding of *Torah* upon his conversion, which had not received direct attention since the Liberal psychologizing portraits of Paul's development had fallen out of favor.[92]

As is well-known, Bultmann regards all of Paul's theological expressions to involve the articulation of the possibility of believing human existence, that is, that one 'sich selbst an Gott preisgebend, sein Selbst gewinnt.'[93] Such a premise, which is undergirded by both exegetical and theological argumentation, permits Bultmann to gain his sweeping explication of Paul's thought. Paul, according to Bultmann, whether he makes use of the juridical

---

[91] Rudolf Bultmann, *Theologie des Neuen Testaments*[9] (Tübingen, J. C. B. Mohr [Paul Siebeck], 1984), pp. 191–192.

[92] The most important works by Bultmann relating to Paul's understanding of Judaism include: 'Römer 7 und die Anthropologie des Paulus,' in *Exegetica*, ed. Erich Dinkler (Tübingen: J. C. B. Mohr, 1967), pp. 198–209; 'Christus des Gesetzes Ende,' *Gesammelte Aufsätze* II (Tübingen: J. C. B. Mohr [Paul Siebeck], 1952), pp. 33–58; 'Paulus,' in *Die Religion in Geschichte und Gegenwart*[2], 7 vols., edited by Hermann Gunkel and Leopold Zscharnack (Tübingen: J. C. B. Mohr [Paul Siebeck], 1930),4:1019–1045; *Theologie des Neuen Testaments*, pp. 187–353.

[93] Bultmann, *Theologie des Neuen Testaments*, p. 271.

language of Judaism, or borrows from the terminology of Gnostic mythology, works from this *Grundposition*. This single interpretive insight therefore allows Bultmann to fuse the disparate elements of Paul's thought together and to assign the theme of justification a central role in it.

According to Bultmann, this single aim encompasses the whole of Paul's theological endeavor, including his analysis of human existence before and outside of faith:

> Es versteht sich dabei, gemäß dem Ursprung der theologischen Er-
> kenntnis im Glauben, daß der Mensch vor der Offenbarung der
> πίστις von Paulus so gezeichnet wird, wie er vom Glauben her sicht-
> bar geworden ist.[94]

Bultmann's construal of Paul's theology is therefore of critical importance not only for his assessment of the theme of 'justification' within Paul's thought, but also for the understanding of Judaism which he ascribes to Paul.

This portrayal of Judaism has come under heavy fire from E. P. Sanders, who has suggested that his work suffers from a persistent and pernicious Protestant misinterpretation of Jewish devotion to the Law. Several related questions concerning Paul's conception of sin, his relationship to Judaism, and his conversion are problematic for Bultmann's position, as we shall see in the following analysis. However, some of the criticisms which Sanders has leveled against Bultmann's work are not convincing and, in large measure, fail to comprehend Bultmann's explication of Paul.

Part of the difficulty arises from the fact that Sanders incorrectly presents Bultmann's depiction of Judaism as a continuation of Bousset's line of thought. As we have seen, the description of Paul which Bultmann presents is dependent on the revised understanding of first-century Judaism which began to have influence in the earlier part of this century through the influence of scholars such as George Foot Moore.

In his mature period, Bultmann repeatedly rejects Protestant portraits of Paul in which Paul's conversion was depicted as the result of a desire to be free from the burden of the Law or as stemming from a guilt-ridden conscience:

> Man verwechselt leicht Paulus mit Luther und übersieht die histor-
> ische situation, in der Paulus schreibt. Was die äußere Belastung
> durch das Gesetz betrifft, so haben die jüdischen Erklärer des Neuen

---

[94] Bultmann, *Theologie des Neuen Testaments*, p. 192.

Testaments die christlichen Exegeten öfter darauf hingewiesen, daß sie sich ein falsches Bild vor der jüdischen Gesetzlichkeit als einer drückenden Last machen. Sie sagen mit Recht: wer im Judentum aufgewachsen ist, wer von klein auf in der Familie in der Ordnung solcher Bräuche gelebt hat, wie das Gesetz sie fordert, für den bedeuten sie gar keine Last, . . . Und so freut sich der fromme Jude des Gesetzes, das sein Leben regelt.[95]

Consciousness of sin did not lead to doubt concerning the validity of the Law in early Judaism. It was instead a prod to repentance and to greater joyous zeal.[96]

Some unfair characterizations of Judaism continue in Bultmann's work, but for the most part Bultmann's portrait of Paul does not suffer from them.[97] Bultmann attributes to Jews an *Angst*

---

[95] Bultmann, 'Christus des Gesetzes Ende,' pp. 33–34; cf. 'Paulus,' col. 1022.

[96] Bultmann, 'Christus des Gesetzes Ende,' p. 35.

[97] E. P. Sanders's complaint that Bultmann short-sightedly ignores the alternative views of writers such as Moore and Erik Sjöberg is only partially justified. And it has little to do with Bultmann's description of Paul. See, Sanders's *Paul and Palestinian Judaism: A Comparison of Patterns of Religion*, (Philadelphia: Fortress, 1977), pp. 43–47.

Sanders attacks, in particular, the views expressed in Bultmann's *Das Urchristentum* (Zürich: Artemis Verlag, 1949), especially pp. 68–75. Bultmann maintains that 'radical obedience' was not possible within Judaism because many of the commands of *Torah* had become irrelevant to the life of Jews in the first century, and because moral and ritual demands are given equal force in the Law. This judgment springs largely from Bultmann's Marburg Neo-Kantianism. The fact that at an earlier stage in his career, Bultmann was willing to attribute a defective moralism to Jesus himself shows that he did not proceed from a simple bias against Judaism (cf. 'Ethische und mystische Religion,' cols. 741–742). Bultmann's position is theologically questionable, and to attribute such a stance to Judaism as a whole is reductionistic, but Bultmann's statements do not represent a thoughtless dismissal of Judaism.

Bultmann's use of Jewish sources concerning uncertainty about salvation, repentance as merit, and a juridical conception of divine retribution misrepresent the materials, but only partially. The actual references from Jewish sources which Bultmann cites indicate, for example (b. Berakoth 28b), that Jews of the first century *could* entertain doubts and fears about salvation. It would be unusual if they did not, on occasion, experience qualms of conscience. Bultmann's point is that such uncertainty, the consciousness of sin, and the need for repentance, are occasioned by the legal conception of obedience inherent to *Torah*. It is hard to deny that the concrete demands contained in *Torah* might lead to such results, however one-sided Bultmann's portrayal might be.

Likewise, Bultmann's treatment of Erik Sjöberg's, *Gott und die Sünder im Paläs-tinischen Judentum*, BWANT 49 (Stuttgart: W. Kohlhammer, 1938) cannot be fully dismissed. Sanders charges Bultmann with misrepresenting Sjöberg's ideas in two respects. First, Bultmann supposedly ignores Sjöberg's references to God's mercy toward sinful Israelites. Yet Sjöberg closes his chapter, 'Die Güte Gottes gegen die sündigen Israeliten,' with the following: 'Weil der Erwählungsglaube sich hier auswirkt, kann man behaupten, daß sie (the sinful Israelites) auch dem letzten Gericht entrinnen werden und trotz ihrer Sünden mit ihrem Volke Anteil an der zukünftigen Welt haben werden. Dieser Gedanke setzt sich jedoch verhältnismäßig selten durch. *Meistens gilt auch von den Israeliten, daß die Sünder unter ihnen*

which was merely a fear of punishment, and not a true self-judgment, yet elsewhere he denies that *Paul* experienced anxiety in this
manner.[98] Bultmann's reading of Paul is more subtle. The sort of
Angst the preconversion Paul experienced was unconscious, manifesting itself in the attempt to secure life by obedience to the Law.[99]
Paul's conflict with Judaism then is over the question of whether
the Law is to be regarded as the way to salvation.[100] Boasting in
Torah as a means of securing salvation is the basic sin of the Jew.[101]

It is not as if Bultmann singles out Judaism as being especially
faulty. The situation of the Jew is no different from that of any
human being prior to faith. The Law only illuminates a problem
common to all human existence.[102] Like the rest of humankind, the
Jew is unaware of this problem. While aiming at life through

*beim letzten Gericht keine Barmherzigkeit finden werden, sondern nach ihren bösen Taten
gerichtet und mit endgültiger Verdammnis bestraft werden.'* (p. 124, emphasis mine) Cf.
pp. 188–190, where in summary of Tannaitic religion, Sjöberg maintains that
obedience was demanded, although this concept was accompanied by ideas of
undeserved mercy. Sjöberg does not agree with Moore as closely as Sanders
thinks, and his conclusions affirm what Bultmann suggests they do.

Sanders is on firmer ground when he argues that Bultmann misconstrues Sjöberg by citing him in support of the argument that repentance came to be
regarded as a meritorious work. As Sanders points out, Sjöberg contends that
the view then current among Protestant scholars, that *Judaism as a whole* adhered
to the notion that repentance was a meritorious work, was false and had to be
discarded. But Sjöberg goes on to acknowledge that: 'Es gibt tatsächlich auch
Zeugnisse dafür, daß ein solches Verständnis der Umkehr sich in gewissem Maße
im Judentum, auch im rabbinischen Judentum, geltend gemacht hat.' (p. 157,
examples follow) Bultmann, in his use of Sjöberg, implicitly and wrongly represents Judaism as a whole as maintaining this conception. It is crucial to note,
however, that Bultmann's portrayal of Judaism at this juncture leads up to his
description of Jesus' preaching, not of Paul's theology.

[98] Bultmann, 'Paulus,' col. 1022: 'So weiß er (Paul) nichts davon, daß das
Gesetz für das subjektive Empfinden des Juden eine Last sei, und niemals in
seinem christlichen Kampf gegen das Gesetz stellt er den Glauben als die Befreiung von solcher Last dar. Mit der 'Angst', in der der Mensch vor dem
Glauben steht, ist nicht das subjektive, durch falsche religiöse Vorstellungen
verursachte Angstgefühl gemeint.' Cf. 'Christus des Gesetzes Ende,' p. 35.

[99] Bultmann, *Theologie des Neuen Testaments*, p. 242.

[100] Bultmann, 'Christus des Gesetzes Ende,' p. 37: 'Sein Vorwurf ist der, daß
die Juden durch Erfüllung des Gesetzes das Heil gewinnen wollen. Er bestreitet
ihnen, *daß die Erfüllung des Gesetzes der Heilsweg sei.'*

[101] Bultmann, *Theologie des Neuen Testaments*, pp. 239–270; 'Römer 7,'
p. 200: 'Was ist aber die eigentliche Sünde der Juden? Worin besteht die Ver-
kehrtheit des Gesetzesweges?–Sobald Paulus die Lehre von der δικαιοσύνη Θεοῦ
auf Grund der πίστις χωρίς νόμου zu erstenmal vorgetragen hat (Röm 3,21–26), ist
die erste Frage: ποῦ οὖν ἡ καύχησις; (V.27). Das καυχᾶσθαι, das πεποιθέναι ἐν σαρκί
(Phil 3,3 f) charakterisiert die jüdische Haltung unter dem Gesetz, und zwar in
der Weise, daß der Jude gerade das Gehorsam fordernde Gesetz zum Mittel der
καύχησις macht.'

[102] Bultmann, 'Christus des Gesetzes Ende,' pp. 38-40; *Theologie des Neuen
Testaments*, p. 246: 'Darin, daß der Mensch ein Ich ist, dem es um seine ζωή,
sein Selbst, geht und gehen soll, liegt die Möglichkeit der Sünde. Darin, daß der

obedience to the Law, he or she is unaware that such a path actually leads to death.[103]

Bultmann's position should not be misunderstood as charging Judaism with being devoid of any conception of God's mercy or of the role of repentance. These ideas are themselves a part of Paul's basic conflict with Judaism.[104] The fundamental theological difference between Paul and Judaism, according to Bultmann, is not whether God is merciful at all, but whether God's grace and human obedience to *Torah* are cooperative in securing salvation.[105]

Some assessment of the weaknesses of Bultmann's description of Paul's relationship to Judaism is in order. Bultmann strongly emphasizes that Paul, in his conflicts with Judaizers, proceeds from an understanding of Judaism constructed within his existence in faith. Paul's judgments are therefore isolated from objective criteria having to do with first-century Judaism. They are instead bound up with 'the self-understanding inherent to faith,' i.e. with fundamental theological presuppositions. Nevertheless, at one point, Bultmann's depiction of Paul's disagreement with Judaism enters an arena where it may be tested historically. Paul's rejection of the Law, according to Bultmann, depends on the potentially verifiable claim that early Jewish obedience to the

---

Anspruch der ἐντολή Gottes auf die ζωή des Menschen geht, ist die Möglichkeit des Misverständnisses begründet: der zum Selbst berufene Mensch will von sich selbst sein und verliert so sein Selbst, seine ζωή und rennt in den Tod. Das ist die Herrschaft der Sünde, daß alles Tun des Menschen gegen seine eigentliche Intention gerichtet ist.'

[103] Bultmann, 'Römer 7,' p. 206: 'Es dürfte also klar sein, was ὁ γάρ κατεργάζομαι οὐ γινώσκω (V. 15) bedeutet: der Mensch weiß nicht, daß sein δουλεύειν ἐν παλαιότητι γράμματος in den Tod führt, wie nach 2Kor 3,14f der Jude nicht weiß, was der Sinn des Gesetzesdienst ist: seine νοήματα sind verstockt, eine Hülle liegt über dem Gesetz.'

[104] Bultmann, *Theologie des Neuen Testaments*, p. 264: "Der Jude würde schon der Behauptung des Paulus widersprechen, daß ein Mensch nur auf Grund schlechthin vollkommener Gesetzerfüllung (ὅς . . . ἐμμένει πᾶσιν . . . Gl 3. 10) gerechtfertigt werden kann; er würde vollends mit dem Satz widersprechen, daß sich Rechtfertigung aus Gesetzeswerken und aus göttlicher, im Glauben des Menschen ergriffener Gnade ausschließen. Das aber ist die entscheidende These des Paulus: τέλος γάρ νόμου Χριστὸς εἰς δικαιοσύνην παντί πιστεύοντι (Rom 10, 4), d.h. 'Christus bedeutet das Ende des Gesetzes und führt zur Gerechtigkeit jeden, der glaubt.'"

[105] Bultmann, *Theologie des Neuen Testaments*, pp. 122–123: 'Kommt die vergebende Gnade Gottes der menschlichen Tat ergänzend zu Hilfe? Oder wird das menschliche Tun des Guten überhaupt erst begründet durch die zuvorkommende Gnade Gottes? Das Problem kann auch als das des Verhältnisses zwischen der Tat des Menschen, die Gottes Wohlgefallen gewinnt, und seinem Glauben, der die Gnade ergreift, formuliert werden. . . . Gibt auf diese Frage einerseits die paulinischen Lehre von der Rechtfertigung aus Glauben allein die Antwort, so andrerseits die Entstehung des kirchlichen Bußinstituts.'

Law was driven by the basic aim of securing righteousness and life.

Such a characterization of Judaism is reductionistic. One may easily find examples which indicate the contrary to Bultmann's assumption. E.g. the saying found in m.Aboth 1.3:

> Antigonos of Socho received from Simon the Just. He used to say: Be not like slaves that minister to the Master for the sake of receiving a reward, but be like slaves that minister to the Master not for the sake of receiving a reward; and let the fear of Heaven be upon you.[106]

Since this saying was taken up in Rabbinic tradition, one may presume that the Tannaitic rabbis (and those before them) had both encountered such attitudes and sought to avoid them. Some Jews no doubt developed an attitude of the sort Bultmann describes, but others lived with higher motives. As Neugebauer has noted, Bultmann's analysis of human existence has difficulty in accounting for a plurality of human motives in relation to God, especially love for God.[107] Bultmann's Paul, as a result, entertains a simplistic and misleading view of the Jewish religion.

It is not clear, moreover, that Paul actually maintained the views Bultmann ascribes to him. For Bultmann, the ἰδία δικαι-οσύνη which the Jew pursues is *the conscious attempt to secure one's position before God by one's own efforts*, an attitude which Paul rejects.[108] However, this judgment, that the righteousness obtained through obedience to the Law is 'one's own' *and not from God*, is determined by Paul's *postconversion* analysis of his life under the Law. It is true that Phil 3, especially verse 7, shows that a part of Paul's aim prior to conversion was 'having his own righteousness.' But it is likely that Paul regarded such a righteousness as a cooperatively-given gift of God. The κέρδη of which Paul makes mention in Phil 3:4–7 includes not only his zeal for *Torah*, but the privileges of his birth and childhood, which he surely looked upon as gifts of God. It is only διὰ τὸν Χριστόν that Paul regards such privileges as loss, as a πεποίθησις ἐν σαρκί. Therefore it is only in the light of faith in Christ that ἐμὴ

---

[106] Cf. Sanders, *Paul and Palestinian Judaism*, pp. 117–122. Sanders is just as reductionistic as Bultmann in his idealistic portrait: he denies that such a problem can be found in Judaism. The very fact that the rabbinic literature is conscious of the problem indicates that Judaism (like Christianity) was susceptible to it.

[107] Fritz Neugebauer, 'Die hermeneutischen Voraussetzungen Rudolf Bultmanns in ihrem Verhältnis zur Paulinischen Theologie,' *KuD* 5 (1959):299–300.

[108] Rom 10:3, cf. Phil 3:9.

δικαιοσύνη stands in opposition to a righteousness given by God.[109]

Moreover, the postconversion Paul did not reject the notion that one's pursuit of obedience and life would determine the outcome of the final judgment. Each one would have to give an account to God.[110] The debate Paul carried on with first-century Judaism was not simply over the surrender of one's status before God. It was over the means by which God granted the gift of salvation, and the relationship of that gift to human effort.

The same discrepancy lies between Bultmann's construal of καύχησις and Paul's own usage of the expression. It is true that Paul excludes any boasting in works as a basis for righteousness.[111] But he does embrace a proper boasting, which includes human obedience as the product of divine grace. It is a boasting in God and in that accomplished by the proclamation of the Gospel, a boasting which will ultimately be subject to divine appraisal.[112]

A further problem resides in Bultmann's conception of Jewish 'boasting.' As will be borne out in later chapters of this study, he rightly indicates that Paul's perception of the relation between salvation and human effort was a central feature of his conversion and his later conflicts with Judaizers. But Bultmann, influenced perhaps by the traditional Lutheran dichotomy between Law and Gospel, wrongly attributes to Paul the conception of *Torah* as simply an occasion for human self-striving. This reading of Paul cannot be sustained. The dispute with Judaism which Paul carries out in Romans has to do with the *legitimacy* of the Jewish boast in *Torah*, just as the καύχησις of Rom 3:27 signifies Jewish privileges, not the abstract concept.[113] In Romans, *Torah* must be understood as a God-given gift and not merely a means by which divine approval might be won.[114]

In light of these considerations it may be said that Bultmann wrongly underplays Paul's understanding of *Torah* as a divine gift. He does not deny that there was a consciousness of divine grace in early Judaism, but he wrongly subsumes divine gifts to Israel along

---

[109] Cf. Phil 3:9 and see Chapter 3, Section II.C. The same may be said concerning Rom 10:3. Paul states that Israel pursued the Law (νόμος δικαιοσύνης, 9:31) and that the Jewish people were zealous for God (10:2), not that they attempted to establish themselves by means of the 'Sichtbar-Vorfindlich.' His characterization of their effort as τὴν ἰδίαν δικαιοσύνην ζητοῦντες is bound up with his own confession of the δικαιοσύνη Θεοῦ manifest in Christ.

[110] Cf. Rom 2:5–11, 14:10–12; 1 Cor 3:8, 14, 15, 4:5; 2 Cor 5:10; Gal 6:5.

[111] E.g. Rom 3:27–4:8, esp. 4:2.

[112] Gal 6:4, 13–14; 1 Cor 15:31; 2 Cor 1:12, 14; 10:8, 13; 11:10–12; 12:6; Phil 1:26, 2:16; 3:3; Rom 5:2, 3, 11; 15:17; 1 Thess 2:19.

[113] See Rom 2:17, 23; 3:27; 5:2, 3, 11.

[114] See Rom 2:17–20.

with Jewish zeal for the Law under Paul's concept of σάρξ. For
Bultmann, pride in titles and national privilege represent the
desire to establish the self in independence from God, just as much
as the pursuit of the Law.[115] Here he makes an unmistakable and
illegitimate jump in categories. Paul never fully rejects the reality
of Jewish privilege.[116] And chief among the gifts to Israel is
Torah.[117]

Bultmann's misconstrual of early Jewish understanding of *Torah*
is particularly significant with regard to the preconversion Paul.
His basic idea, that Paul's conversion was 'das Opfer dessen, was
bisher sein Stolz gewesen war,' is clearly correct, given Paul's own
references to his practice of Judaism.[118] But the reasons why and
how this radical *Umkehr* could have taken place must be asked
again. Paul did not regard his obtaining righteousness in the Law
to have taken place apart from the gracious help of God. Therefore his conversion was not a simple rejection of self-striving.

For Bultmann, Paul's theology is a mirror in which his conversion '*spiegelt sich wieder*,' because Paul assumes a theological continuity between his own conversion and what is demanded of every
human being.[119] Therefore Bultmann's defective representation of
Paul's view of Judaism calls into question his entire construal of
Pauline theology. In his interpretation, the 'power' of sin is reduced to the issue of securing one's existence.[120] However, if Paul's
language of sin as personified power cannot be summed up as an

---

[115] See Bultmann, *Theologie des Neuen Testaments*, p. 240.
[116] E.g. Rom 9:4, 5.
[117] Rom 3:1, 2.
[118] Gal 1:13, 14; Phil 3:4–7. Bultmann, *Theologie des Neuen Testaments*, p. 189.
Paul's radical rejection of his former life in Judaism leads Bultmann to the conclusion that the preaching of the Hellenistic Christian community constitutes the
historical background of Paul's conversion. It was here that Paul first heard the
message of Christianity as one of abrogation of the Law. See, Bultmann, 'Paulus,'
cols. 1021–1023; *Theologie des Neuen Testaments*, pp. 109-123, 188-189. One might
well dispute Bultmann's logic on several grounds. Paul himself denies that he
received the theological content of his Gospel from any human (Gal 1:12). As
Bultmann rightly notes, we have no record of any other segment of earliest
Christianity which formulated the relation between δικαιοσύνη διὰ πίστεως Χριστοῦ and δικαιοσύνη ἐξ ἔργων (νόμου) as an *Entweder-Oder* in the manner of Paul.
Moreover, Paul always explains his conversion theologically, and as the result of
an appearance of Christ, not on the basis of the preaching of others, in distinction
to the conversion of his congregations (e.g. Gal 1:15, 16; 1 Cor 15:1–11). See
Chapter 3.
[119] Bultmann, 'Paulus,' col. 1027: 'Denn indem er aus dem Verfolger zum
Gläubigen, verwirklicht sich nach seiner Auffassung und in extremer Weise,
was sich grundsätzlich überall vollzieht, wo ein Mensch vom 'Worte' getroffen
wird und sich glaubend entschließt, sein altes Ich preiszugeben und sich unter
Gottes Gnade zu stellen, wie Phil 3 4-16, II Kor 4 3–6 deutlich zeigen.'
[120] The simple fact that Paul frequently speaks of sins and transgressions (in the

attack upon a basic human existential dilemma, the problem of the relationship between being declared and being made righteous reemerges and Bultmann's comprehensive center no longer suffices as an explanation for the whole of Paul's thought.[121]

Nevertheless, a central aspect of Bultmann's proposal would seem to have some validity. Paul's conversion involved the reevaluation of the role of *Torah* and of Israel's privileges in the divine granting of righteousness.[122] If this is so, then Bultmann's description of Paul's dissent from Jewish ideas concerning the relation between the gift of salvation and obedience may well form a theologically significant element of his conversion. How did the Judaism which Paul knew prior to his conversion understand the relation between divine saving mercy and human effort? And to what extent did Paul's conversion involve the rethinking of this relation?

V. JUSTIFICATION AS CHRIST'S SAVING LORDSHIP: ERNST KÄSEMANN

Ernst Käsemann developed his influential reappraisal of Paul's concept of 'justification' as a challenge to Bultmann's description of Paul's theology. In contrast to Bultmann, he draws attention to the cosmic and theocentric aspects of redemption in Paul's thought. However, precisely because he is concerned to develop a unified presentation of Paul's theology as a rival to Bultmann's synthesis, he refuses to surrender 'justification' as the center of the Pauline Gospel or to give up Bultmann's focus on the Pauline address to the individual. He therefore attempts to subsume all

---

plural) from which redemption is necessary suggests that sin as an act played an important role in his thought (Gal 1:4; 1 Cor 15:3, 17; Rom 2:12; 3:25; 4:7; 5:16; 7:5; 8:13; 11:27).

[121] See Bultmann, *Theologie des Neuen Testaments*, pp. 244–246. Despite his emphasis on the juridical conception of sin in Judaism, he himself qualifies the extent to which this form of thinking influenced Paul's thought. The concept of death as a natural outgrowth of fleshly existence is given an independent status alongside juridical ideas. If the juridical concept of sin as transgression is allowed a broader role in Paul's thought, a more theocentric description of Paul's soteriology results. The problem of guilt as an objective phenomenon, and the effects of divine judgment as an act external to humans must be given a place within the logic of Paul's argumentation. This sort of thinking surfaces repeatedly in Paul's letters. See e.g. Gal 3:22, Rom 1:26, 5:16, 11:32 and the important article by Ulrich Wilckens, 'Was heißt bei Paulus: "Aus Werken des Gesetzes wird kein Mensch gerecht"?' in *EKKNT: Vorarbeiten* (Neukirchen: Neukirchener, 1969), 1:51–77. The ultimate effect of questioning Bultmann's understanding of Judaism then, is that a larger role must be allowed the '*umgekehrt*' of Bultmann's characterization of Paul's thought: 'Jeder Satz über Gott ist zugleich ein Satz über den Menschen und umgekehrt.' Bultmann, *Theologie des Neuen Testaments*, p. 192.

[122] E.g. Phil 3:9.

aspects of Paul's soteriology under the rubric of 'justification.' This fusion, which involves the traditional categories of 'sanctification' and 'justification,' is accomplished exegetically.[123]

Käsemann has predecessors in this approach to Paul. Adolf Schlatter's construal of δικαιοσύνη Θεοῦ as 'the creative power of God,' provides the theological background for Käsemann, who developed a religio-historical setting for the conceptual framework which Schlatter provided, and reasserted this broadened understanding of 'justification' in the discussion of Paul's thought.[124] His views have gained a broad range of followers, including some Roman Catholic interpreters of Paul, who, because of Käsemann's joining of *gerecht erklären* and *gerecht machen*, are able with Käsemann to describe 'justification' as the center of Paul's theology.[125]

Like Schlatter, Käsemann begins with Romans and Paul's theme of the manifestation of the 'righteousness of God,' which, according to Käsemann, one must interpret properly in order to understand not only Romans, but the whole of Paul's thought. He notes that in some passages, Paul clearly speaks of a righteousness given by God.[126] In other passages, Käsemann finds δικαιοσύνη Θεοῦ personified as a power,[127] as the fellowship of the redeemed on earth,[128] or as God's own being and acting.[129] He then poses the

---

[123] Naturally such a fusion also bridges the gap between the *ethisch-juridisch and sakramental-mystisch* sides of Paul's thought, which played such a large role for Liberal interpreters of the later nineteenth century. See Ernst Käsemann, 'Gottesgerechtigkeit bei Paulus,' in *Exegetische Versuche und Besinnungen*, 2 vols. (Göttingen: Vandenhoeck & Ruprecht, 1965), 2:184.

[124] Adolf Schlatter, *Gottes Gerechtigkeit: Ein Kommentar zum Römerbrief* (Stuttgart: Calwer Vereinsbuchhandlung, 1935). H.-D. Wendland also attempted to establish a theological relation between *Rechtfertigung* and other aspects of Paul's thought, including anthropology, eschatology, christology and ecclesiology, *Die Mitte der paulinischen Botschaft: Die Rechtfertigungslehre des Paulus im Zusammenhange seiner Theologie* (Göttingen: Vandenhoeck & Ruprecht, 1935).

[125] See Karl Kertelge, *'Rechtfertigung' bei Paulus: Studien zur Struktur und zum Bedeutungsgehalt des paulinischen Rechtfertigungsbegriffs* (Münster: Aschendorff, 1967); 'δικαιοσύνη, δικαιόω,' in *Exegetisches Wörterbuch zum Neuen Testament*, 3 vols., ed. H. Balz and G. Schneider (Stuttgart: W. Kohlhammer, 1980), 1:784–807. Cf. the Lutheran, John Reumann, *'Righteousness' in the New Testament* (Philadelphia: Fortress, 1982). While Reumann questions Käsemann's claim that Paul's usage of δικαιοσύνη Θεοῦ represents the borrowing of a technical term, he follows Käsemann's exegesis of the Pauline texts. In dependence on Karl Kertelge, he also broadens the category of 'justification' by distinguishing between a *Rechtfertigungsbegriff* and a *Rechtfertigungsbotschaft*. The whole of Paul's soteriology, with its varied expressions, may be included under the latter heading (p. 41–91, esp. p. 91). Cf. also Manfred Brauch, "God's Righteousness' in Recent German Discussion,' in *Paul and Palestinian Judaism*, pp. 523–542.

[126] E.g. Rom 5:17, Phil 3:9.

[127] Rom 1:17, 10:3.

question, whether Paul might have been inconsistent, or whether a unifying factor might be found which might account for the various senses in which δικαιοσύνη Θεοῦ must be understood in Paul's writings.

For an answer Käsemann turns to Paul's conception of salvation. For Paul:

> Nicht einmal Rechtfertigung und Heiligung lassen sich sachlich oder chronologisch trennen.[130]

The gift of righteousness includes the Giver himself. It is the gift of Christ's lordship. Forensic justification and the *Stand in der Gerechtigkeit* are mutually established by one and the same divine salvific act.[131] In so far as they refer to the advance of God's cause on earth, the gift of righteousness, of God's glory, and of the Spirit are identical to one another.[132] One therefore possesses this all-embracing gift of righteousness by remaining under Christ's lordship:

> Nur indem wir unterwegs bleiben und täglich neu in die Herrschaft Christi gerufen werden, bleiben wir in der empfangenen Gabe, und bleibt diese in uns lebendig und mächtig.[133]

Nevertheless, this 'remaining under Christ's lordship' should not be considered as one's own doing. It remains the gift of God. Pauline soteriology, especially as it it expressed in Romans, binds *gerecht erklären* and *gerecht machen* together, not merely as cause and result, but in the essence of a divinely-worked salvation:

> Die ganze Botschaft des Briefes läßt sich im Rückgriff auf die Kyrios-Akklamation in die ebenso knappe wie paradoxe Aussage bringen, der Gottessohn sei als unser Kyrios die eine eschatologische Gabe Gottes an uns und darin offenbare sich zugleich Gottes Recht auf uns wie unser Heil.[134]

---

[128] 2 Cor 5:21.
[129] Rom 3:5, 25. Cf. Käsemann, 'Gottesgerechtigkeit,' 2:182.
[130] Käsemann, 'Gottesgerechtigkeit,' 2:184.
[131] Käsemann, 'Gottesgerechtigkeit,' 2:184.
[132] Käsemann, *An die Römer*, p. 28.
[133] Käsemann, 'Gottesgerechtigkeit,' 2:188.
[134] Käsemann, *An die Römer*, p. 26. In a curious manner, Käsemann's understanding of justification, in which forensic and behavioral righteousness are fused, represents a form of return to a pre-Reformation position. Despite his theocentric framework, which stresses the in-breaking of the kingdom of God, Käsemann's reading of Paul also emphasizes the bringing of the individual into submission to Christ's lordship. In contrast, the Reformers' emphasis was on the change in the divine disposition toward the individual. See Alister McGrath, *Iustitia Dei:*

According to Käsemann, this unified view of salvation has its
origins in apocalyptic Judaism, where, he contends, the expression
'righteousness of God' carries the sense of 'God's saving power.'
Here it was a technical term, a personification, in which the conceptions of power and gift were already present. Bearing this meaning, the term was taken up by Paul and given his characteristic
christocentric emphasis.[135] While Käsemann admits that the number of texts in which 'the righteousness of God' appears as a
technical term is relatively small, he nevertheless claims that it is
probable that Paul was familiar with it.[136]

A History of the Christian Doctrine of Justification, 2 vols. (Cambridge: Cambridge
University Press, 1986), 1:51: '. . . the notional distinction between *iustificatio* and
regeneratio provides one of the best *differentiae* between Catholic and Protestant
understandings of justification, marking the Reformers' complete discontinuity
with the earlier western theological tradition. From its beginning to end, the
medieval period saw justification as involving a real change in the sinner—a
understanding which precludes the Reformation distinction between *iustificatio*
and *regeneratio* from the outset.'

[135] Käsemann, *An die Römer*, pp. 25–27.

[136] In Käsemann's view, only Test. Dan 6:10, Matt 6:33, Jas 1:20, 1QS 10:25,
11:12, 1QM 4:6 contain the technical usage. Käsemann is dependent on the
work of Peter Stuhlmacher for his evidence. See, *Gerechtigkeit Gottes bei Paulus*
(Göttingen: Vandenhoeck & Ruprecht, 1965). Stuhlmacher's dissertation,
which is important not only for its research into the background of the expression 'righteousness of God' but for its extensive survey of the history of its
interpretation, uncovered relatively few examples. Stuhlmacher himself, moreover, has distanced himself somewhat from his earlier views, having accepted
Eduard Lohse's critique. See Peter Stuhlmacher, 'Zur neueren Exegese von Röm
3,24–26,' in *Jesus und Paulus*, ed. E. Earle Ellis and Erich Gräßer (Göttingen:
Vandenhoeck & Ruprecht, 1975), p. 331 n. 62; also 'Die Gerechtigkeitsanschauung des Apostels Paulus,' in *Versöhnung, Gesetz und Gerechtigkeit* (Göttingen:
Vandenhoeck & Ruprecht, 1981), pp. 85–116. While appreciating Stuhlmacher's contribution, we want to distance our work here from him somewhat.
Despite the shift in Stuhlmacher's position, his understanding of Paul's word-
usage still seems to be in danger of engaging in what James Barr has called
'illegitimate totality transfer.' Stuhlmacher insists on a 'synthetic' understanding
of all Paul's righteousness language, which nevertheless may shift in its stress
upon divine or human righteousness from context to context ('Gerechtigkeitsanschauung,' p. 105). Behind his assertion lies the analysis of צדקה in the
Hebrew Bible by K. Hj. Fahlgren in which a divine pronouncement and reality
are considered as inescapably (synthetically) connected (See 'Die Gegensätze von
sedaqa im Alten Testament,' in *Um das Prinzip der Vergeltung in Religion und Recht
des Alten Testaments*, WdF 125, ed. Klaus Koch (Darmstadt: Wissenschaftlichebuchgesellschaft, 1972), pp. 87-129). Even if one accepts Fahlgren's assessment,
it is improper to transfer the theological concept (expressed by word-combina-
tions) to the usage of individual terms. Stuhlmacher's appeal to changing emphasis in Paul's use of 'the righteousness of God' belies his insistence on a unified
concept behind the expression, although he is entirely correct to claim that a link
exists for Paul between God's own righteousness, which makes a claim upon the
human being, and the righteousness given as a gift to faith. Cf. Eduard Lohse,
'Gerechtigkeit Gottes in der paulinischen Theologie,' in *Die Einheit des Neuen
Testaments: Exegetische Studien zur Theologie des Neuen Testaments*, pp. 209–227
(Göttingen: Vandenhoeck & Ruprecht, 1973); Udo Schnelle, *Gerechtigkeit und*

In his commentary on Romans, Käsemann attempts to broaden the religio-historical basis for his position somewhat. He observes that the conception of salvation *sola gratia* was not peculiar to Paul. It appears in some traditions of apocalyptic Judaism, especially in some of the writings of the Qumran community. Paul's difference with his adversaries, therefore, was not over the presence of eschatological salvation. 'Justification by faith' was Paul's theological variation of the early Jewish- Christian proclamation of the in-breaking of the kingdom of God in Christ. The gap between Paul and the apocalyptic Judaism represented in the Qumran materials was essentially christological, manifesting itself anthropologically in Paul's Gospel of salvation *sine legis, sola fide*. The christological focus of Paul's message therefore accounts for both the proximity of his views to those of Qumran Judaism (since both conceived of an eschatological manifestation of God's righteousness in the present) and for the distance of Paul's views from this form of apocalyptic Judaism (since $\delta\iota\kappa\alpha\iota\sigma\sigma\acute{\nu}\nu\eta$ $\Theta\epsilon\sigma\hat{\nu}$ is for Paul manifest in Christ, and appropriated by faith, apart from the Law).

Käsemann's proposal has received not only wide reception, but considerable criticism.[137] The particular historical background which Käsemann suggests lies behind $\delta\iota\kappa\alpha\iota\sigma\sigma\acute{\nu}\nu\eta$ $\Theta\epsilon\sigma\hat{\nu}$, viz., that it is a technical term arising from apocalyptic Judaism, has been strongly questioned. This aspect of his thesis remains highly problematic. Furthermore, as we shall see in the following discussion, the conceptual broadening of 'justification' which Käsemann proposes fails to match the nature of Paul's argument in his letter to Rome.

Without a doubt, Käsemann's emphasis on Paul's interest in the establishment of God's lordship over the world through Christ is an important corrective to Bultmann's construal of Paul's theology. One also can readily affirm with him that: 'Paulus kennt keine Gabe Gottes, die uns nicht zum Dienst verpflichtete und unsern Dienst ermöglichte.'[138] For Paul, the *nova obedientia* necessarily issues from the Gospel, and is not subsequent to or of lesser importance than forensic justification.[139] Further, it is doubtlessly

Christusgegenwart: Vorpaulinische und paulinische Tauftheologie, GTA 24 (Göttingen, Vandenhoeck & Ruprecht, 1983), pp. 92–100; Klaus Berger, 'Neues Material zur 'Gerechtigkeit Gottes',' *ZThK* 68 (1977):266–276; David Hill, *Greek Words and Hebrew Meanings: Studies in the Semantics of Soteriological Terms* (Cambridge: Cambridge University Press, 1967), pp. 82–162.
[137] For a survey of reactions to Käsemann's views, see Hübner, 'Paulusforschung seit 1945,' pp. 2694–2709.
[138] Käsemann, 'Gottesgerechtigkeit,' p. 183.
[139] See Victor Paul Furnish, *Theology and Ethics in Paul* (Nashville: Abingdon, 1968), pp. 153–157.

true that Paul's usage of δικαιοσύνη Θεοῦ in some manner reflects apocalyptic Jewish tradition of his day. There are clear overtones of God's covenant faithfulness in some passages where the expression occurs (e.g. Rom 3:5), a theme which is prominent in the Hebrew Bible, and recurs in early Jewish apocalyptic materials.

Specific aspects of Käsemann's thesis are troubling, however. He proceeds from the notion that Paul would be guilty of *Inkonsequenz* if no unifying concept could be found for his varying usage of δικαιοσύνη Θεοῦ.[140] But the accidental nature of language requires no necessary conceptual unity between the various usages of terms or expressions.[141] One might then allow that some occurrences of δικαιοσύνη Θεοῦ bear the sense of an authorial genitive, while others are to be interpreted as genitives of possession or belonging, without charging Paul with logical inconsistency.[142]

Moreover, Käsemann overlooks the difficulties inherent to the detection of technical terms. Even if a term takes on a technical usage, non-technical meanings may appear alongside the technical one in a text, making exegesis a difficult task. Interpreters are all too aware of this phenomenon with regard to Paul's use of the term νόμος.[143] When, therefore, Käsemann speaks of Paul taking over a formula in which he combines the senses of both gift and power, one immediately suspects that Käsemann is engaging in what James Barr has called 'illegitimate totality transfer,' i.e. adding the semantic value which a word bears in one context to that which it has in another.[144]

Furthermore, it is questionable whether the technical sense which Käsemann gives to the expression 'righteousness of God'

---

[140] Käsemann, 'Gottesgerechtigkeit,' pp. 182–183.

[141] E.g. simply because it is unthinkable for Paul that Jesus should die δωρεάν in Gal 2:21, does not mean that he contradicts himself in Rom 3:24 when he states that believers have been justified δωρεάν. Nor does it mean that one must search for a single meaning which might join the two usages for Paul.

[142] This does not precipitate one into Lietzmann's *schillernde Doppelbedeutung* for the expression δικαιοσύνη Θεοῦ. See *An die Römer*[4], HNT 8 (Tübingen: J. C. B. Mohr [Paul Siebeck], 1933), p. 30. Käsemann rightly notes that grammatical labels are of only limited help in describing the significance of δικαιοσύνη Θεοῦ. The authorial genitive may be simultaneously understood as a genitive of possession, i.e. the righteousness from God is God's own righteousness, since it does not derive from the human being. On the proper categories for describing this genitive, see Chapter 4, Section III.A.

[143] I am indebted to Dr. Moisés Silva for this important observation.

[144] James Barr, *The Semantics of Biblical Language* (Oxford: Oxford University Press, 1961), p. 218. Cf. Käsemann, 'Gottesgerechtigkeit,' p. 185: Die von Paulus übernommene Formel spricht jedoch zunächst vom Heilshandeln Gottes, das sich in der Gabe niederschlägt, ohne darin völlig aufzugehen. Selbstverständlich wird der ganze Nachdruck auf die Gabe fallen, wenn Glaubens- und Werkgerechtigkeit scharf kontrastiert werden müssen.

may be found in the examples from apocalyptic Judaism which he cites.[145] If this is so, then the religio-historical connection which Käsemann proposes is severed, and the particular manner in which he links Paul to apocalyptic Judaism is rendered void.

In this case, the problem reemerges as to whether the 'center' which Käsemann proposes can account for the whole of Paul's soteriology. Once the basis for Paul's use of δικαιοσύνη Θεοῦ in a borrowed formula is removed, it becomes more difficult to sustain the claim that the expression bears the sense of *Macht* in all its Pauline contexts.[146] Käsemann's contention that forensic justification is *never* materially independent of sanctification for Paul rests heavily on the idea that δικαιοσύνη Θεοῦ bears the sense of power. If such a sense is lacking in even *some* contexts, a conception of forensic justification distinct from behavioral sanctification reappears.

We will treat general problems with Käsemann's thesis as it relates to Paul's letter to Rome below. More detailed consideration of some of the passages in which the 'righteousness of God' appears in Romans is reserved for the discussion of the function of 'justification' in Romans in Chapter 4.

Käsemann's claim that Paul employs δικαιοσύνη Θεοῦ in Rom 1:17 as a reference to an apocalyptic conception of God's salvation-creating power runs into difficulties with the argument of Romans itself. Paul here supposedly refers to a tradition in which the 'righteousness of God' was understood as an obedience producing power. At one point in his commentary, Käsemann seems to presume that Paul's opponents and addressees at Rome were familiar with the apocalyptic traditions found at Qumran, in which the

---

[145] We will examine the instances of the expression 'righteousness of God' which Käsemann claims as evidence for a technical use in a later excursus. Since a number of these occurrences appear in 1QS, this excursus has been placed in Chapter 2, at the conclusion of a discussion of the soteriology of 1QS. For a critique of the method of investigation employed by Käsemann and Stuhlmacher, see G. Klein, 'Righteousness in the NT,' in *Interpreter's Dictionary of the Bible*, Supplement (Nashville: Abingdon, 1975), pp. 750-752; Erhardt Güttgemanns, 'Gottesgerechtigkeit' und strukturale Semantik: Linguistische Analyse zu δικαιοσύνη Θεοῦ,' in *Studia Linguistica Neotestamentica* BEvT 60 (München: Chr. Kaiser, 1971), pp. 75–82.

[146] See the following, who challenge Käsemann's reading in various contexts: Lohse, 'Gerechtigkeit Gottes,' pp. 218–227; Rudolf Bultmann, 'ΔΙΚΑΙΟΣΥΝΗ ΘΕΟΥ,' *JBL* 83 (1964):12–16; Hans Conzelmann, 'Die Rechtfertigungslehre des Paulus: Theologie oder Anthropologie?' *EvT* 28 (1968):389-404, esp. 398–403; John Piper, *The Justification of God: An Exegetical and Theological Study of Romans* 9:1–23 (Grand Rapids: Baker, 1983), pp. 103-130; Sam K. Williams, 'The 'Righteousness of God' in Romans,' *JBL* 99 (1980):241–290, esp. 243–244, 258, 282–284.

grace of God was regarded as the ultimate source of salvation.[147] Usually however, much like Bultmann, he understands Paul's opponents as Jews or Jewish Christians who sought 'their own righteousness' in the Law.[148] In either case, it is difficult to imagine that Paul was relying on the tradition which Käsemann has described.

The burden of proof clearly rests with Käsemann and those who adopt his position, since, as noted already, non-technical uses may appear alongside technical terms, requiring that the technical meaning be demonstrated in every context. Moreover, since it is unlikely that a technical usage existed, it is crucial for those who maintain that Paul appeals to such a tradition to show that the idea of a obedience-creating power is present in each context in which δικαιοσύνη Θεοῦ or δικαιοσύνη appears. Solid proof for this claim is lacking, however.

Since Paul introduces the expression δικαιοσύνη Θεοῦ in Rom 1:17 without explanation, one must assume either that he thought his word usage would be understandable to his audience, or that he intended to unfold the significance of his language in the body of the letter which follows. Yet no expansion or explanation of δικαιοσύνη Θεοῦ appears in the letter. And when in Rom 6 Paul explicates the call to obedience inherent to his Gospel, he does so in specifically *christological*, not Jewish apocalyptic, terms. Given the detailed and consciously worked-out argumentation of Romans, it therefore seems likely that Paul introduced δικαιοσύνη Θεοῦ in Rom 1:17 assuming his audience was familiar with the meaning he intended to convey by it.

However, it is unlikely that Paul assumed that his audience was familiar with the background to δικαιοσύνη Θεοῦ which Käsemann suggests. If Paul's addressees had been familiar with a tradition in which the idea of 'God's saving and obedience-producing power' was expressed by δικαιοσύνη Θεοῦ, there would have been no need for the argument of Rom 6. The chapter is clearly addressed to an

---

[147] Käsemann, *An die Römer*, p. 23: 'Im sola gratia sind die Gegner sich einig.' Stuhlmacher expressly appeals to the Jewish heritage of the community in Rome as the basis of their knowledge of such a tradition, 'Gerechtigkeitsanschauung,' p. 108.

[148] See e.g. Käsemann, *An die Römer*, pp. 77–80; also Ernst Käsemann, 'Rechtfertigung und Heilsgeschichte im Römerbrief,' in *Paulinische Perspektiven*, pp. 127–128 (Tübingen: J. C. B. Mohr [Paul Siebeck], 1969): 'Wir haben zu fragen: Wen repräsentiert der jüdische Nomismus, gegen den Paulus sich wandte? Dann ist jedoch zu antworten: Er vertritt jene Gemeinschaft frommer Menschen, welche Gottes Verheißungen zu ihrem Privileg und Gottes Gebote zum Mittel ihrer Selbstheiligung machen.'

audience for whom the gift of δικαιοσύνη seemed to encourage licentious behavior.[149] Such a concern is unthinkable for one who knows of δικαιοσύνη Θεοῦ as the establishment of God's right as Creator in the obedience of the creature. The argument of Rom 6 indicates, then, that Paul's first readers were ignorant of the tradition which Käsemann proposes. It is by all means likely that Paul alluded to some common Jewish ideas with his various references to δικαιοσύνη Θεοῦ, but the nature of these allusions must be understood in a manner other than that of an 'obedience-producing power.'

The difficulty from which Käsemann's thesis suffers in Paul's letter to Rome indicates that Käsemann's merging of *gerecht erklären* and *gerecht machen* cannot bridge what must be regarded as an unavoidable gap. While δικαιωθέντες νῦν (Rom 5:1) and 'death with Christ to sin and resurrection to service' (Rom 6) are obviously connected for Paul, he does not equate them. He rather argues in Rom 6 that union with Christ's death and resurrection effects and demands the obedience of the believer. Moreover, he does not present his argument purely in terms of Jewish apocalyptic thought, nor in terms of 'justification' (the expression appears only in v 7), but as a fresh analysis of the significance of the Gospel which proclaims Christ as crucified and risen. Käsemann and others are entirely correct in affirming that in Paul's theology as a whole forensic justification is never envisioned as an isolated gift to the individual divorced from other participatory aspects of salvation. But one cannot legitimately collapse 'justification' and 'sanctification' in Paul's letters. Therefore, despite Käsemann's legitimate concern to emphasize the apocalyptic dimension of Paul's thought, his attempt to construe a comprehensive theological 'center' entails serious weaknesses.

This conclusion brings the discussion of the place of 'justification' in Paul's thought to a critical juncture. In spite of qualifications given above, it is clear that Käsemann's assertion that the gift of forensic justification and the obligation to Christ's service were inseparable for Paul is legitimate.[150] One might then attempt to assess the *significance* of forensic justification for other aspects of the Pauline 'indicative' (as opposed to Käsemann's construal of the

---

[149] Cf. Rom 3:8 in which the argument of Rom 6 is anticipated, and 6:1, 15, 19.

[150] An independent forensic conception of justification does not necessarily rob Paul's theology of its cosmic dimensions. Nor should any of the following discussion be taken to imply a rejection of an apocalyptic framework for understanding Paul's thought.

whole of Paul's soteriology as essential to the *nature* of justification).[151] But since the religio-historical background which Käsemann has proposed for comprehending the whole of Paul's
soteriology is wanting, one runs the risk of being reduced to a
terminological discussion, as Reumann has rightly observed.[152]
The only means by which a full resolution of the relation between
'being declared' and 'being made righteous' might be accomplished is through a fresh reconstruction of a religious background
to explain the inherent but invisible link between the forensic and
behavioral/participatory aspects of salvation for Paul.

Even if such an investigation were completed, however, little
would be accomplished with regard to the place of 'justification'
in Paul's thought, if the origin and function of Paul's arguments
regarding a forensic, juridical justification were not addressed. *It is
the place of this aspect of Paul's thought which has been the subject of
controversy since the time of Baur.* The concept of forensic justification
appears in distinct rhetorical situations in Paul's letters, involving
his rejection of the Law as a way of salvation. Only if the significance of this theme to Paul's life and thought is assessed, will it
become possible to treat the issue of the meaning and implications
of Pauline 'justification by faith' adequately. This study therefore
will restrict itself to the question of whether or not Paul's arguments for a forensic *justification* may be regarded as 'central' to
Paul's thought.

VI. SALVATION IN CHRIST FOR ALL AS THE ESSENCE OF PAULINE
SOTERIOLOGY: E. P. SANDERS AND CURRENT PAULINE RESEARCH

While E. P. Sanders's *Paul and Palestinian Judaism* was not the first
investigation to challenge the central role which Bultmann and his
school assigned to the theme of 'justification by faith' in Paul's
thought, this monograph has become one of the most influential
treatments of Pauline theology in current scholarly discussion.[153]

---

[151] Prof. Paul W. Meyer has pointed out to me that the similarity in structure
between the indicative of forensic justification and other Pauline indicatives is
already an important argument for correlating the two aspects of Paul's soteriology. Cf. Bultmann 'Das Problem der Ethik bei Paulus,' pp. 179–199.

[152] Reumann, *Righteousness in the New Testament*, pp. 122–123. E. P. Sanders has
probingly suggested that once the whole of Paul's soteriology has been placed
under the umbrella of 'justification,' it is questionable whether one may legitimately use this term and not another to designate the essence of Paul's thought:
Paul and Palestinian Judaism, p. 438, n. 41, pp. 507–508.

[153] In addition to *Paul and Palestinian Judaism*, Sanders has produced a number
of articles and a second monograph on Paul. Most of the following discussion is
based on Paul and Palestinian Judaism, since Sanders's basic view is developed

Sanders has won a broad hearing in part because of his revision of the view of first-century Judaism which typified much of Christian scholarship during the late nineteenth and early twentieth centuries. The image of that Judaism as a religion of strict legalism, in which merits and demerits were strictly weighed, now can be seen to be a crude caricature. As Sanders and others before him have shown, much of early Judaism envisioned a God whose mercy and graciousness outweighed any requirement for strict retribution of misdeeds.

Sanders was by no means the first to call attention to this misrepresentation of early Judaism frequently found in Protestant scholarship. G. F. Moore, C. Montefiore, H. J. Schoeps, and others had done so before him.[154] Much of the interest in Sanders's work is the result of the direct comparison he has made of Paul with the Judaism of Paul's day. Earlier studies which rejected the commonly accepted view of Judaism, e.g. H. J. Schoeps's *Paulus*, generally posited that Paul was a Hellenistic Jew, foreign to the Judaism in which the covenant and the graciousness of God played a larger role.[155] Sanders, in contrast, attempts to assess Paul's relationship to a general pattern of religion found in virtually all elements of early Judaism.

Sanders's reading of Paul is no less revisionist than his treatment of Judaism. Taking up major aspects of Schweitzer's work, he attacks Bultmann's reading of Paul directly and turns Käsemann's

---

there, with later modifications noted when necessary. For further reference see: E. P. Sanders, 'Patterns of Religion in Paul and Rabbinic Judaism: A Holistic Method of Comparison,' *HTR* 66 (1973):455–478; 'The Covenant as a Soteriological Category and the Nature of Salvation in Palestinian and Hellenistic Judaism,' in *Jews, Greeks, and Christians: Religious Cultures in Late Antiquity*, ed. Robert Hamerton-Kelly and Robin Scroggs (Leiden: E. J. Brill, 1976), pp. 11–44; 'Paul's Attitude Toward the Jewish People,' *USQR* 33 (1978):175–187; 'On the Question of Fulfilling the Law in Paul and Rabbinic Judaism,' in *Donum Genticilium: New Testament Studies in Honour of David Daube*, ed. E. Bammel, et al. (Oxford: Clarendon, 1978), pp. 103–126; 'Jesus, Paul, and Judaism,' in *ANRW* II, 25.1, ed. W. Haase (Berlin: de Gruyter, 1982), pp. 432–433; *Paul, the Law, and the Jewish People* (Philadelphia: Fortress, 1983).

[154] See C. G. Montefiore, *Judaism and St. Paul: Two Essays* (London: M. Goschen, 1914; reprint ed., New York: Arno Press, 1973); G. F. Moore, 'Christian Writers on Judaism,' *HTR* 14 (1921):197–254; Schoeps, *Paulus*. Donald A. Hagner offers a survey of recent works on Paul by Jewish authors, 'Paul in Modern Jewish Thought,' in *Pauline Studies: Essays Presented to Professor F. F. Bruce on his 70th Birthday*, ed. D. A. Hagner and M. J. Harris (Grand Rapids, Eerdmans, 1980), pp. 143–165.

[155] G. F. Moore stands out as the exception. Schoeps constructs his own thesis despite the fact that he acknowledges Paul's contact with Palestinian Judaism. Cf. *Paulus*, pp. 1–42, esp. 38–42. For a survey of various descriptions of Paul's relationship to Judaism represented in this century, see Thielman, *From Plight to Solution*, pp. 1–27.

analysis on its head by declaring that 'participation,' not 'justification' is the proper term for describing the central theme of Paul's soteriology. The resulting, radical, new image of Paul has commanded a great deal of interest and debate.

A third reason for the considerable impact which Sanders's work has made lies in the general tendency in present scholarship to assign a lesser role to the topic of 'justification by faith' in Paul's life and thought. Krister Stendahl, for example, has explained Paul's apocalyptic conception of salvation-history and his resulting missionary aims as the motivation for this idea.[156] A number of interpreters propose that Paul's arguments on 'justification' were the result of his missionary experience and conflicts with Judaizers. In different ways and to varying degrees, it is suggested that Paul created the theme of forensic justification in response to crises within Gentile churches.

Therefore, while Sanders's position was anticipated by others (e.g. Moore and Stendahl), it was his extensive research in which he described Judaism in relation to Paul which broke the ground for a new reading of Paul. On account of its pioneering nature, Sanders's work heads this final section of our survey. While a number of current scholars differ from Sanders in positing mission activity as the source of Paul's understanding of 'justification,' their work is generically related to that of Sanders since they too divorce the topic from his conversion. Some of the more important of these interpretations are discussed at the end of this section.

A. Sanders's Description of Pauline Soteriology

According to Sanders, Paul operated from a few readily identifiable convictions:

> (1) that Jesus Christ is Lord, that in him God has provided for the salvation of all who believe (in the general sense of 'be converted'), and that he will soon return to bring all things to an end; (2) that he, Paul, was called to be the apostle to the Gentiles.[157]

Paul's analysis of the human plight, his rejection of the Law as a means of salvation, and his assertion that one may be justified by faith all proceed from these prior commitments. The resulting Pauline 'pattern of religion' can be best described as 'participationist

---

[156] Krister Stendahl, 'The Apostle Paul and the Introspective Conscience of the West,' *HTR* 56 (1963):199–215.
[157] Sanders, *Paul and Palestinian Judaism*, pp. 441–442.

eschatology.'[158] Language about 'justification' or 'righteousness by faith' does not express any one doctrine. It overlaps with participationistic conceptions such as having the Spirit, having life, and being cleansed. Such language serves primarily as an argument against the necessity of keeping the Law in order to participate in salvation. This conviction in turn is dependent on Paul's prior commitment to Christ as Savior of all, both Jew and Gentile.[159]

While Paul himself did not distinguish between juristic and participationistic categories, the emphasis of his religious thought lay in 'participation.' Believers were transferred into Christ, to live under his lordship, whereas before they had been under the power of sin. Although Paul sometimes characterizes the problem of sin as guilt, the idea of bondage, or of a union which precludes union with Christ represents his fundamental understanding of transgression. Participation in Christ as Savior, i.e. in his death and resurrection, is the guarantee of the eschatological salvation which Paul expected imminently. Christians must guard against allowing that salvific union to be disrupted by incompatible unions, such as the one formed in the worship of idols. While disobedience may be overcome by repentance, correct behavior is required for remaining in the state of salvation.[160] The concept of forensic justification therefore plays virtually no role in Paul's most basic convictions.

The problem of explaining Paul's conversion strikingly reappears in Sanders's study. Like Wrede, Sanders postulates a personal and private origin to Paul's theology. All that one can know about how Paul came to his 'basic convictions' is that he had a revelation.[161] His theological tenets are without parallel in his

---

[158] Sanders, *Paul and Palestinian Judaism*, p. 549: 'God has sent Christ to be saviour of all, both Jew and Gentile (and has called Paul to be the apostle to the Gentiles); one participates in salvation by becoming one person with Christ, dying with him to sin and sharing the promise of his resurrection; the transformation, however, will not be completed until the Lord returns; meanwhile one who is in Christ has been freed from the power of sin and the uncleanness of transgression, and his behaviour should be determined by this new situation; since Christ died to save all, men must have been under the domination of sin, 'in the flesh' as opposed to being in the Spirit.'

[159] Sanders, *Paul and Palestinian Judaism*, pp. 491–492.

[160] Sanders, *Paul and Palestinian Judaism*, pp. 548–549 (cf. pp. 452–453, 453–458).

[161] Sanders, *Paul, the Law, and the Jewish People*, p. 208: 'While we can see that Paul, in discussing membership in the people of God, always insists on the equality of Jew and Gentile and faith in Christ alone, and thus conclude that these are the two interrelated convictions which lie immediately behind his denial of righteousness by the law, there is a real sense in which we cannot explain in detail why Paul came to that position. He appeals to revelation. God revealed his son to (or in) him, and as a result he knew that it was through faith in Christ that God intended to save the world.' Cf. 'Jesus, Paul, and Judaism,' pp. 432–433; and Anton Fridrichsen, 'The Apostle and His Message,' *UUÅ* 3 (1947):1–23, who maintains that Paul received his Gospel that Christ is Lord of all in vision, though not at his conversion.

religious environment and unique in the history of early Christianity. With Sanders then, one is strongly reminded of Schweitzer's complaint against Wrede that he made Paul's teaching *eine isolierte Größe* without connection to his environment forwards or backwards.

As a consequence, the same troubling questions arise in relation to Sanders's portrait of Paul, as did in relation to Wrede's. How did a Jew, zealous for his ancestral religion, blameless in the righteousness of the Law, one who enjoyed the graciousness of God in the 'covenantal nomism' which Sanders describes, come to reject this entire pattern of religion to which he had been so fully devoted?[162] How is it that this pious Jew could ever conceive of the Messiah as Savior apart from *Torah*? Likewise, how is it that the Messiah became the Savior of the Gentiles for Paul apart from their incorporation into the nation of Israel?[163]

As we shall see in further discussion, Sanders passes over such questions largely because the image of Paul's preconversion Judaism which he has reconstructed seems to render a non-soteriological interpretation of Paul's conversion necessary. Yet it is clear that Paul did not create a religion *ex nihilo*, but interpreted the Christ-event as the fulfillment of the values and hopes of Judaism. According to Paul, God's son 'from the seed of David according to the flesh' appointed him as apostle to the Gentiles.[164] And while the Law brings condemnation, death, and wrath, it is nevertheless 'holy, righteous, and good.'[165] Moreover, the covenant with Israel given to the patriarchs remains valid.[166] Since Paul viewed faith in Jesus as Messiah as a fulfillment of Israel's hopes, it is insufficient simply to say that he adopted another 'pattern of

---

[162] Gal 1:13, 14; Phil 3:6.

[163] James Dunn, 'The New Perspective on Paul,' *BJRL* 65 (1983):101, comments: 'The Lutheran Paul has been replaced by an idiosyncratic Paul who in arbitrary and irrational manner turns his face against the glory and greatness of Judaism's covenant theology and abandons Judaism simply because it is not Christianity.'

[164] Rom 1:3, 5.

[165] Rom 7:9–12.

[166] Rom 11:28, 29. Cf. Rom 9:4, 5. In contrast, Sanders claims: 'Taken together, Paul's positions on the law and on the Jewish people mean that he explicitly denied the saving efficacy of the covenant between God and Israel, confidence in which was the heart of covenantal nomism which we described as basic to the Judaism of the period. He accepts the terminology (the sons of Abraham will inherit the promises), but systematically redefines the crucial terms ('Jesus, Paul, and Judaism,' p. 434).' But in view of Rom 11:28, 29, it is impossible to sustain the notion that Paul simply redefines all the crucial terms of Judaism. Cf. Morna Hooker, 'Paul and Covenantal Nomism,' in *Paul and Paulinism: Essays in Honor of C. K. Barrett*, ed. M. D. Hooker and S. G. Wilson (London: SPCK, 1982), pp. 51–52.

religion' or that he rejected Judaism merely because it was not Christianity. Some account must be given as to how his conversion affected his prior understanding of salvation.

The implicit assumption of Wrede and Schweitzer, that Paul relies exclusively on *ad hominem* argumentation in opposing Judaism and Judaizers, also reappears in Sanders's work. According to Sanders's reading, Paul in his debates with Judaizing Christians *never* uses the arguments which led him as a Jew to his fundamental soteriology, despite the fact that Sanders acknowledges that Paul was directly engaged in debates with 'covenantal nomism.' Sanders's Paul simply does not express to other Jewish Christians why he has taken his odd stance.[167] To explain Paul, Sanders merely asserts the logical priority of Paul's conviction that Christ was Savior of all.[168] Such a reconstruction is both deficient and unlikely in the extreme.

While Sanders's study is similar to Wrede's *Paulus* in creating a Paul oddly detached from his environment, his image of Paul also is closely related to that of Schweitzer, to whom he explicitly refers. As a result, his Paul inherits many of the weaknesses of Schweitzer's work. Sanders displaces Schweitzer's 'eschatological mysticism' as a descriptive term for Paul's theology with 'participation in Christ.' He also rejects Schweitzer's attempt to locate Paul's background in apocalyptic Judaism, as is apparent in the preceding description of his views. But Sanders's 'participation in Christ' is materially not very different from Schweitzer's characterization of Paul's thought. Both Schweitzer and Sanders contend that the notion of 'sharing in Christ' has precedence over juristic conceptions for Paul. Sanders, furthermore, takes up Schweitzer's argument that 'justification by faith' is detached from ethical demands in Paul's letters, and hence cannot be regarded as central to Paul's thought.[169]

We have seen, however, that Schweitzer's arguments are not particularly weighty.[170] The consideration to which Sanders makes special appeal, i.e. that no theme which does not explain other concepts may be regarded as 'central,' does not help to

---

[167] Cf. Sanders, *Paul, the Law, and the Jewish People* , p. 46.

[168] Sanders, *Paul, the Law, and the Jewish People*, p. 47: 'I have elsewhere written that his real attack on Judaism is against the idea of the covenant and that what he finds wrong in Judaism is that it lacks Christ. Perhaps putting the matter in terms of God's plan of salvation formulates those ideas in a more precise and more understandable way. What is wrong with the law, and thus with Judaism, is that it does not provide for God's ultimate purpose, that of saving the entire world through faith in Christ, and without the privilege accorded to Jews through the promises, the covenants, and the law.'

[169] Sanders, *Paul and Palestinian Judaism*, p. 440.

[170] Cf. Section III, above.

decide the place of forensic justification in Paul's thinking.[171] It is
not clear that Paul developed his thought deductively nor that the
letters which have been preserved reveal precisely how his theology
as a whole developed. One should not expect, then, that it will be
possible to reconstruct Paul's thought so that it will unfold like a
treatise of systematic theology. There are a variety of themes which
cannot be derived by deductive reasoning from Sanders's own
construction: Paul's belief in the uniqueness of the God of Israel,
in the fact of a final judgment, in the holiness of *Torah*, or in the
faithfulness of God to his promises. It is not necessary then, to
suppose that one must be able to derive the entirety of Paul's
soteriology by deductive means from the topic of forensic justification, in order for this concept to be of importance to Paul.[172]

As we have noted, the 'participationist eschatology' which Sanders attributes to Paul incurs the weaknesses common to the
naturhaft conceptions of Paul's soteriology. Sanders takes up

---

[171] Sanders's claim that, because δικαιοσύνη and cognate terms have a range of
meanings in Pauline usage, 'justification by faith' is not one doctrine but a
'heuristic category' used to refute Judaizers, is nonsensical. The semantic field
of the expressions has nothing to do with whether or not Paul entertained a
particular understanding of 'being justified,' forensic or otherwise. Sanders's concept of 'participation' is itself nothing more than a 'heuristic category.' The real
issue at stake is whether or not Paul employs arguments concerning forensic
justification merely as an *ad hominem* strategy.

[172] It is not true that the idea of being justified by faith is independent of all
other elements of Paul's thought. Sanders himself allows that faith touches upon
ethics in Gal 5:6 and Rom 14:23. One may add other passages to this brief list.
Whether or not one accepts the well-attested subjunctive ἔχωμεν in Rom 5:1, the
context in which it appears is clearly hortatory, urging perseverance in affliction.
Here, then, is a passage in which forensic justification itself is connected to an
exhortation. And as Käsemann and Stuhlmacher have rightly pointed out, for
Paul forensic justification cannot be isolated from obedience to Christ. See. e.g. 2
Cor 5:11-6:18; Phil 3:7-16. Likewise, the ὑπακοὴ πίστεως (Rom 1:5, 16:26),
although sometimes interpreted as an epexegetic genitive, is most likely a genitive
of origin. The ὑπακοή which the believers at Rome displayed was not that of faith
as mere *notitia*, but of active submission to the message of the Gospel (Rom 6:17,
18; cf. 1 Thess 1:8–10). Paul elsewhere in Romans makes the claim that Christ
worked the obedience of the Gentiles in word and deed through him (Rom 15:17):
the λόγῳ καὶ ἔργῳ is most naturally taken as an adjectival modifier of ὑπακοή, not
as an adverbial phrase (cf. Phil 2:12–18, 2 Cor 10:1–6). Faith, then, is more
closely related to ethics for Paul than Sanders allows.

Sanders is blatantly incorrect in claiming that guilt, repentance and forgiveness play no role in Paul's soteriology. Regarding Rom 4, Hans Hübner rightly
observes: 'Rechtfertigung bedeutet eben, daß die Zurechnung der Gerechtigkeit
ein Akt der Tilgung der Schuld ist, in dem der Gerechtfertigte zugleich der
Herrschaft der Sündenmacht entnommen ist.' Hans Hübner, 'Pauli Theologiae
Proprium,' *NTS* 26 (1980):468; also Karl T. Cooper, 'Paul and Rabbinic
Soteriology: A Review Article,' *WTJ* 44 (1982):131–132. See Rom 2:4–5; 4:7;
2 Cor 7:9–10; 1 Thess 1:9; 2 Cor 3:16. Cf. Sanders, *Paul and Palestinian Judaism*,
p. 503.

Schweitzer's thesis, that for Paul union with Christ might be disrupted by incompatible unions. But we have seen already that this misrepresents Paul, since the imperatives in Paul's letters generally do not assume the possibility of a falling back into existence prior to faith.[173] Sanders's reconstruction of a Pauline 'center' therefore fails to adequately represent the relation between the 'indicative' and 'imperative.'[174]

Likewise, the discussion of Käsemann's thesis has indicated that the claim that Paul did not distinguish between juristic and participatory categories cannot be sustained. Käsemann introduces the initial argument against Bultmann, but retains the centrality of juristic language. Sanders inverts the terminology, making 'participation' primary.[175] Following Sanders, Reumann again retrieves Paul's righteousness terminology and claims on a historical and systematic basis that, when righteousness is defined in participatory categories, it may be claimed as a proper description of Paul's theology.[176] These flip-flops may go on *ad infinitum*, but once one argues that Paul did not distinguish between juridical and participatory soteriology, it is ludicrous to assert the priority of one over the other in a historical assessment of Paul's thought.

Sanders's method of demonstrating that 'participationist eschatology' is Paul's 'real concern' is also faulty. His important, yet misdirected debate with Bultmann contains a fallacy which seriously weakens his thesis and highlights the need for a better

---

[173] See above, Section III. Cf. Sanders, *Paul and Palestinian Judaism*, pp. 454–456.

[174] Sanders's comment, that Bultmann's formulation of the relationship between the 'indicative' and 'imperative' is 'absolutely correct, except for one thing' (i.e. that the indicative is 'living in the Spirit'), can only amount to an instance of confusion on Sanders's part. To affirm Bultmann's description is to deny the 'participationist eschatology' which Sanders attributes to Paul. Cf. *Paul and Palestinian Judaism*, pp. 439–440.

[175] Yet Sanders acknowledges that in Gal 3:1–5, the gift of the Spirit is the result of faith. One cannot simply say then, as Sanders does, that Paul did not distinguish between juristic and participatory ideas. On occasion, Paul can speak of 'participation' as deriving from faith, thus making a distinction between the two. See Sanders, *Paul, the Law, and the Jewish People*, pp. 12–13 n. 4, where he corrects his statement in *Paul and Palestinian Judaism*, p. 441, that righteousness by faith can be derived from participatory aspects of Paul's thought. He continues to claim, however, that Paul did not distinguish between the two motifs. Hübner, 'Pauli Theologiae Proprium,' pp. 445–473, rightly notes that Rom 6 introduces 'participationist' ideas as a means of warding off false conclusions which might be drawn from the preceding juristic discussion. It is incorrect, therefore, to claim as Sanders does, that juristic language is made to serve participationist language, but not vice versa. Cf. Sanders, *Paul and Palestinian Judaism*, p. 503.

[176] Reumann, *Righteousness in the New Testament*, pp. 120–123.

method for the identification of Paul's 'concerns.'[177] The flaw in his argument is best seen in his statement of disagreement with Bultmann. Sanders sets out to:

> exclude one of the traditional ways of setting up the discussion of Paul's theology: by describing first the plight of man to which Paul saw Christ as offering a solution.[178]

He claims that the reverse is true:

> It seems likely, however, that Paul's thought did not run from plight to solution, but rather from solution to plight. The attempts to argue that Romans 7 shows the frustration which Paul felt during his life as a practicing Jew have now mostly been given up, and one may rightly and safely maintain that the chapter cannot be understood in this way.[179]

The implicit error in Sanders's work, recognizable in these citations, is his equating of the reasoning by which Paul came to his convictions with his later theology.

This assumption is faulty on two counts. First, Sanders incorrectly presumes that the beliefs which Paul adopted subsequent to his conversion would not become of primary importance to his theology. He is undoubtedly correct in asserting that it was Paul's encounter with Christ, not a disappointment with the Law which prompted his conversion. Yet when Paul came to new, radical conclusions regarding the nature of sin, the Law, and righteousness, is it likely that such ideas would not have become constitutive elements of his theology?

Secondly, Sanders overlooks the fact that 'Paul's thought' is 'sub-textual,' an abstraction from the arguments of Paul's letters. These letters were written for concrete purposes in specific situations. 'Paul's thought' is accessible therefore only through reconstruction and interpretation of his aims. Sanders, in contrast, rather naively assumes that the argument of Galatians represents

---

[177] Thielman, *From Plight to Solution*, p. 7, rightly recognizes that Bultmann's synthesis of Paul's thought is coherent with Sanders's claim that Paul worked from the conviction that 'Christ is Savior.' As we have observed, the crucial element of Bultmann's synthesis is his contention that in all Paul's writings the self-understanding inherent to faith comes to expression. Formally, this is not different from Sanders's claim that Paul always worked from his conviction that Christ was 'Savior of all.' Sanders's oversight in this matter underscores the weakness of his method for reconstructing Paul's thought.

[178] Sanders, *Paul and Palestinian Judaism*, p. 442.

[179] Sanders, *Paul and Palestinian Judaism*, p. 443. Cf. p. 474: "On page after page of Bultmann's discussion of Paul's conception of 'man prior to faith' I have marked 'backwards'. . . ."

an unfolding of Paul's thought-processes.[180] He dissociates the structure of Romans from Paul's theology by linking its argument to Jew-Gentile relations. This is not an implausible suggestion for the purpose of Romans, although we will present an alternative reading. How is it, however, that the polemical letter to Galatia, which itself has to do with Jew-Gentile relations, reveals Paul's logic while Romans does not?[181]

It is clear then, that the resolution to Sanders's dispute with Bultmann over the nature of Paul's theology lies in a reexamination of Paul's aims in writing Galatians and Romans, especially the latter. Even if it could be shown that Galatians is a theological treatise, reflecting a basic 'participatory' theology, Sanders's argument that 'participation' *and not* 'justification' was of primary importance to Paul could be established only if it is shown that the particular circumstances of Romans *alone*, and not Paul's theological concerns, call forth Paul's arguments for a forensic justification by faith there.

B. Sanders's Description of Early Judaism

Despite the deficiencies of Sanders's discussion of the 'center' of Paul's theology, his work on early Judaism opens up a number of questions concerning the validity of Bultmann's portrait of Paul. Although Bultmann took into account newer research into early Judaism, his thesis concerning Paul's conversion and his subsequent theology rests on a misrepresentation, as we have observed already.[182] It is widely acknowledged that Sanders has performed a significant service by pointing out the inherently biassed treatment of early Judaism which appears in a number of older Protestant works on the subject. More precisely stated, Sanders has dispelled the notion that the Tannaitic materials, as

---

[180] Sanders is undoubtedly influenced by Schweitzer, who views Galatians as the prime representation of Paul's *Sein in Christo* soteriology.

[181] Sanders's analysis of Galatians leads him to conclude that Paul's argument proceeds from the exclusivity of salvation in Christ, which appears especially in Gal 2:21; 3:2, 5, 11: 'Throughout, the argument is *dogmatic*; there is no analysis of the human situation which results in the conclusion that doing the law leads to boasting and estrangement from God (Sanders, *Paul and Palestinian Judaism*, p. 484; emphasis Sanders's.)' In contrast, he finds that Paul's basic intent is to establish the equality of Jew and Gentile in Romans, that the argument for faith, which varies in its definition, is actually an argument directed against the Law, and that 'righteousness by faith' serves primarily as a refutation of the idea that one needs to keep the Law (Sanders, *Paul and Palestinian Judaism*, pp. 485–497). Cf. Hübner's insightful critique of Schweitzer's reading of Galatians, 'Pauli Theologiae Proprium,' pp. 450–454.

[182] See above, Section IV.B.

well as other early Jewish sources, reveal a Judaism in which the
hope for salvation depended on the exacting measurement of merits versus transgressions.[183] The 'pattern of religion,' i.e. 'covenantal nomism' which Sanders finds in early Judaism has been widely,
although not universally, acknowledged as valid:

> The 'pattern' or 'structure' of covenantal nomism is this: (1) God has
> chosen Israel and (2) given the law. The law implies both (3) God's
> promise to maintain the election and (4) the requirement to obey.
> (5) God rewards obedience and punishes transgression. (6) The law
> provides for means of atonement, and atonement results in (7) main-
> tenance or re-establishment of the covenantal relationship. (8) All
> those who are maintained in the covenant by obedience, atonement
> and God's mercy belong to the group which will be saved. An impor-
> tant interpretation of the first and last points is that election and ul-
> timately salvation are considered to be by God's mercy rather than
> human achievement.[184]

The broad acceptance of Sanders's views on early Judaism has
had a significant impact on the study of Paul. Because he has
stressed the abiding belief in God's mercy in early Judaism, Sanders has left most scholars without a category by which to describe
the immediate effect of Paul's coming to faith in Christ upon his
understanding of salvation. A number of recent studies on Paul
have concluded with Sanders that Paul's conversion consisted
simply in his affirmation of Jesus as Messiah, or perhaps as a
supernatural 'Savior of all humanity.' Questions as to the role of
Torah and the plight of humanity were answered later, in defense of
the universalism which Paul had adopted or as an extrapolation of
Paul's belief in the limitation of salvation to those who belonged to
Christ.

As we have seen however, Paul's postconversion Jewish self-
identification requires that one account for the impact of his
conversion on his earlier devotion to *Torah*. It is here that
serious questions arise concerning the means by which Sanders
compares Paul with the Judaism Paul knew. Just as Protestant
depictions of Judaism in the past century or so wrongly indic-
ted the religion as a whole, Sanders's study, redolent of the

---

[183] See Sanders, *Paul and Palestinian Judaism*, pp. 128–147. The portrait of
Judaism which took root in Protestant exegesis in the later nineteenth and earlier
twentieth centuries consisted in a gross oversimplification and misunderstanding
of the sources. Sanders points to Emil Schürer's *Geschichte des Jüdischen Volkes im
Zeitalter Jesu Christi*, Ferdinand Weber's *Jüdische Theologie auf Grund des Talmud und
verwandter Schriften*, and Wilhelm Bousset's *Die Religion des Judentums im neutestamentlichen Zeitalter* as having particular influence.
[184] Sanders, *Paul and Palestinian Judaism*, p. 422.

work of George Foote Moore, seeks to vindicate the religion in its entirety.[185] While the former studies overlook the genuine piety and moral insights which are found in early Judaism, the latter gloss over the imperfections which are a part of the practice of all religions. Both approaches bring to the historical task theological and philosophical prejudgments which are assumed more than discussed and defended. Sanders's approach is not appropriate to a study of Paul, who was not engaged in debate with 'the whole' of Judaism. For the purposes of historical study it is of greater importance to correctly identify and describe the particular forms of Judaism and Jewish Christianity from which Paul dissented and with which he debated.

Similarly, the question with which Sanders addresses the texts, that of 'how one gets 'in' and stays 'in'' ultimately imposes a theological, not historical question on many of his sources, particularly the Tannaitic materials.[186] As Neusner has noted, Sanders's bypassing of the bulk of the halakhic corpus in favor of the haggadic materials is questionable if one's aim is to understand Judaism 'on its own terms': Sanders does not engage the 'generative problematic' of the materials themselves. Neusner's methodological solution also is eminently reasonable: through careful descriptive work, one must 'tease out a range of questions' common to both sides of the comparison.[187] But in this case, a comparison with Paul in the area of soteriology is hardly fitting for the writings of the Tannaitic period, since as Sanders admits, that concern rarely comes to the surface in the Rabbinic literature.[188]

---

[185] See G. F. Moore, 'Christian Writers on Judaism,' *HTR* 14 (1921):198–254. Westerholm's discussion of Sanders's views suffers from the same weakness, *Israel's Law*, pp. 148–150.

[186] Cf. Wayne Meeks, 'Toward a Social Description of Pauline Christianity,' in *Approaches to Ancient Judaism 2*, ed. William S. Green (Chico, CA: Scholars Press, 1980), p. 27: ". . . his own book, monumental as it is, shows how powerful are the habits of our religious and scholarly tradition. For Sanders' definition of 'pattern of religion' turns out instead to be a pattern of theology, an ordo salutis that can be reduced– despite Sanders' own strictures in the introduction to his book– to its essentials: 'covenantal nomism' on the one hand, 'participationist eschatology' on the other. These may be useful catchwords to summarize some recurrent patterns of language, but they are not apt descriptions of 'the way the religion works.'"

[187] See, Jacob Neusner, 'The Use of the Later Rabbinic Evidence for the Study of Paul,' in *Approaches to Ancient Judaism 2*, ed. William S. Green (Chico, CA: Scholars Press, 1980), pp. 43–59 esp. 45–47: 'To state matters simply, How do we know that 'the Rabbis' and Paul are talking about the same thing, so that we may compare what they have to say? And if it should turn out that 'the Rabbis' and Paul are not talking about the same thing, then what is it that we have to compare (p. 56)?'

[188] Sanders, *Paul and Palestinian Judaism*, p. 75, 211–212, 235–237.

There is fairly broad agreement that Sanders's analysis fits the general assumptions of the Rabbis of the Tannaitic period. He finds the same pattern in the Qumran literature and most other early Jewish apocalyptic writings.[189] Yet Sanders misses important nuances to the 'covenantal nomism' which he describes, particularly in the apocalyptic materials.

It is not at all clear that the upheavals of the late first and early second centuries with which Judaism had to contend, the destruction of Jerusalem by Rome, the rise of Christianity, and the further destruction incurred during the Bar Kokhba revolt, would not have strikingly influenced the expression of the Jewish religion.[190] Indeed, some of the most important differences between literature with pronounced emphasis on apocalyptic eschatology and later Tannaitic materials are immediately apparent. Unlike the Rabbis, the apocalyptic writers often were directly concerned with questions of soteriology. It was in such terms that the struggle against Hellenistic influence (which long preceded Roman occupation) was carried out by various sects and movements seeking to preserve Jewish identity and religion.[191] Sanders himself admits that it is in this literature that soteriological questions come to the fore:

> It is noteworthy that it is in polemical literature that the topics of election and the requirement of strict obedience to the Mosaic code come to most explicit expression. I have in mind, for example, Jubilees, the principal Dead Sea Scrolls, and the letters of Paul. . . . When one turns to Rabbinic literature, which is relatively non-polemical

---

[189] The boundaries for what constitutes 'apocalyptic writings' are notoriously difficult to define. See the treatment of this issue in Chapter 2, Section I.

[190] Cf. Frank C. Porter's criticism of Moore: 'Great events happened during the three centuries from Antiochus IV to Hadrian, events which deeply affected Judaism as a religion. But of these events and their influence Moore has little to say. It is of course in connection with these events that the Apocalypses were written. In regard to these writings it would be possible to call in question the entire consistency of Moore's position ('Judaism in New Testament Times,' *Journal of Religion* 8 [1928]:42–43).'

[191] Cf. Martin Hengel, *Judentum und Hellenismus: Studien zu ihrer Begegnungen unter besonderer Berücksichtigung Palästina bis zur Mitte des 2.Jh. v. Chr.* WUNT 10 (Tübingen: J. C. B. Mohr [Paul Siebeck], 1969), p. 459: 'Zwar war von jetzt (the end of the second century BCE) an jede Bewegung, die in grundsätzlicher Weise Kritik an der *Tora* übte, in Palästina zum Scheitern verurteilt; jedoch gab die Frage nach ihrer autoritativen Deutung ständig Anlaß zu erbitterten Streitigkeiten. Der durch die Abwehr des hellenistischen Überfremdungsversuches entfachte religiöse Rigorismus wirkte als beunruhigendes Element weiter bis hin zur zealotischen Bewegung im 1.Jh.n.Chr. Man wird daher das palästinische Judentum zwischen 200 v. und 70 n.Chr. keinesfalls als einheitliche Größe unter dem Aspekt der späteren rabbinischen Gesetzesauffassung betrachten dürfen, zumal die stärkste Partei, die der Pharisäer, selbst in sich gespalten war.'

toward outsiders, it is quite understandable to find that these inherited, common features were taken for granted and discussed relatively little.[192]

Yet Sanders's study glosses over the various ways in which
covenant and election, obedience and mercy were understood in
materials which stress apocalyptic eschatology. When such concepts are in flux, it is relatively unimportant (although correct)
to say that Palestinian Judaism as a whole may be described as
'covenantal nomism.' As D. A. Carson has observed, the crux of
the matter lies in the various ways in which these concepts involving the covenant are construed.[193]

Sanders's interaction with the work of Hartwig Thyen provides
a good example of the interpretive difficulties which arise with the
use of the category of 'covenantal nomism.' Part of the difference
between Sanders and Thyen, whom Sanders strongly criticizes, lies
in their opposing evaluations of the conclusions of Erik Sjöberg.[194]

Thyen implicitly accepts the conclusion of Sjöberg who maintains that ideas of retribution and mercy lie side-by-side in the
materials. This juxtaposition results in the idea that God's undeserved mercy is extended to the obedient and repentant:

> So bleibt die jüdische Religion, wie sie von den Tannaiten dargestellt
> wird, eine Religion, in der das normale Gottesverhältnis auf die Ger-
> echtigkeit des Menschen und das dadurch gewonnene Wohlgefallen
> Gottes aufgebaut ist. Das steht unbedingt fest, und es gibt keine An-
> sätze zur Aufhebung dieses Grundfaktums. Zu einem solchen Gottes-
> verhältnis soll der Sünder umkehren. Aber trotzdem weiß man nicht

---

[192] E. P. Sanders, 'Puzzling Out Rabbinic Judaism,' in *Approaches to Ancient
Judaism*, vol. 2, ed. William S. Green (Chico, CA: Scholars Press, 1980), pp. 72–
73.

[193] We shall see that his assertion that notions of grace and mercy are diluted in
apocalyptic materials is confirmed in the Psalms of Solomon, *Divine Sovereignty and
Human Responsibility: Biblical Perspectives in Tension* (Atlanta: John Knox. 1981), pp.
68–69.

[194] Sanders charges Thyen both with misrepresenting Erik Sjöberg and with
rejecting Judaism 'because it is not Lutheranism' (Sanders, *Paul and Palestinian
Judaism*, p. 53). But Thyen explicitly affirms Sjöberg's conclusion that Palestinian
Judaism maintained a belief in God's mercy alongside his justice. In the section
which Sanders cites, Thyen asserts only that since the slightest trace of merit
theology or synergism corrupts the idea of grace, it is not surprising that
gelegentlich one finds repentance regarded as a meritorious deed. Thyen finds that
on the whole Judaism retained a consciousness of real forgiveness. Because the
requirement of obedience remains alongside the idea of mercy, Thyen comes to
the theological conclusion that the whole of early Judaism was synergistic in its
soteriology. Sanders disagrees with Thyen, but that does not mean that Thyen has
ignored the data. Cf. Hartwig Thyen, *Studien zur Sündenvergebung im Neuen Testament und seinen alttestamentlichen und jüdischen Voraussetzungen*, FRLANT 96 (Göttingen: Vandenhoeck & Ruprecht, 1970), pp. 74–76.

nur davon zu reden, daß Gott den Sünder, wie er es verdient hat, bestraft, sondern auch davon, daß er ihn auf vielerlei Weise seine unverdiente Güte spüren läßt.[195]

Sanders disputes this analysis however, claiming that:

> . . . the *universal* view is that every *individual Israelite* who indicates his intention to remain in the covenant by repenting, observing the Day of Atonement and the like, will be forgiven for *all* his transgressions. The passages on repenting and atoning in order to return to God, which are ubiquitous in the literature, *presuppose* the covenantal relationship between God and all the members of Israel (emphasis by Sanders).[196]

Sanders's language here, as elsewhere, is somewhat vague. On the one hand, he can say that 'intention and effort' are necessary to remaining in the covenant.[197] Yet he also claims that the Tannaitic materials have a broader conception of mercy than apocalyptic literature in which the theme of mercy extended to the righteous appears.[198] Obviously the nature and degree of obedience required differs between various documents. This allows Sanders to say occasionally that one is 'in' unless by 'heinous transgression' one opts out of the covenant.[199] Sanders's categories gloss over significant differences between various materials, and permit him to speak rather generally about the relation between mercy and obedience.

But the concepts of 'mercy,' 'obedience' and 'covenant' are fundamental to the disagreement between Sanders and Sjöberg (and Thyen). Sanders claims that throughout the materials the 'covenant' is the presupposition for salvation. But Sjöberg regards the restrictions applied to the salvation of 'all Israel,' and similar statements elsewhere as introducing individualism into the soter-

---

[195] Sjöberg, *Gott und die Sünder*, p. 190.

[196] Sanders, *Paul and Palestinian Judaism*, p. 182; cf. Sjöberg, *Gott und die Sünder*, pp. 118–124. Sjöberg's views are not as easily dismissed as Sanders indicates. Sjöberg does not merely argue that M. Sanh. 10.1 ('All Israel has a portion in the world to come. . .') deals with Israel collectively and not individually. He also contends that the exceptions which follow show the rule is qualified by the concept of retribution. And he reminds the reader that the Rabbis did not develop a unified system: there are other references in which it is said that sinners in Israel will be punished along with the Gentiles. (Sjöberg refers back to his chapter on God's treatment of sinners, pp. 108–109, and as evidence points to T. Sanh. 13.) He observes that the matter of forgiveness of transgressions is not really dealt with in M. Sanh. 10.1. The concept of election displaces the question of guilt.

[197] E.g. Sanders, *Paul and Palestinian Judaism*, pp. 146–147.

[198] Sanders, *Paul and Palestinian Judaism*, p. 421.

[199] Sanders, *Paul and Palestinian Judaism* pp. 136-137.

iological equation. And Sanders himself contradictorily indicates that obedience remains a requirement for participation in this covenant. Yet the Tannaim do not suggest that God's covenant with the nation as a whole has been displaced. Inherent tensions surround the concept: the 'covenant' is assumed by the Rabbis, but do restrictions to it subvert the notion of grace implied by it?[200]

The problem of determining the significance of God's covenantal 'mercy' is sharpened when one moves from the relatively irenic Tannaitic materials to the more combative writings such as the Psalms of Solomon.[201] Here a clear distinction emerges between the righteous and wicked within Israel. An appeal to God's strict justice can be directed against 'sinners,' while a plea is made for God's mercy upon the 'pious.' The question arises as to whether notions of unmerited favor are qualified by the restrictions placed upon the sphere of operation of God's mercy.

Sanders resolves the matter by contrasting sayings which speak 'of God' with those which speak 'to God.'[202] He is undoubtedly correct in maintaining that the texts show no awareness of a tension between 'free' and 'earned' mercy. Yet the concept of mercy obviously differs between the two types of expression in the Psalms: a thought-provoking ambivalence to which we will return in Chapter 2.

Moreover, it is in materials such as the Pss. Sol. that one finds the most appropriate source for comparison with Paul. The determination of the proper dating and original *Sitz im Leben* of the Tannaitic materials is notoriously difficult.[203] And it is only in conjunction with these parameters that the real significance of 'covenantal nomism' can be weighed. Furthermore, soteriological themes are often consciously developed in writings with pronounced apocalyptic eschatology. By using this literature as a

---

[200] Sanders's presentation tends to cover over some of the logical tensions between the various views expressed in the Tannaitic material. At times God's election of Israel could be based on meritorious grounds (*Paul and Palestinian Judaism*, pp. 87–91). Even though Rabbinic soteriology does not generally rest on the weighing of deeds, some expressions indicate that the amount of work (even one deed) is taken into account, e.g. M. Aboth 3:15 (cf. *Paul and Palestinian Judaism*, p. 139). Good deeds are said to be able to suspend punishment (*Paul and Palestinian Judaism*, p. 146). Pharisees may have regarded Sadducees to have been excluded from salvation (*Paul and Palestinian Judaism*, pp. 150–151). There are underlying problems within these materials which deserve further exploration.

[201] See Sanders's interaction with Braun's views, *Paul and Palestinian Judaism*, pp. 392–397.

[202] Sanders, *Paul and Palestinian Judaism*, p. 395.

[203] See, e.g. Neusner, 'Rabbinic Evidence and Paul,' pp. 43-45; Philip Alexander, 'Rabbinic Judaism and the New Testament,' *ZNW* 74 (1983):235–245.

basis for comparison one is better able to avoid the trap into which
Sanders falls, of imposing one's own agenda on the texts.

What we know of Paul encourages this comparison as well. His
persecution of believers in Jesus as Messiah prior to his conversion
strongly suggests that he regarded adherence to this early movement as incompatible with the covenantal obligations laid upon
Israel. His reaction then was not unlike other early Jewish sects
and movements which sought to defend Judaism against Helleniz-
ing influences. Consequently, sources which display some form of
polemical stance against other Jews are the proper point of depar-
ture for a comparison with Paul.

One need not dispute Sanders's claim that 'covenantal nomism'
applies to apocalyptic literature as well as to that of the Rabbis to
recognize that significant tensions surrounding the ideas of mercy,
covenant, election, and the like often emerge with particular
strength in apocalyptic writings. The change of views which took
place in the course of Paul's coming to faith clearly involved the
shifting of such ideas. Unfortunately, the comparison of 'wholes'
which Sanders carries out misses the particular historical matrix
which gave these conceptions associated with 'covenantal nomism'
their significance in life for Paul. As a result Sanders fails to carry
out a true comparison of Paul with his Jewish background. G. B.
Caird insightfully comments on Sanders's conclusions:

> What we are led to expect is the thesis that the Judaism Paul rejects is
> not the spurious Judaism of Weber and Bousset but the genuine Ju-
> daism as expounded by Moore and Sanders. Instead we find only the
> lame conclusion: 'This is what Paul finds wrong in Judaism: it is not
> Christianity' (p. 552). Yet what a splendid case could have been
> made for the bolder hypothesis.[204]

C. Sanders's Work and Current Pauline Research

While Sanders's thesis posits a basic theological motivation behind
Paul's letters, much of current research asserts instead that Paul's
pragmatic concerns were the source of his arguments concerning
forensic justification. Yet such studies share with Sanders the common judgment that Paul's commitment to 'justification by faith
alone' did not spring from his conversion. It rather was employed
solely to defend the rights of Gentile congregations and the Gentile
mission.

---

[204] G. B. Caird, review of *Paul and Palestinian Judaism: a Comparison of Patterns of
Religion* by E. P. Sanders, in *JTS* 29 (1978):541–542.

A brief survey of some of recent proposals follows. We have attempted to describe a broad and representative (although not exhaustive) array of positions which supplement Sanders's work. The issues which they raise will form the subject matter of the remainder of this investigation. Our aim here is simply to point out some of the questions which such studies leave unanswered.

1. Krister Stendahl. Krister Stendahl has been perhaps as influential as Sanders in bringing about what James Dunn has called the 'new perspective on Paul.'[205] Stendahl correctly points out the lack of evidence that Paul ever suffered from 'an introspective conscience.' He also rightly argues that much of Romans has to do with Jew-Gentile relations. From this observation he draws the conclusion that Paul's arguments on (forensic) justification and his coming to faith had little or no personal soteriological significance. One should speak of Paul's 'call' not his 'conversion.' One must further bear in mind that 'justification' has to do with Jews and Gentiles, not the human predicament.

But the dichotomies which Stendahl has created have not been shown to be legitimate. While Paul did not seem to suffer acutely from the pangs of guilt, one need not conclude that his coming to faith did not have implications for his self-understanding. The very notion of a call to preach salvation in a risen Messiah to Gentiles is a radical turnabout for one who as a Jew persecuted early believers in Jesus. There is no known parallel in Judaism to Paul's evangelistic efforts among Gentiles.[206] It is therefore difficult to believe that his efforts to resolve Jew-Gentile relations were merely a matter of church politics without any personal relevance. The identity of the individual and the status of the group are not mutually exclusive categories. Stendahl's observations are basically correct, but they do not necessarily lead to the conclusions he draws.

2. James D. G. Dunn. James D. G. Dunn's position is not unlike that of Stendahl, although his view involves a criticism of early

---

[205] See Krister Stendahl, 'The Apostle Paul and the Introspective Conscience of the West,' *HTR* 56 (1963):199–215; *Paul Among Jews and Gentiles* (Philadelphia: Fortress, 1976).

[206] Behind Stendahl's characterization of Paul's conversion stands Johannes Munck, *Paul and the Salvation of Mankind* (Richmond, Virginia: John Knox, 1959), who maintained that Paul's basic insight was a salvation-historical one. The influx of the Gentiles into the people of God was to precede the salvation of Israel. But the notion of Gentiles *en masse* enjoying equal status with Jews without commitment to *Torah* is unheard of in first-century Judaism. It is therefore difficult to imagine Paul's call as having merely salvation-historical implications.

Judaism.[207] He accepts Sanders's critique of earlier Protestant interpretations of early Judaism, yet rightly claims that Sanders does not go far enough in explaining how Paul's differences with Judaism arose. For Dunn, this breach is found in Paul's combating particularism and nationalism, rather than activism and merit theology. A major thrust of his argument is that ἔργα νόμου does not signify general deeds of obedience, but the marks of being Jewish, especially circumcision.[208]

Yet we have seen that Wrede's similar assertion regarding ἔργα νόμου is entirely unconvincing.[209] And, as Nils Dahl has observed,

> Jewish monotheism at the time of Paul was universalistic in its own way, and Christian monotheism remained exclusive.[210]

Thus the false dichotomy which Dunn draws between universalism (Paul) and particularism (Judaism) obscures the issues at stake. It was possible both for Gentiles to be incorporated into the covenant with Israel and for some Jews to regard others as disqualified from the covenant, on the basis of adherence to the Law.[211] It is true that Paul does not regard his opponents as seeking to secure salvation solely by their own efforts, but that does not mean that 'merit theology' is thereby excluded.[212]

Bruce Longenecker's recent Durham dissertation, which follows the line laid out by Dunn, offers a good example of the weaknesses inherent to such an interpretation of Paul.[213] Longenecker rightly gives considerable attention to Rom 2 in his attempt to sustain his thesis that Paul combats 'ethnocentric covenantalism.'[214] It is here that Paul addresses the question of Jewish superiority. But to limit Paul's argument to purely ethnic concerns is to miss the thrust of the passage. If Paul was fundamentally concerned with nationalis-

---

[207] James D. G. Dunn, *Romans*, WBC 38 (Dallas, Tx: Word, 1988), 1:lxiii-lxii; J. D. G. Dunn, 'Works of the Law and the Curse of the Law,' *NTS* 31 (1985):523–542; Dunn, 'The New Perspective on Paul,' pp. 95–122.

[208] Dunn recognizes that Paul is able to vary between the use of ἔργα νόμου and νόμος in his argument, without any apparent shift in meaning. See Gal 2:16, 21; 3:11; 5:4; Rom 3:20, 28. Cf. Westerholm, *Israel's Law*, pp. 117–119.

[209] See Section II, above.

[210] Nils A. Dahl, 'The One God of Jews and Gentiles,' in *Studies in Paul* (Minneapolis: Augsburg, 1977), p. 191.

[211] E.g. the circumcision of Izates reported by Josephus, Ant. 20.34–48; the distinction between the pious and the wicked in the Pss. Sol. See Chapter 2, Section III.B.

[212] See Thielman's critique of Dunn, *From Plight to Solution*, p. 24.

[213] Bruce W. Longenecker, *Eschatology and the Covenant: A Comparison of 4 Ezra and Romans 1–11*, JSNTSup 57 (Sheffield: JSOT Press, 1991).

[214] Longenecker, *Eschatology and the Covenant*, pp. 174–202.

tic sentiment, why does he begin by addressing the human being, not the Jew?[215] Why does he begin with the personal soteriological implications of passing moral judgment on others?[216] Even when Paul speaks rhetorically to the Jew, he does not deal with simple ethnic pride, but with the assumption that the knowledge of God's will mediated by the Law brings moral superiority.[217] Longenecker himself recognizes that the issue at stake goes beyond ethnicity to ethics, but fails to draw the necessary conclusion.[218] Circumcision was indeed a 'national boundary marker,' but Paul here assumes that it also was a claim to religious preeminence mediated by the Law, and consequently constituted an assurance of salvation.[219] It is this claim which he attacks in Rom 2.

3. Lloyd Gaston. In a manner similar to Stendahl, Lloyd Gaston has argued that Paul's fundamental theological concern was the defense of the status of Gentile Christians as partakers of salvation, not the relationship of faith in Christ to the Law:

> Paul said nothing against the *Torah* and Israel, but simply bypassed them as irrelevant to his gospel.[220]

According to Gaston, it was uncertainty regarding the relation of God-fearers to the covenant which brought about legalistic practices (i.e. the doing of works in order to win God's favor).[221] Thus the problem which Paul addresses is a Gentile one, and not Jewish.

Gaston further postulates that Paul was a Shammaite, who viewed the only hope of salvation for Gentiles to rest in their proselytization, and makes much of Paul's rhetorical protasis 'if I still preach circumcision . . .'[222] Before his Damascus experience, according to Gaston, Paul was desperately concerned for the salvation of the Gentiles around him. His encounter with Christ provided him with the solution to the dilemma in which he found himself: Gentiles could be saved apart from *Torah*.

---

[215] Rom 2:1–11. Ultimately Paul does have the question of Jewish superiority in mind even here. But his choice of ὦ ἄνθρωπε πᾶς ὁ κρίνων indicates that he is attacking a principle beyond ethnicity.

[216] Rom 2:1–11.

[217] Rom 2:17–24.

[218] Longenecker, *Eschatology and the Covenant*, pp. 174–192.

[219] Rom 2:17–29.

[220] Lloyd Gaston, 'Paul and the Torah,' in *Antisemitism and the Foundations of Christianity*, ed. Alan Davies (New York: Paulist, 1979), p. 66. See also his *Paul and the Torah* (Vancouver: University of British Columbia, 1987).

[221] Cf. Markus Barth, 'Die Stellung des Paulus zu Gesetz und Ordnung,' *EvT* 33 (1973):496–526, who argues that ἔργα νόμου refers to Gentile adoption of Jewish practices.

[222] Gal 5:11.

Here Gaston makes much of very little data. Paul's brief reference
to 'preaching circumcision' is slim evidence for the passionate
missionary effort Gaston attributes to him. It does not appear that
there are any substantiating parallels of Jews actively engaged in
mission to Gentiles.[223] Moreover, Paul's tacit admission to having
'preached circumcision' must be understood differently. As we shall
see, the statement does not disclose earlier missionary activity
(before or after conversion) in which Paul asked Gentiles to accept
circumcision.[224]

In the end, Gaston's thesis can be maintained only by ignoring
Paul's statements relating his Gospel to Judaism. In the first place,
Paul explicitly states that his Gospel includes the salvation of Jews
within its scope.[225] And he characterizes Jewish rejection of his
message as a 'stumbl-ing' over the proclamation of salvation
through faith in a crucified Messiah.[226] The issue at stake here
goes beyond evangelization of Gentiles. The same is the case in
Paul's confrontation of Cephas in Antioch. For Paul, the manner in
which Cephas and other Jewish-Christians related to Gentiles implicitly expressed a faulty understanding of salvation.[227] Moreover,
given Gaston's reading of Paul, it is difficult to make any sense out
of Rom 7, in which Paul claims that believers have died to the
Law, an argument directed toward Jewish members of the church
at Rome.[228] Paul likewise describes the Mosaic covenant as a
ministry of condemnation and death, in contrast to the new covenant which mediates righteousness.[229] It would be wrong to ignore
Paul's abiding expectation of the salvation of Israel expressed in
Rom 11.[230] But it is equally incorrect to push aside his conspicu-
ously particularistic statements found in Rom 9 and Gal 4.[231]
Above all else, Paul's description in Phil 3:7–9 of the reversal of
his Jewish soteriological values which faith in Christ brought to
him indicates that Gaston's thesis is inadequate.

---

[223] See now the thorough treatment of this question by Scot McKnight, *A Light
Among the Gentiles: Jewish Missionary Activity in the Second Temple Period* (Philadelphia: Fortress, 1991).
[224] See the discussion of this passage in Chapter 3, Section I.
[225] Rom 1:16.
[226] 1 Cor 1:18–25.
[227] Gal 2:14–21.
[228] See Chapter 4, especially the discussion of Rom 7:14–25. It is true, of
course, that Paul never demands that Jewish believers refrain from keeping the
Law, as his treatment of the 'weak' and the 'strong' in Rom 14:1–15:7 shows.
[229] 2 Cor 3:4–11.
[230] Rom 11:25–27.
[231] See Rom 9:1-5, 27-29; Gal 4:21–31.

4. Francis Watson. According to Francis Watson, Antioch Christianity, which Paul represents, passed through the stages of a sociological paradigm (reforming movement—rejection—sect) in the process of developing a Gentile mission.[232] Paul began his missionary activity among Jews. When he and other missionaries like him met with failure, they purportedly decided to preach to the Gentiles. In order to prevent the repetition of the rejection they had faced among Jews, they decided to jettison the requirements of *Torah*, thus making it easier for Gentiles to accept their message.[233] Paul's later arguments in Romans and Galatians served to legitimate the social reality of sectarian Gentile communities, which resulted from these endeavors.

Unfortunately, the most pressing questions go answered in this model. Watson overlooks Paul's persecution of believers and thus fails to grapple with the theological dynamic of Paul's coming to faith. Likewise, he offers no reconstruction of the message which Paul and the Antioch community proclaimed among Jews, which is essential to understanding why it was rejected. Even more striking is the absence of explanation for the turn to Gentile mission. There is no inherent reason why a Jewish movement would adopt this unparalleled practice in the process of becoming a sect. And given Watson's thesis, one wonders why this supposed sociological phenomenon did not repeat itself across the Mediterranean world. These rather noticeable gaps render Watson's proposal unsatisfactory.

His exegetical observations, although sometimes thought-provoking, do not lead to the conclusions which he suggests. There might have been a period in which Paul preached only to Jews, as Watson argues, but Paul's report suggests that if there was one, it was relatively short. Watson's most convincing evidence for a purely Jewish mission is found in Paul's rehearsal of his earliest visit to Jerusalem after his conversion. Paul gives no indication that the question of Gentile circumcision was discussed at this time.[234] But like many arguments from silence, this one is fragile. Paul indicates that it was under the special condition of a revelation (κατὰ ἀποκάλυψιν) that he later took the issue to Jerusalem.[235] One cannot draw too much from his report that he did not deal with the problem earlier. His limited contact with the Jerusalem church in

---

[232] Francis Watson, *Paul, Judaism and the Gentiles: A Sociological Approach* (Cambridge: Cambridge University Press, 1986).
[233] Watson, *Paul, Judaism and the Gentiles*, p. 36.
[234] Gal 1:18–20.
[235] Gal 2:2.

his early period of mission indicates that he was already pursuing an independent course. And his decision to meet with the Jerusalem apostles in order to resolve the uncertainty which he developed over his Law-free Gospel to the Gentiles, indicates that his Gentile mission was not the product of sectarianism.[236]

Watson too easily dismisses the likelihood that Paul continued to witness to Christ within synagogues during the period of his Gentile mission. It is illegitimate to translate Paul's retrospective assessment of God's providential dealings with Israel in Rom 11 into a description of Paul's own practice.[237] Paul tells the Thessalonian church that his work among Gentiles was hindered by Jewish resistance, which is hard to imagine apart from a continuing contact with the synagogue.[238] He indicates to the Corinthians that he at times *returned* to Jewish practices in order to evangelize Jews, having accepted already a basically new identity.[239] His earlier statements in 1 Cor strongly imply that he still preached to Jews.[240] It is hard to imagine that Paul did nothing to reach out to his people, given his powerful expression of concern for them in Rom 9, and his statement in Rom 11 that he hoped to 'save some of them.'[241] Paul's five lashings from the Jews need not have been associated with a mission purely to them.[242] In fact, the attempt to carry out a dual outreach might well have been the provocation for such treatment.

5. Gerd Lüdemann. Gerd Lüdemann has offered a rather vague assessment of the origins of Paul's understanding of forensic

---

[236] One cannot sweep away Paul's admission to uncertainty in Gal 2:2: μή πως εἰς κενὸν τρέχω ἢ ἔδραμον.

[237] See Rom 11:11–36.

[238] 1 Thess 1:16.

[239] 1 Cor 9:20,21: Καὶ ἐγενόμην τοῖς Ἰουδαίοις ὡς Ἰουδαῖος, ἵνα Ἰουδαίους κερδήσω· τοῖς ὑπὸ νόμον ὡς ὑπὸ νόμον, μὴ ὢν αὐτὸς ὑπὸ νόμον, ἵνα τοὺς ὑπὸ νόμον κερδήσω. Paul here indicates that as an act of service he gave up his freedom and lived as a Jew, in order to evangelize (9:19). He is conscious that his practice is not entirely Jewish, as his use of ὡς and the restrictive datives (τοῖς Ἰουδαίοις, τοῖς ὑπὸ νόμον) indicate. Therefore Paul's statement here means precisely what Watson says it cannot, cf. *Paul, Judaism and the Gentiles*, p. 29. Tomson, *Paul and the Jewish Law*, pp. 274–281, has argued that one should read, 'I was born the Jews a Jew, that I shall win Jews; those under Law as under the Law, that I shall win those under the Law.' But this interpretation 1) ignores v. 19 where Paul states that his practice was a volitional act in which he gave up his freedom to do otherwise; 2) likewise fails to account for the datives, which inform the reading of ὡς; 3) necessarily adopts the weakly attested omission of μὴ ὢν αὐτὸς ὑπὸ νόμον.

[240] 1 Cor 1:22–24.

[241] Rom 9:1–5; 11:14.

[242] 2 Cor 11:24.

justification.[243] He denies that the concept was entailed in Paul's conversion, primarily because it first appears after Gal 2:15. It was first formulated by Paul in response to the Galatian conflict.[244] Nevertheless, Paul was called at his conversion to be an apostle to the Gentiles: there he recognized a promised eschatological event in Christ. Thus the later conflict with *Torah* and Judaism was inherent to his conversion, even if it did not enter in as an explicit theological element.[245] *Torah* was '*relativiert*' by Paul's conversion, but the later rejection of the Law in Paul's teaching on justification was the result of the Gentile mission.[246]

The observation which Lüdemann brings to bear, that Paul's arguments concerning justification by faith first come to expression in Galatians, is important. But unless one defines more precisely the statement that in Paul's Damascus experience 'für den ehemaligen Pharisäer die Tora relativiert wurde,' one has not answered the question of the relation of Paul's conversion to his later teaching.

6. Heikki Räisänen. Heikki Räisänen's *Paul and the Law* sets out the problems inherent to Paul's language about the Law with admirable clarity.[247] However, his own characterization of how Paul arrived at a rejection of the Law is somewhat wanting. Räisänen's description very much represents a return to the psychological portraits of Paul popular in the last century, in which intuition and experience are played off against any theological element in Paul's motivations. He thus raises the complaint that German exegetes exclude psychological data:

> This naïve trust on a man's testimony about himself is a curious fundamentalistic survival within critical scholarship.[248]

Even granted that one must critically assess Paul's statements about himself, Räisänen's appeal fails to make a point. Refusal to

---

[243] Gerd Lüdemann, *Paulus und das Judentum*, Theologische Existenz heute 215 (München: Chr. Kaiser, 1983).
[244] Gerd Lüdemann, *Paulus und das Judentum*, p. 21. Georg Strecker argues similarly, that since the theme does not appear in 1 Thess, it represents a later polemical development. See 'Befreiung und Rechtfertigung: Zur Stellung der Rechtfertigungslehre in der Theologie des Paulus,' in *Rechtfertigung: Festschrift für Ernst Käsemann*, ed. J. Friedrich, W. Pöhlmann, P. Stuhlmacher (Tübingen: J. C. B. Mohr [Paul Siebeck], 1976), pp.479–508.
[245] Gerd Lüdemann, *Paulus und das Judentum*, pp. 21–22.
[246] Gerd Lüdemann, *Paulus und das Judentum*, p. 41.
[247] Heikki Räisänen, *Paul and the Law* (Philadelphia: Fortress, 1986).
[248] Räisänen, *Paul and the Law*, p. 232.

base one's description of Paul on a psychological analysis has to do
with the lack of data for such an undertaking, not with a retreat
from critical questions. The rejection of this means of approaching
Paul is verified all the more by Räisänen's discussion. He resorts to
the unsubstantiated and tentative proposal that Paul before his
conversion was a 'Pharisee of fear,' who as a Jew of the Diaspora
had entertained doubts about the ritual aspects of *Torah*. Of course,
'it is not impossible that Paul the Pharisee had (suppressed) doubts
about some of the ritual stipulations,' but it is not demonstrable
either![249] Speculative appeals of this sort do not present a convincing argument. As Sanders has rightly underscored, Paul gives no
indication that anything other than his encounter with Christ
dinted his zealous love for *Torah*. The widespread confidence in
God's mercy in early Judaism, which Sanders and others before
him have pointed out, calls this aspect of Räisänen's thesis into
question.

According to Räisänen, at Paul's conversion he adopted 'a more
or less lax attitude toward *Torah* observance.'[250] Meanwhile Gentiles entered the circle of believers in droves, while Paul, *mirabile
dictu*, observed and joined in the process of mission to them, accepting that these new believers need not be circumcised and adopt full
observance of his formerly cherished *Torah*! Over the years Paul
became alienated from 'the ritual aspects of the Law.'[251] When the
status of Gentiles was challenged at Antioch, Paul, being unable to
retrace his steps because of the social realities which then existed,
had to develop a radical critique of the Law as a whole in his
defense of the Gentile position.[252]

It must be asked whether the image Räisänen presents of Paul
initially adopting an attitude of indifference toward the Law is
plausible. If Paul persecuted believers in Jesus because he somehow regarded this movement as incompatible with *Torah*, the
cessation of his persecution at his conversion most likely meant
that he concluded that they were in conformity with the Law after
all, or that the meaning of the Law itself had to be radically
rethought. It is hard to envision Paul taking the middle ground
which Räisänen suggests, of adhering to the Law rather loosely. It
is true, as Räisänen argues, that it is possible for a person to shift

---

[249] Räisänen, *Paul and the Law*, p. 236.
[250] Räisänen, *Paul and the Law*, p. 236. Thus one finds the same sort of impreci-
sion here as with Lüdemann. What would this 'laxness' mean to one who earlier
had been zealously attached to Torah?
[251] Räisänen, *Paul and the Law*, p. 258.
[252] Räisänen, *Paul and the Law*, pp. 260–263.

ideas in stages.[253] That is not the question, however. The question is whether *Paul*, who persecuted believers out of devotion to the Law, could have suddenly taken this mediating stance.

Räisänen further operates with a misleading conception of Paul's relationship to Judaism. On the one hand, Räisänen is able to affirm Sanders's view, which allows that in general some minimal form of obedience was regarded as necessary for remaining in the covenant.[254] He nevertheless charges that Paul is opposed to a 'soft legalism,' in which salvation is based on obedience. This 'legalism' is unrepresentative of the Judaism of Paul's day.[255] Räisänen here obviously sets up a straw man. He himself regards early Judaism as having looked upon some extent of obedience as necessary to salvation. Therefore, Paul need not have opposed a 'legalism' in which salvation was *based* on obedience to have dissented from a Judaism in which obedience was regarded as a *necessary supplement* to God's covenantal mercies.

If Paul did reject a form of early Judaism in which obedience was regarded as integral to salvation, yet which on the whole was not boastfully self-reliant, an integral picture of Paul's conversion and of his later arguments might be constructed. His later conflicts with Judaizers might then reflect the values which he himself held prior to his conversion.

7. Recent Challenges to Sanders's Portrait of Paul. Two significant responses to Sanders's work appeared after a considerable portion of the present study had been completed. Since each of these investigations provides an alternative to Sanders's interpretation of Paul, it seems appropriate to offer an assessment of these proposals before proceeding with the study at hand.

a. Stephen Westerholm: Stephen Westerholm has produced a reconstruction of Paul's theology joined to a discussion of recent interpreters of Paul which is well-written, informative, and often insightful.[256] His treatment of Paul's usage of νόμος (which fre-

---

[253] Heikki Räisänen, 'Paul's Call Experience and His Later View of the Law,' in *The Torah and Christ: Essays in German and English on the Problem of the Law in Early Christianity*, Publications of the Finnish Exegetical Society 45 (Helsinki: Finnish Exegetical Society, 1986), p. 66.

[254] Heikki Räisänen, 'Legalism and Salvation by the Law,' in *The Torah and Christ: Essays in German and English on the Problem of the Law in Early Christianity*, Publications of the Finnish Exegetical Society 45 (Helsinki: Finnish Exegetical Society, 1986), pp. 29–32; also Räisänen, 'Paul's Call,' p. 78.

[255] Räisänen, *Paul and the Law*, pp. 177–181; 'Legalism,' pp. 37–38; cf. p. 26: A 'soft' legalist would be one whose system of salvation consists of the observance of precepts but who is free of any boasting or self-righteous attitude.

[256] Stephen Westerholm, *Israel's Law and the Church's Faith: Paul and his Recent Interpreters* (Grand Rapids: Eerdmans, 1988).

quently bears the sense of 'Mosaic covenant,' with promises of blessings and punishment) is very helpful, as is his description of the Pauline opposition between grace (faith, promise, Spirit) and the Law. But, as the title of Westerholm's monograph (*Israel's Law and the Church's Faith*) suggests, his work analyzes 'Paul's theology' as a cohesive whole.[257] This limitation results in an interpretation of Paul which is unsatisfying in the end.

Although Westerholm is aware of the questioning of the unity of Paul's thought by Räisänen and others, he treats 'Paul's theology' as an abstract entity.[258] This unfortunate decision has the effect of blocking out not only the sort of issues which Räisänen raises, but also any allowance for the development of Paul's thought (which Westerholm acknowledges) or the recognition that Paul's letters were contingent upon specific situations (which Westerholm also recognizes).

Westerholm's approach also renders his challenge to Sanders's work ineffective. He wrongly construes Sanders's description of Paul as being based on 'the starting point of Paul's thought, the conviction that occasioned his reassessment of the law.'[259] As we have seen, Sanders does not merely claim that Paul initially came to view Judaism differently on the basis of his belief that 'Christ is Savior of all,' he also claims that Paul consistently argues from this position. Therefore Westerholm's counter-proposal, that one may reconstruct Paul's thought as 'a description of (one variety of) first-century Christian theology' in which human dependence on divine grace is the central affirmation, constitutes a *petitio principii*.[260]

Other problems arise in the details of Westerholm's work as a result of the ahistorical method which he adopts. Two examples deserve mention.

In attempting to show that Paul's thought involved, from the start, a conviction regarding humanity's 'plight,' Westerholm asserts that Paul's acceptance of the tradition that Jesus' death was 'for our sins' forced him to a radical understanding of sin.[261] There is some value to this view, as the discussion of Paul's conversion in Chapter 3 will show. However, it is not at all clear that acceptance of the interpretation of Jesus' death as an atonement would have automatically led a Jew to Paul's position regarding the Law. The

---

[257] Cf. Westerholm, *Israel's Law and the Church's Faith*, pp. 152–153.

[258] Cf. Westerholm, *Israel's Law and the Church's Faith*, p. 152, where he refers to the 'achievement of the apostle.' Presumably, Westerholm regards Paul's 'mature' thought as 'Paul's theology.' What demarcates this stage of Paul's thinking?

[259] Westerholm, *Israel's Law and the Church's Faith*, p. 152.

[260] Westerholm, *Israel's Law and the Church's Faith*, p. 152–153.

[26'] Westerholm, *Israel's Law and the Church's Faith*, p. 161.

fact that Paul was such a solitary figure in the early Church attests
to the faulty logic which Westerholm employs here.

Likewise, Westerholm claims without much substantiation that:

> . . . the fundamental principle affirmed by Paul's thesis of justifica-
> tion by faith, not works of the law, is that of humanity's dependence
> on divine grace; and that conviction, it may be safely said, underlies
> everything Paul wrote.[262]

One is uncertain as to whether one ought to interpret this remark as Westerholm's theological analysis (a theology based on
Paul) or as an attribution to Paul himself (Paul's 'conviction').
Does Westerholm mean to tell us that Paul regularly employed
his arguments regarding 'justification by faith' for the purpose of
affirming humanity's dependence on grace? Or does he mean to
say that all Paul's statements cohere with this idea? Given an
Augustinian theological framework, there is no doubt that the
latter may be shown to be the case (as it is, one might add, with
the writings of the Qumran community). However, an attempt to
show that Paul himself wrote to defend an abstract notion of divine
grace would most likely prove unfruitful.

In light of these considerations, it seems fair to say that despite
Westerholm's perceptive discussion of Paul and his interpreters, he
fails to provide a satisfactory reply to Sanders's description of Paul.
Historical questions essential to grappling with Sanders's work go
unanswered.

b. Frank Thielman: In his monograph, *From Plight to Solution: A
Jewish Framework for Understanding Paul's View of the Law in Galatians
and Romans*, Frank Thielman attempts to explicate Paul's view of
the Law on the basis of early Jewish expectations of an eschatological purification of Israel. Employing both canonical (e.g. Jer 31,
Ezek 20) and non-canonical materials, Thielman suggests that
certain first-century Jews awaited a divine intervention which
would end Israel's rebelliousness and create new obedience. One
such Jew was Paul, who interpreted Jesus' death and resurrection
as constituting this eschatological act of God. Those who believe in
Jesus now truly obey the Law—albeit in a reduced, Hellenistic
form. Thus Paul operated from a traditional Jewish pattern of
thought which moved from 'plight to solution,' rather than from
'solution to plight,' as Sanders has suggested.

Despite the cleverness of Thielman's appeal to early Jewish
traditions, several problems attend his use of the materials. In

---

[262] Westerholm, *Israel's Law and the Church's Faith*, p. 167.

the first place, he does not show that in his sources pessimism
regarding human ability to keep the Law is joined with an eschatological hope for the nation of Israel. The radical pessimism of the
Qumran writings is set within the context of the sect's identification
of itself as the true locus of salvation, excluding Israel as a whole.[263]
Where one does find hope for the nation (as in the Pss. Sol. and
4 Ezra, which Thielman cites), one finds it in a specific form: Israel
will be delivered as a nation of the pious and obedient, from which
sinners will be removed.[264] Therefore, Thielman has not shown that
Israel could be portrayed as stubbornly disobedient and still expect
eschatological deliverance, aside from the canonical materials.

Secondly, Thielman's claim to have located a religio-historical
background to Paul's soteriology is predicated on his relating
Paul's 'reduction' of the Law to the expectations of certain circles
in Diasporic Judaism.[265] But, as Thielman admits, there is no
precedent in Jewish religious practice for Paul's forbidding circumcision, food laws, and the like for Gentiles.[266] Moreover, Thielman
can produce no evidence that circles existed in which emphasis on
human moral inability, eschatological hope for Israel, and mini-
mization of Jewish observances were joined, as they are in Paul's
letters. Such a combination of ideas is of the utmost importance to
Thielman's case, since Paul does not attempt, like one such as
Philo, to demonstrate the coherence of the important aspects of
the Law with Hellenistic ideals. Paul rather bases his 'reduction'
of the Law (granting, for the moment, Thielman's reading) *precisely
on God's eschatological act of deliverance.*[267] Where are the other early
Jewish sources which do the same? More importantly, if such
traditions existed, why doesn't Paul appeal to them?[268] Thielman
has produced an interesting assortment of parallels, but has not
provided an early Jewish background to Paul.

Finally, one may seriously question Thielman's claim that Paul
regarded believers as obeying the Law by means of the Spirit.
None of the three passages which form the linchpin of Thielman's
argument (Gal 5:14, Rom 8:4, Rom 13:8–10) provide direct evidence for his view.[269]

---

[263] See the discussion of 1QS in Chapter 2.
[264] See the discussion of the Pss. Sol. in Chapter 2.
[265] Thielman, *From Plight to Solution*, pp. 54–59.
[266] Thielman, *From Plight to Solution*, p. 56.
[267] E.g. Gal 3:19–29; Rom 7:1–6.
[268] Paul does not even appeal to the canonical materials such as Jer 31 and
Ezek 20 as evidence of an expected divine intervention.
[269] Although the purpose clause of 8:4 is usually taken to mean that Paul
expects believers to fulfill the Law, the passive sense of a *iustitia aliena* is to be
preferred. See the discussion of this text in Chapter 4, Section III.C.

Contrary to Thielman's claim, in Gal 5:14 Paul does not admonish believers to fulfill the Law. Rather, Paul asserts that the (whole) Law is fulfilled in the command, 'You shall love your neighbor as yourself.' This pronouncement is not an exhortation, but a theological argument built upon the Galatian desire to obey the Law. Obedience to the love commandment, which fulfills the Law's overall intent, is to *substitute* for the Galatian longing for adherence to the Law. Believers have been called to 'freedom,' which must be understood in context as signifying 'freedom from the Law.'[270] Those led by the Spirit are not 'under Law,' which must mean 'under the strictures of the Mosaic covenant,' and not (as Thielman suggests) 'under the curse of the Law,' since Paul applies this phrase to the birth of the son of God.[271]

Similar objections may be made to Thielman's reading of Rom 13:8–10. The assertion that, 'one who loves the neighbor has fulfilled the Law,' is contingent upon Paul's 'summing up' all commands of the Law in love for the neighbor. The shift in tense in 13:8 from present to perfect should not be overlooked: ὁ γὰρ ἀγαπῶν τὸν ἕτερον νόμον πεπλήρωκεν. Paul represents the Law here as containing a series of prohibitions against harming others. Love, which must be understood as including beneficence, by definition satisfies these demands.[272] The one actively engaged in loving the neighbor, has *already fulfilled* these prohibitions against harming others, and does more. Love, as Paul understands it, is the 'fulfillment' of the Law, in that it obviates it, as the Law itself it attests in the summary love command.[273]

These objections are sufficient to show that Thielman's thesis is tenuous from both early Jewish and Pauline perspectives. His attempt to show the 'Jewishness' of Paul over against Sanders's work is unconvincing as a result.

VII. SUMMARY AND PROSPECTUS

We have seen in our survey of interpreters of Paul, that attempts to employ 'justification' as a conceptual center from which the whole of Paul's theology may be explained, have failed to produce

---

[270] Gal 5:1, 13.
[271] Gal 5:18, cf. 4:4.
[272] The idea of active love is implicit in 13:8, where believers are said to be indebted to love others.
[273] The reference to the Law is most likely made in anticipation of Paul's discussion of disagreements between the 'weak' (conservative Jewish Christians) and the 'strong' (the remainder of the church). Cf. the reference to love (not Law) in Rom 14:15.

satisfactory results. The same has been shown to be the case for *naturhaft* or 'participatory' construals of Paul's thought.

The inability of various major proposals to produce an encompassing idea to which the whole of Paul's thought may be logically related leaves the door open for a much more modest endeavor. As we suggested in the introduction to this chapter, there is room for a more historically-oriented approach to the question of the place of forensic justification in Paul's thought. Questions of the logical relation of this topic to the remainder of Paul's theology may be held in abeyance, while two crucial issues related to the 'history of ideas' are raised: the origin of Paul's concept of being justified by faith, and the function of this concept in Paul's letters. Although Käsemann's interpretation of Paul represents a historical approach to determining the place of 'justification' in Paul's thought, we have seen that the religio-historical background for which he contends is lacking in Paul's letter to Rome, and we shall see that it is lacking also in the texts in which he claims a technical usage appears.[274] There is a need therefore for a fresh attempt to answer these questions regarding the meaning of 'justification by faith' for Paul. We have suggested at a number of points in the preceding discussion that Paul's conversion deserves to be the focal point for a reconsideration of the origin of his ideas regarding 'justification by faith.' Beginning with Wrede, and continuing until the present, there have been steady attempts to understand Paul's conversion in fundamentally christological and not soteriological terms. Where soteriology is involved with Paul's conversion in such constructions, it appears as a logical conclusion drawn from christological premises, *not as a radical rethinking of the ideas concerning salvation which Paul held prior to his vision of the risen Jesus.* This reading of Paul has received tremendous impetus from the work of E. P. Sanders, who through his often insightful critique of Protestant portraits of Paul, has reminded the scholarly world of the conscious dependence on God and his mercies present within early Judaism.

Despite the appeal of Sanders's work, there is room for a reexamination of Paul's conversion. At a number of points in the preceding discussion, we have observed that both Paul's preconversion devotion to *Torah* and his continuing Jewish identity after his conversion require that some account be given for the change in his views. Whatever his conversion involved, his soteriology was not a simple continuation of preconversion views in a new christological

---

[274] See Chapter 2, Section II, Excursus.

modification. Nor did Paul completely overthrow his past for an entirely new religion.

Another reason for reevaluating the soteriological aspect of Paul's conversion, is the deficiency of Sanders's comparison of Paul to his background. On the one hand, the preconversion Paul seems more closely related to the somewhat combative apocalyptic materials than Sanders's general survey allows. On the other, Sanders has not inductively investigated the concepts of mercy, covenant, obedience, and the like, in which the crux of a comparison of Paul with his background lies.

Chapters 2 and 3 represent a new attempt to describe the soteriological factor in Paul's conversion on the basis of a comparison of his own statements with selected apocalyptic materials. In these chapters, we shall see that Paul's conception of the relation between divine mercy and human response underwent a significant shift at his conversion. His coming to faith in Jesus as Messiah did not leave his previous soteriology intact.

The decision to devote attention to the function of 'justification' in Paul's letter to Rome also may be substantiated from the preceding discussion. We have seen that a curious image of Paul emerges from the work of Wrede, Schweitzer and Sanders. The 'Paul' whom they reconstruct cannot communicate to his contemporaries how he himself came to regard the observance of *Torah* as unnecessary to salvation. Much of the reason for this unlikely portrait of Paul lies in the lack of adequate criteria for distinguishing between Paul's convictions (which had relevance to him as a Jewish Christian) and the arguments which he employs solely for the sake of his opponents. The difficulty comes to a head in Sanders's misdirected argument against Bultmann's description of Paul's theology. The dispute between Sanders and Bultmann cannot be resolved in the fashion which Sanders attempts, by playing off the structure of Galatians (as representative of what 'Paul really thought') against that of Romans. The place of 'justification' in Paul's mature thought can only be determined by reexamining its function within Paul's aim in writing to Rome. Chapter 4 of this study will be devoted to this task.

A final chapter will be given to consideration of the role which may be ascribed to 'justification' in Paul's thought in the light of the conclusions of the preceding chapters. We shall see that although the idea of forensic justification by faith is not a theological 'center' from which the whole of Paul's thought may be derived, concepts associated with this theme were integral to his conversion and to his later interpretation of the Gospel.

CHAPTER TWO

THE COMMUNITY RULE
AND THE PSALMS OF SOLOMON
AS BACKGROUND TO
THE APOCALYPTIC JUDAISM OF PAUL

I. THE SELECTION OF SOURCES AND THE AIM OF THE DISCUSSION

We have argued in our discussion of Sanders's description of early Judaism, that materials in which apocalyptic eschatology is prominent provide a better basis for comparison with Paul than Tannaitic writings.[1] Such materials more closely conform to Neusner's well-founded demand that a range of common questions be drawn from both elements of a comparison: with Paul, apocalyptic materials often share an explicit interest in questions of soteriology.[2] We are especially interested in those writings which take some type of polemical stance toward other Jews, as did the preconversion Paul in his persecution of the earliest believers. Generally, the chronological precision which an adequate comparison requires also is more easily attained in apocalyptic materials. The date of a number of such writings can be shown to be relatively close to the first century, and in a number of instances even pre-70 CE Usually the original *Sitz im Leben* of these materials can be better defined than that of Tannaitic traditions. There is good reason then, for turning to early Jewish writings which emphasize apocalyptic eschatology as sources for comparison with Paul.

The investigation which follows is not an attempt to exhaustively categorize early Judaism. Our effort is limited to the reconstruction of the soteriology of selected documents for the purposes of comparison and contrast with Paul's references to his Judaism and his preconversion life. On the basis of his reading of Paul, Räisänen

---

[1] See Chapter 1, Section VI.B. The important factor here is not that the transcendent character of the age to come is stressed, but that a decisive divine intervention vindicating his people is anticipated.

[2] We have noted the apparent ambiguity of the Mishna on the extent of the covenant in our discussion of Sanders's description of early Judaism, Chapter 1, Section VI.B.

has provocatively asked whether any sector of early Judaism regarded salvation as *based on* obedience. Although he formulates the matter improperly, one may pose a similar question: Was righteous behavior ever regarded as *contributing to* salvation within early Judaism?[3] This issue will guide our analysis of early Jewish materials.

The results of the following study will not serve as a means of making generalizations about apocalyptic Judaism or even about Pharisaism. Although the writings investigated below are widely regarded as being of Palestinian origin, no claim will be made to have found characteristics which apply to the whole of the Palestinian Judaism of Paul's day. The sole aim is to discover if the Judaism reflected in Paul's letters might be found in any other pre-70 CE Palestinian sources.

Naturally, those writings which may be shown to be nearest to Paul in provenance ought to be selected for a comparison with him. Therefore materials such as 4 Ezra and 2 Baruch, which were composed under obviously altered conditions a generation after the destruction of the Temple are of lesser importance than writings which were composed prior to 70 CE.[4] Other material is potentially early, but cannot easily be demonstrated to be contemporaneous with Paul.[5] Likewise, essentially non-Palestinian sources (e.g. the Jewish Sibyllines) are also of lesser value for a comparison with Paul, who despite his familiarity with the Hellenistic world, had Palestinian roots.[6] As we have noted, those writings which give evidence of some form of polemics are more desirable for a comparison with the preconversion Paul than neutral or speculative materials. His persecution of the early Church, which was motivated by his devotion to Judaism, suggests that he was linked to circles which drew sharp boundaries between acceptable and unacceptable behavior.[7]

As we shall see in the following discussion, considerable linguistic precision is required for a proper construal of the soteriology of apocalyptic materials. Therefore writings which in their bulk are

---

[3] Räisänen, 'Legalism,' p. 26. Cf. Chapter 1, Section VI.C.6. Paul's statements about his preconversion life and his attacks on his opponents assume this type of Judaism. If it did not exist, Paul's picture of Judaism is a complete misrepresentation.

[4] See the discussion of the soteriology of 4 Ezra in the excursus at the close of this chapter.

[5] E.g. a considerable portion of the Enochic traditions.

[6] See now Martin Hengel, *The Pre–Christian Paul*, trans. John Bowden (Philadelphia: Trinity Press International, 1991), pp. 18–39.

[7] For this reason a writing such as the soteriologically-oriented Vita Adam et Eva (ApMos), which is potentially (although perhaps not demonstrably) contemporaneous with Paul, is not of primary important for the following comparison.

extant only in Ethiopic (e.g. Ethiopic Enoch, Jubilees) are not as useful as those which have gone through fewer translations.[8] Likewise, the existence of Christian interpolation in some writings (e.g. Testaments of the Twelve Patriarchs) lends a degree of uncertainty to any interpretation, rendering them somewhat less desirable as a basis of this sort of comparison with Paul.

Two writings seem particularly appropriate for a comparison with Paul: the Community Rule (1QS) and the Psalms of Solomon (Pss. Sol.). Both are pre-Pauline, yet fairly close to Paul chronologically. Both have a Palestinian provenance. The original *Sitz im Leben* of both writings can be fairly well determined.

Since its discovery, the Qumran literature has been favored for comparison with Paul because of its emphasis on themes of grace, election and a divinely-given righteousness. Käsemann's reading of Paul, for example, takes its starting point from the conceptions found in Qumran literature. From the varied writings of the Qumran community, 1QS is especially useful for purposes of comparison because of the central role it played for the sect. For these reasons 1QS has been selected as representing a form of Judaism potentially related to Paul.

We shall see that the suggested connection between Paul's conception of the gift of righteousness and that of the Qumran community is not as close as has often been supposed. Nevertheless, a number of the features of the soteriology represented in 1QS characterized the preconversion Paul, as Chapter 3 will show.

The Psalms of Solomon not only meet the criteria mentioned above, but like 1QS, may be included in this comparison for the particular link which they have to Paul. The Pss. Sol. have long been regarded as Pharisaic writings. We shall see that despite some qualifications to the traditional view, these psalms may still be regarded as representative of some Pharisaic group. They therefore are of considerable value for understanding Paul, the Pharisee, even if due caution must be exercised not to read one into the other.

1QS and the Pss. Sol. represent two quite different communities. This fact will become all the more obvious in the following description of the soteriological ideas of these writings. The following study therefore involves the comparison and contrast of two

---

[8] Extensive portions of 1 Enoch are extant in Greek, of course. And numerous Aramaic fragments have been found at Qumran. But an assessment of the soteriology of 1 Enoch adequate for the type of investigation undertaken here is made very difficult by the fact that approximately two-thirds of the material exists only in Ethiopic.

groups which themselves were only a part of the diversity which characterized pre-70 Judaism.

The effort has been made in the treatment of these two writings to follow the themes which are prominent in each piece, rather than imposing the categories of one upon the other. Therefore the headings which appear under 1QS do not correspond to those under the Pss. Sol. This dissimilarity in approach to the documents is perhaps most noticeable in the contrast between the 'covenant' in 1QS and 'Israel,' which receives far more stress as a theological topic in the Pss. Sol. A synthesis of the essential points of agreement and consideration of the differences between the two writings is reserved for the final section of the chapter.

According to Bultmann, the difference between Paul and the Judaism which Paul knew consists in how they construe the relationship between grace and obedience. This chapter, together with the treatment of Paul's conversion in Chapter 3, will show that this proposal retains its validity. In both 1QS and the Pss. Sol. salvific value is accorded to righteous behavior. Moreover, in the Pss. Sol., which represents the form of Judaism to which the preconversion Paul would have been related, God's grace and human obedience work cooperatively in securing salvation.[9]

II. 1QS: THE COMMUNITY RULE

A. Introduction

The eleven column scroll found in Cave 1 at Qumran, commonly called 'the Community Rule' on the basis of the (reconstructed) opening . . . . ספר סרך היחד . . ., represents a document which was clearly of foundational importance to the community which occupied the site, particularly in the earlier period (Ib). Not only does this writing appear to have been repeatedly recopied over a considerable period of time (from 100–75 BCE to late first century BCE), but its catechetical and liturgical content mark it as being integral to the self-understanding of the

---

[9] No association with the ideas of accumulating or weighing deeds is intended by this statement. Sanders and others have rightly dismissed the older Protestant understanding of זכות in the Tannaitic materials. Nor is it the aim of the following discussion to bring the technical distinctions of medieval Christian theology into the first century. Neither 1QS nor the Pss. Sol. give any evidence of having reflected actively on the question of 'merit' in a manner in which later Christian theologians did. The idea of 'merit' as a preparation for justification, or as an essential element of it, is therefore extraneous to the following discussion.

Qumran community.[10] It appears likely, moreover, that a section of the document, comprising basically columns 8 and 9 (the precise limit of the section is difficult to determine) contains a statement of the ideals which lay behind the founding of the community. An analysis of the contents of 1QS should therefore yield important insights into the basic thought of the Judaism practiced at Qumran.

We will make no attempt in the following discussion to describe a course of development of ideas within the material contained in 1QS. It is not clear that the progressive stages of the community postulated by such scholars as J. Murphy-O'Connor and J. Pouilly involve shifts in the basic soteriology adopted by the group.[11] Nor is the evidence which they produce for their detailed proposal unequivocal. It is generally recognized that 1QS represents a compilation of various once-independent materials. But beyond this observation, it seems speculative to work out a precise description of the social development of the community on the basis of the material in 1QS.

In the following discussion, we will analyze four themes significant to the understanding of the soteriology of 1QS. Each of these themes, drawn from the material itself, contributes to the question at hand: How was the covenant and the graciousness of God which is expressed in it thought to operate in the Judaism at Qumran? Two of the themes treated below, 'covenant' and 'election,' relate to the extent of the covenant, and the means by which its salvific blessings are obtained. The other two themes, 'atonement' and

---

[10] On the paleographic analysis of the Qumran materials see Frank Moore Cross, Jr., 'The Development of the Jewish Scripts,' in *The Bible and the Ancient Near East*, ed. G. E. Wright (Garden City, NY: Doubleday, 1961), pp. 133–202. Helpful discussions of the various copies of the material represented by 1QS along with brief treatments of dating and compositional questions may be found in Devorah Dimant, 'Qumran Sectarian Literature,' in *Jewish Writings of the Second Temple Period* CRINT 2, ed. Michael E. Stone (Philadelphia: Fortress, 1984), pp. 497–502; Schürer, *The History of the Jewish People*, rev. and ed. Vermes, Millar, and Black, 3:1:381–386; A. R. C. Leaney, *The Rule of Qumran and Its Meaning* (London: SCM, 1966), pp. 111–116; and M. Delcor, 'Qumrân. Règle de Communauté,' in *Dictionnaire de la Bible: Supplément*, 10 vols., ed. H. Cazelles and A. Feuillet (Paris: Letouzey and Ané, 1979), 9:851–859.

[11] See J. Murphy-O'Connor, 'La Genèse Littéraire de la Règle de la Communauté,' *RB* 76 (1969):528–549; J. Pouilly, *La Règle de la Communauté de Qumrân: son évolution littéraire*, CahRB 17 (Paris: Gabalde et Cie, 1976). The development in the dualism of the sect from an *Endkampfdualismus* (1QM) to an *ethisch orientierter Dualismus* (1QS) suggested by Peter von der Osten–Sacken, *Gott und Belial: traditionsgeschichtliche Untersuchungen zum Dualismus in den Texten aus Qumran*, SUNT 6 (Göttingen: Vandenhoeck & Ruprecht, 1969), is hard to prove. One finds the ethical element in 1QM (e.g. 1:2), and the anticipated destruction of the wicked by the community found in 1QS (8:6, 7) echoes the eschatological dualism of 1QM. The different emphases of the two writings may have nothing to do with development in the conception of dualism at Qumran.

'purity/righteousness' have to do with how the saving provisions of the covenant were thought to operate.

We shall see that while salvation is clearly based on divine grace in 1QS, the life of the community is given an explicit role to play in securing salvation. Moreover, the covenant does not include all of Israel, but is limited to those who enter into its Qumran form.

B. The Covenant

In 1QS, the Qumran community frequently expresses the belief that the divine covenant with Israel now belongs to the community, and to it alone.[12] Since this theme figures so prominently in 1QS, one finds in it a particularly strong expression of exclusivistic soteriology.

The idea that the community alone possesses the divine covenant is expressed in the opening section (1QS 1:1–15). The community declares its aims in terms of an exclusively conceived covenant:

ולהבי את כול הנדבים לעשות חוקי אל בברית חסד	. . . and to bring all those willing to do the statutes of God into the covenant of grace. 1QS 1:7, 8a

The second section of 1QS, 1:16–3:12, describes the covenantal ritual by which new members were inducted into the community and an annual celebration of covenant renewal, ceremonies which were most likely held in conjunction with one another. Participation in the community life and its rites of atonement was limited to those who publicly expressed their commitment through this entrance ritual:

וכול הבאים בסרך היחד יעבורו בברית לפני אל לעשות ככול אשר צוה . . .	And all who come into the rule of the Community shall enter into the covenant before God to do according to all he has commanded 1QS 1:16, 17a

Those outside the covenant were thought to be lost and accursed, belonging to the dominion of Belial.[13] As a part of the covenantal ceremony, which was obviously shaped by Deuteronomic imagery, the Levites were to curse those 'of Belial's lot,' their pronouncement to be followed by an antiphonal 'Amen'

---

[12] The theme of the divine covenant with the community figures largely in the Damascus Document (CD), the *Hodayoth*, and the Messianic Rule (1QM) as well.
[13] 1QS 1:21–24; 2:4b–10.

from those entering into the covenant.[14] Likewise, the covenant itself was thought to bear a curse for one who entered it with duplicity: a further curse was ceremonially invoked on one who entertained thoughts of rebellion while outwardly adopting the obligations of the covenant.[15]

The closing portion of the covenantal rite reasserts the rule that one who did not enter into the covenant had no share in the saving knowledge, cultus, or spirit of the community.[16] Only in 'humbling the soul under the divine statutes, to walk in all God's ways,' could one be accepted by God. This very act of expressing one's commitment to the *halakhoth* of the community was the essence of the covenant:

והיתה לו לברית יחד עולמים   And it will be to him the covenant of the eternal Community. 1QS 3:11, 12

The instruction concerning the two spirits (3:13–4:26), which constitutes a self-contained catechetical statement, also refers to the divine covenant as the basic structure of salvation. The 'sons of light,' those who have their origin in the 'spirit of truth' (also characterized as 'sons of righteousness'), are the 'upright' (ישרים, 4:22), whom God chose for an eternal covenant.[17]

The significance of this division of humanity into groupings based on the spirits of light and darkness should not be overlooked:

> Au schéma traditionnel de partage de l'humanité: Israël et les nations, se superpose un autre critère de division, une division selon 'l'esprit.'[18]

The human race is bifurcated on the basis of membership in the Qumran community.[19] The 'sons of light,' to whom the spirit of light has been appointed, are the members of the community.[20]

---

[14] 1QS 2:4b–10; cf. Deut 27.
[15] 1QS 2:11–18.
[16] This statement presupposes that בברית אל is to be supplied for the lacuna at the beginning of line 2 in column 2. Most commentators adopt this reading, given that the edge of a ל appears at the end of the gap, and the section closes with a reference to the covenant in 3:11.
[17] 1QS 4:22 כיא בם בחר אל לברית עולמים.
[18] Annie Jaubert, *La notion d'Alliance dans le Judaïsme aux abords de l'ère chrétienne*, Patristica Sorbonensia 6 (Paris: Seuil, 1963), p. 132.
[19] See the discussion by J. H. Charlesworth, 'A Critical Comparison of the Dualism in 1QS III, 13– IV, 26 and the 'Dualism' in the Fourth Gospel,' *NTS* 15 (1972):389–418.
[20] 1QS 3:13.

The divine covenant made with them therefore implicitly supersedes the divine covenant with Israel, which the Qumran sectarians believed had been radically transgressed.[21]

An element of individualism therefore displaces the notion of a covenant with all Israel here. Salvation is now thought to depend on whether one had been appointed to truth or to error, not on physical descent alone.[22]

Twice in the fourth section of 1QS (5:1–7:25) there appears the unusual expression, 'the priests and *their covenant*.'[23] The pronominal suffix attached to ברית obviously refers to the priests. Yet the sense of the expression is difficult to decipher. Norbert Ilg has suggested that such language reflects the covenant given to Phineas on the basis of his zeal for God.[24] All the community members are envisioned as sharing in a priestly covenant on the basis of their zealous devotion to the 'Rule of the Community.'[25] Alternatively, one might interpret the pronoun 'their' as implying that the covenant belongs to the priests in the community, in so far as they keep it and ensure that it is maintained. In 5:9 the priests are described as שומרי הברית ודורשי רצונו, 'those who keep the covenant and seek his (God's) will.'[26] In either reading, it is clear that participation in the divine covenant is based upon obedience to the community statutes.

The sub-section of 1QS 5:7b–20a consists of an elaboration of two requirements for entrance into the covenant. Alongside an oath to return to the observation of the Law of Moses within the Qumran community, the entrant covenanted a strict separation from אנשי העול, 'the men of evil,' fellow Jews who were not a part of the covenant community.[27] On the basis of this section of 1QS, Wilfried Paschen has persuasively argued that the sharing of goods and meals at Qumran is to be interpreted as deriving from the desire to maintain the purity of the community, not from

---

[21] 1QS 1:22–26.

[22] N.b. election is portrayed in individualized terms in 1QS 3:13–4:26, not in terms of the community as a whole.

[23] 1QS 5:9; 6:19 (הכוהנים ורוב אנשי בריתם).

[24] Cf. Num 25:6–13.

[25] Norbert Ilg, 'Überlegungen zum Verständnis von ברית in den Qumrantexten,' in *Qumrân: Sa piété, sa théologie et son mileau*, ed. M. Delcor (Paris-Gembloux: Duculot, 1978), pp. 257–263. Ilg interprets the phrase as (p. 263): "'. . . die Priester, und die Männer, die dasselbe Recht haben wie sie," nämlich auf Grund ihrer persönlichen Lebensführung in den ברית כהנת עולם mit hineingehören.'

[26] Elsewhere in column 5 (11,18,19,22) the covenant is referred to as 'his covenant' (i.e. God's).

[27] 1QS 5:10.

aspirations after a common life.[28] The very life of the community is
constructed on the basis of its strictly exclusivistic views. Contact
with outsiders was thought to defile, and had to be avoided in
order to maintain the purity of those within the covenant.[29]

The fifth major section of 1QS, which may be regarded as
consisting of 8:1–9:26a, is generally regarded as representing the
aims of the Qumran Essenes prior to the founding of the community at Qumran. The material represents the 'manifesto' (so
J. Murphy-O'Connor) or 'program' for the community which
was realized in the establishment at Qumran. It is therefore of
significance that in this section the 'council of the Community'
(עצת היחד, 8:1, 5) is said to exist in order to 'establish a
covenant for the eternal statutes' (להקם ברית לחוקות עולם,
8:10).[30] From its very inception, the community life at Qumran
was thought to embody the covenantal obligations given in
Torah.[31]

The concept of the divine covenant with the Qumran community also makes its appearance in the final hymn (10:8–11:22).
Here the speaker resolves:

עם מבוא יום ולילה אבואה   Upon the arrival of the day
בברית אל ועם מוצא ערב   and of the night, I will enter
ובוקר אמר חוקיו   into the covenant of God, and
                                     with the going forth of the eve-
                                     ning and of the morning I will
                                     pronounce his statutes.
                                     1QS 10:10

The pious devotion of the representative of the community who

---

[28] Wilfried Paschen, *Rein und Unrein: Untersuchung zur biblischen Wortgeschichte*,
SANT 24 (München: Kösel, 1970), pp. 85–124. He comments, p. 198: 'Für die
Einigungsleute stand nicht ein gemeinsames Leben im Vordergrund, vielmehr die
Absonderung von den anderen Juden, die wegen falscher Toraauffassung als
Irrungsleute verworfen wurden. Insbesondere bei den Waschungen, bei Toraerk-
lärung und Gebet, bei den Mahlzeiten, bei Arbeit und Handel mußten die
Einungsleute strengstens auf Trennung von den Gemeindefremden achten. So
ergab sich zwangsläufig, daß sie aufeinander angewiesen waren und auch im
täglichen Leben fast nur mit ihresgleichen verkehren konnten.'

[29] Such practices are closely related to the atoning function which the community assigned to itself, which is discussed below.

[30] 'Council of the community' probably signifies the community as a whole,
not merely the inner circle mentioned in 8:1. See P. Wernberg-Møller, *The
Manual of Discipline* STDJ 1 (Leiden: Brill, 1957), pp. 122–123; Leaney, *The Rule
of Qumran*, p. 211; Michael A. Knibb, *The Qumran Community*, CCWJCW 2
(Cambridge: Cambridge University Press, 1987), p. 129.

[31] Cf. 8:9, where the community is said to provide a holy of holies for Aaron:
'with eternal knowledge for the covenant of justice,' בדעת כולם לברית משפט
כולם should most likely be read as עולם.

speaks in this hymn is expressed in terms of a daily recommitment to the covenant. In the parallel clause which follows, this covenant is associated with the observances of the community. One cannot miss the individualization of the concept of the covenant here. The pledge of the speaker is regarded as an entrance into the covenant, which is to be continually renewed. Given that this hymn was very likely used liturgically, the consciousness of personal obligation to the covenant would have been ingrained within the community.[32] If the Qumran community maintained an exclusivistic conception of the covenant, how did it conceive of 'Israel'? Did it identify itself with 'Israel,' and reinterpret the traditional use of the term? Or, as E. P. Sanders has argued, did the Qumran sect *avoid* designating itself by the title 'Israel'?[33]

Sanders rightly points out that in some contexts יִשְׂרָאֵל clearly signifies the nation at large.[34] However, in other contexts it is difficult to determine whether the community or the nation is in view. In 2:22, for example, the ordering of the covenant ritual is given, so that each person 'in Israel' might know his/(her?) place. Does the passage have a view to the eschatological incorporation of the nation into the community? Or is the community regarded as Israel here? Likewise, in 1QS 5:5 it is difficult to discern whether לִיַחַד בְּרִית עוֹלָם is appositional or if it further defines the purpose of the community.[35]

In other instances, however, it is likely that the Qumran community used the title 'Israel' in reference to itself. For the expression רֹב יִשְׂרָאֵל הַמִּתְנַדְּבִים (5:22), Sanders prefers the translation 'the multitude *from* Israel, those who volunteer.'[36] But the genitive relation may just as well be appositional.[37] Moreover, Sanders's translation demands that a somewhat pejorative sense be attached to 'Israel,' a requirement which is not only unlikely but which runs against Sanders's own overall reading.[38] Furthermore, the parallel expression in 5:21 characterizes the priestly leaders of the community who have devoted themselves to establishing the

---

[32] Note that liturgical ordinances precede this hymn (10:1–8a).
[33] Sanders, *Paul and Palestinian Judaism*, pp. 244–247.
[34] 1QS 1:22, 23; 6:13; 8:11.
[35] לִיַסֵּד מוֹסַד אֱמֶת לְיִשְׂרָאֵל לְיַחַד בְּרִית עוֹלָם
[36] Sanders, *Paul and Palestinian Judaism*, p. 246.
[37] The expression וְכֹל הַמִּתְנַדֵּב מִיִשְׂרָאֵל in 6:13 provides only ambiguous evidence for assessing the sense of the genitive relation in 5:22. On the one hand, the meaning is clearly, 'anyone *from* Israel who volunteers.' But unlike the phrase in 5:22, the preposition מִן is used to express the partitive idea. And the individual, not the multitude, is the subject.
[38] Prof. J. H. Charlesworth brought this observation to my attention.

divine covenant as 'the sons of Aaron.'[39] This identification of the leaders with the priesthood strongly suggests that in 5:22 the multitude is metaphorically regarded as Israel. Likewise, in the teaching on the two spirits, help comes to the sons of light from 'the God of Israel' implying that the community members constituted Israel.[40] In a number of instances then, 1QS regards the Qumran community as 'Israel.'[41]

In so far as references in 1QS to 'Israel' signify the nation as a whole, the nation is viewed as an empirical phenomenon, not as a structure of salvation. In the context of 1QS 3:24, where soteriological overtones appear, the community, not the nation is the focal point.[42] Moreover, Sanders's case clearly breaks down when one moves to 1QM. Jews disobedient to the Qumran covenant are expected to ally themselves with the Gentiles in the final eschatological battle.[43] The remnant, שארית, consisting of the covenant community, is regarded as the people of God.[44] At the eschaton the Qumran group clearly becomes identical with Israel.

Sanders's further argument, that the Qumran community envisioned a final salvation of all of Israel despite its exclusivism, is unconvincing. His contention that in 1QM the enemies of the sect are referred to as Gentiles, and that the saved are called 'Israel' does not establish the identity of the groups. On the contrary, as noted above, the 'Israel' pictured in 1QM consists in the members of the Qumran covenant. Likewise, Sanders's appeal that 'the wicked Israelites will only be punished, and perhaps even redeemed,' rests on a weak *argumentum e silencio* from 1QpHab 5:3–6.[45]

The strongest argument which Sanders offers for his thesis that a final salvation of all Israel was anticipated at Qumran derives from his reference to Vermes's translation of 1QSa 1:1:

> This is the Rule for all the congregation of Israel in the last days, when they shall join [the Community to wa]lk . . .

---

[39] Loren Stuckenbruck has called my attention to the importance of taking this parallel into account: בני אהרון המתנדבים ביחד להקים את בריתו.

[40] 1QS 3:24.

[41] A number of occurrences are difficult to interpret in this regard: e.g. 1QS 8:4, 5, 9, 12; 9:3, 6, 11.

[42] The God of 'Israel' and his angel help the sons of light.

[43] 1QM 1:2.

[44] 1QM 13:7, 8. Cf. Jaubert, *La notion d'Alliance*, pp. 129–131.

[45] Sanders, *Paul and Palestinian Judaism*, p. 254. The commentary on Hab 1:12b (למשפט שמתו וצור למוכיחו יסדתו) states that God will not destroy his people by the hand of the Gentiles. He will rather render judgment on the nations through his elect, who will also effect a chastisement through which the wicked of his people will make expiation. The destiny of wicked Jews is not clearly stated.

According to Sanders, this passage indicates that the community anticipated that the whole of Israel would join the sect in the eschatological period. But Vermes's translation of the verb אסף as 'join' is an unfortunate choice. The word signifies the idea of gathering, not that of entering into membership. It is used with regard to the assembling of the community (1QS 5:7), and to the eschatological gathering of the elect (1QM 3:4, 10; 18:4) and of the wicked (1QM 14:5). Furthermore, the whole of 1QSa is given to the discussion of the gathering together and organization of the eschatological congregation, the עדת ישראל, which does not refer to the nation at large, but to the community.[46] Hence the appearance of this expression in 1QSa 1:1 does not provide information about how the Qumran group regarded the nation as a whole. While a final assembly of a large number of persons is anticipated, the material gives no indication that a salvation of all of Israel is expected. On the contrary, any person thought to bring impurity to the congregation is to be excluded.[47]

One finds then in 1QS, that the community regarded itself as possessing the divine covenant. The nature of the relationship between this covenant and the covenant given to the patriarchs is not made completely clear: the Qumran covenant might either replace the former one or serve as the eschatological expression of it.[48] In any case, it is certain that the Qumran covenant was understood to displace the covenant with Israel as a salvific structure. This shift in ideas brought a concomitant individualism. One's willingness to adhere to the Qumran community determined whether or not one shared in the sphere of salvation.[49] Salvation and forgiveness come only to those who have taken on the practices of the community: *extra ecclesiam nulla salus*.[50]

C. Election

The individualism of the Qumran conception of the covenant did not lead to a soteriology based on 'merit'. Quite the contrary, belief

---

[46] See 1QSa 2:12 where the עדת ישראל before which the Messiah and the priests enter is clearly the community, not the nation at large.

[47] 1QSa 2:3b–11a.

[48] Cf. Jaubert, *La notion d'Alliance*, pp. 209–249. The occurrences of הברית החדשה in CD 6:19; 8:21; 19:33, 34; 20:11, 12 do not resolve this issue.

[49] Cf. Hermann Lichtenberger, *Studien zum Menschenbild in Texten der Qumrangemeinde*, SUNT 15 (Göttingen: Vandenhoeck & Ruprecht, 1980), pp. 212–218.

[50] I have borrowed the application of this Cyprianic reference to the Qumran literature from D. A. Carson. See his discussion of Qumran soteriology in *Divine Sovereignty and Human Responsibility: Biblical Perspectives in Tension* (Atlanta: John Knox, 1981), pp. 75–83.

in a strict determinism and (soteriological) predestination makes the soteriology of 1QS firmly and explicitly *sola gratia* in its basic formulation.

Election, a theme which is naturally interwoven with that of the divine covenant, is expressed in starkly individualized terms in 1QS. Membership in the community is regarded as a lot which has been given and determined by God.[51] The 'sons of light' have been chosen by God for an eternal covenant.[52] The idea is likewise expressed in 11:7:

לאשר בחר אל נתנם לאוחזת   Whom God chose, he appoin-
עולם וינחילם בגורל קדשים   ted to an eternal possession. And he gave them a portion in the lot of the holy ones.

The other aspect of (double) predestination, i.e. reprobation, which follows logically from this position, also finds expression in 1QS. The wicked are said to belong to the lot apportioned to Belial.[53]

In contrast to the election of the patriarchs in the Hebrew Bible, the individualized soteriological predestination of 1QS is explicitly linked to the order of creation. It is this joining of determinism and predestination in the teaching on the two spirits (3:13–4:26) and in briefer form in the closing hymn (11:7–11, 16–22) which provides an unmistakable indication that salvation was regarded as gratuitous in 1QS. 'From the God of knowledge comes all that is and that will be.'[54] He created the human race and appointed for it two spirits in which to walk.[55] The behavior of each individual is linked to a corresponding, divinely-given share in truth or in error.[56] The two opposing camps of humanity will exist in strife with one another until the appointed time of divine visitation and the new creation.[57] Participation in the community of the saved is therefore regarded as deriving from the fixed order of creation.

Sanders, who is generally concerned to emphasize that early Judaism conceived of salvation as a gracious gift, argues, oddly enough, that the affirmations of election and determinism by the Qumran community were not, 'understood in such a way as to

---

[51] 1QS 1:10; 2:2.
[52] 1QS 4:22.
[53] 1QS 2:4b, 5; cf. 3:24.
[54] 1QS 3:15, cf. 11:11b, 17b.
[55] 1QS 3:17b, 18; cf. 3:25; 4:15.
[56] 1QS 4:16, 24.
[57] 1QS 4:25, 26.

exclude man's ability to choose which of the two ways he would follow.'[58] But given the highly individualized conception of the covenant, and the atoning significance which the community assigned to its practices (to be discussed below), it is only the priority assigned to the divine election of the members of the sect which preserves the soteriology of the community from making the obedience of its members the source of salvation. Sanders therefore strikes at the root of his own thesis by overstating the manner in which freedom was conceived at Qumran.[59]

He is quite correct in pointing out that the question of freedom of the will is not *per se* the question addressed in 1QS as a whole, or in 3:13–4:26. The passage has far more to do with the problem of human evil, since it not only contrasts the saved and the lost, but provides a means for accounting for the misdeeds of the elect.

The adoption of the idea of a divine covenant with the community no doubt would have provided the Qumran group with considerable logical and psychological motivation toward addressing the problem of evil. Given the exclusivistic stance of the community, one would have been immediately cast back upon the idea of a divine determination of the course of history (leading to final apocalyptic victory) as a means of deflecting the unthinkable notion that God was responsible for the past and present failures of the nation. To conclude that the formation and growth of the community was an element of the predetermined plan of God would not only protect the concept of God from any taint of wrong, but it would also (perhaps more importantly) solidify the self–understanding of the community as the appointed locus of salvation, rather than a mere attempt at renewal of piety.

The preceding considerations are only a preliminary reflection on the reasons why the Qumran community adopted such a stance. Comparative studies of similar phenomena in religious reforming movements would be necessary in order to give any concrete answer to the question. But it is crucial to note that any strict voluntarism (i.e. the idea that the formation of, or membership in the community was effected by personal choice) could only serve to undermine the idea that the community was a 'divine planting.' God would then seem to lag behind the initiative of the pious at Qumran in his response to the errors of Israel.

---

[58] Sanders, *Paul and Palestinian Judaism*, p. 261. See his discussion of election and predestination in the Qumran writings, pp. 257–270. Cf. A. Marx, 'Y-a-t-il une prédestination Qumrân?' *RevQ* 6 (1967- 9):163–181.

[59] See Sanders, *Paul and Palestinian Judaism*, p. 294, where he argues that the those who were not elect might repent and join the sect.

In light of these observations, Sanders's explanation for the interest of the community in divine predestination is far too simple. Predestinarian statements do not *merely* have to do with providing a means of asserting that the members of the community were graciously elected.[60] The presence and duration of evil and the proclivity of the elect to err receive explicit attention in the teaching on the two spirits, ideas which are hardly essential to the notion of grace, but which are integral to the problem of evil.

The problem of human evil and its relationship to salvation, moreover, while not limited to the question of the nature of human freedom, are in large measure dependent upon how freedom is construed. While human freedom is not the primary consideration in 3:13–4:26 or in the remainder of 1QS, the issue is implicitly present.[61]

Obviously, predestination is not conceived in purely mechanistic terms in 1QS, since humans are clearly portrayed as responsible and free from psychological constraint in, for example, the decision to repent and join the community.[62] But the relationship between this sort of freedom and the deterministic expressions of 1QS is not worked out. Therefore, one should not impose upon the text a modern conception of human freedom as absolute power to choose good or evil. Not too much can be made of the designation of the community members as 'those who are willing.'[63] As Gerhard Maier rightly observes, this terminology is drawn from Biblical language, and should not be taken to provide an answer to the question of human freedom.[64] It is overstepping the constraints imposed by the texts then, to formulate human freedom in 1QS as Sanders does, as 'the ability to choose' one of the two ways, irrespective of divine determination.[65]

---

[60] Sanders, *Paul and Palestinian Judaism* , pp 267– 268.

[61] Therefore, while freedom of the will should not be regarded as the *topos* around which the discussion is centered, Gerhard Maier's insistence that the question played an important role in early Judaism may not be dismissed. See Gerhard Maier, *Mensch und freier Wille nach den jüdischen Religionsparteien zwischen Ben Sira und Paulus*, WUNT 12 (Tübingen: J. C. B. Mohr [Paul Siebeck], 1971), pp. 165–263. Cf. Lichtenberger, *Menschenbild*, pp. 184–189.

[62] 1QS 1:11; 3:8; 5:13b, 14.

[63] נדב 1QS 1:7, 11; 5:1,6,8,10,21,22; 6:13; cf. 9:5, 24.

[64] Maier, *Mensch und freier Wille*, p. 207: 'Die 'Willigen' des AT sind also für Qumran typologische Vorbilder gewesen und es ergibt sich wieder, daß man diese Terminologie gebrauchte, um sich als die gehorsame Gemeinde vom ungehorsamen Israel abzugrenzen.' Cf. Neh 11:2; Ezra 7:13; 2 Chron 17:16; Psalm 110:3.

[65] On predestination in the Qumran materials see Carson, *Divine Sovereignty*, pp. 75–83; Maier, *Mensch und freier Wille*, pp. 165–263; H. Ringgren, *The Faith of Qumran*, trans. E. Sander (Philadelphia: Fortress, 1963), pp. 109–112; H. W. Huppenbauer, *Der Mensch zwischen zwei Welten*, ATANT 34

Participation in the covenant of grace (ברית חסד, 1:8) ultimately hinges upon a divinely appointed election to that covenant. Therefore the gracious blessings of the covenant and the praise which the community member offers to God for the merciful benefits of salvation, can in no way be attributed to the effort or intent of the beneficiary.[66] One therefore must conclude precisely the opposite of Herbert Braun, who rhetorically asks:

> Ist die Einsicht in das Angewiesensein auf Gottes חסד, צדקה und רחמים wirklich durchgeführt und radikal verstanden? Diese Frage wird man eindeutig verneinen müssen.[67]

The idea of grace *is* radically carried through in 1QS by means of a deterministic conception of election. Attribution of atoning value to deeds of obedience, which we will examine below, are limited in scope by this belief.

D. Atonement

Since in the view of the Qumran community the Temple had been defiled by the unworthy practices of the Jerusalem priesthood, the sect withdrew from participation in the official cult. Yet rather than rejecting cultic practices, the Qumran community reinterpreted them, regarding its own ordered life as the true Temple, erected in defiance of the cult rendered illegitimate by disobedient Jews outside the sect.[68] The community did not give up its hope for a restoration of the Jerusalem Temple, of course. That is made obvious by the Temple Scroll (11QTemple 19–47) in which a cleansed and reconstituted eschatological Temple in a

---

(Zürich:Zwingli, 1959), pp. 30–44; E. H. Merrill, *Qumran and Predestination: A Theological Study of the Thanksgiving Hymns*, STDJ 8 (Leiden: Brill, 1975). For a thorough rebuttal of Wernberg-Møller's attempt to read the dualism of 1QS as a psychological one, see Charlesworth, 'The Dualism in 1QS III, 13–IV, 26 and the 'Dualism' in the Fourth Gospel,' pp. 389–418.

[66] 1QS 2:4, 7; 10:4, 6; 11:12,13. The concepts of election and grace are directly connected to one another in 11:13. As Otto Betz has noted, the verb נגש there most likely signifies 'being brought into the covenant community,' as it does in 9:16. ברחמיו הגישני, 'Through his mercies he has brought me near, i.e into the covenant community.' See Otto Betz, 'Rechtfertigung und Heiligung,' in *Rechtfertigung, Realismus, Universalimus in biblischer Sicht*, ed. G. Müller (Darmstadt: Wissenschaftliche Buchgesellschaft, 1978), p. 35.

[67] Herbert Braun, *Spätjüdisch-häretischer und frühchristlicher Radikalismus*, 2 vols., BHT 24 (Tübingen: J. C. B. Mohr [Paul Siebeck], 1969), 1:46.

[68] See especially Georg Klinzing, *Die Umdeutung des Kultus in der Qumrangemeinde und im Neuen Testament*, SUNT 7 (Göttingen: Vandenhoeck & Ruprecht, 1971), pp. 8–155; Bertil Gärtner, *The Temple and Community in Qumran and the New Testament*, SNTSMS 1 (Cambridge: Cambridge University Press, 1965), pp. 1–46; Paschen, *Rein und Unrein*, pp. 134–152.

pure and holy Jerusalem is envisioned. But until God brought about the final cleansing of the Temple, the undefiled observance of God's commands within the Qumran community was viewed as the very equivalent of the Temple.[69] This transposition of the atoning function of Temple sacrifices into the obedient life of the community results in an unmistakable attribution of salvific value to human behavior.

The proper observance of *Torah* maintained by the community was thought to atone for sins, not only for those of the members of the sect, but also for 'the Land'[70] (1QS 3:6, 8; 5:6, 7;[71] 8:6, 10; 9:4[72]). The righteous deeds of the Qumran psalmist were looked

---

[69] See Lawrence H. Schiffmann, *Sectarian Law in the Dead Sea Scrolls Courts, Testimony and the Penal Code*, BJS 33 (Chico, Ca.: Scholars Press, 1983), pp. 216–217.

[70] On the theme of atonement in the Qumran writings see Bernd Janowski and Hermann Lichtenberger, 'Enderwartung und Reinheitsidee: Zur eschatologischen Deutung von Reinheit und Sühne in der Qumrangemeinde,' *JJS* 34 (1983):31–62; Bernd Janowski, *Sühne als Heilsgeschehen: Studien zur Sühnetheologie der Priesterschrift und zur Wurzel KPR im Alten Orient und im Alten Testament*, WMANT 55 (Neukirchen-Vluyn: Neukirchner, 1982), pp. 259–265; Hermann Lichtenberger, 'Atonement and Sacrifice in the Qumran Community,' in *Approaches to Ancient Judaism: Volume II*, BJS 9, ed. W. S. Green (Chico, Ca: Scholars, 1980), pp. 159–171; Paul Garnet, *Salvation and Atonement in the Qumrancrolls*, WUNT2 3 (Tübingen: J. C. B. Mohr [Paul Siebeck], 1977); Lang, 'כפר' in *Theologisches Wörterbuch zum Alten Testament*, ed. G. Botterweck, H. Ringgren H.–J. Fabry (Stuttgart: Kohlhammer, 1984), 4:317–318; Paschen, *Rein und Unrein*, pp. 134–152; Klinzing, *Umdeutung des Kultus*, pp. 93–106.

[71] The reading of the text is under dispute. Contra Garnet, *Salvation and Atonement*, pp. 60–64, who is overly concerned to deny any traces of the idea of substitutionary atonement in the Qumran materials, the ריאם/ו in 5:5 should probably be read as כיא אם. The sense of the passage is then that those in the community are to 'circumcise the foreskin of the (evil) inclination and stiffness of neck, . . .' in order to atone . . .' The purpose clauses in lines 6, 7 which follow are very similar to the aims of the community described in 8:6, 7 (to atone for 'the Land' and to bring vengeance upon the wicked). It is not unreasonable to suppose that the community would regard its life together as providing mutual atonement. Nor is the sentence structure awkward. Furthermore, contra Garnet, it is not clear whether the initial letter is a *waw* or a *yodh*. Brownlee's interpretation of אאם as a reference to God, which Garnet prefers, cannot be substantiated. Cf. Klinzing, *Umdeutung des Kultus*, p. 67; Janowski and Lichtenberger, 'Enderwartung,' p. 50. On the efficacy of intercessory prayer in Qumran thought see, Bernd Janowski, 'Sündenvergebung 'um Hiobs willen' Fürbitte und Vergebung in 11QtgJob 38:2f. und Hi 42:9f. LXX,' *ZNW* 73 (1982):251–280.

[72] The expression ולרצון מבשר לארץ עולות most likely should be translated, 'and to make expiation for the Land without the flesh of burnt-offerings.' To read the preposition מן instrumentally here (Wernberg-Møller, Carmignac) would make the syntax of כפר vary considerably from the Hebrew Bible. The instrumental use of מן with כפר also lacks attestation in the Qumran writings. See Paschen, *Rein und Unrein*, pp. 139–140. The context further suggests the privative (Klinzing, Lichtenberger) over against the comparative sense (Lohse, Jaubert). See the discussions by Klinzing, *Umdeutung des Kultus*, pp. 38–41; Janowski and Lichtenberger, 'Enderwartung,' pp. 50–53.

upon as a means by which God wiped away sin.[73] This singular statement in the closing hymn of 1QS is an expression of the more frequently appearing idea that the 'perfection of way' of the community members served as a means of atonement. The inner circle of the community was to be 'perfect in all which is revealed from all the *Torah*' in order to 'expiate guilt with just deeds and with the crucible of affliction.'[74] The covenant itself is said to be founded on the perfection of the community.[75]

The rituals and rules of the community were not thought to work *ex opere operato*. Community regulations were to be observed with an inward sense of devotion and humility.[76] Likewise, the community member was to endure affliction and oppression with humility and patience.[77]

This practical inseparability of the inward and outward may be seen in the concept of 'spirit.' The term רוח signifies an independently existing being in 1QS. Yet, according to Qumran thought, רוח manifests itself in the demeanor of human beings, and in their adherence to the practices of the sect.[78] The life of the Qumran community therefore was a concrete expression of the holy spirit.[79] The spirit, present in both inward life and outward practice, was the means by which atonement was made for sin:[80]

כיא ברוח עצת אמת אל דרכי איש יכופרו כול עוונותו	For with the spirit of the council of God's truth atonement is made for one's ways, for all one's guilty deeds. 1QS 3:6b, 7a

The atonement worked by the community therefore resulted from the whole of the pious life of the group, not merely from the outward ritual observances.

In accord with the Qumran belief in predestination, this atoning work of the community was considered to be a gracious gift of God. Thus in the closing hymn of 1QS the psalmist can speak of God's

---

[73] This interpretation hinges on reading 1QS 11:3 as ובצדקותי ימח פשעי. For a defense of this interpretation, see below.

[74] 1QS 8:3, 4a ולרצת עוון בעושי משפט וצרת מצרף. Note the string of telic infinitives which connect the perfection of the inner circle to its atoning service: לעשות אמת (8:2), לשמור אמונה (8:3a), ולרצת עוון (8:3b).

[75] 1QS 8:9b, 10.

[76] 1QS 3:8; 4:2–8; 8:1–3; and the closing hymn 10:8– 11:21.

[77] 1QS 1:17, 18; 11:1b–3a.

[78] 1QS 3:13–4:26, cf. 5:21, 24; 9:14, 15, 18; 10:18; 11:1.

[79] 1QS 8:3; 9:3.

[80] See J. H. Charlesworth, 'Les Odes de Salomon et les Manuscrits de la Mer Morte,' *RB* 77 (1970):522–549.

goodness and righteousness as the source of cleansing and atonement.[81] It is likely that the underlying thought here is of God's covenant faithfulness as a source of salvation, since הגישני(11:13) probably signifies being brought into the covenantal community, and in 11:14 the speaker looks forward to being judged 'in his (God's) righteous truth,' i.e. within the saving covenantal provisions.[82] Other references to God's righteousness in the closing hymn of 1QS signify his covenant faithfulness or the righteous ordinances of the covenant.[83] Likewise, in 4:20 'his (God's) truth' is spoken of as the source of cleansing. Here the idea is very likely that of God's faithfulness to his plan, which includes the purification of the righteous (4:22). God then is looked upon as the ultimate source of the atonement worked within the Qumran community.

The exclusivism of the sect extended to its conception of atonement as well. Those unwilling to enter into the covenant could not be purified through the cultic practices and devotion of the community.[84] Separation from outsiders was necessary for cleansing, as was strict observance of the regulations of the community.[85] Alongside the atoning purpose of the community was the expectation that it would condemn and bring eschatological vengeance upon the disobedient.[86]

The Qumran conception of atonement represented by 1QS therefore assigned salvific value to obedience.[87] The life of the community was thought to provide the sole means of cleansing from sin. Nevertheless, the resultant salvation which the community enjoyed was thought to be a creation of God and a product of his grace.

---

[81] 1QS 11:14, 15; cf. 10:11b–12.

[82] On הגישני (11:13) see Betz, 'Rechtfertigung und Heiligung,' p. 35.

[83] 1QS 10:25; 11:4b, 5; 11:13. Cf. 1QH 4:37–40 where atonement through God's righteousness and the Qumran covenant are associated. For a full list of the means of atonement expressed in the Qumran materials, see Janowski, *Sühne als Heilsgeschehen*, pp. 264–265.

[84] 1QS 3:4, 5.

[85] 1QS 5:13, 14; 8:16b–19.

[86] 1QS 5:6, 7; 8:6, 7. For this reason, הארץ לכפר בעד in 8:6 should not be interpreted to refer to Jews outside the Qumran covenant, but to the land of Israel itself, the concept of atoning for it most likely deriving from Num 35:33. See Paschen, *Rein und Unrein*, pp. 147–152.

[87] Prof. J. H. Charlesworth has rightly called my attention to the annual ranking of community members according to 'understanding and deeds,' a practice which would have been impossible unless religious status was attached to obedience. See 1QS 5:20–24. This yearly examination of the behavior of the community members therefore corroborates the thesis developed in this section in that it shows that the community consciously linked religious standing to the deeds of the individual.

E. Purity and Righteousness

It is crucial for modern commentators to bear in mind that the righteousness in which the member of the Qumran community participated was conceived of in behavioral, not merely forensic terms.[88] 'Righteousness'[89] is regularly coupled with 'perfection of way'[90] and 'holiness'[91] in 1QS as a description of the ideals of conduct for the members of the community. Therefore when the Qumran psalmist appeals to God as 'my righteousness' (צדקי 1QS 10:11), it is improper to interpret such a righteousness as one imparted alongside of or apart from *Torah*.

One important aspect of this behavioral understanding of righteousness is the value placed upon ritual purity. In 1QS, interestingly, the concepts of purity and righteousness are regarded as equivalent in value. Likewise, impurity and transgression are equally serious offenses.[92] This linkage may be largely attributed to the group's self–identification with the Temple.[93]

Whatever the cause for the importance assigned to purity at Qumran might have been, it reinforces the preceding observations

---

[88] See especially, Betz, 'Rechtfertigung und Heiligung,' pp. 30–41.

[89] 1QS 3:3; 2:4; 4:2, 4, 24; cf. 4:9; 1:5; 5:4; 8:2.

[90] 1QS 1:8; 2:2; 3:9, 20, 22; 4:22; 8:1, 9, 10, 18, 20, 21; 9:2, 5, 14, 19.

[91] 1QS 2:25; 5:6, 13, 18, 20; 8:5, 6, 8, 17, 20, 21, 23; 9:2, 6, 8.

[92] E.g. 1QS 5:10–20, where separation from outsiders is regarded as necessary to membership; 6:24–7:25. The remarkable feature here is not that of the defilement resulting from sin, but of a sin of defilement. See Jacob Neusner, *The Idea of Purity in Ancient Judaism*, SJLA 1 (Leiden: Brill, 1973), pp. 50–55; Janowski and Lichtenberger, 'Enderwartung,' pp. 30–41; Michael Newton, *The Concept of Purity at Qumran and in the Letters of Paul*, SNTSMS 53 (Cambridge: Cambridge University Press, 1985), pp. 2–51. Newton's study disappointingly neglects what is probably the most important issue for a comparison of Paul with Qumran in this regard: why the concept of purity is not of central concern to Paul, while it is to the Qumran community.

[93] But then the question must be posed as to why this reinterpretation of the Temple occurred within the Qumran community. Mary Douglas very likely touches upon an explanation in terms of comparative religious phenomena: Any sect tends to define itself by purity rules. . . . the further from membership of a sectarian group, the more tendency to turn purity rules into metaphors of spiritual good instead of regulations for daily entrances and exits and rankings. ('Critique and Commentary,' in Neusner, *The Idea of Purity*, p. 141.) If Douglas's analysis is correct, the emphasis on purity at Qumran was a function of the sectarian nature of the group. Similarly, the emphasis in 1QS upon 'truth' as faithfulness to the covenant, used as an equivalent to righteousness (cf. Isa 48:1, Jer 4:2, Zech 8:8), is probably motivated by the attempt of the community to place a clear demarcation between its participation in salvation and Jews on the outside (n.b. the stress which the polarity of truth and error receives in the teaching on the two spirits). Contra B. Przybylski, *Righteousness in Matthew and His World of Thought*, SNTSMS 41 (Cambridge: Cambridge University Press, 1980), p. 28, it is not clear that the concept of righteousness is subordinate to that of truth in 1QS.

on the community's conception of righteousness in behavioral terms. The regulated life of the Qumran community created and maintained the purity and righteousness of its members through proper observance of *Torah*, discipline of errors, and separation from those outside.[94]

The significance given to purity at Qumran results in a blurring of a distinction between personal faults and external sources of defilement. In 1QS 11:12, 13, the threat to the sanctity of the Qumran psalmist is depicted as an assault by external enemies: not merely the transgressions of the individual, but interaction with the wicked brought defilement.[95] A number of the expressions of human nothingness in the Qumran materials are undoubtedly related to the linking of transgression and defilement. The human body itself, through its natural functions, presented a constant danger of decay, corruption, and disorder.[96] The resulting defilement, which was regarded as equivalent to transgression, could be removed only by the divinely-ordered life of the sect.

The member therefore remained capable of transgression and defilement from which cleansing and forgiveness was required. Consequently, the claim to righteousness, holiness and 'perfection of way,' in 1QS should not be understood in terms of absolute sinlessness. Such terms describe rather the divine requirements for purity and holiness, embodied and fulfilled in the covenant and rules of the community.

F. Summary

Three basic features of the soteriology of 1QS may be highlighted. The sect clearly regarded the divinely ordained plan for the elect as the ultimate source of salvation. The absolute priority assigned to this gift of divine election is in no way qualified by statements about

---

[94] It is therefore incorrect to draw a close connection between Paul's conception of justification through faith in Christ apart from the Law and the Qumran view of the divine gift of righteousness, so e.g. Siegfried Schulz, 'Zur Rechtfertigung aus Gnaden in Qumran und bei Paulus,' *ZThK* 56 (1959):155– 185; Becker, *Das Heil Gottes*, pp. 276–279. Even Jürgen Becker, who recognizes that 'righteousness' at Qumran was displayed in obedience to the community interpretation of *Torah*, fails to appreciate this observation when he speaks of a צדקה *neben dem Gesetz* ' or of the accent in the Qumran understanding of righteousness shifting '*auf geistig-personale Beziehung*' in 1QS (*Das Heil Gottes*, pp. 115–126). The inward and outward were obviously *conceptually* distinguishable, since 1QS addresses the problem of false motives (1QS 2:11–18). But the life of obedience to the practices of the community mediated the righteousness which the Qumran sectarian possessed. Paul's conception of righteousness as a gift given to faith represents a radically different understanding of salvation.

[95] 1QS 11:14b, 15.

[96] E.g. 1QS 11:10.

human response in 1QS. Yet within this encompassing framework, salvific, i.e. atoning, value is attributed to the practices of the community in a startlingly explicit manner. Furthermore, submission to the Community Rule is an essential prerequisite to the righteousness and purity necessary for salvation. The rules of the community provided a 'sphere' of saving sanctity, expressed in identification with the Temple, into which the outsider could not enter.

EXCURSUS: EVIDENCE FOR A TECHNICAL USAGE OF 'THE RIGHTEOUSNESS OF GOD'

Because of the importance of the expression 'the righteousness of God' in apocalyptic Judaism to Käsemann's claim that Paul takes up a technical term, a brief examination of its meaning in relevant texts is in order. We shall see that evidence for a technical usage is lacking.

A. 1QS 10:25

The unusual expression 'a strong judgment for the righteousness of God' (ומשפט עוז לצדקת אל) bears a significant resemblance to a number of passages in the Hebrew Bible. The priestly leaders of the Qumran community were to preserve the correct observance of *Torah*, which was characterized as truth, righteousness, (just) judgment, and love of faithfulness: לעשות אמת וצדקה ומשפט ואהבת חסד.[97] This model for the leadership of the Qumran community was drawn from the ideals of kingship.[98] The cumbersome expression of 1QS, ומשפט עוז לצדקת אל, may therefore have its origin in the linking of משפט and צדקה in such texts.[99] A reference to this Biblical idiom fits the context well. The speaker views himself as the leader of the people of God gathered in the community. In line 25 one finds a personal dedication to uphold the strict observance of *Torah*. The speaker assumes the responsibility for instruction and judgment, including comfort to the oppressed: אהבת חסד לניכעים, which again is reminiscent of the kingship ideals of the Hebrew Bible.[100] The צדקת אל in this reading of the text signifies the righteous judgment or determina-

---

[97] 1QS 8:2 see 1:1–9; 5:1–4; 8:1–4.
[98] E.g. 2 Sam 146; 8:15; 1 Kings 10:9; Isa 16:5; 2 Chron 9:8; Jer 22:2–3, 15–16; 23:5; 33:15; Prov 1:1–4.
[99] Psalm 72:1, 2 is particularly close to 1QS 10:25, since in pronominal form it also refers to 'the righteousness of God': אלהים משפטיך למלך תן וצדקתך לבן מלך ידין עמך בצדק וענייך במשפט
[100] Cf. Isa 11:4; Jer 22:2–3, 15–16.

tion of God, similar to the sense of צדקה in the parallel references to the monarchical pattern found in the Hebrew Bible.[101] The sense of a 'saving power' of God which Stuhlmacher suggests for צדקת אל in 1QS 10:25 is lacking in this case, as is the parallelism to line 23.[102]

B. 1QS 11:3

Despite the virtually identical appearance of *waw* and *yodh* in 1QS, the the reading צדקותו (his righteous deeds) has been universally adopted. However, the (apparently) previously unconsidered reading צדקותי (my righteous deeds) is to be preferred. This interpretation not only excludes a technical usage of the '-righteousness of God' in this line, but bears major significance for the assessment of the soteriology of 1QS. The passage should be read:

כיא אני לאל משפטי ובידו תום דרכי עם ישׁור לבבי 3ובצדקותי ימח פשׁעי כיא ממקור דעתו פתח אורי ובנפלאותיו הביטה עיני . . .	For I belong to the God of my vindication and the perfection of my way is in his hand with the uprightness of my heart.[3] And *with my righteous deeds* he will wipe away my transgressions, for he opened my light from the well of his knowledge and with his wonderful deeds he caused my eyes to see . . .

According to Elisha Qimron, approximately thirty cases of ו- in place of י- appear in the Qumran literature (indicating identical pronunciation), but, 'The scribes however, almost always succeed in preserving the orthographic distinction.'[103] When the endings used with the singular are joined to plural nouns in 1QS, it is

---

[101] See the reading offered by Udo Schnelle (*Gerechtigkeit und Christusgegenwart*, p. 94): Da . . . drei von dreizehn Wörtern der folgenden Zeile zerstört sind, ist die Zuordnung von צדקת אל zum Kontext sehr problematisch. Wahrscheinlich aber ist eine Beziehung auf das vorhergehende אמנים und משׁפט עוז. Danach wäre die צדקת אל Maß und Grund des durch Treue gekennzeichneten Verhaltens des Beters.

[102] Stuhlmacher argues that *parallelismus membrorum* requires that לצדקת אל in 10:25 be read as the beginning of a new clause, *Gerechtigkeit Gottes*, pp. 155–159. This is not necessary, however, since a strict parallel is lacking between the infinitive שׁמור and the noun צדקה. He also reads the singular לצדקת אל as a parallel to the plural וצדקות אל in line 23, despite the difference in number.

[103] Elisha Qimron, *The Hebrew of the Dead Sea Scrolls*, HSS 29 (Atlanta: Scholars Press, 1986), pp. 33–35, 59. As is well-known, in Biblical Hebrew feminine plural nouns generally take the pronominal endings used with plural nouns, but the endings used with singular nouns also appear. See E. Kautsch, *Gesenius' Hebrew Grammar*, trans. and rev. A. E. Cowley (Oxford: Clarendon, 1980), 91 m,n.

generally the third person masculine plural form, in which the use of the ending ‏ם-‏ (instead of ‏יהם-‏), does not result in semantic ambiguity. Two occurrences of the form of ending used with the singular appear with a feminine plural, and two with a preposition taking endings used with the plural. The immediate context of these expressions prevents any semantic confusion.[104]

It seems likely that the copyist of 1QS avoided the ‏ו-‏ to signify the third person masculine singular with plural nouns in instances in which ambiguity might result. In the closing hymn of 1QS 10:8–11:22 in particular, only the ‏יו-‏ ending appears with plural nouns.[105] Moreover, nouns with first-person common singular pronominal endings surround ‏משפטי דרכי, ישור לבבי, פשעי‏, ‏בצדקותו/י‏: requiring the use of the ‏יו-‏ if the reading 'his righteous deeds' is to be made explicit (given the similarity of appearance of *waw* and *yodh* in 1QS). In the same line a feminine plural form with a third-person masculine singular suffix is given the form of the ending used with the plural: ‏נפלאותיו‏, presumably to avoid ambiguity. The endings used with the plural may be expected then, when the context is unclear. If the expression 'his righteousness' was intended in line 3, one would expect ‏צדקותיו‏.

The context of 1QS confirms this judgment. It should not be overlooked that the plural form ‏צדקות‏ consistently maintains the sense of 'righteous deeds' in the Qumran literature, which when applied to God the community is devoted to recounting, i.e. *past* events are contemplated.[106] In contrast, the singular ‏צדקה‏ is the form predicated of God when he is appealed to as the (future) source of a hoped-for vindication or cleansing.[107] This observation further inclines one toward the interpretation of the suffix as a first person singular, since in 1QS 11:3 it is clear that a future hope is expressed.[108] It would be unusual if 1QS applied the noun ‏צדקות‏ to God in this instance.

The Qumran psalmist's confidence in God's future action on his behalf (expressed by the verb ‏ימח‏) springs from what God has already done in him. The train of thought in line 3 clearly shifts back from the expression of confidence in God to an acknowledgment of his previous illumination of the psalmist. The reading ‏בצדקותי‏ fits this transition well, since the divine revelation which brought salvation to the psalmist ('for he opened my light

---

[104] 1QS 3:7, 8 (‏עוונותו‏ his guilty deeds). See also ‏מאחרו‏ 1QS 1:17; 6:3.
[105] ‏חוקיו, חסדיו, מעשיו, נפלאותיו, רחמיו‏.
[106] 1QS 1:21; 10:23; 1QH 17:17.
[107] E.g. 1QS 11:5, 14.
[108] ‏ובצדקותי ימח פשעי‏.

from the well of his knowledge . . .'), was linked to the righteous behavior maintained within the community.[109]

The idea that righteous deeds serve as a source of cleansing might seem to run against the grain of Qumran theology. But in fact there is a distinct thematic link between our reading and the atoning function assigned to the community which we have found elsewhere in 1QS. The community regarded its practice of צדקה ומשפט ואהבת חסד to serve as atonement for those who volunteered allegiance to the community.[110] This obligation fell with special emphasis on the priestly leaders.[111]

The Qumran community undoubtedly found precedent for its appeal to the deeds of the righteous in the Hebrew Bible, where divine favor upon צדקות is expressed in a number of passages.[112] The most likely source for the thought of 1QS 11:3 is the book of Ezekiel, where expressions of individualized retribution appear. God warns the righteous that their righteousness (or, if read as a plural, their righteous deeds) will not 'be remembered,' if they turn aside to iniquity.[113] Likewise, the wicked are called on to repent and promised that if they do so, they will live by the 'righteousness' which they do.[114] The idea of atoning for iniquity by one's obedience is not present here, but the idea could be derived easily from these passages. It might be inferred that if the 'righteous' continue their obedience, their righteous deeds would be 'remembered' in their favor, and that they thereby would be cleansed from iniquity and would live. Just as the transgressions of the repentant sinner are forgotten on the basis of righteous behavior, the speaker in 1QS 11:3 trusts that his transgressions will be done away with on the basis of his righteous deeds.

It might be objected that an appeal to one's righteous deeds would be unthinkable for a group in which righteousness was attributed to God alone.[115] It should not be overlooked, however, that in the same breath in which the *Hodayoth* deny human righteousness, it is confessed that God 'perfects the way of the sons

---

[109] E.g. 1QS 4:20–22.

[110] 1QS 5:4, 6.

[111] Cf. 1QS 8:1–6, 10; 9:4, e.g. 8:4: ולרצת עוון בעושי משפט.

[112] Isa 33:15; 64:5; Ps 11:7. Cf. Dan 9:18.

[113] Ezek 3:20; 18:24; 33:13. The plural reading צדקתיו which the Masoretes adopted (קרי) is clearly early, since it is attested by manuscripts from the Cairo Geniza (Ezek 18:24) and by the Septuagint, Vulgate and Targum. It may well represent the Qumran reading as well, given the borrowing of thought from these passages in 1QS 11:3, where the plural appears.

[114] Ezek 18:22: כל־פשעיו אשר עשה לא יזכרו לו בצדקתו אשר־עשה יחיה cf. 18:21, 27; 33:14–19.

[115] Cf. 1QH 1:26, 27; 4:29–32.

of his good pleasure.'[116] In 1QS 11:2 the Qumran Psalmist's 'perfection of way' and upright heart are affirmed, while in 1QH 4:30 it is denied that humans may attain to תום דרך. Moreover, the Biblical Psalms themselves, upon which the Qumran community based their psalmody, alternate between claims to vindication on account of righteousness, and denial that human beings can be righteous.[117] Therefore the appeal to one's righteous deeds in 1QS 11:3 is not in conflict with the thought expressed elsewhere that no human being is righteous.[118]

C. 1QS 11:12

It is likely that 1QS 11:12 and its context allude to Psalm 119 and to the idea of צדקת אל as God's covenantal faithfulness which is found there. The proximity of 1QS 11:12 to Ps 119:142, 143 is readily recognized:[119]

ואני אם 12 אמוט חסדי אל
ישועתי לעד ואם אכשול בעוון
בשר משפטי בצדקת אל תעמוד
לנצחים 13 ואם יפתח צרתי
וממשחת יחלץ נפשי ויכן לדרך
פעמי ברחמיו הגישני ובחסדיו
יבוא 14 משפטי בצדקת אמתו
שפטני וברוב טובו יכפר בעד
כול עוונותי ובצדקתו יטהרני
מנדת 15 אנוש וחטאת בני אדם
להודות לאל צדקו ולעליון
תפארתו

And when 12 I am caused to totter, the lovingkindnesses of God deliver me forever. And when I am caused to stumble by the iniquity of flesh, my vindication is with the *righteousness of God* which stands forever. 13 And when my distress is opened he both rescues my soul from destruction and establishes the way of my steps. With his compassionate deeds he draws me near. And with his acts of lovingkindness comes 14 my judgment. By *the righteousness of his truth* he will judge me. And in the plenitude of his goodness he will atone for all my iniquities forever. And *in his righteousness* he will purify me from the pollution of 15 humanity and the sin of the sons of Adam to give praises to God for *his righteousness* and to the Most High for his majesty.

---

[116] 1QH 4:31–32.

[117] E.g. Psalm 7:9; 18:21, 25; 143:2; 130:3.

[118] The following context leaves no doubt, of course, that God is the ultimate source of the speaker's goodness (cf. 1QS 11:13). The reading adopted here in no way alters the fundamental *sola gratia* stance of Qumran thought.

[119] Cf. Ps 111:3.

צדקתך צדק לעולם 142   142 Your righteousness is an
ותורתך אמת 143   צר־ומצק   everlasting righteousness and
מצאוני מצותיך שעשעי   your *Torah* is truth. 143 Although trouble and anguish
have come upon me, your
commands are my delight.

The context of 1QS 11:12 further contains remarkable similarities in expression and vocabulary to the latter portions of Psalm 119: e.g. חסדי אל (119:159: save my life, according to your lovingkindness!), משפט (119:160: every judgment of your righteousness is forever!), חלץ (119:153: see my oppression and deliver me!), רחם (119:156: your compassions are great!), ויכן לדרך פעמי (119:133: direct my footsteps in your words!), אמת (the sum of your word is truth!). Even the appeal for deliverance from oppression by others appears in Psalm 119:134. Given these similarities, the prominence of the theme of the covenant in 1QS, and the appeal to the speaker's righteous deeds in 1QS 11:3, it is likely that the confidence in צדקת אל in 11:12, along with the further references to God's צדקה, represent a trust in God's covenant faithfulness.[120] For the Qumran community this faithfulness was concretized in his sovereign election and preservation of the Qumran community and its practice of righteousness.[121]

It is hard to find convincing proof for the meaning 'saving power' which Käsemann assigns to צדקת אל in 11:12. In the expression בצדקת אמתו (11:13), the *nomen regens* most likely functions adjectivally: 'his righteous truth.' Elsewhere in 1QS, אמת is treated as a concrete referent, signifying the true will of God concretized in his plan for the course of history, or in the ordinances of the Qumran covenant, the knowledge of which was necessary for salvation.[122] In 11:13 then, צדקת אמתו most likely refers to the righteous plan of God, which was expressed in his covenant with the community.[123] This 'righteous truth of God,'

---

[120] On the concept of the covenant in 1QS, see above.

[121] Sanders rightly points out that צדקה and חסד overlap in meaning in this context. But the parallelism between the expressions in 1QS 11 does not require that the two words are precisely equivalent. If this were the case, which sense should one choose to give to both? Sanders argues that צדקה should be understood as 'mercy.' Given Sanders reasoning the reverse is just as plausible. חסד, טוב, רחם all might be understood as 'righteousness.' In this context צדקה and חסד function in approximately the same way, but the parallel structure should not be robbed of its poetic force by reducing the statements to the same sense. The variation in expression is intentional, bringing out slightly varied perspectives. Cf. *Paul and Palestinian Judaism*, pp. 305–312.

[122] E.g. 1:5, 11, 12, 15, 19; 3:6; 4:6, 17, 20; 5:3, 6, 10; 6:15; 7:18; 8:2, 6.

[123] Cf. 1QS 1:13b–17.

i.e. his saving purpose expressed in the Qumran covenant, is the source of the Qumran Psalmist's vindicating judgment by God.[124]

The two references to צדקה which follow in 11:14, 15 may be elucidated by their parallels. וברוב טובו יכפר (in the plenitude of his goodness he will atone) corresponds to ובצדקתו יטהרני (in his righteousness he will purify me). Likewise, להודות לאל לצדקו (to give praises to God for his righteousness) parallels ולעליון תפארתו (and to the Most High for his majesty). The other instances of צדקה in this context therefore provide no solid support to the idea that in 1QS 11:12 צדקת אל signifies a saving act of God. There is no compelling reason then to understand צדקת אל as God's apocalyptic intervention.[125]

A dissimilarity to Paul's thought with regard to the expressions עוון בשר (the iniquity of flesh, 1QS 11:12) and the statement ובצדקתו יטהרני מנדת אנוש (And in his righteousness he will purify me from the pollution of humanity, 1QS 11:14, 15a) should be noted. One finds a curious mixture of themes in 1QS 11:9--15, reflective of the seriousness with which impurity was regarded at Qumran. The speaker trusts in God for forgiveness of sin, but the sin in this instance is not regarded as the responsibility of the individual.[126] It is rather the result of being placed among the human race.[127] Deliverance from עוון בשר (1QS 11:12) then is not regarded as the expunging of strictly personal sins, but as victory over the onslaught of sinful human beings, who as the source of the Psalmist's sin, are regarded as enemies.[128] Likewise, the verbs אמוט and אכשול express the effects of sin, but not the idea of transgression: 'when I am caused to totter, . . . when I am caused to stumble.'[129] The Qumran Psalmist is assaulted and

---

[124] Cf. 4:2 where צדק אמת clearly signifies the behavior of a member of the Qumran community.

[125] Stuhlmacher appeals to חסדי אל as a parallel to support this claim, *Gerechtigkeit Gottes*, pp. 154–155. But parallelism is lacking, since צדקה is in the singular.

[126] 1QS 11:10.

[127] 1QS 11:9, 10.

[128] In the immediate context בשר denotes the whole of sinful humanity, not the existence of the individual (1QS 11:7, 9). Jürgen Becker recognizes that בשר may bear this meaning in the Qumran materials, but fails to apply it to 1QS 11, *Das Heil Gottes: Heils- und Sündenbegriffe in den Qumrantexten und im Neuen Testament*, SUNT 3 (Göttingen, Vandenhoeck & Ruprecht, 1964), pp. 111–112. Both the imagery and the usage of בשר in 1QS 11 argue for the meaning adopted here. Cf. Rudolf Meyer, 'σάρξ' in *Theologisches Wörterbuch zum Neuen Testament*, 10 vols., ed. G. Kittel and G. Friedrich, (Stuttgart: Kohlhammer, 1964), 7:109–118.

[129] The verb כשל in Biblical Hebrew does not usually refer to sin as transgression, but to sin in its effects, i.e. the loss of strength and security. Cf. Hos 5:5; 14:2, 10; Prov 4:19; 24:16; Dan 11:33. The Hiphil הכשיל in 1QS 3:24 bears this significance: the angel of darkness causes the sons of light to stumble.

brought into iniquity and its plagues by the sinful humans among
whom he lives. The imagery of physical danger is employed: God
rescues him as from distress and destruction. As we have seen
already, this equating of impurity to transgression in 1QS strictly
qualifies the manner in which the Qumran concept of saving grace
may be related to Paul. The pollution from which the Qumran
Psalmist is saved here is his own, yet the fault for it is assigned to
the sinful human race, so that the speaker can appeal for deliverance from sin like the Psalmists of the Hebrew Bible appeal for
rescue from physical danger.[130]

D. 1QM 4:6

The reference to **צדקת אל** in 1QM 4:6 deserves only brief
mention. The context simply does not allow one to determine
whether a display of God's power or a divine quality is signified.
There is a series of construct relations with **אל** as the *nomen rectum* in
1QM 4. These instances display a considerable variety in the sense
of the construct relations, e.g. **ימין אל** (the right hand of God: act
or metaphorical attribute?), **חללי אל** (those slain by God), **עדת**
אל (assembly of God). It is seemingly impossible to sort out
whether a quality of God (e.g. his covenant faithfulness) or a
divine saving power is contemplated by the four examples in 4:6:
אמת אל צדק אל כבוד אל משפט אל.[131]

E. Test. Dan 6:10

The final example of a technical usage of δικαιοσύνη Θεοῦ to which
Käsemann appeals is found in Test. Dan 6:10. In this case, the
reading which Käsemann has chosen is problematic text-critically.
If the lemma which M. de Jonge has reconstructed is correct, an
alternative reading of the passage is clearly original. The reading
κολλήθητε τῇ δικαιοσύνῃ τοῦ νόμου κυρίου would in this case have
attestation in families I and II.[132] In any event, mss. *b*, which is
now generally regarded as the representative of the earliest form of

---

[130] God's acts of lovingkindness in 11:12 may not signify acts of forgiveness of
sin, but rescue from enemies (1QH 2:23, 25; 5:22). Moreover, it should not be
overlooked that the **חסדי אל** are not dispensed to humanity at large, but only to
those who belong to the Qumran community (1QS 1:8; 2:1b–4; 2:25, 26).

[131] Stuhlmacher (*Gerechtigkeit Gottes*, p. 163) maintains that with **צדקת אל**: '. . .
taucht der Begriff Gottesgerechtigkeit zum dritten Mal in den Texten auf. Die
Parallellesungen machen es unzweifelbar, daß damit Gottes eigenes Recht und
nicht Gottes Gabe gemeint ist.' He criticizes Jürgen Becker for his translation:
'innerhalb und aufgrund des Bundes gewährtes Heil Gottes,' *Das Heil Gottes*, p. 83.
Neither translation can be convincingly demonstrated from the context.

[132] Only *c h i j* lack τοῦ νόμου, κυρίου is found in *b* [I] and in *l* [II].

the text, contains this reading, not the reference to δικαιοσύνη Θεοῦ to which Käsemann appeals.[133] Moreover, the presence of τοῦ νόμου in the text has broad attestation.[134]

In the passage, the patriarch Dan warns his children to be wary of Satan and his schemes. Dan's children are to follow his example of obedience to the Law: ἐκδιδάσκων (Dan) διὰ τῶν ἔργων νόμον Θεοῦ (6:9). This will ensure their salvation (or that of those who imitate them):

6:10 ἀπόστητε οὖν ἀπὸ πάσης ἀδικίας καὶ κολλήθητε τῇ δικαιοσύνῃ τοῦ νόμου κυρίου, καὶ ἔσται τὸ γένος μου εἰς σωτηρίαν ἕως τοῦ αἰῶνος.

The righteous Law is regarded as a source of salvation, but only for those who cling to it. Even if the reading which Käsemann prefers is accepted, the δικαιοσύνη Θεοῦ could only be regarded as the means to salvation, and not a salvation-creating *Macht*. Therefore none of the instances of a technical usage to which Käsemann appeals are convincing.

F. Psalm 142 (LXX)

Richard B. Hays claims that while the texts which Käsemann uses for examples of a technical usage are questionable, Paul himself takes up a reference to δικαιοσύνη Θεοῦ as a 'saving power' found in Psalm 143 (LXX 142).[135] Hays's own case is unconvincing, however.

He interprets the δικαιοσύνη Θεοῦ of Rom 3:5 as 'God's covenant faithfulness,' but insists that the idea of power is at hand, since 'God's faithfulness/righteousness is manifested in his saving activity.'[136] However, the fact that God's covenant faithfulness might be manifested as a saving power does not attest to the *meaning*, 'saving power' for the expression δικαιοσύνη Θεοῦ. Moreover, Hays's appeal to an instrumental sense for ἐν τῇ δικαιοσύνῃ σου in v. 11 is weak. There is no inherent difference between the sense of the phrase in v. 11 and in v. 1, where Hays allows that the instrumental sense is merely 'possible.' In both cases a modal sense, i.e. the notion of God responding in covenant faithfulness, is equally likely. It is

---

[133] Cf. H. Dixon Slingerland, *The Testaments of the Twelve Patriarchs: A Critical History of Research*, SBLMS 21 (Missoula, Mont.: Scholars Press, 1977), pp. 95–96.
[134] Cf. M. de Jonge, *The Testaments of the Twelve Patriarchs: A Critical Edition of the Greek Text* Pseudepigrapha Veteris Testamenti Graece 1 (Leiden: E. J. Brill, 1978), pp. xxxiii–xli, 110–111, 187.
[135] Richard B. Hays, 'Psalm 143 and the Logic of Romans 3,' *JBL* 99 (1980):107–115.
[136] Hays, 'Psalm 143,' p. 111.

unwarranted therefore to insist on an instrumental usage in this context.

It is important to observe that in the Psalm the deliverance which is sought is that from physical danger from a personal enemy. The Psalm is distant from the topic of salvation from the 'power' of sin which is found in Romans 3 and the Qumran texts.

G. Targum Jonathan (Isaiah)

Klaus Koch has claimed to find three distinct conceptions of 'righteousness' in three different Aramaic words which translate the Hebrew צדק/צדקה in the book of Isaiah of the Targum Jonathan.[137] It is worth noting that the Targum's use of three different terms indicates that the translator intuitively recognized that the Hebrew צדק/צדקה could signify a number of ideas (at least three if Koch is correct), undermining any attempt to synthesize an overarching conception for the expression. According to Koch, the expression זכי (and related vocables) is used in for human deeds of righteousness, צדיקיא for the community of those who (although beset by sin) seek to be faithful to the covenant, and קושטא for God's 'truth,' i.e. his covenant faithfulness. This third idea, which is the logical source of the other two, constitutes the means by which they are actuated, and consequently is salvific in scope.

However, Koch's analysis is not satisfactory for a number of reasons. First, as Koch notes, קושטא is frequently associated with divine judgment (e.g. 1:24–26; 16:5), which implies not only saving vindication of the people of God, but his punitive acts against his foes. Moreover, human beings may and ought to do קושטא (26:9, 10; 32:8). God will fill Zion with the (human) service of true and righteousness judgment (עבדי דין דקשוט יזכו, 33:5). The expression therefore does not univocally convey the sense of a saving covenant faithfulness, since it may either refer to human acts or include divine retribution. Koch therefore has not shown that a technical use of קושטא analogous to Käsemann's conception of the 'righteousness of God' appears in Isaiah of Targum Jonathan.

---

[137] Klaus Koch, 'Die drei Gerechtigkeiten: Die Umformung einer hebräischen Idee im aramäischen Denken nach dem Jesajatargum,' in *Rechtfertigung: Festschrift für Ernst Käsemann zum 70. Geburtstag*, ed. Johannes Friedrich, Wolfgang Pöhlmann, and Peter Stuhlmacher (Tübingen: J. C. B. Mohr [Paul Siebeck], 1976), pp. 245–267.

III. THE PSALMS OF SOLOMON

A. Introduction

A collection of eighteen psalms, preserved in eleven Greek and four Syriac manuscripts, which may be dated from the tenth to the sixteenth centuries, are known as the 'Psalms of Solomon' through the pseudepigraphal attributions appended to the psalms at a very early stage in the transmission of the material.[138] On the basis of subject matter and historical allusions, these psalms are generally regarded as deriving from the late Hasmonean and early Roman periods in Palestine (from approximately 75 to 40 BCE), with Jerusalem itself being the likely place of composition.[139] It is commonly agreed that the Pss. Sol. were composed in Hebrew or Aramaic, from which the Greek version was translated.

We will investigate four prominent themes which relate to the soteriology of the Pss. Sol. Two of these themes, 'the pious/sinners' and 'Israel' provide an indication of how traditional ideas regarding the divine covenant were interpreted by the group which produced the psalms. The other pair of themes, 'God's righteousness' and 'God's mercy' reveal how divine grace and human obedience were thought to function in providing salvation. We shall see that again in the Pss. Sol. the behavior of the 'pious' is accorded

---

[138] On introductory matters regarding the text, see R. B. Wright, 'Psalms of Solomon,' in *The Old Testament Pseudepigrapha*, 2 vols., ed. J. H. Charlesworth (Garden City, NY: Doubleday, 1985), 2:639–640, or another of the recent introductions to the material by Brock, Holm–Nielsen, or Schüpphaus. Robert R. Hann (*The Manuscript History of the Psalms of Solomon*, SBLSCS 13 [Chico, CA: Scholars Press, 1982]) and Joseph L. Trafton (*The Syriac Version of the Psalms of Solomon*, SBLSCS 11 [Atlanta, GA: Scholars Press, 1985]) have produced fresh studies of the textual history of Pss. Sol., the former revising von Gebhardt's stemma, the latter substantially confirming K. G. Kuhn's contention that the Syriac version was based in some places on a Hebrew *Vorlage*.

[139] See Wright, 'Psalms of Solomon,' pp. 640–642; Sebastian Brock, 'The Psalms of Solomon,' in *The Apocryphal Old Testament*, ed. H. F. D. Sparks (Oxford: Clarendon, 1984), p. 651; M. Delcor, 'Psaumes de Salomon,' in *Dictionnaire de la Bible: Supplément* 10 vols., ed. H. Cazelles and A. Feuillet (Paris: Letouzey and Ané, 1979), 9:232–236; Joachim Schüpphaus, *Die Psalmen Salomos: Ein Zeugnis Jerusalemer Theologie und Frömmigkeit in der Mitte des Vorchristlichen Jahrhunderts*, ALGHJ 7 (Leiden: Brill, 1977), pp. 5–8; Svend Holm–Nielsen, 'Die Psalmen Salomos,' in *Poetische Schriften*, JSHRZ 4, ed. W. G. Kümmel (Gütersloh: Gerd Mohn, 1977), pp. 58–59; Maier, *Mensch und freier Wille*, pp. 264–280; G. B. Gray, 'The Psalms of Solomon,' in *The Apocrypha and Pseudepigrapha of the Old Testament*, 2 vols., ed. R. H. Charles (Oxford: Clarendon, 1913), pp. 627–630; J. Viteau, *Les Psaumes de Salomon*, Documents pour l'etude de la Bible 4 (Paris: Letouzey et Ané, 1911); G. Kittel, 'Die Psalmen Salomos,' in *Die Apokryphen und Pseudepigraphen des Alten Testaments*, 2 vols, ed. E. Kautzsch (Tübingen: J. C. B. Mohr [Paul Siebeck], 1900), pp. 127–128; H. E. Ryle and M. R. James, Ψαλμοὶ Σολομῶντος *Psalms of the Pharisees, Commonly Called the Psalms of Solomon* (Cambridge: Cambridge University Press, 1891), pp. xxxvii–xliv.

a saving significance. Likewise, the extent of covenant is restricted
to the 'pious': God's 'mercy' is applicable only to those who fulfill
its righteous demands.

Since Wellhausen's investigation, *Die Pharisäer und die Sadducäer*,
in which he employed the Pss. Sol. as a source for the description of
Pharisaic thought, the ὅσιοι ('pious'), who take a central position in
the psalms, have traditionally been taken to represent the Pharisees, who express in the psalms their bitter opposition to the Hasmoneans and their Sadducean allies.[140] There has been a recent
shift away from this view in light of the Qumran finds, with a
number of scholars adopting a more cautious stance, claiming that
the evidence does not permit one to assign the material to any
particular group.[141] Most of the recent investigators who continue
to ascribe the Pss. Sol. to Pharisaic circles rightly refrain from
categorizing the opponents of the 'pious' as Sadducees. There are
no direct references to a Sadducean party within the psalms, and
the material is primarily directed toward the instruction and edification of the community in which it was composed.[142]

Legitimate criticisms have been brought to bear upon a number of the arguments for regarding the Pss. Sol. as Pharisaic in
origin. As Charlesworth and others have pointed out, it is incorrect to use the Psalms of Solomon as a 'classical source' for the
description of Pharisaism, or to force the Psalms into a mold of
traditional assumptions about Pharisaic beliefs.[143] Nevertheless,

---

[140] J. Wellhausen, *Die Pharisäer und die Sadducäer: Eine Untersuchung zur inneren
jüdischen Geschichte* (Greifswald: Bamberg, 1874). So, e.g. Ryle and James, *The
Psalms of the Pharisees* , pp. xliv–lii.

[141] So, e.g. P. N. Franklyn, 'The Cultic and Pious Climax of Eschatology in the
Psalms of Solomon,' *JSJ* 18 (1987):15–17; Robert Wright, 'The Psalms of
Solomon, the Pharisees, and the Essenes,' in *The 1972 Proceedings of the International
Organization for Septuagint and Cognate Studies*, SBLSCS 2, ed. Robert A. Kraft (Los
Angeles, CA: Scholars Press, 1972), pp. 136–147; Jerry O'Dell, 'The Religious
Background of the Psalms of Solomon,' *RevQ* 3 (1961–62):241–257. The claim
that the Pss. Sol. are Pharisaic has by no means disappeared, however. See Dieter
Lührmann, 'Paul and the Pharisaic Tradition,' *JSNT* 36 (1989):75–94.

[142] Maier, *Mensch und freier Wille*, pp. 282–300; Schüpphaus, *Die Psalmen
Salomos*, pp. 5–11; Holm-Nielsen, *Die Psalmen Salomos*, pp. 58–59.

[143] See Charlesworth's editorial note in R. B. Wright, 'Psalms of Solomon,' in
The Old Testament Pseudepigrapha, 2 vols., ed. J. H. Charlesworth (Garden City,
NY: Doubleday, 1985), 2:642.

[144] See Josephus, *Ant.* 13.408–418, 14.4–7. Aristobulus' animosity toward the
Pharisees reflects the earlier relationship of his father, Alexander Jannaeus, to the
Pharisees and the Jewish people. See Josephus, *Ant.* 13.372–383. Schüpphaus, who
regards the Pss. Sol. as Pharisaic, relates Ps. Sol. 17:16 to experiences of the
Pharisees under Alexander Jannaeus (*Die Psalmen Salomos*, pp. 130–131), but this
is hardly likely, since 17:11–17 almost certainly refers to Roman occupation of
Jerusalem. André Caquot (following *inter alia*, Adolf Schlatter) has recently argued
that Ps. Sol. 17 reflects events of the early Herodian period ('Les Hasmonéens, les

these psalms may, with due caution, be ascribed to Pharisaic circles.

It is clear that ideas such as an expectation of a Messiah, or the differentiation which is made between the 'righteous' and the 'wicked,' can not be used as evidence for (or against) the thesis that the Pss. Sol. represent an early Pharisaic group. Too little is known about the Pharisees and other movements within early Judaism to make a judgment on solely theological grounds.

But given the widely acknowledged setting of the Pss. Sol. in the late Hasmonean period, a Pharisaic group is the most likely source of these writings. The group responsible for the psalms not only opposed the Hasmoneans, but had suffered expulsion from Jerusalem at their hands (17:5). If, as seems likely, the passage following 17:5 refers to the conflict between Aristobulus II and Hyrcanus II, then the 'sinners' of verse 5, who expelled the group which authored the psalms, are probably the followers of Aristobulus. Given the hostility that existed between Aristobulus and the Pharisees, they, and those in sympathy with them, would have fared poorly after his forceful acquisition of kingship.[144]

It is clear from the Qumran writings that not only the Pharisees, but also those who formed the Qumran community in the early first century BCE, came into conflict with the Hasmonean rulers and their associates. On the basis of the opposition to the Hasmoneans alone, the Essenes or another grouping of which we are presently unaware might still be thought of as the source of the Pss. Sol.

However, if the earliest historical situation reflected in the psalms may be dated to the time immediately prior to the capture of Jerusalem by Pompei (as presupposed in the preceding inter-

---

Romains, et Hérode: Observations sur Ps. Sal. 17,' in *Hellenica et Judaica*, ed. A. Caquot, M. Hadas–Lebel, and J. Riaud [Leuven: Peeters, 1986], pp. 213–218). But the psalm's reference to the searching out and capture of Hasmoneans, the desolation of the land, and the exile to the west fit Pompei's capture of Jerusalem better than that of Herod.

[145] Ἵνα τί σύ, βέβηλε, κάθησαι ἐν συνεδρίῳ ὁσίων (4:1). Given that the provenance of the psalms was Jerusalem, συνέδριον most likely signifies the Great Sanhedrin. Maier, following Aberbach, interprets Ps. Sol. 4 as an attack upon the Idumean Antipater (*Mensch und freier Wille*, pp. 275–277). But the psalm is not directed against a particular figure. It rather holds up a model which is to be avoided, a role which a number of 'sinners' may fill (4:8, 20–22, 23–24). Contra Robert R. Hann, 'The Community of the Pious: the Social Setting of the Psalms of Solomon,' *SR* 17 (1988):169–189, the group which authored the psalms has not withdrawn from society and retains considerable influence. The psalms assume a continuing contact with 'sinners,' and presumes a setting in a city (Jerusalem). See e.g. Pss. Sol. 4:5–8; 7:2; 11:1–9; 12:1–6; 16:7, 8. This situation is reflected in the soteriology of the psalms which we will examine below.

pretation of 17:5), the Pharisees emerge as the most likely source of
the Pss. Sol. As noted above, their changing fortunes after the
death of Alexandra Salome are specifically mentioned by Josephus. While it is possible that some unnamed group which suffered
parallel experiences in the vicissitudes of Palestinian politics was
responsible for the Pss. Sol., the congruence of the material with
what may be known from Josephus of the Pharisees' lot in this
period gives some credence to the thesis that the Psalms are Pharisaic.

A further consideration strengthens this argument considerably.
The circle of the 'pious' seems to have been one of considerable
influence in the late Hasmonean period despite the low economic
status which they endured, since they regarded themselves as
dominant in the Great Sanhedrin.[145] It is unlikely that another
group with such political power in Jerusalem, whose fate in the late
Hasmonean period paralleled that of the Pharisees, would receive
no mention in Josephus. Therefore, while it remains possible that
an unknown group composed the Pss. Sol., it is probable that the
Pss. Sol. are Pharisaic.[146]

It is in any case unlikely that the Pss. Sol. represent the work of
an Essene group.[147] While a number of parallels of thought and
language are shared by the Qumran writings and the Pss. Sol.,
significant theological differences between them make it unlikely
that they are related. Chief among these are the assertion of the
freedom of the human will, and the absence of a radical rejection of
the Temple cult in the Pss. Sol.[148]

---

[146] Josephus' report (*Ant.* 13.408–418, 14.4–7) concerning the fate of the Pharisees in this period does not reflect any desire on his part to vindicate them. On the
contrary, where they do appear in this material, it is in a negative light. Hence,
one can hardly claim that Josephus, who is generally concerned to put the
Pharisees in a good light, is tendentious in his report.

[147] Contra Hann, 'The Community of the Pious,' pp. 184–189. There is no
indication that the group which produced the psalms was composed of priests nor
that they were focussed on the cult. On the contrary, they were willing to regard
fasting as making atonement (Ps. Sol. 3:6–8). Ryle and James place a full stop
after ἀδικίαν in verse 7, rather than after ἐν παραπτώματι αὐτοῦ, creating a suggestion of atonement by sin-offering (*Psalms of the Pharisees*, pp. 34–35). But since this
punctuation necessitates a emendation by the transposition of ἐν νηστείᾳ and καὶ,
the punctuation offered by von Gebhardt and Rahlfs is to be preferred. As in the
case of 1QS, atonement is made by the 'pious,' apart from the Temple cult,
although here it is likely that these penitential acts are regarded as a necessary
supplement to, rather than a replacement for sacrifices, since no outright rejection
of the Temple is expressed in the Pss. Sol.

[148] A number of other thematic variations between Qumran and the Pss. Sol.,
which need not be mentioned here, have been noted by various scholars. See
Delcor, 'Psaumes de Salomon,' 9:236–242, and his well-argued dismissal of objections to Pharisaic authorship of Pss. Sol.

To these theological differences further observations by Delcor and Holm–Nielsen may be added. If the Pss. Sol. sprang from Essene circles, it is highly likely that some of the materials would have made their way to Qumran.[149] Yet no copies of the Pss. Sol. have been found at Qumran.[150] This argument is admittedly *e silencio*, and one must take into account the possibility of a variety of Essene groups. Yet one would expect that at least some of these psalms would have been taken up into the worship of the Qumran community and would have left some trace of influence. The radical differences between the Pss. Sol. and the *Hodayot* in genre and style make it extremely unlikely that they were related to the same type of group.[151] Since the Qumran writings constitute the primary evidence of the nature of Essene thought, it seems improbable that the Pss. Sol. are Essenic in origin.

A certain amount of caution must be exercised in relating these materials to the Pharisee Paul. It is likely that there were various shadings of thought within Pharisaic circles. The Pss. Sol. can hardly be taken to represent a dogmatic confession of the whole of first-century BCE Pharisaism. Moreover, a half century, at minimum, separates Paul from these writings, so that the possibility of development in Pharisaism also must be taken into account. Nevertheless, the Pss. Sol. must be counted as an important source for the illumination of early Pharisaism, including that of Paul, since if the preceding arguments hold, the Pss. Sol. represent the only direct evidence for Pharisaic thought from this early period.

The extensive amount of didactic material within the Pss. Sol., and the fact that they were composed in the psalmodic genre, indicate that they were intended for purposes of instruction and edification, most likely being employed in Pharisaic synagogues.[152] The interest in divine justice, which figures prominently in the psalms, is not an actual wrestling with theodicean questions raised by Pompei's capture of Jerusalem. Rather, interpretation of these

---

[149] The flight of the 'pious' from Jerusalem to the wilderness is explicitly mentioned, Ps. Sol. 17:16, 17.

[150] Delcor, 'Psaumes de Salomon,' 9:242.

[151] See Svend Holm–Nielsen, 'Erwägungen zu dem Verhältnis zwischen den Hodajot und den Psalmen Salomos,' in *Bibel und Qumran*, ed. Siegfried Wagner (Berlin: Evangelische Haupt-Bibelgesellschaft, 1968), pp. 112–131.

[152] See Svend Holm–Nielsen, 'The Importance of Late Jewish Psalmody for the Understanding of Old Testament Psalmodic Tradition,' *ST* 14 (1960):1–53, esp. 4–11; also his 'Die Psalmen Salomos,' pp. 59–60; Franklyn, 'Psalms of Solomon,' pp. 2–7. Franklyn's suggestion that the entire collection took its form on the basis of liturgical practice is an over-interpretation, however. The didactic character of the material weighs against this thesis, which, in any case, is undemonstrable.

events is employed for the purpose of admonition and encouragement. Likewise, the eschatological hope which is held out for the
'pious' and for Israel in many of these psalms, is meant to instill
present perseverance and devotion.[153]

Several important insights are connected to this observation.
First, it is improper to characterize the castigation of the
'wicked' and the rehearsal of their faults as a mere attack upon
the Hasmoneans or a Sadducean 'party.'[154] It is true that specific
opponents are the focus of some of the polemics (e.g. 2:22–30; 17:5–
10), but the moralizing is meant for purposes internal to the group
which produced the psalms. The downfall of such people is interpreted as a display of divine justice, and thus a source of hope and
religious instruction. Further, some of the depictions of the 'wicked'
seem to be generic portraits meant to encourage avoidance of
certain faults, since the 'pious' themselves are susceptible to the
same sins.[155] Thus while the division between 'righteous' and
'sinner' was very likely prompted by concrete adversaries, this
polarity is employed in the Pss. Sol. for the admonition within
the circles in which the psalms were read.[156]

The group which created these psalms for synagogal usage
regarded itself as economically deprived.[157] The eschatological
orientation of the hope expressed in the psalms is certainly a
reflection of the group status. This group self-perception, together
with the uncertain situation of the Jewish people in this period, also
served to shape the manner in which salvation was conceived.[158]
Finally, because of the hortatory and practical character of the
material, a number of lines of thought which are of considerable
importance to the understanding of the theology of the Pss. Sol. receive incomplete development. In particular, the relations between

---

[153] As is widely recognized, the placement of these psalms at the end of the
collection is probably intentional, reflecting either liturgical or catechetical usage
of the material.

[154] It is unlikely in any case that the Sadducees formed an organized religious
party.

[155] Pss. Sol. 3:9–12; 4:1–25; 12:1–6; 14:6–10, cf. 16:1–15.

[156] In terms of rhetorical categories, the Pss. Sol. are epideictic, although there
is no evidence that a Hellenistic scheme of argument was consciously employed.
Franklyn's attempt to distinguish between the 'righteous/wicked' polarity in the
canonical psalms and in the Pss. Sol., i.e. his characterization of the former as
'qualitative,' and the latter as 'nominalizing concrete groups of people,' is therefore incorrect ('Psalms of Solomon,' p. 9). So also, incorrectly, Schüpphaus, *Die
Psalmen Salomos*, p. 96.

[157] See e.g. the references to God as the hope of the poor and needy (5:2, 11;
10:6; 15:1; 18:2). Moderate means are held up as an ideal (5:16). Endurance of
poverty is necessary (16:12–15). The wicked greedily defraud them (4:20–22).

[158] See the discussion of 'mercy,' in Section III.E, below.

a complex of crucial soteriological ideas are left unstated: the relation between God's role as righteous judge, who administers a *iustitia distributiva*, and the mercy which he reserves for the 'pious'; the relation between this divine righteousness and the hope which is expressed for Israel; and the relation between the theological categories 'pious' and 'sinners.' Much of following discussion will address these ambiguities.[159] Caution must be exercised not to draw conclusions from the psalms which they themselves do not allow. Nevertheless, the pietistic aims of the Pss. Sol. which limit and shape their theological expression should not be allowed to obscure their essentially didactic character: it is precisely through instruction that the psalms seek to edify. The very silence of the Pss. Sol. on matters such as those enunciated above reveals important aspects of the soteriology of the group which produced them.

Attempts to further define the genre of the psalms, in a manner which might lead to a more precise understanding of their *Sitz im Leben* have not proved fruitful.[160] Nickelsburg's distinction between 'Psalms of the Nation,' and 'Psalms of the Individual,' which is adopted by Franklyn is too simple.[161] Aside from Pss. Sol. 7, 11, 18, individualizing statements appear in the psalms described as 'national.'[162] Israel's fate is addressed in psalms classed among the 'Psalms of the Individual.'[163] Therefore, a description of genre cannot be made on the basis of these themes. Holm–Nielsen concludes his excellent discussion of the classification of the various Pss. Sol. with the observation:

> Aus dieser Übersicht sollte hervorgehen, daß man vom Subjekt der Psalmen aus nicht auf die Gattungen der Psalmen oder ihren individuellen oder kollectiven Charakter schließen kann.[164]

Likewise, Schüpphaus's elucidation of two *Themenkreise*, one holding out hope for divine help in distress, and one expressing belief in the vindicating and recompensing righteousness of God, cannot be employed as a reliable means by which to recover the

---

[159] We have touched upon the conflict between Sanders and Braun over the meaning of 'mercy' in the Pss. Sol. already. See Chapter 1, Section VI.B.

[160] This includes the work of H. L. Jansen despite its overall value. See *Die Spätjüdische Psalmendichtung ihr Entstehungskreis und ihr 'Sitz im Leben'* Skrifter utgitt av Det Norske Videnskaps-Akademi i Oslo II. Hist.-Filos. Klasse 3 (Oslo: Jacob Dybwad, 1937), pp. 95–132.

[161] See George W. Nickelsburg, *Jewish Literature Between the Bible and the Mishna* (Philadelphia: Fortress, 1981), pp. 203–214; Franklyn, 'Psalms of Solomon,' pp. 2-5.

[162] E.g. 1:7, 8; 2:16, 17; 8:8, 23–25; 17:22, 25, 27, 36.

[163] So 5:18; 12:6; 14:5 and especially Pss. Sol. 9, 10 where the two elements are unmistakably present.

[164] Holm–Nielsen, 'Hodajot und Psalmen Salomos,' p. 128.

original *Sitz im Leben* of individual psalms. Schüpphaus connects
the psalms containing the former *Themenkreis* to a time of continuing distress, i.e. in the period immediately following the capture of
Jerusalem by the Romans. The psalms in which the latter
Themenkreis appears must have been written, according to Schüpphaus, in a period between 48 and 43/42 BCE, after the murder of
Pompei, which to the 'pious' would have been a display of divine
justice.[165] This group of psalms, moreover, are basically unified in
their composition, while psalms of the group from the earlier
period show redactional additions from the time in which the
distress of the Roman conquest had eased.

Schüpphaus's theory builds on the premise that the core of
psalms such as 1/2, 4, 8, 17 were composed as the result of an
actual wrestling with difficulties following Pompei's capture of
Jerusalem. This assumption not only cannot be demonstrated,
but is inherently unlikely.

Contrary to Schüpphaus's interpretation, Ps. Sol. 1:1–3 does not
reflect the confidence of the 'pious' in Jerusalem's righteousness
prior to the shattering experience of Pompei's capture of the city.
The introduction to this psalm more likely is meant to reflect the
perspective of the naive, which the teaching contained in the subsequent psalms is intended to correct. Given that the Pss. Sol.
reflect the opposition of the Pharisees to the Hasmoneans, it is
unlikely that Pharisaic circles would have regarded Jerusalem as
'full of righteousness' (1:3) prior to Pompei's appearance. Ps. Sol. 8
rehearses the sins of the priestly class which brought destruction,
sins of which the 'pious' could hardly have been ignorant.

Holm–Nielsen's observations regarding the psalms characterized
as *Klagepsalmen* by Jansen (4, 5, 7, 8, 9, 12, 17), also work against
Schüpphaus's theory. All of these psalms directly or indirectly
express the desire for deliverance from distress, and are included
in Schüpphaus's group of early psalms. But they vary widely in
their construction, with Pss. Sol. 4, 5, 8, 9, 17 containing large
sections of didactic material.[166] Some of this material Schüpphaus
classifies as later redaction, but he does not account for all of it.
The instructive element in these psalms adds weight to the notion
that even the psalms which Schüpphaus regards as a response to
crisis were composed for the admonition of those associated with

---

[165] See Schüpphaus, *Die Psalmen Salomos*, pp. 74– 82, 105–107, 115–117, 138–
151. The theme of God as righteous judge appears primarily in Pss. Sol. 3, 5, 6,
10, 13, 14, 16, 18; that of God as help in distress in Pss. Sol. 1/2, 4, 5:5–7/7, 8/9/11,
12, 17.

[166] Holm–Nielsen,'Hodajot undPsalmen Salomos,' pp. 128–129.

the 'pious,' so that the theme of hope for God's help cannot be assigned to a distinct *Sitz im Leben*.

It is historically unlikely in any case, that the period following Pompei's capture of Jerusalem would have been one of distress for those associated with the Pharisees. Pompei removed Aristobulus, who was a threat to the Pharisees, and installed as High Priest, the weaker Hyrcanus. Although there was initial loss of life and deportation of prisoners, misfortunes which were largely limited to the followers of Aristobulus and the priests serving in the Temple at the time of Pompei's attack (groups of which the Pharisees would not have been a part), the immediately following period was fairly peaceful.[167] Moreover, Jews appear as oppressors in the psalms which Schüpphaus designates as early (e.g. Pss. Sol. 4, 12), but given the conditions just described, this state of affairs is somewhat less likely, rather than more so, in the period immediately following Pompei's conquest.

It is best then to regard all the psalms as having arisen for purposes of instruction and exhortation within synagogues associated with the Pharisees in and around Jerusalem. The diverse theological themes which emerge from these psalms, including both an eschatological hope for Israel, and the individualizing concept of a divine *iustitia distributiva*, are directed toward the exhortation of the 'pious,' and must be interpreted in this light. It is instructive to note that despite their partitioning of the material, both Schüpphaus and Franklyn admit that the theology of the Pss. Sol. must be treated as a whole.[168] The intertwining of seemingly disparate themes is so complete that in practice it is hard to escape this approach.

B. Divine Righteousness

As Schüpphaus rightly observes, 'the righteousness of God,' stands out as the most prominent theme in the Pss. Sol.[169] More specifically stated, the belief appears again and again that God is

---

[167] See Josephus, *Ant.* 14.77–81, whose silence about affairs in Palestine in this period probably indicates that all was quiet.

[168] See Schüpphaus, *Die Psalmen Salomos*, pp. 126–127; Franklyn, 'Psalms of Solomon,' pp. 14–15.

[169] Schüpphaus, *Die Psalmen Salomos*, pp. 83–84. The motif of God as a righteous judge appears in a few of the canonical psalms as well Pss. 7, 50, 75. Cf. Sir 35:11–24. On the theology of the Pss. Sol., see also Sanders, *Paul and Palestinian Judaism*, pp. 387–409; Herbert Braun, 'Vom Erbarmen Gottes über den Gerechten: Zur Theologie der Psalmen Salomos,' in *Gesammelte Studien zum Neuen Testament und seiner Umwelt²* (Tübingen: J. C. B. Mohr [Paul Siebeck], 1967), pp. 8–65; Adolf Büchler, *Types of Jewish-Palestinian Piety from 70 B.C.E to 70 C.E.* (London: Oxford University Press, 1922), pp. 128–195.

a righteous judge who brings retribution for evil, and so displays
his justice.

The interest in divine justice moves between essentially two
points of reference. On the one hand, the Pss. Sol. interpret God's
acts within history, the catastrophic experience under Pompei in
particular, as divine judgments upon sin.[170] On the other hand, the
psalms reveal a belief that divine visitation occurs at an individual
level: the 'pious' expect to see God's justice in the case of each
person, and not merely in political and military events.[171] The
Pss. Sol. especially look for divine retribution upon the 'wicked,'
among whom the 'pious' must live.[172] Thus the past events in
which God made his righteous judgments known against 'sinners'
are proleptic signs of the coming eschatological judgment in which
each person will receive recompense.[173] As Braun remarks:

> Diese Strafgerichte Gottes an den Sündern sind vorweggenommene
> Apokalypsen, in den Zeitlauf hineingezerrte Bilder dessen, was eigen-
> tlich erst der dies irae an den Tag bringen soll.[174]

The Pss. Sol. therefore orient themselves along an axis which
runs from God's past display of righteous judgment to its full and
future manifestation. At the same time, the psalms also bring
constant reminders that presently, too, God is a righteous and
powerful judge, from whose scrutiny none can escape.[175]

---

[170] Pss. Sol. 2:10, 15, 32; 8:7, 8, 23– 26; 9:1–2; 17:8.

[171] See Pss. Sol. 5:4; 9:4, 5. The statement of 5:4 (ὅτι ἄνθρωπος καὶ ἡ μερὶς αὐτοῦ
παρὰ σοῦ ἐν σταθμῷ· οὐ προσθήσει τοῦ πλεονάσει παρὰ τὸ κρίμα σου, ὁ θεός), is best
interpreted as an acknowledgment that God's judgments (5:1) determine one's lot
in life. Therefore the earthly state of each person is dependent solely on God
(5:2, 8–19). God's 'judgment' is not his foreordination of the eternal state of the
individual, but his recompense for behavior, therefore, pace Maier, the verse is not
predestinarian (cf. Mensch und freier Wille, pp. 325–328). Ps. Sol. 9:4b, καὶ ἐν τῇ
δικαιοσύνῃ σου ἐπισκέπτῃ υἱοὺς ἀνθρώπων, refers to divine visitation upon the
individual (so Brock, Holm–Nielsen), not God's supervision (Wright).
Ps. Sol. 9:5b is clearly a restatement of this theme: τὰ γὰ κρίματα κυρίου ἐν
δικαιοσύνῃ κατ ἄνδρα καὶ οἶκον.

[172] Ps. Sol. 4:6–8, 14–25.

[173] Pss. Sol. 15:4–13; 17:21–25.

[174] Herbert Braun, 'Vom Erbarmen Gottes,' pp. 41–42. Braun also rightly
notes that the Pss. Sol. contain the additional theme of the righteous Messiah,
who will guide his people in righteousness, and keep them from wickedness. But
this work of the Messiah follows upon his role as eschatological judge through
whom divine justice is administered, and by whom 'sinners' are removed and
destroyed (17:22–32, 36–41; 18:7, 8).

[175] See Pss. Sol. 2:32–35; 4:24; 8:24; 9:2, 3; 14:8, 9; 15:8; 17:10. Schüpphaus
suggests that God's righteousness in the Pss. Sol. is characterized by his mercy,
which on the one hand proceeds from the Creator toward all his creatures, and on
the other hand is especially directed toward Israel, the covenant people. So God's
righteousness works punitively against 'sinners,' but toward the 'pious' it functions

These regular appeals to divine justice obviously serve a variety of hortatory functions. The 'pious' are comforted in the hope that their present demeaned condition (which, in part, is attributed to the wickedness of 'sinners') will be relieved. Their faithful obedience will result in their being blessed.[176] At the same time, the penalty for evil behavior is brought repeatedly to mind, discouraging the 'pious' from sin.[177] Perhaps most importantly, the prosperity and successes of 'sinners' (both Jew and Gentile) is shown to be only temporary, since they too will be subject to God's searching justice.[178] The almost uniform appearance of formulaic prayers/promises of blessing on the 'pious' and recompense for the 'wicked' at the close of the psalms strongly attests to these practical functions to which the theme of God's righteousness was put in the Pss. Sol.

One of the most striking features of the appeal to God's righteousness in the Pss. Sol. is the complete absence of the idea of saving righteousness, Cremer's *iustitia salutifera*, which obviously continued to live in Jewish traditions of the period, especially in the Qumran materials.[179] Usually the loss of the concept is attributed to the shift from the Hebrew צדקה to the Greek δικαιοσύνη. Those who translated the Hebrew Bible into Greek lacked a category in the semantic field of the Greek term for such a saving righteousness, and so chose in a number of instances to render צדקה as ἔλεος or ἐλεημοσύνη.[180] That may be the case in four instances in the Pss. Sol. as well, although the syntax of the majority of the contexts in which 'mercy' appears in the Pss. Sol. shows that חסד, חנן and the like were most likely the terms used in the Hebrew.[181]

The conception of divine righteousness as a *iustitia distributiva* introduces a strong element of individualism and universalism into

---

'als erbarmend-züchtigende Gerechtigkeit' (*Die Psalmen Salomos*, p. 89). But divine providence is not described as 'God's righteousness,' and the discipline which God exerts upon the 'pious' is never called 'mercy,' in the Pss. Sol. The categories which Schüpphaus introduces represent his own theologizing.

[176] Pss. Sol. 2:33–37; 3:11, 12; 4:23–25; 5:18; 7:9, 10; 8:33, 34; 9:3–5; 10:5–8; 12:4–6; 13:6–12; 14; 15; 16:15.
[177] See especially Ps. Sol. 16.
[178] Pss. Sol. 2:16–17, 26–27; 8:8–16; 17:5–20.
[179] See, e.g. the discussion of 1QS above. Sanders rightly observes, '*dikaiosyne = tsedaqah* never refers in the Psalms of Solomon to leniency or charity,' *Paul and Palestinian Judaism*, p. 407.
[180] See LXX Isa 1:27; 56:1; 59:16.
[181] See Pss. Sol. 2:36; 10:4; 16:3; 18:3. While the Greek translation may hide this link to covenantal thought in these four instances, it hardly obscures a prominent feature of the theology of the psalms. See the discussion of Israel below.

the soteriology of the Pss. Sol. Thus the destiny of the individual can be said to be contingent upon behavior, and not merely membership in the nation:

ὁ ποιῶν δικαιοσύνην θησαυρίζει ζωὴν αὑτῷ παρὰ κυρίῳ, καὶ ὁ ποιῶν ἀδικίαν αὐτὸς αἴτιος τῆς ψυχῆς ἐν ἀπωλείᾳ· τὰ γὰρ κρίματα κυρίου ἐν δικαιοσύνῃ κατ' ἄνδρα καὶ οἶκον. (9:5)[182]

The division between the 'pious' and the 'wicked,' which runs throughout the psalms, is an example of the same individualized soteriology.[183] Correspondingly, to a small extent, a universalistic perspective enters into the psalms:[184]

ὅτι σὺ κριτὴς δίκαιος ἐπὶ πάντας τοὺς λαοὺς τῆς γῆς.(9:2b)[185]

It is clear then, that the concept of God's righteousness found in the Pss. Sol. encroaches upon the idea of the covenant as a promise of salvation to the whole of Israel, and replaces it.[186]

Despite the prominence which is given to the theme of *iustitia distributiva*, the concept of God as a righteous judge is not carried to the conclusion one might think. Braun, for example, regards the contrast in the psalms between expected judgment upon 'sinners' and mercy for the 'pious' as a paradox:

---

[182] N.b. There is no suggestion here of weighing of good versus evil deeds to determine one's eternal state. The statement closest to this concept in Pss. Sol. is found in 5:4, but there is no indication there that deeds are weighed against one another, and the passage is primarily directed toward the status of the individual in life, not eternal reward.

[183] See the discussion of 'the pious' and 'the sinners' below.

[184] Even obedient Gentiles will become objects of mercy for the Messiah: καὶ ἐλεήσει πάντα τὰ ἔθνη ἐνώπιον αὐτοῦ ἐν φόβῳ.(17:34b) This and 9:2b are isolated statements, however. There is no real interest in the salvation of Gentiles in the psalms. It should be noted that while the theme of God as an impartial judge adds an aspect of universalism to the Pss. Sol., in another sense an element of universalism found in the Hebrew Bible is attenuated, in that the promises for the pilgrimage of the Gentiles to Jerusalem, and to Israel's God are lost.

[185] Charlesworth rightly cautions that in a number of instances ἡ γῆ might be interpreted as a reference to the land of Israel and not the earth as a whole. See his, 'Review of *Die Psalmen Salomos* by Joachim Schüpphaus,' in *JAAR* 50 (1982):292–293. This reading seems particularly fitting in 8:23 (ἐδικαιώθη ὁ θεὸς ἐν τοῖς κρίμασιν αὐτοῦ ἐν τοῖς ἔθνεσιν τῆς γῆς), which, given its context, might well mean, 'God was justified in his judgments (upon sinful Jews) among the Gentiles of the Land (i.e. Gentiles who were living in Palestine). In 9:2, however, γῆ clearly signifies 'the earth.'

[186] See the discussion of 'Israel' below. Therefore, in contrast to Maier's statement that the 'dualistische Aufspaltung aller Menschen in Gerechte und Sünder findet hier (i.e. in the covenantal concept) ihre Grenze' (*Mensch und freier Wille*, p. 321), the relation appears to be nearly the reverse: the notion of God as an impartial judge over all persons apparently limits the concept of covenant. Ryle and James likewise interpret the relation wrongly, *Psalms of Solomon*, pp. l–li.

Gerade nach der Betonung der Gerechtigkeit Gottes in diesen Gerichten sollten wir erwarten, der Fromme würde nun nach dem Maß-
stab dieser Gerichte bestehen und seinen Lohn in ihnen empfangen,
so wie Psalm 9 ja auch davon redet. Aber wider alle angekündigte
Logik der Gerichtsterminologie empfängt der Gottesfürchtige in diesen Gerichten nicht sein Recht und seinen Lohn; diese Gerichte gehen als Strafgerichte an ihm vielmehr vorbei, er empfängt in ihnen
von Gottes Barmherzigkeit.[187]

That the 'pious' do not appeal to God for just reward is not an
isolated phenomenon, however. The 'pious' are not without sin
themselves.[188] Thus according to the canons of strict justice, one
might expect (in complete reversal of Braun's statement) that
divine condemnation might fall on them along with 'sinners.'
That is not the case in the Pss. Sol either. The 'righteous' rather
experience a limited form of divine justice, a discipline by God,
which preserves them for salvation, rather than destroying them
along with 'sinners.'[189]

Clearly then, the psalms operate with an understanding of God
as impartial judge which is not based on anything like the later
Stoic concept of *iustitia*. I.e., the justice which is to be dealt out to
each person in the Pss. Sol. is not based on a common sense of right
joined to an egalitarian ideal.[190] Rather, God is thought to operate
according to 'covenantal' standards, which manifest themselves in
(what appears to deductive reasoning as) 'partial' treatment for
the 'righteous.'[191] In the Pss. Sol., impartial and universal divine
justice is expressly defined in terms of 'the word of God,' linking it
implicitly to notions of promise and covenant:

---

[187] Braun, 'Vom Erbarmen Gottes,' p. 43.
[188] E.g. Pss. Sol. 3:3–8; 9:6–7.
[189] Pss. Sol. 13:6–10; 10:1–3.
[190] Braun therefore errs when he argues that the appeal by the 'pious' to divine
mercy, rather than to a just reward, reveals an uncertainty about obtaining final
salvation. Braun, 'Vom Erbarmen Gottes,' pp. 49–50. Because he reasons here on
a deductive basis, it appears to him that the notion of receiving one's just due
ought to form the basis of hope of the 'righteous.' He takes the absence of such a
claim as evidence of *Heilsunsicherheit*. But we have seen that in a least a few
instances it is possible that the Greek ἔλεος hides צדקה. Two of these cases
refer to God's salvation of the pious (2:36; 10:4): the Pss. Sol. may then in fact
twice speak of (saving) justice as the recompense of the 'pious.' It should be noted
that the same phenomenon appears elsewhere in the LXX: καὶ ἐλεημοσύνη ἔσται
ἡμῖν, ἐὰν φυλασσώμεθα πάσας τὰς ἐντολὰς ταύτας ἐναντίον κυρίου τοῦ θεοῦ ἡμῶν
(Deut 6:25, cf. Deut 24:13; Ps. 23:5).
[191] The Pss. Sol. remind one of the medieval Christian voluntarist interpretation of God's righteousness. God operates with strict justice, but the just standard
by which he judges is determined by his sovereign will. Cf. McGrath, *Iustitia Dei*,
1:64.

ἐν παντὶ ἔθνει ἡ διασπορὰ τοῦ Ἰσραηλ κατὰ τὸ ῥῆμα τοῦ θεοῦ, ἵνα δι-
καιωθῇς, ὁ θεός, ἐν τῇ δικαιοσύνῃ σου ἐν ταῖς ἀνομίαις ἡμῶν, ὅτι σὺ
κριτὴς δίκαιος ἐπὶ πάντας τοὺς λαοὺς τῆς γῆς (9:2).

Likewise, the Law can be regarded as the source of life for those
who live 'in the righteousness of its ordinances.'[192] Wellhausen is
therefore closer to the mark than Braun, when he comments on the
hope of the 'pious':

> Es ist wohl die Hoffnung auf Lohn, aber der Lohn ist die Erbarmung,
> die Gnade.[193]

C. The 'Pious' and the 'Sinners'

The theme of divine justice, around which the Pss. Sol. are oriented, results in the fundamental anthropological polarity of the
material. Humanity is divided into two basic categories: οἱ ὅσιοι
(החסידים 'the pious')/ οἱ δίκαιοι (הצדיקים 'the righteous') who
are also described as οἱ φοβούμενοι/ἀγάποντες/ἐπικαλομένοι τὸν
κύριον, δοῦλοι κυρίου versus ἁμαρτωλοί (החטאים 'sinners') who are
also called παράνομοι, πονηροί .[194]

A corresponding soteriology is built upon this division of humanity. As we have noted, the Pss. Sol. expect that 'sinners' will be
punished κατὰ τὰ ἔργα αὐτῶν καὶ κατὰ τὰς ἁμαρτίας αὐτῶν. They
will receive eternal destruction in the darkness of *Sheol*.[195] The
'righteous' will be delivered from their devices.[196] God will repay
'sinners' for what they did to the 'righteous.'[197] Divine judgment
upon them takes place in public, exposing their sins.[198] The 'pious'
in contrast, will receive God's mercy and 'inherit' eternal life.[199] In
place of the public judgment which destroys 'sinners,' the 'pious'
receive private discipline which atones for their sins and purifies
them.[200] God forgives the transgressions of the 'pious,' in contrast
to the strict retribution upon 'sinners.'[201] Moreover, he preserves

---

[192] 'Ἐν δικαιοσύνῃ προσταγμάτων αὐτοῦ,' 14:2. See 14:1–5, and the discussions of
'Israel' and 'mercy,' below.
[193] Wellhausen, *Pharisäer und Sadducäer*, pp. 118–119.
[194] This dichotomy is found in the canonical psalms and other sections of the
Hebrew Bible as well, originating in cultic distinctions perhaps, but developing
through the influence of wisdom traditions. See e.g. Pss 1:5, 6; 26:1–12; 52:11,
149:1; Prov 11:5, 6; 13:21; Isa 1:27, 28; 33:14, 15; 37:16–22; Ezek 3:16–21; Amos 9:10;
Mal 4:2.
[195] Pss. Sol. 3:11; 9:5; 13:11; 14:9; 15:10–13.
[196] Ps. Sol. 4:23.
[197] Ps. Sol. 2:35.
[198] Ps. Sol. 13:6, 7.
[199] Pss. Sol. 2:33–36; 3:12; 4:25; 6:6; 10:3; 13:11– 12; 14:10; 15:13; 16:15.
[200] Pss. Sol. 10:1–4; 13:7–10.

them from transgression.[202] Thus despite the fact that the 'right-eous' sin, they are not 'sinners.'

It is not possible to determine precisely what those who com-posed the psalms regarded as boundaries between 'pious' and 'sinner.' The psalms were written for the purpose of exhortation of the 'pious,' not in order to provide a theological statement detailing the distinction between the two groups.[203] The dichoto-my clearly transcends the division between Jew and Gentile, since both Gentiles (e.g. 2:1) and, more frequently, Jews (e.g. 4:1–8) are called 'sinners.'

Not surprisingly, the faults of 'sinners' are often described, pro-viding examples of divine judgment and/or behavior to be avoided by the 'pious': sexual immorality, hypocrisy, slander, greed and oppression, cavalier disregard for the sanctity of the Temple.[204] In some cases an accusatory tone is clearly present, as for example in Ps. Sol. 8:11–13, where the priests are clearly the object of the charge. But on the whole, the transgressions which are described serve as moral lessons for the 'pious.' By means of the threats of judgment, one is urged to abstain not only from the above men-tioned sins, but from all kinds of unrighteousness.[205]

The Pss. Sol. largely presume that the 'pious' are aware of the behavior which is expected of them. Since the psalms were written for the encouragement of the 'in-group,' there was no need to delineate what was already common knowledge. Some aspects of the behavior expected of the 'pious' are defined by prohibition in the reproach given to trespasses of 'sinners.' Sexual immorality in particular is regarded as a potential downfall.[206] But the positive characteristics enjoined upon the 'pious' are expressed in quite general terms. The righteous person does not allow sins to remain unaddressed, but searches out and atones for sins of ignorance by fasting and humbling of the soul.[207] The 'pious' are further expec-

---

[201] Pss. Sol. 9:6, 7; 13:10.

[202] Pss. Sol. 16:1–15.

[203] As argued above, it is unlikely that the distinction between the two groups was made along the lines of a Pharisaic versus Sadducean party.

[204] Sexual immorality: 2:11–14; 4:4, 5; 8:9, 10; 16:7–8; hypocrisy: 4:2, 8; slan-der: 12:1, 2; greed and oppression: 4:9–13; pollution of the Temple: 2:3–5; 8:11–13.

[205] Pss. Sol. 4:24; 14:6–10.

[206] Ps. Sol. 16:7, 8.

[207] Ps. Sol. 3:6–8. Trafton points out that in the Syriac version God is made the subject of the first clause in verse 7 ('The Psalms of Solomon: New Light from the Syriac Version?' *JBL* 105 [1986]:236). But this reading is most likely inferior, since it suggests that God is the subject of the following Syriac clauses as well: 'And he saved his soul in the case when he sinned in ignorance, with fasting and

ted to submit to and embrace the just discipline which God brings
into their lives, including poverty.[208] Such submission to judgment
also results in atonement for their sin.[209] In Ps. Sol. 3:8 the righteous person is portrayed as incurring only sins of ignorance
(ἐξιλάσατο περὶ ἀγνοίας). But one cannot use this portrait of the
'righteous' to attribute a dogmatic position on this point to the
Pss. Sol., since the image presented is clearly exemplary, intended
as a model of morality for the 'pious.'[210]

Not infrequently the 'pious' and 'sinners' are described on the
basis of their attitudes. 'Sinners' act in arrogant ignorance of God's
righteous judgment, and refuse to repent.[211] The 'pious' constantly
confess God's righteous judgments, even those given to discipline
them.[212] Nevertheless, in practice, attitudes and acts are inseparable for the Pss. Sol.[213] So, for example, God judges the 'wicked' by
the thoughts in their hearts and according to their deeds.[214] The
attitudes which are enjoined on the 'righteous' are concretized in
specific acts of repentance, prayer, and a life of piety.[215]

It is misleading then to characterize the polarity of 'pious/sinner'
in the Pss. Sol. as *Verhältnisbegriffe* in contrast to *Qualitätsbegriffe* as
Schüpphaus does.[216] It is true that in the Pss. Sol. one is not
necessarily constituted a 'sinner' by a single act of sin. The 'righteous' themselves may be said to transgress. Likewise, the righteousness which is attributed to the 'pious' is not conceived on the basis
of an abstract ideal, but on that of essentially relational covenantal
concepts. As noted already however, the Pss. Sol. were composed
for purposes of edification. They partially reflect, yet do not fully
express group standards. Hence the absence of a description of the
deeds required of the 'righteous,' does not mean that there were no
behavioral norms by which the circle of the 'pious' marked their

---

humiliation.' Trafton himself confusingly indicates that the Syriac is to be preferred on pp. 56–57 of his dissertation, but lists the Greek as more reliable on
p. 212 (*The Syriac Version of the Psalms of Solomon*).
[208] Pss. Sol. 3:3–5; 16:12–15.
[209] Pss. Sol. 10:1, 2; 13:6–10.
[210] Both Schüpphaus (*Die Psalmen Salomos*, p. 102), and Braun, ('Vom Erbarmen Gottes,' p. 35) wrongly interpret this statement as descriptive anthropological dogma.
[211] E.g. Pss. Sol. 1:6, 3:9–10; 4:21.
[212] E.g. Pss. Sol. 3:3–5; 4:23; 6:1, 4, 6; 9:6– 7; 10:2; 14:1.
[213] The same is the case in 1QS, as we have seen above.
[214] See Ps. Sol. 17:25, cf. 2:16, 34; 17:8.
[215] E.g. Pss. Sol. 3:7, 8; 6:2, 4–5; 9:6–7; 10:3; 14:2.
[216] Schüpphaus, *Die Psalmen Salomos*, pp. 94–105, 121–122. It may be doubted
that an absolute distinction between the two concepts applies in the canonical
materials as well.

boundary. As Braun points out, in the Pss. Sol. 'righteousness' may be said to consist in individual deeds (to be accompanied, to be sure, by the proper attitude) which, it is affirmed, God will justly reward.[217] Therefore the condition of being 'pious' or a 'sinner' cannot be reduced to a positive or negative *Grundhaltung zu dem Gott Israels*.[218] The designation 'pious' or 'sinner' is based on behavior.

Furthermore, Schüpphaus's claim that the 'pious' display a consciousness of their inadequacy before God's demands for righteousness is incorrect.[219] That sentiment never comes to concrete expression in the psalms. Rather, the 'righteous' are granted the blessings of forgiveness and deliverance from temptation.[220] The 'pious' are assured of the recompense which their righteous deeds will receive.[221]

While the faults of 'sinners' are more completely described than the virtues of the 'righteous,' there is no reason to think that the list of vices attributed to them in the Pss. Sol. is complete. Sanders is therefore incorrect when he asserts that 'sinners' are those Jews alone who 'sin worse than the Gentiles,' and that those who did not commit one of three cardinal sins (robbing the Temple, sexual immorality, or ritual impurity in Temple service), 'can be counted among the pious.'[222] Such a conclusion completely misses the fact that group boundaries were implicitly understood and required no elaboration in the material. For rhetorical purposes the whole nation can be said to be sinful.[223] Furthermore, in one instance 'sinners' are distinguished from the 'impious,' indicating that the categories of 'pious' and 'sinner' were not exhaustive. In a certain

---

[217] See Braun, 'Vom Erbarmen Gottes,' pp. 27–29; Pss. Sol. 9:3, 5; 17:19 also 1:2 and 8:6, despite the fact that the psalmist presents these statements as false predications about Jerusalem.

[218] Schüpphaus, *Die Psalmen Salomos*, p. 122. This interpretation, which misses the hortatory character of the material goes back to Wellhausen, *Pharisäer und Sadducäer*, pp. 117–119.

[219] Schüpphaus, *Die Psalmen Salomos*, pp. 101–102.

[220] See esp. 9:6, 7 (τίνι χρηστεύσῃ, ὁ θεός, εἰ μὴ τοῖς ἐπικαλουμένοις τὸν κύριον; ... δικαίους εὐλογήσεις καὶ οὐκ εὐθυνεῖς περὶ ὧν ἡμάρτοσαν, καὶ ἡ χρηστότης σου ἐπὶ ἁμαρτάνοντας ἐν μεταμελείᾳ) and 16:5 (ἐξομολογήσομαί σοι, ὁ θεός, ὅτι ἀντελάβου μου εἰς σωτηρίαν καὶ οὐκ ἐλογίσω με μετὰ τῶν ἁμαρτωλῶν εἰς ἀπώλειαν). In the light of the preceding discussion then, the reception of such benefits is dependent on obedient behavior.

[221] In making his claim that the 'pious' regard themselves as incomplete against the standard of divine righteousness, Schüpphaus himself slips into the conception of righteousness as a norm derived from an ideal of human perfection. But the understanding of human righteousness found in the Pss. Sol. is derived from concrete covenantal demands, which the 'pious' were thought to fulfill: καὶ αἱ δικαιοσύναι τῶν ὁσίων σου ἐνώπιόν σου, κύριε (9:3b).

[222] Sanders, *Paul and Palestinian Judaism*, p. 405.

[223] Ps. Sol. 17:19, 20.

sense at least, one might not be 'pious' even if one was not a
'sinner.'[224] The distinction between the two groups is a theological
category which the Pss. Sol. introduce for purposes of exhortation.
The empirical boundaries were not of importance, the significance
of the demarcation rests in the ideal image which is presented.

In accordance with the purposes of edification for which the
Pss. Sol. were composed, the question of whether or not one is
'pious' or a 'sinner' is made to rest ultimately on the choice of
the individual:

τὰ ἔργα ἡμῶν ἐν ἐκλογῇ καὶ ἐξουσίᾳ τῆς ψυχῆς ἡμῶν τοῦ ποιῆσαι δικαιοσύνην καὶ ἀδικίαν ἐν ἔργοις χειρῶν ἡμῶν· καὶ ἐν τῇ δικαιοσύνῃ σου
ἐπισκέπτῃ υἱοὺς ἀνθρώπων. ὁ ποιῶν δικαιοσύνην θησαυρίζει ζωὴν αὑτῷ
παρὰ κυρίῳ, καὶ ὁ ποιῶν ἀδικίαν αὐτὸς αἴτιος τῆς ψυχῆς ἐν ἀπωλείᾳ·
τὰ γὰρ κρίματα κυρίου ἐν δικαιοσύνῃ κατ' ἄνδρα καὶ οἶκον (9:4, 5).

Schüpphaus unsuccessfully attempts to weaken the sense of this
passage by claiming that if one interprets these verses as teaching
the free will of a human being who stands in a neutral position
before God, the verses do not fit the following context in which the
'righteous' are said to receive forgiveness. According to Schüpphaus, verses 4 and 5 are intended to underscore the responsibility
of the 'righteous' for their acts, for which they will have to render
account.[225]

Here again, Schüpphaus illegitimately operates with a preconceived notion of impartial justice in ideal terms. Already in 9:2,
God's righteousness is measured against his word to Israel. Likewise, in 9:6, 7 divine promises form the basis for the assurance that
God will cleanse from sin and forgive. And the following appeal for
mercy shows a covenantal orientation.[226] We have seen that the
Pss. Sol. employ a concept of divine righteousness linked to covenantal ideas. This understanding of the righteousness of God does
not at all preclude the maintenance of justice along with the dispensation of forgiveness to the 'pious,' since the standards for recompense are in this case the stipulations of the covenant.

---

[224] The impious person is said to fear on account of personal transgressions,
when the destruction of 'sinners' occurs: ἐταράχθη ὁ ἀσεβὴς διὰ τὰ παραπτώματα
αὐτοῦ, μήποτε συμπαραληφθῇ μετὰ τῶν ἁμαρτωλῶν. The 'sinners' in this case are
the ones upon whom God's judgment falls: the distinction here between 'impious'
and 'sinner' is not behavioral. Von Gebhardt suggests the emended reading
εὐσεβής for ἀσεβής, which is unnecessary.

[225] Schüpphaus, *Die Psalmen Salomos*, pp. 102– 104, n. 257.

[226] Ps. Sol. 9:8–10. It is clear that with the rhetorical questions τίνι χρηστεύσῃ, ὁ
θεός; and καὶ τίνι ἀφήσεις ἁμαρτίας; promises of divine goodness and forgiveness
such as those found in Pss. 86, 103, 130 are contemplated.

Furthermore, the import of 9:4, 5 cannot be limited to a reminder to the 'righteous' of their answerability to God for their acts. Human beings are responsible, not merely for their *deeds*, according to verse 5, but for the *destinies* to which those deeds lead: life or destruction. The explicit enunciation of human freedom in 9:4, 5 is intended to urge the act of repentance which will lead to promised forgiveness.[227]

Although the status of the individual, 'pious' or 'sinner,' is contingent upon personal choice in the Pss. Sol., one finds no expressions of boasting or of uncertainty regarding salvation. On the one hand, the 'pious' are conscious of the need for divine help, protection, and forgiveness, for which the conclusions of the psalms make regular appeal. On the other, the 'pious' of the psalms are also confident that God will act righteously and mercifully to fulfill his promises to deliver them. While the 'righteous' are warned against wavering, only the 'impious' person is made to feel that salvation is in doubt.[228]

D. Israel

The Pss. Sol., unlike 1QS, retain the term 'Israel' in soteriological expressions. In contrast, the concept of 'covenant,' which is a primary feature of 1QS, recedes significantly, although it does not disappear. These dissimilarities are probably the result of the differing degrees to which the Qumran community and the Pharisaic circles in which the Pss. Sol. arose were sectarian in nature. For the more exclusivistic Qumran community, the boundaries were more firmly drawn. Hence the notion of a community covenant predominates and 'Israel' for all practical purposes drops out as a means of affirming eschatological hope. The Pharisaic circles in which the Pss. Sol. were composed had a more open stance toward outsiders, and for this reason most likely, gravitated toward articulation of divine promises for the nation.[229]

Nevertheless, in the Pss. Sol. the soteriology based on the categories of 'pious' versus 'sinner' encroaches upon that based on a polarity between Israel and the Gentiles. As a result, traditions expressing hope for the nation provide the apocalyptic framework

[227] The passage may reflect Sir 15:11–20. Cf. Maier, *Mensch und freier Wille,* pp. 333–340.

[228] See Ps. Sol. 6, cf. 13:5.

[229] The dependence of the Pss. Sol. on Biblical traditions to express trust in God for Israel's destiny extends beyond language to genre. Psalms such as Pss. Sol. 7, 11 in which the theme of Israel's deliverance is central most closely approach canonical psalms in form. Cf. Jansen, *Die spätjüdische Psalmendichtung,* pp. 80, 123, who classifies the former as a *Klagepsalm,* the latter as a *Hymn.*

for the Pss. Sol., but the actual content of terms such as 'Israel,'
'seed of Abraham' and the like must be read in the light of the
overall 'pious/sinner' dichotomy.

That this polarity intrudes upon that of Israel/Gentiles as a
soteriological category, and not the reverse, is apparent from two
fundamental considerations. First, as we have observed, Jews are
included among the 'sinners.' Furthermore, the Pss. Sol. explicitly
interpret the traditional hope for Israel in terms of the 'pious/
sinner' dichotomy. Promises of eschatological salvation to Israel
are restricted to the 'pious':

τοῦ κυρίου ἡ σωτηρία ἐπὶ Ἰσραηλ παῖδα αὐτοῦ εἰς τὸν αἰῶνα· καὶ
ἀπόλοιντο οἱ ἁμαρτωλοὶ ἀπὸ προσώπου κυρίου ἅπαξ, καὶ ὅσιοι κυρίου
κληρονομήσαισαν ἐπαγγελίας κυρίου (12:6).

ἐν σοφίᾳ δικαιοσύνης ἐξῶσαι ἁμαρτωλοὺς ἀπὸ κληρονομίας, ἐκτρῖψαι
ὑπερηφανίαν ἁμαρτωλοῦ ὡς σκεύη κεραμέως (17:23).[230]

Correspondingly, the Israel of the Messianic kingdom is conceived as a sanctified body, from which 'sinners' have been removed.[231]

Nevertheless, the psalms also address prayers to God, in which
the present Israel is conceived in idealized terms, as a nation which
turns to God in repentance and trust.[232] This phenomenon is very
likely due to the fact that those who composed the psalms had not
withdrawn from the social life of the nation. Hence a hope for the
purification of the society in its contemporary structure, to be
accomplished in part through the efforts of the 'pious,' could be
retained.[233]

The idea of divine justice as it relates to Israel is divided in the
Pss. Sol., expressing itself according to both aspects of the 'pious/
sinner' dichotomy. God can be said to judge Israel for disciplinary
purposes and with mercy, just as he does the 'righteous.'[234] But he
can also be said to make Israel a public display of his righteousness,
exposing its transgressions, a treatment which is reserved for 'sinners.'[235] This ambiguity reflects the tension between the interpreta-

---

[230] The same narrowing of the concept of Israel is implicitly the case in 14:5,
where in context Israel must be taken to signify the 'pious' (cf. 14:1–4).

[231] Pss. Sol. 17:26–27, 43–44;18:1–5. Ps. Sol. 17 should most likely be read as
an expression of eschatological blessing, the past tense due to the use of the *per-
fectum propheticum* in the Hebrew.

[232] Pss. Sol. 7; 8:27–34; 9:8–11; 10:5–8.

[233] Contrast 1QS where no idealization of a holy Israel in the *present* appears.

[234] E.g. Pss. Sol. 8:26; 18:3.

[235] Ps. Sol. 9:1–2; cf. Ps. Sol. 13:7

tion of past disasters, as divine acts of judgment on 'sinners,' and the hope which the psalms retain for the nation. Since eschatological judgment upon Israel includes the removal of 'sinners,' it is clear that this hope for the nation is restricted by the soteriological frame-work of the 'pious/sinner' polarity.[236] The 'Israel' that in God's justice is expected to receive mercy is a nation of the 'pious.'

Likewise, the few references to the covenant in the Pss. Sol. show the same bifurcation. The covenant is used in an appeal for God's mercy on the nation in the face of a threat from Gentiles. However, it is an idealized nation speaking in this context, one which in its soul turns toward God.[237] In another psalm, the 'sons of the cove-nant' are said to have adopted the practices of Gentiles and to have become transgressors. The covenant in their case becomes irrele-vant as a salvific structure.[238] Elsewhere, the covenant, like the term 'Israel,' is interpreted as applying to the 'pious' alone:

καὶ μνησθήσεται κύριος τῶν δούλων αὐτοῦ ἐν ἐλέει· ἡ γὰρ μαρτυρία ἐν νόμῳ διαθήκης αἰωνίου, ἡ μαρτυρία κυρίου ἐπὶ ὁδοὺς ἀνθρώπων ἐν ἐπισκοπῇ (10:4).

Here the covenant is understood nomistically. It provides a witness of a divine visitation (of justice, cf. 10:5) upon human behavior: the Lord's servants, who in the preceding verse are identified as the 'righteous,' will receive the mercy to which the covenantal Law attests.[239]

Sanders's treatment of the Pss. Sol. is therefore misdirected considerably by his use of the category of 'being in (or out of) the covenant.' Not only does the term hardly appear in the Pss. Sol., but the use of the expression reflects the soteriological scheme of 'pious versus sinner,' not 'Israel versus the Gentiles.'[240]

E. Mercy

In a number of ways, the concept of salvation operative in the Pss. Sol. reveals itself as covenantal in structure. As we have ob-served above, Ps. Sol. 10:4 indicates that while the expression 'covenant' is infrequent, a specific understanding of a divine cove-nant with Israel lies behind the soteriology of the Pss. Sol. We have seen that the concept of divine justice likewise is dependent on the idea of promise and fulfillment, covenantal ideas. Moreover, the

---

[236] Pss. Sol. 17:26–27, 43–44; 18:1–5.
[237] Pss. Sol. 9:8–10.
[238] Pss. Sol. 17:15, 18, 20.
[239] N.b. the Deuteronomistic language of the passage, e.g. Deut 30:19, 20.
[240] Sanders, *Paul and Palestinian Judaism*, pp. 404–409.

anticipated blessing of the 'righteous' may be characterized as an 'inheritance of life/the promises,' or also absolutely as, 'the inheritance' (κληρονομία, נחלה), a clearly covenantal idea.[241] The dispensing of mercy is regarded as the fulfillment of promise.[242] The 'pious' look forward to the eschatological visitation as a divinely promised 'Day.'[243] Thus there is strong reason for regarding the soteriology of the Pss. Sol., represented by the 'pious/sinner' dichotomy, as a specific interpretation of the covenantal idea.

'Mercy' (represented by ἔλεος and its cognates) serves as the primary means of expressing this covenantally based hope of salvation in the Pss. Sol.[244] The predominance of the term 'mercy' may to some extent reflect the preference of the Greek translator(s), but for the most part it represents the historical setting in which the psalms were composed. The 'pious' of the Pss. Sol. regarded themselves as needy and oppressed by 'sinners.' The hope for deliverance from such a condition naturally shaped the language of salvation.[245] Likewise, the Israel of the psalms is beset by Gentile enemies. The longed-for relief, security, and blessing are understandably regarded as the products of divine mercy.[246] It is therefore the precarious position in which the nation as a whole, and the 'pious' in particular, found themselves in the early Roman period, which determined the manner in which salvation was conceived. This feature of the soteriology of the Pss. Sol. manifests itself not only in the choice of the term 'mercy,' but also in the very image of eschatological hope which the psalms present: the coming Messiah will deliver Israel from Gentile oppressors and will drive out 'sinners' from among the people.

As with 'Israel' and 'covenant,' the term 'mercy' gives evidence of a tension deriving from the pull of the soteriology of the Pss. Sol. on traditional concepts.[247] Just as hope for 'Israel' is conditioned by the 'pious/sinner' soteriology of the psalms, so the idea of 'mercy' is altered in contrast to its roots. While the Pss. Sol. contemplate God

---

[241] Pss. Sol. 14:10; 12:6; 17:23, respectively. The punishment which 'sinners' receive may likewise be described as an inheritance or lot (μερίς, חלק): 14:9; 15:10; 3:12; 4:14; 14:5.

[242] Pss. Sol. 7:10.

[243] Pss. Sol. 14:9; 15:12; 18:5, 9.

[244] As noted above, while ἔλεος may represent צדקה in a few instances, the syntax of most contexts in which ἔλεος or a cognate word appears suggests that it usually represents חסד, חנן, רחם and the like.

[245] Pss. Sol. 2:35; 4:23–25; 5:2, 5; 10:6; 12:5, 6.

[246] E.g. Pss. Sol. 7:6; 9:8; 17:45.

[247] Braun, 'Vom Erbarmen Gottes,' pp. 18–29, touches upon the two-fold understanding of 'mercy' in the Pss. Sol., but does not formulate the polarity properly.

showing mercy to the nation despite its sin,[248] the 'Israel' which is the object of such mercy is always a people which turns to God in repentance. In other words, when Israel receives mercy in the Pss. Sol., it is treated as 'pious,' not as rebellious.[249] Thus the divine judgments from which the nation appeals for relief are viewed as the discipline which God sends on the 'righteous.'[250] The eschatological hope for divine mercy on Israel is envisioned as coming upon a purified, not a rebellious people.[251] Therefore the Pss. Sol. lack an important aspect of the traditional conception of 'mercy.' The term no longer serves to express deliverance *in spite of* justice, but deliverance *as justice* rendered by God.[252]

F. Summary

We have seen that the concept of God as righteous judge functions as the central element of the covenantal soteriology of the Pss. Sol. In particular, the psalms await the hope of his eschatological judgment against 'sinners,' both Jew and Gentile, who flagrantly disobey him, and who oppress the 'pious.' The manner in which the psalms regard salvation as an act of deliverance, and a display of divine mercy, is probably due to the uncertainties which both Israel and the Pharisaic movement faced in the late Hasmonean and early Roman periods.

The polarity between 'pious' and 'sinner' marks the distinctive interpretation of covenantal ideas in the Pss. Sol. Divine promises for salvation no longer apply to the whole of Israel, but to the 'pious' alone.

Despite the emphasis on the universality and impartiality of divine justice, righteousness in the Pss. Sol. should not be confused with philosophically derived egalitarian ideals. Divine justice here is instead based on covenantal ideas: the 'pious' and 'sinners' receive what is due them according to promises given by God.

---

[248] Pss. Sol. 7:5, 10; 8:27, 28; 9:8–11; 11:1–9. 250. E.g. Ps. Sol. 9:4–11. While it is true that the 'righteous' sin, they also themselves make atonement for transgression and submit to divine discipline, which result in their being cleansed. Hence they, in contrast to 'sinners,' are prepared for salvation.

[249] See e.g. Ps. Sol. 3:5–12. Even when it is necessary for God's mercy to preserve them from their own temptations, God acts in their behalf because he does not regard them as 'sinners': ἐξομολογήσομαί σοι, ὁ θεός, ὅτι ἀντελάβου μου εἰς σωτηρίαν καὶ οὐκ ἐλογίσω με μετὰ τῶν ἁμαρτωλῶν εἰς ἀπώλειαν (16:5).

[250] E.g. Pss. Sol. 7, 8.

[251] Pss. Sol. 17, 18.

[252] See Carson, *Divine Sovereignty*, pp. 68–69. The idea of mercy in defiance of justice is well-known in the canonical materials, of course. One thinks immediately of Psalm 51 and of the book of Hosea. There are various other instances in which 'mercy' is associated with this concept, e.g. 2 Sam 12:22; 24:14; Hab 3:2; Ezek 39:25; Micah 7:18, 19; Dan 9:18.

Furthermore, while the 'pious' remain conscious of their dependence on God, the category 'pious' or 'righteous' is based on
behavioral ideals. These ideals find only partial expression in the
Pss. Sol., since the material served as an exhortation to insiders,
who were aware of the boundaries of acceptable behavior.

IV. SYNTHESIS

The most outstanding feature common to 1QS and the Pss. Sol. is
that they both introduce a new bifurcation of humanity in place of
'Israel versus the Gentiles.' For 1QS, the polarity is based on the
'spirits of light and darkness.' The Pss. Sol. distinguish between
'pious' and 'sinner.' Concomitantly, the concept of a divine covenant with all of Israel is reinterpreted in both writings. The covenant is now seen to apply to a limited group within the nation, who
maintained fidelity to *Torah* in an age of impiety.

Both 1QS and the Pss. Sol. therefore include a strong measure of
individualism in their soteriology. The promise of eschatological
blessing is regarded as contingent upon personal righteousness. In
1QS, that righteousness was embodied in the life of the community.
We have seen that the Pss. Sol. contain a concept of righteousness
that was no less behavioral, even if it was not defined so narrowly.

The expression of this 'pattern of religion' differs in the two
documents, of course. In Pss. Sol. the idea of a divine saving righteousness recedes. Likewise, in the Pss. Sol. notions of a special
covenant with the community and of saving predestination are
absent. These dissimilarities are very likely due to the degree to
which those who composed these writings marked themselves off
from the rest of society. The reforming movement which 1QS
represents had rejected the structure of contemporary Judaism,
and in essence constituted a radical new beginning. The Pss. Sol.
are the work of a renewal movement, which looked for the purification of the nation *within existing structures*. Hence the Pss. Sol.
could express eschatological hope in terms of 'Israel,' while 1QS
focuses on the sphere of the community. For the same reason, the
concept of community atonement appears in 1QS, while in Pss. Sol.
atonement receives little attention, and, where present, is expressed
in individualized terms.

These distinctions give rise to one especially significant difference
between the soteriology of 1QS and that of the Pss. Sol. As we have
seen, the stress on divine predestination shields Qumran soteriology
from locating the ultimate cause of salvation in the atoning conduct of the community. This is not the case for the Pss. Sol. The

exclusivistic soteriology of the psalms implicitly attaches salvific value to the behavior of the 'pious.' The concept of 'mercy' is here constricted. It does not include mercy in the face of impiety, but mercy because of piety.

In contradiction to Sanders's assumptions, we have seen that an emphasis on 'mercy' did not necessarily exclude the idea that obedience was a prerequisite to salvation in early Judaism. Therefore, if Paul knew this form of Judaism, his conversion may well have had a soteriological element, since the postconversion Paul understands divine grace and mercy in a manner which prohibits saving value from being attached to obedience.[253] And given this fact, contrary to Räisänen's views, Paul's arguments with Judaizers need not have radically misrepresented his adversaries.

EXCURSUS: AN ASSESSMENT OF LONGENECKER'S TREATMENT OF 4 EZRA

Working against the backdrop of covenantal nomism, and Sanders's admission that 4 Ezra does not fit this 'pattern of religion,' Bruce Longenecker has argued that the author of 4 Ezra rejects an 'ethnocentric covenantalism' in favor of a 'rigid individualistic legalism.'[254]

It is doubtful, however, that 'ethnocentric covenantalism,' the expression by which Longenecker prefers to describe virtually the whole of early Judaism, is the proper term for much of early Jewish literature. Most writings deal with or are addressed to the nation of Israel. But generally it is not their concern to assert some form of intrinsic ethnic privilege. We have seen that in 1QS and the Pss. Sol. the authors define a restricted group within Israel to whom the covenant belongs. Conformity to behavioral norms, not ethnicity, are of central concern. Longenecker recognizes that non-ethnic restrictions to covenantal membership appear in a number of writings, but fails to see the clear implication that ethnicity is not the operative category.[255] How can one describe a writing as having a 'ethnocentric' focus when its intent is to draw distinctions within Israel based on behavior? His imposition of this scheme on the materials is belied by the occasional mention of Gentiles as within the scope of divine judgment and mercy: although there is no real interest in Gentiles, the shift to behavior

---

[253] See e.g. Rom 4:16; 9:16; 11:6, 32; Gal 2:21; 5:4.
[254] Bruce W. Longenecker, *Eschatology and the Covenant: A Comparison of 4 Ezra and Romans 1–11*, JSNTSup 57 (Sheffield: JSOT Press, 1991).
[255] See Longenecker, *Eschatology and the Covenant*, pp. 26–27.

and individualism brings a concomitant form of universalism.[256]

Such universalistic statements appear in 4 Ezra, even in the mouth of Ezra who purportedly voices the 'covenantal ethnocentrism' which the author of 4 Ezra rejects.[257] Longenecker fails to explain why in these instances Ezra sets Israel on the same footing as all humanity, even though elsewhere he is concerned for the salvation of the nation and asserts its unique status. Longenecker is correct in his claim against A. L. Thompson that Ezra is not interested in the salvation of the Gentiles (e.g. 6:55–59), but he does not take into account that for Ezra Israel's identity is bound up with its keeping the Law.[258] Universalism is implicitly expressed in 4 Ezra, even though the message of the apocalypse is addressed to Jews. It is those who are obedient to the divine mandates who will be saved, *de facto* this means Jews, but Gentiles are not excluded *de jure*.

Contrary to Longenecker's claim that there is no 'covenantal efficacy' or mercy operative in 4 Ezra, its soteriology ultimately remains covenantal in structure. In reality, one form of mercy is rejected in favor of another. Ezra appeals for God to show mercy at the judgment to those who do not obey the Law. Uriel rejects this appeal, but does not deny all forms of divine mercy.[259] He implicitly accepts Ezra's assumption that the Law, which retains its promissory and covenantal status, is the vehicle by which divine mercy is obtained.[260] Both figures acknowledge that God's patience and mercy are operative in the present age.[261] Only at the time of judgment will mercy be withdrawn.[262] Freedom to obey the Law remains, despite the pessimistic assessment of the present state of the world shared by Uriel and Ezra.[263] There is room for repentance.[264] The righteous, like Ezra feel that they are unrighteous, but God sees true piety beyond such humble doubting.[265] More-

---

[256] We have seen this in Pss. Sol. 9:2; 17:34b.

[257] E.g. 4 Ezra 3:36; 7:62–69; 116–131.

[258] See 4 Ezra 3:35.

[259] 4 Ezra 8:19–36. One wonders if in part one is witnessing here an aftershock to the rise of Jewish Christianity which found forgiveness apart from the Law.

[260] 4 Ezra 4:22–25. Uriel simply transposes the time of salvation to the age to come (4 Ezra 4:27).

[261] This is how Ezra's statement and Uriel's response must be interpreted: 4 Ezra 7:132–8:3, cf. 8:12, 45.

[262] 4 Ezra 7:33–35.

[263] 4 Ezra 9:11. The various statements about the perishing of the nation (e.g. 9:36) cannot be taken to imply that all are lost. The hortatory character of the writing would be meaningless then.

[264] 4 Ezra 7:82.

[265] 4 Ezra 8:47–55.

over, the company of the saved in 4 Ezra is represented by the twelve tribes of Israel, indicating that the author did not discard his belief in the efficacy of covenantal promises, despite the individualism which he adopted.[266] It is true that Uriel stresses the necessity of obedience and the expectation of eschatological reward and punishment, but this does not mean that for the author of 4 Ezra salvation is not an expression of divine mercy.[267] It is very doubtful that the author of 4 Ezra intended Uriel's statement in 7:89 to convey the idea that the righteous had not transgressed.[268] Such an interpretation contradicts Ezra's repeated assertions elsewhere that all have sinned.[269] The context itself indicates that the righteous resist *danger* in keeping the Law, not temptation. Faithfulness to the Law in a hostile (Gentile) environment is envisioned here, not moral perfection. The way to life is indeed narrow and the path straight and few are those who find it, according to the author of 4 Ezra. But this stance does not eliminate divine mercy from the present age. The covenant is highly constricted in 4 Ezra, but it is not eliminated.

---

[266] Longenecker rightly points out that it is a reduced Israel which appears here (*Eschatology and Covenant*, pp. 150–151), but that is to miss the point. 4 Ezra merely exemplifies the restriction of the covenantal promises to an obedient group within the nation, it does not embrace a multitude from every tribe and tongue like the Apocalypse of John (7:1–10).

[267] 4 Ezra 12:34.

[268] In eo tempore commoratae servierunt cum labore Altissimo et omni hora sustinuerunt periculum, uti perfecte custodirent legislatoris legem.

[269] 4 Ezra 3:21; 7:46, 68, 120.

CHAPTER THREE

'JUSTIFICATION BY FAITH'
AND PAUL'S CONVERSION

I. THE AIM OF THE DISCUSSION AND THE PROBLEM OF
RECONSTRUCTING PAUL'S CONVERSION
FROM HIS SELF-REFERENCES

We shall see that Paul's references to his life prior to his faith in Christ cohere quite well with the 'pattern' of Judaism found in the Pss. Sol. Like the pious of the Pss. Sol., Paul regarded obedience as cooperative with divine mercy in securing salvation. In this respect, his preconversion views differed from the thought expressed in 1QS, which despite its explicit attachment of salvific value to obedience, attributed the whole of salvation to the predestinating grace of God. Yet despite the place which Paul allowed to obedience in securing salvation, he, like the pious of the Pss. Sol., does not seem to have struggled over uncertainty with regard to his salvation. Nor is it likely that he boasted in the hope of salvation as a self-accomplishment.

This linking of Paul with the form of Judaism found in the Pss. Sol. reopens the possibility that his conversion involved a soteriological element. Our concern, therefore, in the following analysis is to explore the effect of Paul's coming to faith in Christ on his understanding of righteousness, and on the obedience to the Law which mediated it to him.

The legitimacy of the use of the term 'conversion' to describe Paul's coming to faith in Christ has been seriously questioned in recent years. Krister Stendahl, among others, has contended that it is better to speak of Paul's 'call' to Gentile mission, since Paul himself describes the beginning of his ministry in this manner.[1] Paula Fredriksen (again with others) prefers to avoid the term because she views the change in Paul as a phenomenon internal to Judaism: Paul merely switched from one party to another.[2] But

---

[1] Gal 1:15, 16.
[2] Paula Fredriksen, 'Paul and Augustine: Conversion Narratives, Orthodox Traditions, and the Retrospective Self,' *JTS* 37n.s. (1986):15.

our study will confirm what Alan Segal has suggested, that Paul's belief in Jesus as Messiah was accompanied by an entrance into a new group, and a 'reconstruction of reality' on Paul's part.[3] One must not fail to appreciate Paul's own judgment expressed in the classical texts on his conversion, that his coming to faith involved a radical transformation of his values.[4] Failure to do so only forces one to look for an alternative cause for this change, for which, we shall see, there is no good evidence. Likewise, one should not overlook that in his letters Paul gives himself and his churches an identity independent of Judaism, despite the fact that in the middle of the first century Christianity was only beginning to emerge from the synagogue.[5] For Paul, the eschatological community of believers in Christ, although a consummation of Jewish hope, is also a *novum*, composed of Jews and Gentiles.[6] 'Conversion' therefore remains an appropriate term to characterize the new 'pattern of religion' which Paul adopted.

It is not necessary, and probably wrong, to think of Paul's conversion simply as a momentary, revolutionary experience.[7] To make this statement does not diminish in the least the significance of the Christophany to which Paul attributes his changed life. It is merely an acknowledgment of what was almost certainly the case. The assimilation of the traditions of the early believing community and the emergence of a new constellation of beliefs must have required some time, even for Paul. It is important to bear this consideration in mind in order to avoid a false conception of the question facing us. The issue at stake is not whether or not Paul received the whole of his theology in a blinding flash, but whether his ideas on justification by faith were derived from and adopted with his coming to faith in Christ.[8]

Along with the fairly regular appearance in the scholarly literature of articles and shorter discussions which wrestle with the

---

[3] Alan F. Segal, *Paul the Convert: The Apostolate and Apostasy of Saul the Pharisee* (New Haven: Yale University Press, 1990), pp. 72–114, 285–300. Segal makes good use of sociological insights into conversion, but stresses community dynamics too strongly. As he acknowledges, Christianity was in a formative stage in the first century. Paul was one who shaped this community by his own theology and mission. See also B.R.Gaventa, *From Darkness to Light: Aspects of Conversion in the New Testament* (Philadelphia: Fortress, 1986).
[4] Gal 1:10–24; Phil 3:2–11.
[5] On Paul's new identity, see Gal 3:14; 4:12; 1 Cor 9:19–21.
[6] See, e.g., Rom 9:23–26; 1 Cor 10:32; Gal 4:21–31.
[7] See Alan Segal, *Paul the Convert*, pp. 285–300.
[8] Cf. Seyoon Kim, *The Origin of Paul's Gospel* (Grand Rapids: Eerdmans, 1982), pp. 334–335.

question of the effects of Paul's conversion on his soteriology, two
monographs on the topic have been published in recent years.[9]
Seyoon Kim has set forth a case for regarding Paul's encounter
with the risen Christ as the catalyst for his theology, especially his
Christology and soteriology.[10] However, Kim gives insufficient
attention to Paul's self-understanding prior to his conversion, with
the result that he falls prey to the false image of the Jew striving
(however confidently) to secure salvation through *Torah*.[11] Christian Dietzfelbinger follows a similar path. Although he deals much

---

[9] Among the shorter treatments of Paul's conversion, see especially
W.G.Kümmel, *Römer 7 und das Bild des Menschen im Neuen Testament* (München:
Chr. Kaiser, 1974), pp. 139–160; Albrecht Oepke, 'Probleme der Vorchristlichen
Zeit des Paulus,' in *Das Paulusbild in der neueren deutschen Forschung*, WdF24, ed.
K.H.Rengstorf (Darmstadt: Wissenschaftliche Buchgesellschaft, 1982), pp. 410–
446; Maurice Goguel, 'Remarques sur un aspect de la conversion de Paul,' *JBL*
53 (1934):257–267; Philippe H. Menoud, 'Revelation and Tradition: the Influ-
ence of Paul's Conversion on His Theology,' *Int* 7 (1953):131–141; H. G. Wood,
'The Conversion of StPaul: its Nature, Antecedents and Consequences,' *NTS*
4(1955):276–282; W. Grundmann, 'Paulus aus dem Volke Israel, Apostel der
Völker,' *NovT* 4 (1960):267–291; Peter Stuhlmacher, "Das Ende des Gesetzes':
Über Ursprung und Ansatz der paulinischen Theologie,' *ZThK* 67 (1970):14–39;
Jacques Dupont, 'La conversion de Paul et son influence sur sa conception du
salut par la foi,' in *Foi et Salut Selon S. Paul*, AnBib 42 (Rome: Pontifical Biblical
Institute, 1970), pp. 77–100; Hans Hübner, 'Gal 3,10 und die Herkunft des
Paulus,' *KuD* 19 (1973):215–231; Klaus Haacker, 'Die Berufung des Verfolgers
und die Rechtfertigung des Gottlosen,' *Theologische Beiträge* 6 (1975):1–19 and
'War Paulus Hillelit?' in *Das Institutum Judaicum der Universität Tübingen 1971–
1972* (Tübingen: Institutum Judaicum, 1973), pp. 106–120; Ulrich Wilckens,
'Die Bekehrung des Paulus als religionsgeschichtliches Problem,' in *Rechtfertigung
als Freiheit: Paulusstudien* (Neukirchen: Neukirchener, 1974), pp. 11–32 and
'Christologie und Anthropologie im Zusammenhang der paulinischen Rechtfer-
tigungslehre,' *ZNW* 67 (1976):64–82; Günther Bornkamm, 'The Revelation of
Christ to Paul on the Damascus Road and Paul's Doctrine of Justification,' in
Reconciliation and Hope, ed. Robert Banks (Grand Rapids: Eerdmans, 1974), pp. 90–
103; Arland J. Hultgren, 'Paul's Pre-Christian Persecutions of the Church: Their
Purpose, Locale, and Nature,' *JBL* 95 (1976):97–111; Otto Betz, 'Paulus als
Pharisäer nach dem Gesetz: Phil.3,5–6 als Beitrag zur Frage des frühen Phari-
säismus,' in *Treue zur Thora: Festschrift für Günther Harder*, ed. Peter von der Osten-
Sacken (Berlin: Institut für Kirche und Judentum, 1977), pp. 54–64; J. G. Gager,
'Some Notes on Paul's Conversion,' *JBL* 27 (1981):697–704; Ulrich Luck, 'Die
Bekehrung des Paulus und das Paulinische Evangelium,' *ZNW* 76 (1985):187–
208; C.M.Tuckett, 'Deuteronomy 2123 and Paul's Conversion,' in *L'Apôtre Paul:
Personalité, Style, et Conception du Ministère* BETL 73, ed. A. Vanhoye (Leuven:
Leuven University, 1986), pp. 345–350; J. D. G. Dunn, "A Light to the Gentiles': the Significance of the Damascus Road Christophany for Paul,' in *The Glory
of Christ in the New Testament*, ed. L. Hurst and N. T. Wright (Oxford: Clarendon,
1987), pp. 251–266; Heikki Räisänen, 'Paul's Conversion and the Development of
his View of the Law,' *NTS* 33(1987):404–419.
[10] Seyoon Kim, *The Origin of Paul's Gospel* (Grand Rapids: Eerdmans, 1982).
[11] See esp. Kim, *The Origin of Paul's Gospel*, pp. 51–55, 298–300. Kim's study
was completed prior to the publication of Sanders's *Paul and Palestinian Judaism* in
1977.

more explicitly with the question of Paul's preconversion Jewish identity, he too remains entrapped in the notion that *Torah* observance was fundamentally a means of self-acquisition of life for the Jew.[12]

At bare minimum, however, these studies underscore the necessity of probing Paul's reports of his conversion for its soteriological aspect, a dimension which Sanders's work, among others, disappointingly neglects.[13]

Two simple observations make it clear that Paul's conversion involved his rethinking the significance of the Law. First, Paul presents his persecution of believers as having been motivated by his devotion to Judaism.[14] His very ceasing to persecute them therefore indicates that his view of the Law was changed in some manner by his coming to faith in Christ. Secondly, Paul consistently attributes his call as apostle to the Gentiles to the Christophany which precipitated his coming to faith.[15] Given that Paul regarded the appearance of the risen Jesus as a commission to preach the Gospel to the Gentiles, and that he regularly represents this Gospel as Law-free, it seems inherently likely that his conversion would have involved a substantial reevaluation of the Law.[16]

In Chapter 1, these two aspects of Paul's self-description have been repeatedly brought up as objections to various reconstructions which detach Paul's new understanding of righteousness from his conversion. These rather obvious features of Paul's reports suggest that it was *improbable* that Paul unreflectively broke with his past (so Sanders), or that he adopted some moderate view in which the Law was regarded as an *adiaphoron* (so Räisänen, et al.), but they do not settle the matter of *how* Paul's conversion influenced his soteriology. Therefore, our investigation will be given primarily to the task of describing the manner in which Paul's conversion changed his views.

The same two considerations also help to define the parameters within which any reconstruction must operate. Some definite

---

[12] Christian Dietzfelbinger, *Die Berufung des Paulus als Ursprung seiner Theologie* WMANT 58 (Neukirchen-Vluyn: Neukirchener, 1985), pp. 22–28, 112–113.

[13] See Chapter 1, Section VI. Cf. J. Christiaan Beker, 'Review of *Paul and Palestinian Judaism* by E.P. Sanders,' *TToday* 35 (1978):108–111.

[14] Gal 1:13; Phil 3:6.

[15] Gal 1:1, 16; 1 Cor 9:1; 1 Cor 15:1–11; 2 Cor 4:3–6. Paul clearly understands God's revelation of Christ to him as an equivalent to the limited post-resurrection appearances of Jesus, *not* as one of the visions or revelations which came to numerous believers.

[16] Contra J. D. G. Dunn, "'A Light to the Gentiles': the Significance of the Damascus Road Christophany for Paul," in *The Glory of Christ in the New Testament*, ed. L.Hurst and N. T. Wright (Oxford: Clarendon, 1987), pp. 251–253.

account for Paul's altered understanding of the Law is necessary
to explain the transformation of Paul from persecutor of the
Church to preacher to the Gentiles. And since Paul refers only
to the appearance of the risen Jesus as the cause for his conversion, the change in his theology must be explicable solely on the
basis of the interaction of his prior theology with his acceptance of
Jesus as Messiah.[17] Moreover, while Paul's change of view need
not have been unique to him, it must have occurred for reasons
which were obvious to very few Jewish believers. Paul was clearly
exceptional: in his letters he makes no appeal for support to a
tradition of Law-free Jewish Christianity.[18]

Recent studies of the rhetorical function of Paul's autobiographical statements have called attention to the fact that Paul's
persuasive aims shaped his remembrance and portrayal of his
conversion. In the extreme form of this approach, Galatians is
read as a pure example of the deliberative genre of argument.
Paul's 'autobiography' is simply a paradigm of the behavior he
wants his readers to adopt: his theology is the cause for his 'conversion.'[19] In similar manner, George Lyons has argued against
what he calls the 'mirror reading' of Galatians, i.e. the use of the
letter to decipher the nature of Paul's opposition.[20] Obviously the
two interpretive issues are related. To the extent that Paul is
defending himself against the charges of adversaries, the narrative
of Gal 1 and 2 has a biographical intent.

---

[17] Ulrich Luck points out quite well the difficulty of finding a link between
Paul's experience of a vision and his theological conclusions. See, 'Die Bekehrung
des Paulus und das Paulinische Evangelium,' *ZNW* 76 (1985):187–208, esp. 187–
190. Dietzfelbinger argues that the appearance of Christ must have been accompanied by an audition (as in Acts), a call to Gentile mission, *Berufung des Paulus*,
pp. 63–64. But Paul's adversaries in Galatia were carrying out a Gentile mission
as well, so that Paul's changed relationship to the Law and to the Greek–speaking
Jewish Christians (as Dietzfelbinger understands them) is not resolved by a brief
audition. One would have to suppose a more lengthy discourse on the Law by the
risen Jesus. In contrast, however, Paul places the weight of his recollections on
Jesus' appearance. This is so despite the fact that Paul's language in Gal 1:15
reflects the calling of the Hebrew prophets. He attributes the change wrought in
him to an Easter-like 'Christophany,' not an audition.
[18] N.b. the tension between 1 Cor 15:3 and Gal 1:12. Our statement should not
be taken to suggest that the reasoning by which Paul came to his Law-free Gospel
would not have been *understandable* to other Jews. Some others like Barnabas were
carrying on a Gentile mission as well as Paul (Gal 2:9). It is only likely that the
reasons which moved Paul were not immediately apparent to many, otherwise
Paul would not appear as such a singular figure.
[19] Beverly R. Gaventa, 'Galatians 1 and 2: Autobiography as Paradigm,' *NovT*
28 (1986):309–326.
[20] George Lyons, *Pauline Autobiography: Toward a New Understanding* SBLDS 73
(Atlanta, Ga: ScholarsPress, 1985).

Clearly one must take into account the rhetorical function of 'autobiographical' remarks in evaluating their historical value. Yet the attempt to make Galatians into a deliberative letter is just as forced as the claim that the letter is entirely apologetic.[21] A variety of persuasive aims, which sometimes overlap, are present.[22] The insight that Paul's autobiographical remarks may serve as paradigms offered for the Galatians to adopt does not in itself mean that some of Paul's 'denials' and 'antitheses' might not simultaneously serve as defenses against charges. It is difficult to make a good case for reading Gal 1:10–2:21 as simply providing a series of models for the Gentile Galatian readers. Paul introduces his argument with the claim that he received his Gospel δι' ἀποκαλύψεως Ἰησοῦ Χριστοῦ.[23] Although this statement implicitly urges his readers to accept it as divine as well, there is an irreproducible element here which Paul's following narrative defends: he was not dependent on the Jerusalem church. The strong statements of Gal 1:19, 20, especially the oath, 'I swear before God that I am not lying,' is hard to understand in any other manner. Likewise, the sudden self-reference in Gal 5:11 stands out from its context so sharply, that no explanation other than that of a defense seems possible.[24] While some aspects of Paul's self-description in Galatians serve exemplary purposes, it is impossible to miss the signals that his rehearsal of his actions represents a response to charges. Paul's 'biography' is part of the basic issue at stake.

A number of considerations further indicate that it is both appropriate and necessary to make use of Paul's statements in reconstructing his conversion. As noted above, Paul consistently attributes his apostolic call to his encounter with the risen Jesus.[25] As we shall see, there was a corresponding consistency in

---

[21] Hans Dieter Betz's *Galatians* (Philadelphia: Fortress, 1979), has been subjected to considerable criticism on this account.

[22] See the balanced discussion by Richard N. Longenecker, *Galatians*,WBC 41 (Dallas, Tx: Word, 1990), pp. c–cxix.

[23] Gal 1:12.

[24] Paul's references to the adversaries suggest that they are Jewish Christians who have infiltrated the congregation (Gal 1:7; 5:12; 6:12, 13). See the discussion of Gal 1:10–24 in Section II.B. Cf. Alfred Suhl, who has recently offered a number of useful insights into Paul's opponents and his autobiographical remarks, 'Der Galaterbrief—Situation und Argumentation,' in *ANRW* 25.4, ed. H. Temporini and W. Haase (Berlin: de Gruyter, 1987), pp. 3067–3134, esp. 3082–3119.

[25] Jack T. Sanders argues on the basis of the apparent conflict between 1 Cor 15:1–3 and Gal 1:12 on the manner in which Paul received his Gospel (viz. through tradition or a vision?), that Paul's statements linking his conversion and call as apostle to the Gentiles are not to be regarded as historically reliable ('Paul's 'Autobiographical' Statements in Galatians 1–2,' *JBL* 85 [1966]:335–343). But Paul obviously could describe the Gospel in varying theological terms

his behavior in the period between his conversion and the writing of Galatians. Theories which postulate a lapse of time between Paul's coming to faith and his recognition of a call to Law-free mission to Gentiles consequently suffer from a severe lack of evidence. Likewise, the link which may be shown to exist between the form of Judaism found in the Pss. Sol. and that known to the preconversion Paul serves to strengthen the conclusion that Paul's reports concerning his conversion in some manner reflect its actual conditions.

Although a number of scholars have suggested that prior to the initial conflict with Judaizers (which is sometimes associated with the writing of Galatians), Paul had not thought through the place of the Law with respect to faith in Christ, the evidence points in the opposite direction.[26] One finds no solid indication that Paul promoted obedience to the Law in his early period of mission.

The strongest potential evidence to the contrary is found in Gal 5:11, where Paul poses the question, 'If I still preach circumcision, why am I still persecuted?' Given the rhetorical nature of Paul's 'admission,' one cannot rule out the possibility that it is a purely hypothetical concession, i.e. a quotation, which is refuted by his cross-examination, 'Why am I still persecuted?'

Even if Paul here implicitly acknowledges that he once 'preached circumcision,' it is highly unlikely that his statement should be understood to refer to his having demanded circumcision of Gentiles in the period following his conversion. His interrogatory remark is obviously prompted by a claim of his adversaries, otherwise the abrupt first-person discourse is inexplicable. It is inherently

---

(e.g. Rom 2:16; 2 Cor 4:4; 8:18; 9:13; Phil 1:5). Even in 1 Cor 15 the rehearsal of the Gospel contains not merely bare historical facts (if such exist), but interpretation, e.g. ὅτι Χριστὸς ἀπέθανεν ὑπὲρ τῶν ἁμαρτιῶν ἡμῶν κατὰ τὰς γραφάς. Paul's particular understanding of this traditional element of the Gospel was at stake at Galatia. He regarded a Law-free position as integral to the message of Christ's atoning death: εἰ γὰρ διὰ νόμου δικαιοσύνη, ἄρα Χριστὸς δωρεὰν ἀπέθανεν (Gal 2:21). He therefore is able to say without contradicting himself that he received the Gospel which he proclaims from God, not from human beings. Moreover, there is a strong connection between 1 Cor 15 and Gal 1 which Sanders does not see: both passages attribute Paul's conversion and call to apostleship to an appearance of the risen Jesus (Gal 1:16; 1 Cor 15:8–11).

[26] In Chapter 1 we suggested, contra Räisänen, that it is unlikely that Paul became indifferent to the Law after his conversion. The same improbability applies to others who suggest that Paul's call as apostle to the Gentiles did not require that he radically rethink the Law. E.g. Dunn, 'A Light to the Gentiles,' pp. 263–264; Georg Strecker, 'Befreiung und Rechtfertigung: Zur Stellung der Rechtfertigungslehre in der Theologie des Paulus,' in *Rechtfertigung: Festschrift für Ernst Käsemann*, ed. J. Friedrich, W. Pöhlmann, P. Stuhlmacher (Tübingen: J. C. B. Mohr [Paul Siebeck], 1976), pp. 479–508.

improbable that Paul, after having argued so vigorously that he has not compromised the Gospel either in Jerusalem or Antioch, should in an offhand manner make such a major concession.[27] In whatever manner one interprets Paul here, the least likely idea is that he confesses to once having taken his opponents' position. 'Preaching circumcision' does not here signify merely a call to perform the act of circumcising, but the proclamation of the saving advantages which result from the act, since in context Paul's other references to περιτομή focus upon its salvific value.[28] The expression περιτομὴν κηρύσσειν parallels Paul's formulaic description of his missionary activity as κηρύσσειν χριστόν (or τὸ εὐαγγέλιον or τὸ ῥῆμα τῆς πίστεως), which involves the proclamation of the *beneficia Christi*.[29] And elsewhere in early Christian tradition, when baptism is the object of κηρύσσειν, the saving graces associated with the act are implied.[30] When one takes into account the lack of evidence for active Jewish mission in the Hellenistic world, Paul's 'preaching circumcision' is best understood as his having once proclaimed the saving benefits of circumcision and full adherence to *Torah* to Jews who had been tempted to assimilate to Hellenistic culture or, perhaps, to God-fearing Gentile visitors to Palestine.[31] Such activity must have taken place prior to his conversion, as we have noted above.

It is possible to venture further in reconstructing the background to Paul's statement. Our interpretation coheres well with Paul's description elsewhere in the letter of his preconversion zeal for Judaism.[32] This pursuit of the Law, which led Paul to persecute believers almost certainly took place in Jerusalem.[33] Moreover, the information which Paul's opponents possessed about him seems to have been centered on his contact with Jerusalem. Their central claim was that he was dependent on a *Torah*-observant believing

---

[27] See especially Gal 2:5, 14.
[28] See Gal 5:6; 6:15.
[29] Rom 10:8; 1 Cor 1:13; 15:12; 2 Cor 1:19; 4:5; Gal 2:2; Phil 1:15; 1 Thess 2:9.
[30] E.g. the 'baptism which John preached' (Acts 10:37) does not convey merely the idea of the necessity of baptism, but of the forgiveness of sins (Luke 3:3).
[31] On the absence of an active Jewish mission see McKnight, *A Light Among the Gentiles*.
[32] See Gal 1:13, 14.
[33] Martin Hengel has convincingly restated the arguments for this conclusion, *The Pre-Christian Paul*, trans. John Bowden (Philadelphia: Trinity Press International, 1991). Paul's reference to Damascus (Gal 1:17) has to do only with the time of his conversion. Those who argue that Paul's persecuting activities must also have taken place in Damascus perhaps unwittingly rely on the testimony of Acts which they reject.

community, led by the 'pillars' in Jerusalem.[34] Included among the pieces of information about Paul's Jerusalem activities which his adversaries possessed and passed along to the Galatian churches was Paul's one-time zeal for the Law. Paul's statement in Gal 1:3, '*You have heard* of my conduct then in Judaism,' probably indicates that his opponents communicated this information to the churches. Paul's use of ἀκούω frequently connotes indirect report, a sense which is reinforced by Paul's choice of alternative expressions to refer to his communication with the Galatians elsewhere in the letter.[35] The report about Paul's 'preaching circumcision' therefore may have derived from the opponents' knowledge of earlier efforts on his part in Jerusalem synagogues among Diaspora Jews (who might have been lax in the practice of circumcision) or among 'God-fearing' pilgrims.[36]

It has been argued that the absence of 'righteousness' language in 1 Thessalonians, which is often taken to have been written prior to Galatians, indicates that Paul had not yet developed his understanding of justification by faith. But the relative dating of Galatians and the Thessalonian correspondence has only a minor bearing on this question. First Thessalonians, whether it was written prior to Galatians or not, evidences Paul's new understanding of the Law and of righteousness. Although one finds no argumentation concerning 'justification by faith,' a reading of the letter makes it apparent that Paul had preached a Gospel which assured these Gentile believers of eschatological salvation without any mention of obligation to the Law.[37] Moreover, Paul plainly had occasion to appeal to the Law in the letter, e.g., in his admonitions regarding sexual morality, yet he does not do so. One must suppose then that Paul was not merely indifferent to the Law at the time of his writing, but that he purposely avoided mention of it. Therefore

---

[34] That is the inescapable conclusion one draws from Paul's protestations in Gal 1:24–2:10.

[35] Cf., e.g., 1 Cor 5:1; 11:18; Gal 1:23; Rom 15:21; Phil 1:27, 30; 2:26. See Gal 1:9, 11; 5:21.

[36] See Hengel, *The Pre-Christian Paul*, pp. 58–59.

[37] E.g. 1 Thess 1:4, 9–10, 12, 16. Reference to the Law is noticeably lacking in the ethical portion of the letter, 1 Thess 4:1–5:22. Richard B. Hays observes, 'though they remain uncircumcised, he has transferred them the communal ascriptions appropriate to Israel.' See 'Crucified with Christ: A Synthesis of 1 and 2 Thessalonians, Philemon, Philippians, and Galatians,' in *Society of Biblical Literature 1988 Seminar Papers*, ed. David J. Lull (Atlanta, Ga.: Scholars Press, 1988), pp. 326–327. Hübner points out that despite the absence of the language of justification, the forensic moment of the argument remains in its strongly eschatological orientation coupled with the promise of salvation, 'Pauli Theologiae Proprium,' pp. 454–458.

the remarkable absence of 'righteousness' language in the Thessalonian correspondence cannot be taken to indicate that Paul had not yet contemplated the issue of the Law. It is better understood as yet another indication of the contingent character of all Paul's epistolary argumentation.

The dating and addressees of Paul's letter to the Galatians, which are notoriously difficult to determine, do not substantially contribute to the question of how Paul's understanding of justification by faith developed either. Paul indicates that prior to his evangelization of 'Galatia,' conflicts with Judaizers had arisen, and that he had warned the Galatian churches against a false Gospel.[38] The Galatians had accepted a Gospel which placed no obligation to the Law on them and had seen Paul live as a Gentile.[39] And as Hübner observes, Paul represents himself as advocating a Law-free Gospel at his meeting with the 'pillars' of the Jerusalem church. Given that Paul's opponents most likely claimed to have the support of the Jerusalem church (and had some connection to it), it is unlikely that in his letter to Galatia Paul would have risked misrepresenting his position at this encounter.[40] Paul's initial confrontation with Judaizers took place well before his writing Galatians.

Paul's narrative in Galatians strongly suggests that it occurred immediately prior to his decision to present his Gospel to the 'so-called pillars' of the Jerusalem church. His statements in Gal 2:24 are of considerable importance in this regard. His uncertainty ($\mu\acute{\eta}$ $\pi\omega\varsigma$ $\epsilon\acute{\iota}\varsigma$ $\kappa\epsilon\nu\grave{o}\nu$ $\tau\rho\acute{\epsilon}\chi\omega$ $\mathring{\eta}$ $\mathring{\epsilon}\delta\rho\alpha\mu\rho\nu$), which should not be overlooked, indicates on the one hand that his views had not been fully tested in debate. On the other hand, he had formulated his ideas in some form in the Gospel which he proclaimed to the Gentiles, which did not require them to be circumcised. And he was prepared to accept a theological correction of his views if it could be shown to be legitimate, indicating that he had reflected on the issue of Gentile circumcision.[41] Although Paul's language in Gal 2:4, 5 reflects his later confidence in his original theological judgment, and although there is no reason to doubt his appeal to a vision as his basis for travel to Jerusalem, it is probable that initial conflict with Jewish

---

[38] Gal 1:9; 2:3–5.

[39] Gal 4:12,13. This is the basis of Paul's appeal $\gamma\acute{\iota}\nu\epsilon\sigma\theta\epsilon$ $\acute{\omega}\varsigma$ $\acute{\epsilon}\gamma\acute{\omega}$, $\mathring{o}\tau\iota$ $\kappa\grave{\alpha}\gamma\acute{\omega}$ $\acute{\omega}\varsigma$ $\acute{\upsilon}\mu\epsilon\hat{\iota}\varsigma$, $\grave{\alpha}\delta\epsilon\lambda\phi\rho\acute{\iota}$, $\delta\acute{\epsilon}\rho\mu\alpha\iota$ $\acute{\upsilon}\mu\hat{\omega}\nu$. Cf. Heinrich Schlier, *Der Brief an die Galater*[4] KEK 7 (Göttingen: Vandenhoeck& Ruprecht, 1965), pp. 208–209; Betz, *Galatians*, p. 223.

[40] See Hübner, 'Pauli Theologiae Proprium,' pp. 454–455.

[41] Gal 2:6.

Christians who demanded that Gentile believers be circumcised prompted this interaction with Jerusalem and solidification of Paul's earlier theology.

Taken cumulatively, our observations point to a rethinking of the Law on Paul's part, stemming from his conversion, prior to engagement with Judaizers.[42] Our aim in what follows is to explore the manner in which this change took place. Naturally, an analysis of the effect of Paul's conversion on his soteriology must begin with Paul's references to his preconversion life and subsequent encounter with Christ, particularly Rom 7:7–13; Gal 1:10–17 and Phil 3:4–9. As Wrede anticipated, as Bultmann later fully acknowledged, and as is now widely accepted, Paul's references to his pre-Christian existence provide virtually no evidence for the psychological portraits of a Paul entrapped in an anxious existence under the Law.[43] Nevertheless, as we have pointed out in the discussion of Sanders's views, it is necessary to press beyond Paul's confession of Jesus as Messiah, and to ask why in the case of Paul, unlike in that of numerous other Jewish Christians of his day, faith in Christ was antithetical to a salvific value for *Torah* observance.

II. PAUL'S REFERENCES TO HIS LIFE AS A JEW AND HIS CONVERSION

A. *Romans 7:7–13*

1. Textual Analysis. Despite the considerable importance attached to Rom 7 for the reconstruction of Paul's conversion in the late nineteenth century, it plays only a minor role in current discussion. W. G. Kümmel's pivotal study, *Römer 7 und die Bekehrung des Paulus*, was especially influential in bringing an end to the widespread reading of this passage as a description of Paul's pre-Christian

---

[42] Stuhlmacher (*Versöhnung*, pp. 90–91) points to the five times Paul received thirty-nine lashes from 'the Jews' as an indication that at an early stage Paul's Gospel was Law-free. If Paul received this treatment at an early stage in his missionary career, it may well have been the result of his stance regarding the Law, but we cannot be certain on this basis.

[43] Despite a number of worthwhile insights, Gerd Theissen's recent psychological analysis of Romans 7 and 8 fails to be convincing. While he carefully distances his thesis from any implication that Paul's relation to *Torah* was a preparation for his conversion, he maintains that Paul's zeal for the Law prior to his conversion was the result of repressed anxiety produced by the threat of an external demand. But such probings of Paul's subliminal state yield little that is demonstrable. If anything, the alternative model of commitment as a means of self-aggrandizement, which Theissen rejects, would seem to fit some of Paul's self-references better (e.g. Gal 1:14; Phil 3:7). Paul, moreover, never argues against Gentile observance of the Law for the reason that it produces anxiety. See *Psychologische Aspekte paulinischer Theologie* (Göttingen: Vandenhoeck & Ruprecht, 1983), pp. 181–268. Cf. the discussion of Rom 7:7–13 below.

struggle with the demands of the Law.[44] In contrast to the biographical interpretation of Rom 7, Kümmel contends that the description of the ἐγώ in Rom 7 is a rhetorical device in which Paul's experience is not in view. Rom 7 pictures the human in general, neither specifically under Adam, nor under Moses, but under the Law.

Kümmel's most forceful arguments may be represented as follows:

1. Rom 7:9, 'I was then alive without the Law,' is irreconcilable with Paul's upbringing as a Jew: it is difficult to conceive of a Jew regarding any period of life without the Law. Further, the pregnant sense of 'life' in this verse contradicts Paul's understanding of pre-Christian existence elsewhere.[45]

2. The wretched person of Rom 7:14–25 does not fit Paul's statements about his past life in Judaism, particularly Phil3:4–6. Paul's self-expressed zeal for the Law (Gal 1:13,14), and his earlier understanding of his ability to accomplish it, weigh heavily against 7:14–25 describing his perception of life under the Law. Nor does Rom 7 correspond to Paul's conception of Christian existence: Pauline imperatives often are set next to indicatives, implying the ability to accomplish them. In contrast, the ἐγώ of 7:14–25 is utterly helpless. Moreover, reference to the Spirit is entirely lacking in this chapter.[46]

3. Paul makes use of a rhetorical *Stilform*, which appears in Hellenistic writings, in Philo, and in Rabbinic texts. This *Stilform* is characterized by the use of the first-person narrator considered solely as a part of humanity. Such a *Stilform* appears elsewhere in the Pauline letters.[47]

While Kümmel's arguments have been persuasive for a majority of scholars for a considerable period, there has been a recent tendency to question his thesis.[48] One of the most significant re-

---

[44] W. G. Kümmel, *Römer 7 und die Bekehrung des Paulus* (Leipzig: J. G. Hinrichs'sche Buchhandlung, 1929; reprint ed., *Römer 7 und das Bild des Menschen im Neuen Testament*, München: Chr. Kaiser, 1974). That Kümmel's dissertation was inspired by Bultmann's Wintersemester 1925/26 seminar on the anthropology of Paul underscores the break Bultmann had made with the portraits of Paul drawn by adherents of the *Religionsgeschichtliche Schule*. Wrede's *Paulus* (Halle, 1904) was also important in this regard.

[45] Kümmel, *Römer 7*, pp. 78–84.

[46] Kümmel, *Römer 7*, pp. 104–117.

[47] Esp. Rom 3:5-9; 1 Cor 6:12,15; 10:29–33; 11:31; 13:13, 11, 12; 14:11, 14, 15; Gal 2:18. Kümmel, *Römer 7*, pp. 117–132.

[48] See especially, J. I. Packer, "The 'Wretched Man' in Romans 7," in *Studia Evangelica II*, TU 87, ed. F.L. Cross (Berlin: Akademie, 1964), pp. 621–627; R. N. Longenecker, *Paul, Apostle of Liberty* (New York: Harper & Row, 1964), p. 88; C. E. B. Cranfield, *The Epistle to the Romans*, ICC (Edinburgh: T. & T. Clark, 1975), 1:342–345; J. D. G. Dunn, 'Rom 7:14–25 in the Theology of Paul,' *TZBas* 31 (1975), pp. 257–273; *Romans*, WBC 38 (Dallas, Tx: Word,

cent investigations is that of Gerd Theissen, who has reintroduced
a psychological interpretation of the text into the current discussion.[49] Unlike the earlier studies, however, Theissen explicitly distances himself from any attempt to portray Paul's pre-Christian
experience as a preparation for the Gospel. Prior to his conversion,
Paul was not conscious that the conflict between norm and desire
described in Rom 7 was intrinsic to the human relationship to the
Law. Only *post Christum* could the inner tension produced by the
Law surface in Paul's consciousness.

The questions which Theissen and others have raised about
Kümmel's interpretation of Rom 7 are weighty enough that one
cannot simply dispense with the chapter in describing Paul's preconversion experience of the Law. As various exegetes have noted,
the claim that the first-person usage of Rom 7:7–25 is entirely
fictive ('*uneigentlich*') runs into difficulties with both the surrounding context and with the thought of the passage itself. Vv.7–25
quite clearly represent an unfolding of Paul's self-inclusive assertion that 'when *we* were in the flesh, the sinful passions which come
about through the Law were at work in *our* members to bear fruit
for Death.' (7:5). Moreover, the section is introduced by the rhetorical deliberative, 'What shall *we* say then?' (7:7). Since Paul here
identifies himself with his readers, his following first-person singular
statements suggest that he is speaking of himself in a typical or
representative manner. And even more importantly, in both 7:7–
13 and 7:14–25 Paul describes the encounter of a human being
with the Law. Kümmel's thesis therefore appears questionable,
since he denies that any element of Paul's experience as a Jew
appears in the passage.

Kümmel's proposed linking of Rom 7 with a fictive *Stilform*, for
which he provided no formal criterion beyond the use of the first-
person singular, now can be seen to be radically flawed as well.
Theissen has pointed out the importance of taking into account
contextual signals when looking for parallels to Paul's usage.[50] He

1988), 1:381–382, 387–388; Ulrich Wilckens, *Der Brief an die Römer*, EKKNT VI
(Zürich: Benziger, 1980), 2:76–78; Beker, *Paul the Apostle*, pp. 240–243.
    [49] Theissen, *Psychologische Aspekte paulinischer Theologie* (Göttingen: Vanden-
hoeck & Ruprecht, 1983).
    [50] Theissen, *Psychologische Aspekte*, pp. 194–204. His claim is reasonable, that
one ought to compare Paul's usage in Rom 7 with other instances in which the
personal pronoun appears and in which indicative statements are made, although
it is hard to see why these markers are essential. And his further assertion that one
must look for passages in which a shift from past to present time (or the reverse)
appears—indicating a move from individualizing to generalizing utterances (or,
correspondingly, the reverse)—is slightly flawed. We shall see in our discussion of
Rom 7:14–25 in Chapter 4 that another marker, the first-person plural, is of

contends that while Paul clearly employs a fictive first-person in conditional statements and rhetorical questions (e.g. Rom 11:19), one should not necessarily conclude that the ἐγώ of the indicative statements of Rom 7 is imaginary.[51] Likewise, Ulrich Wilckens has questioned the applicability of brief Hellenistic and Pauline texts as parallels to Rom 7:7–25, where the first person is employed at length.[52] The only Pauline parallel to this extended usage is found in Gal 2:15–21, where the first person may be seen to function paradigmatically. Both passages begin with a plural form, which refers to a common situation or experience of believers.[53] The argument is then developed by a shift to the 'individual,' who expresses the perspective which Paul wants his audience to adopt. Moreover, in both texts Paul defends Christian freedom from the Law. Thus formal and material parallels strongly imply a typical or representative use of the first person in Rom 7, not a purely fictive one, as Kümmel proposes.

Kümmel's objection to this conclusion has been brilliantly answered by Theissen. Kümmel contends that Paul could not employ, 'ἐγὼ δὲ ἔζων χωρὶς νόμου ποτέ' (7:9) as a self-reference, since as a loyal Jew there was no time in his life in which he was without the Law. Theissen persuasively argues that Paul takes on a role here, which does not correspond precisely with his own history, just as he elsewhere rhetorically takes up roles which only partially fit him.

Theissen's claim may be given further precision. The allusion to Adam's transgression found in 7:9–11 is essentially an argument that trespass of the Law is equivalent to Adam's violation of the divine command, i.e., that transgression brings death. Paul represents himself here as a human being confronted with the demand of the Law, just as Adam was with the prohibition in Eden.[54] The

---

greater importance and that the change to the present tense in Rom 7:14–25 may be described more precisely.

[51] Theissen, *Psychologische Aspekte*, pp. 196–198. E.g. Rom 3:7 and 1 Cor 10:29, 30 contain fictive first–person rhetorical questions, which are followed by first-person expressions which include Paul.

[52] Wilckens, *Der Brief an die Römer*, 2:76–77.

[53] Rom 7:5,6; Gal 2:15–17; Phil 3:3.

[54] Theissen, *Psychologische Aspekte*, 204–213. Like many others, Theissen regards 7:7–12 as picturing Adam. But the allusion to Adam is only mediate. Paul speaks of the giving of the Law (7:7, 8, 9, 12), and elsewhere makes theological use of the temporal gap between Adam's transgression and the giving of the Law. Hence it is unlikely that he would collapse the two here. Moreover, sin is already present within the ἐγώ of 7:8, unlike Adam (5:12). Cf. D. J. Moo, 'Israel and Paul in Romans 7:7–12,' *NTS* 32 (1986):122–135. Paul's obvious reference to Adam, which emerges only in 7:9–11, is based upon his regarding Adam's transgression as typical for disobedience to the Law (5:14). He employs it here not for the sake

entrance of the Law into Paul's personal history is presupposed, but not directly addressed. Instead, Paul's use of the ἐγώ asks the reader to see herself or himself like Adam (and Paul), as a transgressor and under the sentence of death. This image of human encounter with the Law also explains the neutralized meaning of 'dead' and 'alive' in 7:8,9. Elsewhere Paul asserts that without the Law, sin was present in the world, but not 'reckoned.'[55] The subsequent entrance of the Law into history activated sin in acts of disobedience, and brought about death as a divine verdict on transgression.[56] Correspondingly, Paul here speaks of human existence prior to awareness of the Law as 'life,' presumably since apart from the Law there was no possibility of divine wrath and judgment upon trespasses.[57]

To adopt this personal or representative interpretation of the ἐγώ in Rom 7 immediately precipitates one into a further difficulty, which Kümmel articulates. The radical helplessness of the wretched person of Rom 7:14–25 seems to fit neither Paul's life as a Pharisee (Kümmel appeals in particular to Phil 3), nor to Paul's understanding of Christian existence. If a reading of Rom 7 as reflecting Paul's own experience is to be retained, this bifold difficulty must be resolved. We shall see that this problem finds its answer in the recognition that in Rom 7:14–25 Paul describes himself from the limited perspective of a person apart from Christ. Since Rom 7:14–25 adds no information to that which can be gained from a consideration of Rom 7:7–13, we will delay discussion of this passage until our treatment of the argument of Romans in Chapter 4.

2. Historical Reconstruction. The inferences which one may draw from Rom 7:7–13 are limited, since Paul's theological conclusions regarding his earlier experience are the result of his postconversion perspective.[58] Nevertheless, one piece of significant information about the preconversion Paul may be derived from the text. Prior to his conversion (as well as afterward, of course) Paul knew coveting, and illegitimate desire (7:5, 7–9). He knew it, moreover, as a reaction to the command contained in *Torah* (7:5, 7–9).

---

of universalism, which is already inherent to the giving of the Law (cf. 3:19), but because it provides the argument that transgression brings death. The image of Adam is linked to the repeated stress in 7:9–11 upon death as the result of the coming of the commandment (cf. 5:12–14).

[55] Cf. Rom 5:12–14 and Rom 7:8b.
[56] Rom 5:20; 1 Cor 15:56; 2 Cor 3:6–9.
[57] Cf. Rom 4:15.
[58] E.g. Rom 7:10.

Gerd Theissen has made much of this observation, suggesting that the Law's threat of death for transgression worked in combination with its stimulus to rebel, creating anxiety in Paul. Although Paul did not consciously perceive this *Angst*, he responded defensively to it by acting aggressively against the early Christian community in which the Law was not kept fully.[59]

It is possible that the preconversion Paul had such an experience. The fact that he was aware of his internal revolt against the command not to covet means that the potential of his rejecting the Law and divine covenant as a whole might have occurred to him. If one is capable of rebelling against one element of the Law, the possibility exists that one might react against the whole of it. It is unlikely, however, that Paul ever contemplated such a state of affairs actually coming to pass. His upbringing and religious environment would have shielded him from serious consideration of casting off the yoke of *Torah*.

Moreover, Theissen overlooks the fact that Paul's strict reading of the Law, in which the least transgression is met with condemnation, represents Paul's postconversion theology.[60] If prior to his conversion Paul experienced *Angst* with respect to some demands of the Law, he most likely found relief for it in the covenantal promises associated with the Law itself. The fact that Paul could speak of himself as blameless with regard to the Law, while being aware that his own inward response to the Law at times was one of disobedience, strongly suggests that Paul shared the covenantal interpretation of the Law seen already in 1QS and the Pss. Sol.[61] Like earlier Pharisees, Paul knew of atonement, perhaps through the very means mentioned in the Psalms of Solomon: fasting and contrition, and the discipline of hardship. He regarded the forgiveness obtained through such practices as the result of God's gracious covenantal promises.

Nevertheless, Paul's awareness of the problem of coveting in response to the commandment provides important information about the preconversion Paul and the effect of his conversion on him. His construal of sin as a 'power' which has completely overcome the human being is not simply a product of Paul's postconversion soteriology.[62] It has roots in his preconversion experience of rebellion against the Law.

---

[59] Theissen, *Psychologische Aspekte*, pp. 230–244.
[60] Cf. Gal 3:10.
[61] Phil 3:6. See the discussion of this text below, Section II.C.
[62] Cf. Rom 3:9; 5:12, 13, 20, 21; 6:6, 14.

If, however, Paul accorded his unruly desires the status of a
'power' at all prior to his conversion, he seems to have regarded
them as conquerable through adherence to the Law. Only after his
conversion could the phenomenon of sin take on the dimensions it
is accorded in his letters.

His perception of sin clearly changed in at least two respects. He
came to regard any transgression of the Law as working condemnation.[63] He also took a much more pessimistic view of the human
capacity to attain to righteousness. For him, the human being is a
slave to sin, incapable of escaping from domination by transgressions.[64] Hence 'sin' is a formidable 'power' which inexorably works
condemnation and death.[65] The manner in which Paul came to
this radicalized conception of sin will become clear in the following
analysis of his references to his conversion.

B. Galatians 1:10–24

1. Textual Analysis. Paul's letter to the Galatian churches consists of
a defense of his Gospel and of his authority as an apostle in the face
of a challenge from the circumcised, οἱ περιτεμνόμενοι (6:13), Jewish Christians, who claimed to have authority from the churches of
Judea and from the Jerusalem apostles.[66]

These adversaries, who had infiltrated the Galatian churches in
Paul's absence, seemed to have charged Paul with perverting the
Gospel which he had received from his contact with the Jerusalem
church.[67] The probable line of attack was that Paul intentionally
removed the requirement of circumcision for Gentile converts,

---

[63] Rom 7:10–13; cf. Gal 3:10.

[64] Rom 7:14–25.

[65] Rom 5:12; 6:23; 7:13; 7:24; 1 Cor 15:56.

[66] The danger of persecution (6:13) makes it virtually certain that 'the circumcised' are Jewish Christians and have contact with Palestine. Moreover, Paul's
detailed rehearsal of his post-conversion contacts with the churches of Judea and
the Jerusalem apostles makes little sense unless the adversaries had some connection with Jerusalem (Gal 1:15–2:21). See Robert Jewett's well-argued and provocative analysis, 'The Agitators and the Galatian Congregation,' *NTS* 17
(1971):198–212.

[67] F. F. Bruce observes that Paul refers to his adversaries throughout the letter
in the third person. In contrast, in the Corinthian correspondence offenders
within the church are addressed in the second person, those from outside in the
third person (see e.g. 1 Cor 5, 6; cf. 2 Cor 11), *The Epistle to the Galatians* NIGTC
(Grand Rapids: Eerdmans, 1982), pp. 24–25. Given the status which the adversaries have and the role which they seem to play, it seems likely that they were
from outside the congregation (see Gal 1:7, 8; 4:17–19; 5:12–13). *Pace* Stuhlmacher, it is unlikely that Paul would have minimized his contacts with Jerusalem if
he was defending himself against the charge that he was a mere apostle of the
Antiochean community. Cf. *Das paulinische Evangelium* (Göttingen: Vandenhoeck
& Ruprecht, 1968), p. 67.

although he knew better, in order to make the Gospel more acceptable to them.[68] One should not interpret the noun 'defense' too
narrowly, since Paul's advocacy of the Gospel includes a positive
restatement of its content, including the model of the Gospel's
effects, which his self-references provide. Nevertheless, the letter
in all its dimensions is occasioned by Paul's opponents in Galatia.

Gal 1:10–24 represents the first section of the extensive epistolary
self-recommendation (1:10–2:21), in which Paul makes himself
present with the congregation by commending to them a specific
aspect of his character.[69] In this instance, the self-recommendation
serves as a response to charges which had been leveled at Paul by
his adversaries at Galatia. That this is the case is manifest by a
number of Paul's comments within the passage. The rhetorical
question which begins this section is obviously a response to suspi-
cions at Galatia, 'Am I *now* seeking to persuade people or God or
am I *still* trying to please people?' And Paul's asseveration in
Gal 1:20 ('What I write to you, I swear before God, I am not
lying.') strongly suggests that Paul's opponents were accusing
him of being a one-time pupil of the Jerusalem apostles. Moreover, Paul's pointed description of the leaders of the Jerusalem
church as 'those who seemed to be of importance—what they were
makes no difference to me, since God is not impressed by appearance,' suggests that the status of the Jerusalem apostles was of
particular importance to Paul's opponents. Furthermore, Paul's
description of his preconversion practice of Judaism was most likely prompted by the reports which his adversaries had given the
Galatian churches.[70]

Paul's defense in Gal 1:10–24 may be outlined as follows. He
claims that his present missionary activity represents his allegiance
to the Gospel given to him by divine revelation of Christ (1:10–12).
The reports of Paul's earlier commitment to Judaism which the

---

[68] See Gal 1:10; 6:17. The charge may even have been that Paul pandered to
the Galatians alone, in failing to demand their circumcision. Otherwise Gal 5:11 is
difficult to explain. George Lyons, in *Pauline Autobiography*, treats the proposed
charges against Paul, that he was dependent on the Jerusalem apostles and that
he compromised the Gospel, separately. Naturally either one of these, taken on its
own, is insufficient to explain Paul's argument in Galatians. But Lyons fails to
consider the strength of the case for the letter as a response to charges when the
two are taken together: that Paul is under attack as having learned the Jerusalem
Gospel, and yet having knowingly compromised it in Galatia. It is clear that Paul
is responding to the attempts of a third party—not entirely known even to Paul—
to gain the allegiance of the Galatian congregations (1:7; 4:17; 5:12; 6:12, 13).
[69] See Franz Schnider and Werner Stenger, *Studien zum neutestamentlichen
Briefformular*, NTTS 11 (Leiden: Brill, 1987), pp. 50–59.
[70] See the discussion of Gal 5:11 in Section I, above.

Galatians have heard are true (1:13,14). But Paul uses them to
underscore the radical break which the vision of the risen Christ
brought about in him. This reversal included a new independence
from 'flesh and blood,' especially the Jerusalem apostles (1:15–20).
It was accompanied by a recognition by the Judean churches that
God had acted upon Paul (1:21–24). Obviously, Paul's assertion of
freedom from human authority functions as an example for his
readers.[71] But the details of his conversion are unique to him,
and serve to assert his apostolic authority.

2. Historical Reconstruction. Despite the generality of Paul's description of his activities, some insights into his aims as persecutor of
early believers arise from this text. He portrays his persecution as
an integral part of his progress in Judaism, in which he outstripped
his contemporaries. And he attributes the superior status he attained to his abundant zeal for *Torah*, which he in postconversion
language describes as 'my ancestral traditions.'[72] Paul in some
manner regarded faith in Christ and devotion to the Law as antithetical prior to his coming to faith.

His statements also indicate that he was conscious of the status
he was attaining in his practice of Judaism. He contrasts his service
of Christ with his former desire for human commendation, indicating that he once knowingly sought the recognition and approval of
Pharisaic authorities: 'If I were still trying to please people, I
would not be a servant of Christ.'[73] Although Bultmann's depiction of Paul aiming to establish himself before God by his own
effort must be rejected, Paul did attach religious status to pious
behavior, however confident he might have been of the eternal life

---

[71] Cf. Gal 1:8,9.

[72] Gal 1:14. Zeal for *Torah*, even to the point of exerting force against those
who desecrated it, was regarded highly in some segments of first-century Judaism,
having the Biblical narrative of Phineas as its model. See Num 25. Cf. Martin
Hengel, *Die Zeloten: Untersuchungen zur Jüdischen Freiheitsbewegung in der Zeit von
Herodes I. bis 70 n.Chr.2*, AGJU 1 (Leiden: E. J. Brill, 1976), pp. 181–188; Haacker, 'Die Berufung des Verfolgers,' p. 8, argues that in Phil 3:6 it is precisely the
narrow sense of religious intolerance which Paul intends: Es handelt sich bei
diesem Stichwort 'Eifer' offensichtlich um einen festen Begriff für gewaltsame
religiöse Intoleranz, wie Paulus sie vor seiner Berufung vertrat und als Apostel
dann selbst zu spüren bekam. Gager, who rejects psychological approaches, oddly
enough suggests that Paul displayed anger prior to his conversion, unwittingly
perhaps relying on the testimony of Acts 26:9–11, 'Some Notes on Paul's Conversion,' pp. 699–700. To understand 'zeal' solely as anger is to miss the theological significance attached to it.

[73] Gal 1:10. Paul's acknowledgement here should not be taken to imply that
prior to his conversion he was motivated solely by the desire to please others, and
not God. It is more likely that it was precisely through his strict adherence to
Jewish tradition that he strove to serve God.

that was his through the covenant. We will more fully develop this connection with the thought of the Pss. Sol. in our discussion of Phil 3:4–9.[74]

It is difficult to reconstruct the nature of Paul's persecuting activities from the evidence of Paul's letters. Even if his actions were restricted to the disciplinary measures available to the synagogue, it should not be forgotten that the thirty-nine lashes, which Paul himself later experienced, were not a mild slap on the wrist.[75] Whatever means Paul might have employed, his aim was not merely the discipline of some wayward Jews, it was to destroy 'the Church of God.'[76]

This statement found in Gal 1:13 leads directly to the question of the object of Paul's persecution. Bultmann assumes that a purely Hellenistic Christianity, which already proclaimed a Law-free Gospel, became the target of Paul's destructive efforts. His conclusion rests on two fundamental observations. First, Bultmann concludes from the evidence of Paul's letters that Paul's acceptance of the Christian message meant for him from the very start the rejection of the Law.[77] Secondly, Bultmann discounts the

---

[74] Nevertheless, this tendency would have been Paul's fault, and not that of every Jew. Moreover, it is unlikely that it was Paul's only motive for obedience.

[75] Cor 11:24. Cf. m.Makkoth 3:10–14 where the severity of the punishment is apparent.

[76] Gal 1:13. Ἐπόρθουν should most likely be read as a conative imperfect, as in Gal 1:23, BDR, §326. One must not overlook the strong language which Paul uses in describing his persecution of believers. Gaventa (From Darkness to Light, p. 25) wrongly downplays the violence intimated by the word διώκω, which when it bears the sense of 'persecute,' includes the idea of physical harm (Gal 5:11; 6:12 cf. 6:17) and generally for Paul carries the idea of mistreatment of others (Rom 12:14, 1 Cor 4:12, 15:9, 2 Cor 4:9, Gal 4:29). The word πορθέω, which appears only in Gal 1:13,23 and Acts 9:21 in the New Testament, signifies pillage, annihilation, or ravaging. In Hellenistic Greek it is used to describe the sacking of cities, countries and the like, which accompanied military actions. Cf. H. G. Liddell, R. Scott, and H. S. Jones A Greek-English Lexicon[9] (Oxford: Oxford University Press, 1968), s.v. 'πορθέω.' Josephus uses the word solely in this sense. See also 4 Macc 11:4, where the four sons of Eleazar who remain after the death by torture of the first three reply to Antiochus Epiphanes: ὦ μισάρετε καὶ μισάνθρωπε, τί δράσαντας ἡμᾶς τοῦτον πορθεῖς τὸν τρόπον; Philippe Menoud takes pains to point out the violence which the word πορθέω usually signifies, only to conclude that Paul must have meant the term in a moral sense (viz., he sought to undermine the message of faith by his own polemical preaching), since the material means of carrying out a destruction of the early Church would have been unavailable to him. See 'Le sens du verbe πορθεῖν,' in Apophoreta: Festschrift für Ernst Haenchen, BZNW 30, ed. W. Eltester and F. H. Kettler (Berlin: Töpelmann, 1964), pp. 178–186. This conclusion is incorrect. Paul's aim was to destroy the Church (Gal 1:13), not merely 'the faith' (Gal 1:23), nor, as Menoud suggests, merely individuals. Moreover, for the reasons suggested above, it is hard to think that Paul did not mistreat believers.

[77] See, e.g., Bultmann, 'Paulus,' col.1021.

testimony of Acts that a good portion of Paul's action against the fledgling church took place in Jerusalem. He contends on the basis of Gal 1:17 that Paul's persecution of Christians must have taken place in or about Damascus.[78] Likewise he regards Paul's comment in Gal 1:22 (ἤμην δὲ ἀγνοούμενος τῷ προσώπῳ ταῖς ἐκκλησίαις τῆς Ἰουδαίας ταῖς ἐν Χριστῷ) as rendering the claim that Paul had persecuted believers in Jerusalem untenable.[79]

The evidence that Paul persecuted a Law-free Gentile Christianity is weak, however. In asserting that Paul's coming to faith in Christ set him before the decision 'Christ or the Law,' Bultmann relies on Paul's theological description of conversion. But just as Paul consistently portrays conversion in general (and hence his own) as involving a break with *Torah*, he regularly attributes his own conversion to an appearance of the risen Jesus.[80] It is inconsistent therefore on Bultmann's part, to take only part of Paul's testimony into consideration.[81] Furthermore, as others have noted, it is highly unlikely that Paul would have persecuted a purely Gentile movement, since he would not have recognized it as within the bounds of Judaism. It would merely have been one of a number of syncretistic Gentile cults.[82]

The argument based on Gal 1:17, that all of Paul's persecuting activities must have taken place in the vicinity of Damascus bears little weight. Gal 1:17 merely indicates that Paul's conversion took place there, just as it does in the narrative of Acts. There is no necessary geographical connection between Gal 1:15–17, which is set apart by the definite ὅτε ('when'), and the preceding narrative.

The statement of Gal 1:22, ἤμην δὲ ἀγνοούμενος τῷ προσώπῳ ταῖς ἐκκλησίαις τῆς Ἰουδαίας, provides more room for Bultmann's assertion. Paul's usage of πρόσωπον clearly indicates that the idea of direct physical presence is in view.[83] Yet, as Arland Hultgren rightly notes, this reading, i.e. that Paul was 'unknown by face' to the Judaean churches, by no means excludes the possibility that

---

[78] Bultmann, 'Paulus,' col.1021.
[79] Bultmann, 'Paulus,' col.1020–1021. Many others have followed Bultmann's argument, of course.
[80] See 1 Cor 9:1; 15:1, 8–11; 2 Cor 4:3–6. Among the secondary literature see esp. Kümmel, *Römer 7*, pp. 139–160, Kim, *The Origin of Paul's Gospel*, pp. 51–66, and Dietzfelbinger, *Die Berufung des Paulus*, pp. 43–64.
[81] No doubt this hesitancy stems in good measure from Bultmann's unwillingness to allow for supernatural intervention. See, e.g., Bultmann's review of J.G. Machen's *The Origin of Paul's Religion* in *TLZ* 49(1924):13–14.
[82] So, e.g., Hultgren, 'Paul's Pre-Christian Persecutions,' p. 101.
[83] See 1 Cor 13:12; 2 Cor 2:10; 4:6; 5:12; 1 Thess 2:17. Cf. Jas 1:23; Jdt 10:14 (κατανοῶ τὸ πρόσωπον).

Paul persecuted believers in Jerusalem.[84] Jerusalem was a good-sized city in the first century.[85] Paul, furthermore, refers not merely to Jerusalem, but to the churches of Judea as being unfamiliar with his appearance. Thus the circle of believers to which Paul refers is considerable in number. If he did engage in persecution of the Judean believers, there is no reason to think that he would have come into contact with a great many of them. The point in time to which Paul refers in Gal 1:22 is some three years after his conversion, so that one also must reckon with the numerical expansion of the Judaean congregations in this period. Moreover, it should not be forgotten that the dative τῷ προσώπῳ is restrictive: Paul is not saying that he is unknown, he is saying that he had not been in direct contact with these congregations. Nor should it be overlooked that the statements of Gal 1:17–24 are made in a polemical setting. Paul has a vested interest in minimizing his familiarity with the Judaean churches, because his adversaries were claiming that Paul was corrupting the Gospel message he had learned there. If there is any tendency on Paul's part in Galatians, it would be to underplay his connection with Judaean churches and his early contacts with its leaders.

The report which Paul claims the churches of Judea heard about him strongly suggests that they were the focus of his persecuting activities. Attempts to argue that the 'we' of the citation in Gal 1:23 refers to a group other than Jewish Christian believers are not persuasive.[86] Paul gives no indication that a third party is involved, so that reading ἡμᾶς as equivalent to the churches of Judea is the most natural one. And it is hard to think that the Law-observant Jewish Christians of Judea would be in such close contact with a Law-free Gentile church, or with Hellenistic (i.e. Greek-speaking) Jews who had criticized the Law (on which, see below), that they would receive the news of Paul's conversion and subsequently rejoice that his persecution of these wayward groups had ceased. It would seem that Law-observant Jewish Christians might have sympathized with Paul's attack, rather than rejoicing

---

[84] Hultgren, 'Paul's Pre-Christian Persecutions,' p. 106.

[85] Cf. S.Safrai and M. Stern eds., *The Jewish People in the First Century*, 2 vols., CRINT 1 (Philadelphia: Fortress, 1976), 2:683–684. Strecker, 'Befreiung und Rechtfertigung,' p. 482 n.10, in arguing that Paul could not have persecuted the church in Judea, refers to Jeremias's estimate that the population of Jerusalem in the first century was around 25,000. But even if Jerusalem was this size, it is by no means clear that Paul would have been readily recognizable to all the various gatherings of believers in Jerusalem during the relatively short period of his persecution. See now, Hengel, *The Pre-Christian Paul*, pp. 18–39.

[86] μόνον δὲ ἀκούοντες ἦσαν ὅτι ὁ διώκων ἡμᾶς ποτε νῦν εὐαγγελίζεται τὴν πίστιν ἥν ποτε ἐπόρθει. Cf. Ernst Bammel, 'Galater 1 23,' *ZNW* 59 (1969):108–112.

that it had ended, if ἡ πίστις signifies the tenets of those who criticized the Law![87] It is more likely that Paul persecuted the Judean churches.[88]

In place of Bultmann's contention that the (Gentile) Hellenistic community was the focus of Paul's attack, Martin Hengel and others have proposed that the Ἑλληνισταί of Acts 6:1 and 9:29 represent a Christian community of Greek-speaking Jews, who exercised a critique of *Torah* and Temple. It was this group which became the object of Paul's persecuting activities.[89]

Despite the attractiveness of a number of points of Hengel's thesis, some problems exist with both his analysis of Luke's account and the conclusions which he draws regarding the objects of Paul's persecution. In a recent article, Edvin Larsson has highlighted various difficulties with Hengel's description of the Hellenists, which need not be repeated here.[90] One matter deserves attention. Evidence that the Greek-speaking believing community was critical of *Torah* is fairly weak in Acts 6,7. In the first place, the concrete charge presented against Stephen is that he proclaims Jesus' *impending* destruction of the Temple and alteration of the Law.[91] Furthermore, as Hengel recognizes, Jesus appears here not as the end of the Law, but as its authoritative interpreter. Therefore, the text provides no information regarding the practices of the Hellenists, nor does it suggest that they were opposed to

---

[87] The object of Paul's persecution is expressed in theological terms in 1:23: νῦν εὐαγγελίζεται τὴν πίστιν ἥν ποτε ἐπόρθει.

[88] Other evidence can be adduced to support the thesis that Paul had spent considerable time in Jerusalem prior to his conversion. Oepke rightly observes that the importance of Jerusalem to Paul after his conversion would have been even more accentuated prior to it: "Selbst für den Christen Paulus noch steht Jerusalem im Mittelpunkt des Denkens (Röm. 15,19; Gal 4,25ff.). Wieviel mehr mag es bei dem Juden der Fall gewesen sein! Sollte ein Mann, der so bewußt 'Hebräer' war (Phil.3,5), nicht alles getan haben, um die Hochburg seines Volkes kennen zu lernen?'" ('Vorchristliche Zeit,' p. 443.). Moreover, the claim Paul made, to have outstripped the peers of his race in the practice of Judaism, would have been absurd had he not spent extensive periods in Jerusalem, cf. Hengel, *The Pre-Christian Paul*, pp. 18–62, 72–79; Kim, *The Origin of Paul's Gospel*, pp. 33–38.

[89] Martin Hengel, *Between Jesus and Paul* (Philadelphia: Fortress, 1983), pp. 1–29. So also Dietzfelbinger, *Berufung des Paulus*, pp. 16–22; Kim *The Origin of Paul's Gospel*, pp. 44–50. The identity and roll of the Ἑλληνισταί has been under debate since the time of Baur. See the historical surveys of Heinz–Werner Neudorfer, *Der Stephanuskreis in der Forschungsgeschichte seit F. C. Baur* (Giessen/Basel: Brunnen, 1983), pp. 1–218; Gerd Lüdemann, *Paulus, der Heidenapostel*, 2vols. (Göttingen: Vandenhoeck& Ruprecht, 1983), 2:13–57.

[90] Edvin Larsson, 'Die Hellenisten und die Urgemeinde,' *NTS* 33 (1987):205–225.

[91] The general charges against Stephen (Acts 6:11,13) are concretely stated in Acts 6:14: ἀκηκόαμεν γὰρ αὐτοῦ λέγοντος ὅτι Ἰησοῦς Ναζωραῖος οὗτος καταλύσει τὸν τόπον τοῦτον καὶ ἀλλάξει τὰ ἔθη ἃ παρέδωκεν ἡμῖν Μωϋσῆς.

the observance of *Torah* prior to the Messianic act which would effect their envisioned restructuring of Judaism. Stephen places a high value on the Law, and charges his adversaries with failure to keep it![92] Evidence for a critical stance over against the Law is lacking.[93] It appears rather that the Hellenists might have adopted a fresh, apocalyptic interpretation of *Torah* and Temple. Perhaps those who held such a perspective anticipated the eschatological 'spiritualization' of the Law's demands which is represented in Stephen's statements regarding the Temple.[94]

No doubt, this view of the Law might lead to the mission to Gentiles which Luke represents as resulting from the persecution surrounding Stephen.[95] It is also possible that some Greek-speaking Jews from the Diaspora sat loosely with some demands of the Law, and as a result were ready to engage in Gentile mission. Independently of Paul, Hellenistic Jews such as Barnabas were in the forefront of mission to Gentiles.[96] Nevertheless, it is not clear that all those who participated in such a movement rejected the Law.

This conclusion presents a difficulty for an important aspect of Hengel's thesis. He wishes to show that the Hellenists were Paul's theological forebears, thus providing a line of development between Paul and Jesus. But Luke provides little evidence that in the brief period between Jesus' crucifixion and Paul's conversion a movement which challenged the validity of the Law arose.[97] A 'spiritualization' of the Law, or a lax attitude toward some of its provisions is quite different from its abrogation. Some indication that a significant social grouping came to a radical break with the Law prior to Paul's conversion is required for this proposal. Acts simply does not provide such evidence.[98]

When one turns to Paul's letters, the results are much the same. It is hard to find evidence either that he persecuted the Hellenists

---

[92] Acts 7:38,53.

[93] See Hultgren, 'Paul's Pre-Christian Persecutions,' pp. 98–99.

[94] Acts 7:48–50. Cf. Larsson, 'Die Hellenisten,' pp. 218–220.

[95] Acts 11:19–21.

[96] Gal 2:9; 1 Cor 9:6. In view of the lack of evidence that the Roman church was ever troubled by the problem of Gentile circumcision, it would seem likely that it was founded by Greek-speaking Jews who did not require that Gentiles convert to Judaism. See Chapter 4 of this study.

[97] Hengel sets this time gap at three years. See, 'Between Jesus and Paul,' p. 11.

[98] Contra Räisänen ('Paul's Conversion,' p. 406), there is no evidence that the believers whom Paul persecuted were engaged in mission to Gentiles. On the lack of evidence for a Law-free Judaism prior to Paul, see Dunn, 'A Light to the Gentiles,' pp. 255–256. It is possible that Paul perceived a Hellenistic group as *Torah*-critical when in fact it was not. This might explain his persecution of believers, but such a group could not provide Paul with a theological starting point.

solely or that he was influenced by the theology of such a group. As
we noted above, the unity 'in the faith' between the objects of
Paul's persecution and the Judaean churches who received the
report of his conversion renders unlikely the scenario which Hengel and others paint, i.e. that Paul persecuted a distinct movement
which differed from the Hebrew-speaking church.[99] Paul consistently represents his attack to have been directed against the community of faith as a whole.[100] How would Paul have known that
the revelation of the Son of God meant that the Law had been
devalued, if his objection to the early Christian movement had
been directed solely against a segment of the Church which rejected *Torah*? Would he not more likely have adhered to the Law-
observant group of believers after his encounter with Christ?[101]

It is also significant that Paul never appeals to traditions from an
earlier *Torah*-critical Christianity. In fact, he explicitly denies such
a dependence.[102] The fact that he makes no appeal to an earlier
authority for his position regarding the Law, although he readily
does so in other matters (e.g. 1 Cor 15:1–11), seriously weakens the
argument that Paul was initially shaped by the theology of such a
group. It should not be forgotten that Hengel suggests that the
Hellenists provided a link to sayings of Jesus critical of *Torah*.[103]
If Paul was shaped theologically by this group, it is hard to think
why he does not appeal to these sayings. On the other hand, if it is
suggested that Paul was converted to a renegade movement (to
which he could not make appeal, since they carried no authority),
it is hard to explain why and how he was converted to this group
and not those who remained faithful to *Torah*. Räisänen offers a

---

[99]   See Gal 1:23, 24. The assumption that a Law-observant Hebrew-speaking
Christian community could maintain connections with a Law-critical Greek-
speaking community is one of the weakest points of Hengel's reconstruction.
Wouldn't they be just as much at odds with this radical group of Christians as
other Jews?
[100]   Gal 1:13, 23; Phil 3:6; 1 Cor 15:9. Wolfgang Schrage overlooks the fact that
Paul's usage of ἐκκλησία reflects his post-conversion perspective in which the
community of faith is regarded as a unity. Such language cannot be used with
certainty to determine the self-designation of early believers, as Schrage suggests
regarding Gal 1:13 (viz., that ἐκκλησία here reflects the Hellenistic Jewish Christians; "'Ekklesia' und 'Synagoge': Zum Ursprung des urchristlichen Kirchenbegriffs,' *ZThK* 60 [1963]:198).
[101]   Hengel and others who follow this line of argument allow, of course, that
Paul persecuted believers in Jerusalem and not merely in Damascus. It is possible
that Paul made two mistaken assumptions: first, that the Hellenists were critical of
the Law; second, that all those who professed Jesus as Messiah were also critical of
the Law. Then he would have mistakenly persecuted the whole of the early Jewish
Christian community. But he would have been ignorant of their theology.
[102]   Gal 1:12.
[103]   Hengel, *Between Jesus and Paul*, pp. 1–29.

series of examples of statements from Paul's letters which he suggests might represent 'Hellenistic' influence on Paul.[104] However, even if one allows that Paul borrowed these 'spiritualizations' of the Law from other Jewish believers (which is hard to demonstrate), one has not established that his conversion was influenced by their thought.

In summary, it seems unlikely that Paul received a primary impetus from *Torah*-critical Jewish believers. He gives no indication either that he perceived himself as persecuting only a radical wing of the Messianic community or that he received a theological imprint from them at his conversion. Likewise, the book of Acts provides scant evidence that the movement which Hengel suggests developed prior to Paul's conversion. This conclusion is not meant to deny that these 'Hellenists' came into existence, nor does it suggest that they did not represent the sort of theological development which Hengel has proposed. But it appears unlikely that Paul's conversion was shaped by such a theology. Unless one is prepared to engage in speculation, one is reduced to accepting the image which Paul presents: that his persecution was directed against the proclamation of Jesus as Messiah.

One frequently finds the objection to this conclusion, that the mere confession of a certain figure as Messiah would not have been regarded as a cause for opposition in early Judaism.[105] In an insightful and highly significant article, Terence Donaldson has brought important sociological perspectives to bear on this problem.[106] He points to the fact that persecution is the product of a group being perceived as a threat to the social order.[107] As was the case with the Essenes prior to their withdrawal to Qumran, the early Christian movement, through what it taught and did, came to be regarded as dangerous. The persecution of believers in Jesus was engendered not merely by a certain theological confession, but by the presence of a confessing community, whose views and practices brought them into conflict with those who wanted to maintain the *status quo*. Most likely they welcomed into membership and

---

[104] Heikki Räisänen, 'Paul's Conversion,' pp. 414–415. E.g. Phil 3:3; Rom 2:15, 25–29; 12:1; 13:8–10; Gal 3:28; 5:14; 1 Cor 3:16; 6:19; 7:19.
[105] Akiba's acknowledgement of Bar Kokhba, y.Taanith 68d is often cited. See Wilckens, 'Die Bekehrung des Paulus,' p. 18, who argues that for Paul the σκάνδαλον for the Jews was not Jesus' Messianic status, but the devaluation of the Law as the determiner of election. He does not answer the question of *how* Christ came to replace the function of *Torah* in Paul's thought.
[106] Terence L. Donaldson, 'Zealot and Convert: The Origin of Paul's Christ–Torah Antithesis,' *CBQ* 51 (1989):655–682.
[107] Donaldson, 'Zealot and Convert,' p. 670.

gave equal status to those whom Paul, like the Pharisees who
composed the Psalms of Solomon, would have regarded as impious, or 'sinners.' And it is probable, as Donaldson suggests, that
the exclusivism of the earliest believing community evoked a reaction from Paul. In their claim that faith in Jesus as Messiah was
necessary for eschatological salvation, the earliest believers implicitly demoted *Torah*, since even a zealous observer of the Law such
as Paul would have been an 'outsider' to them.[108] The establishment of such groups of believers in Jesus as Messiah challenged the
authority of the Pharisaic party, and the structure of society in
which they were highly influential. In this manner Paul may have
come to regard Christ and *Torah* as antithetical, even though those
whom he persecuted may not have drawn this radical conclusion.[109]

One element of the proclamation of the early believing community which contributed to the hostility it experienced from its
neighbors, including Paul, was that it confessed that one who
had been crucified was Messiah. This reaction is repeatedly reflected in Paul's letters. Even where his polemic is not directed against
Jewish Christian adversaries, but against an 'over-realized' eschatology, Paul distinguishes between Gentiles for whom 'the cross' is
foolishness (μωρία) and Jews for whom the crucified Messiah
(Χριστὸν ἐσταυρωμένον) is an obstacle to faith (σκάνδαλον).[110] In
Galatians, Paul argues, 'if I still preach circumcision, . . . the
scandal of the cross is abolished,' (κατήργηται τὸ σκάνδαλον τοῦ
σταυροῦ).[111] He charges that his opponents have demanded circumcision of the Galatians in order to avoid this sort of persecution (μόνον ἵνα τῷ σταυρῷ τοῦ Χριστοῦ μὴ διώκωνται).[112] Even where
he does not develop his argument on the basis of Jesus' crucifixion,
he presupposes that the message of the crucified Messiah was
incompatible with the inclination of the Galatian churches to

---

[108] Donaldson, 'Zealot and Convert,' p. 679.
[109] Donaldson, 'Zealot and Convert,' p. 680.
[110] 1 Cor 1:23. Cf. Gustav Stählin, 'σκάνδαλον' in *Theologisches Wörterbuch zum
Neuen Testament*, ed. G. Kittel and G. Friedrich (Stuttgart: Kohlhammer, 1964),
7:338–358.
[111] Gal 5:11; cf. 4:29. Paul's adversaries most likely came to the congregation
with the sole message of the necessity of circumcision (without denying faith in
Jesus), since Paul had already proclaimed faith in Christ. Dupont, 'La conversion
de Paul,' pp. 82–84, fails to recognize that the Pauline antithesis between 'the
cross' and circumcision has as its intermediate term the proclamation of the
crucified Jesus as Messiah, σταυρός being an abbreviation for the latter. As a
result he wrongly underestimates the significance of Jesus' Messianic status for
Paul.
[112] Gal 6:12.

adopt Judaism.[113] It is hardly accidental that the greatest concentration of Paul's references to Jesus' cross appear in this letter, where the issue of adherence to the Law is at stake.[114] His statements indicate that the proclamation of a crucified Messiah was a fundamental source of Jewish resistance to the message of the early believing community.

This response to the confession of a 'crucified Messiah' probably had its basis in the threat to society and religion which such a message contained. Since Jesus was put to death under Roman authority, the gathering of believers who waited in hope of his kingdom may well have been alarming to Jewish authorities who wanted to avoid confrontation with Rome. Likewise, if Paul was aware that Jesus had been put to death under the judgment of the Sanhedrin, he would have considered the promulgation of faith in him as an affront to the legitimate interpreters of *Torah*.

The message of a crucified Messiah also carried an intrinsic challenge to *Torah* and the social order, related to the exclusivistic claims of the earliest believers. The Messiah was longed for as a victorious herald of the in-breaking kingdom of God.[115] Jesus' ignominious death and the continuation of the present world not only seemed incompatible with such a hope, but for the pious such as Paul represented a threat. The call to believe in a crucified Messiah meant that all existing structures, in which allegiance to *Torah* was thought to guarantee salvation in the Messianic age, were declared invalid. To many Jews, therefore, the proclamation of a crucified Messiah would have been viewed as a blasphemous attack on the foundations of religion and society.

Judgments concerning a claim to Messianic status undoubtedly would have been grounded in *Torah*, as in fact Paul's characterization of the cross as Ἰουδαίοις σκάνδαλον, i.e. a religious offense, presumes.[116] It is in this light that one must consider Paul's

---

[113] See e.g. Gal 3:1; 6:14–16.

[114] J. Louis Martyn, while rightly noting that the cross is regularly opposed to circumcision in Galatians, and that the crucifixion of Jesus, not his Parousia, is the focus of Paul's apocalypticism, fails to bring the two insights together. The καινὴ κτίσις, the new creation, does away with the distinctions of the present age. But for Paul it has been inaugurated on the basis of Paul's *Torah*-based interpretation of Jesus' death as an atonement, as the following discussion will show. See Martyn's, 'Apocalyptic Antinomies in Paul's Letter to the Galatians,' *NTS* 31 (1985):410–424.

[115] Cf., e.g., 1QS 9:9b–11; 1QSb 5:20–28. Even in those circles in which the Messianic rule was regarded as an *interregnum*, the Messiah's appearance was associated with the inauguration of a period of unparalleled blessing (4 Ezra 12:31–34; 13:32–50; 2 Baruch 72–74).

[116] Cor 1:23.

reference to Deut 21:23 in Gal 3:13. Since Paul in his arguments with the Galatians is to some extent interacting with his own past devotion to Judaism, at some point one would expect to find ideas which had a formative influence on Paul himself. Paul's application of Deut 21:23 to Jesus raises the possibility that prior to his conversion he would have connected this text to the case of a Messianic claimant who had been crucified, and would have concluded that such a person had been accursed by God. It is possible, of course, that other passages of *Torah* could have figured in Paul's theologically-bred antipathy to the early Christian proclamation. But it is certain that Paul's rejection of the crucified Jesus as Messiah had some grounding in *Torah*.

There is good reason for regarding this passage from Deuteronomy, with which Paul was undoubtedly familiar, as having contributed to Paul's preconversion views.[117] The expression ἐπικατάρατος πᾶς ὁ κρεμάμενος ἐπὶ ξύλου appears in Gal 3:13 as substantiation for Paul's claim that Christ bore the curse of the Law for those who were unable to fulfill its demands.[118] The Temple Scroll, by which the Qumran community actualized the book of Deuteronomy at about the beginning of the first century BCE, likewise interprets the passage as a reference to crucifixion. See 11QTemple 64:7–12, especially 10b–12:

10b ותליתמה גם אותו על העץ	10b You shall hang him also
וימות . . . כי 12 מקוללי אלוהים	on the tree, 11 and he shall
ואנשים תלוי על העץ	die . . . . for 12 those hanged on the tree are accursed by God and men.[119]

---

[117] On the connection between this text and Paul's persecution of believers, see Stuhlmacher, 'Das Ende des Gesetzes,' pp. 28–29; Heinz–Wolfgang Kuhn, 'Jesus als Gekreuzigter in der frühchristlichen Verkündigung bis zur Mitte des 2. Jahrhunderts,' *ZThK* 72 (1975):33–36; Kim, *The Origin of Paul's Gospel*, pp. 46–47; Dietzfelbinger, *Die Berufung des Paulus*, pp. 33–36.

[118] On the relation of Paul's reference to the MT and LXX, see Max Wilcox, "'Upon the Tree'—Deut 21:22–23 in the New Testament," *JBL* 96 (1977):85–99. Wilcox argues that a pre-Christian form of the text which connected 'the one hanged' with 'upon the tree' formed the basis of early Christian usage. But the על־העץ which appears at the beginning of v. 23 in the MT, could easily be read interpretively into the later clause apart from a textual tradition.

[119] See Yigael Yadin, ed., *The Temple Scroll* (Jerusalem: Israel Exploration Society, 1983),2:290–291. Cf. Yigael Yadin, 'Pesher Nahum (4Q pNahum) Reconsidered,' *IEJ* 21 (1971):1–11. While it is true that there is continuing debate as to whether hanging or crucifixion is in view, it seems virtually certain that crucifixion is envisaged. As Yadin notes, the transposition of the MT Deut 21:22 (ותליתמה אותו על העץ וימת) in lines 8 and 10 (והומת ותלית אתו על־עץ), strongly supports this conclusion. Furthermore one must also take into account the fact that תלה was interpreted in terms of crucifixion in the LXX, a rendering

More importantly, early Christian use of the expression (κρε-μάσας) ἐπὶ ξύλου as a reference to Jesus' crucifixion,[120] reflects Biblical language, and Deut 21:22, 23 in particular,[121] suggesting that Jewish traditions which connected the text with crucifixion were taken up by the early believing community. From the beginning of the Christian movement, Jewish believers were conscious of the Deuteronomy passage, and attempted to reconcile faith in Jesus with this text in a variety of ways.[122] Thus there is independent, pre-Pauline evidence that Jesus' crucifixion was thought to have marked him as being under a divine curse, and that the early believing community was sensitive to this claim. The hostility toward the proclamation of the crucified Jesus as Messiah, which prior to his conversion Paul shared with a number of the Jews of his day, and which led him to persecute not merely a radical wing of the early believing community, but the movement itself, most likely was motivated in part by the premise that the crucified Jesus had died under the curse of God.

Christopher Tuckett has recently raised five important objections to the association of Deut 21:23 with Paul's conversion.[123]

---

taken up by Josephus: Esth 7:9: εἶπεν δὲ ὁ βασιλεύς Σταυρωθήτω ἐπ' αὐτοῦ; MT ויאמר המלך תלהו עליו. Cf. LXX Esth 8:12r, Josephus *Ant.* 11.266–268. It is also likely that LXX Josh 8:29 interprets תלה as crucifixion: ἐκρέμασεν ἐπὶ ξύλου δίδυμον. Cf. Georg Bertram, 'κρεμάννυμι,' in *Theologisches Wörterbuch zum Neuen Testament*, ed. G.Kittel (Stuttgart: Kohlhammer, 1938), 3:915–920. On the connection between Deut 21:23, crucifixion and Jewish attitudes toward the practice, see Martin Hengel, 'Mors turpissima crucis: Die Kreuzigung in der antiken Welt und die 'Torheit' des 'Wortes vom Kreuz',' in *Rechtfertigung: Festschrift für Ernst Käsemann*, ed. J. Friedrich, W. Pöhlmann, P. Stuhlmacher (Tübingen: J.C.B. Mohr [Paul Siebeck], 1976),pp. 176–178; Gert Jeremias, *Der Lehrer der Gerechtigkeit*, SUNT 2 (Göttingen: Vandenhoeck& Ruprecht, 1963), pp. 131–135. For a broader survey of how crucifixion was regarded in the ancient world, see now besides Hengel, Heinz-Wolfgang Kuhn, 'Die Kreuzesstrafe während der frühen Kaiserzeit: Ihre Wirklichkeit und Wertung in der Umwelt des Urchristentums,' in *ANRW* 25.1, ed. H.Temporini and W.Haase (Berlin: de Gruyter, 1982), pp. 648–793.

[120] Acts 5:30; 10:39; 1 Pet 2:24–25; Gal 3:13.

[121] Cf. Josh 8:29 [and LXX]; Esth 5:14; LXX Esth 7:9 and 8:12r.

[122] Dietzfelbinger argues that early Christian usage of Deut 21:22–23 in relation to the crucified Jesus was originally a response to Jewish polemicists, *Die Berufung des Paulus*, pp. 36–37. But the Acts texts do not really deal with the objection that the Deuteronomy passage would bring to bear. Rather they assert that God raised Jesus, whom the Jews of Jerusalem (so Luke charges) hung on the tree. The allusion to Deuteronomy therefore does not constitute an apologetic response to the charge that Jesus was accursed. Likewise, the reference to Deut 21:23 in 1 Peter clearly has to do with the concept of Jesus' substitutionary suffering for sin, not an apology directed toward Jewish charges.

[123] C. M. Tuckett, 'Deuteronomy 21,23 and Paul's Conversion,' in *L'Apôtre Paul: Personalité, Style, et Conception du Ministère*, BETL 73, ed. A. Vanhoye (Leuven: Leuven University, 1986), pp. 345–350.

His treatment very effectively brings together the most potent arguments of various scholars, which may be listed as follows:

1) It is not clear that *all* victims of crucifixion were regarded as cursed by God (e.g. the 800 Pharisees crucified by Janneus), hence the text need not have been applicable to Jesus.[124]

2) Paul's persecution of the Church is generally regarded as an example of a broader persecution of the 'Hellenists.' But if only one branch of the Church was persecuted, it is unlikely that Deut 21:23 would have figured in such a persecution. On the basis of this text, the claim that Jesus is Messiah would have made all Jewish Christians subject to persecution.

3) According to the logic of this verse, the corollaries which the post-conversion Paul draws about the Law should have been accessible to every Jewish Christian. Yet much of the earliest Church seems to have remained faithful to the Law.

4) Paul's views of the Law need not follow as a logical result of Deut 21:23. One might argue that in this case there was a miscarriage of justice or that the crucifixion was the doing of the Roman authorities.

5) There is little evidence that the text was used polemically by Jews.

Nevertheless, Tuckett's case fails to be convincing:

1) Deut 21:23 need not have been universally applicable to have been relevant to the case of Messianic claimants. It is the particular notion of a crucified Messiah which appears to have been objectionable to Jews according to Paul's statements.

2) Tuckett's criticism, that the verse is incompatible with the persecution of only a segment of the Church is correct. However, we have seen that Paul represents himself as having persecuted the Church as a whole.

3) It is not necessarily the case that the conclusions which Paul might have drawn about the Law from this text would have been transparent to every Jewish Christian. We will argue that Paul would have been led by this text into acceptance of early traditions which interpreted Jesus' death as an atonement, which because of his intense piety, would have had special significance for him.

4) That Paul's views on the Law *need not* have followed from this passage does not mean that they *did not* follow from this passage. Tuckett here repeats a logical fallacy which frequently appears in this connection. For any Jewish Christian who knew the text, some explanation of Jesus' crucifixion was necessary. The fact that Paul in Galatians

---

[124] See Josephus, *Ant.* 13.14.2.

interprets this crucifixion as a death for others suggests that he may have come to understand it in this way at his conversion.

5) The polemical use of the verse is different from rejection of, or re-action against the message of faith in the crucified Jesus. Paul's attri-bution of Jewish resistance to the Gospel to the cross strongly suggests that Deut 21:23 or other similar traditions figured in this negative reaction.

We have argued in the introduction to this chapter that while there is considerable evidence that Paul's conversion involved a soteriological element, a satisfactory explanation of the dynamics of such a change is necessary. Furthermore, we have suggested that such an explanation must operate within a framework which mat-ches Paul's references to his conversion: 1) one must provide a definite account for Paul's reassessment of the Law; 2) the change in Paul's thought must be explicable on the basis of his vision of the risen Jesus; 3) the conditions which allowed such a change must be particular to Paul's situation.

Our thesis allows such a reconstruction. Paul persecuted the early Christian community because he regarded its exclusivism, expressed in the message of forgiveness of sins through a crucified Messiah, as a threat to *Torah*. Paul's encounter with the risen Jesus vindicated the claims of the believing community. The acceptance of Jesus' Messianic status would have demanded that Paul rethink the meaning of the curse of the *Torah* on the crucified Jesus.[125]

Contrary to the opinion of a number of scholars, the state of dissonance in which Paul must have found himself probably did not lead him to regard the Law as perverted or accursed, having wrongly accused Jesus.[126] On the contrary, Gal 3:13, to which

---

[125] It should be noted that our reconstruction of Paul's conversion does not absolutely depend on his having applied Deut 21:23 to the crucified Jesus prior to his conversion. It is necessary only that he have regarded the proclamation of a crucified Messiah as a threat, and that in conjunction with his conversion, he adopted traditions in which Jesus' death was interpreted as an atonement. Never-theless, given Paul's commitment to *Torah*, it is probable prior to his conversion he made the connection between the text and the crucified Jesus.

[126] This perspective, which has enjoyed considerable support among German scholars (having roots which go back at least to Pfleiderer and Bousset), is curiously similar to the concept of the *ius diaboli*, viz. the Devil having acquired rights over humanity through the Fall, overstepped his jurisdiction in bringing about the death of the innocent Jesus, thus forfeiting his legal privilege. Cf. Wolfhart Pan-nenberg, *Grundzüge der Christologie* (Gütersloh: Gerd Mohn, 1964) pp. 283–285; McGrath, *Iustitia Dei*, 1:58–61. Among scholars who have adopted this view see Stuhlmacher, 'Das Ende des Gesetzes,' p. 30; 'Achtzehnthesen Thesen zur pauli-nischen Kreuzestheologie,' in *Rechtfertigung: Festschrift für Ernst Käsemann*, ed. J.Friedrich, W.Pöhlmann, and P. Stuhlmacher (Tübingen: J.C.B. Mohr [Paul Siebeck],1976), pp. 511–512 (Thesis 2); Dietzfelbinger, *Die Berufung des Paulus*,

appeal is often made for this idea, indicates precisely the opposite. At the time of writing Galatians, Paul still understood the crucified Jesus to have been under the curse of the Law: Χριστὸς ἡμᾶς ἐξηγόρασεν ἐκ τῆς κατάρας τοῦ νόμου γενόμενος ὑπὲρ ἡμῶν κατάρα. Moreover, such a depiction of Paul as radically dismissing the Law cannot explain his use of the concept of love as the fulfillment of the Law in the same letter.[127] Further, Paul's citation of Deut 21:23 (ἐπικατάρατος πᾶς κρεμάμενος ἐπὶ ξύλου) carries the implication that God himself—not merely the Law—pronounced the curse on the crucified.[128] Finally, this view fails to provide an explanation that is specific to Paul's situation. The simple deductive reasoning upon which this suggestion is based (i.e. the Law wrongly cursed Jesus, therefore the Law is accursed), assumes an incredible dullness on the part of other Jewish Christians who did not take such a radical stance with respect to the Law.[129] They must have been incapable of this straightforward logic, since, as noted above, the notion of a crucified Messiah was repugnant to a broad segment of the Jewish people, making it unavoidable that other Jewish Christians also would have been confronted with the questions a crucified Messiah raised.[130]

It is probable instead that Paul's encounter with the risen Jesus led him to accept the early Christian interpretation of Jesus' death as an atoning sacrifice, a tradition which undoubtedly took root in the early Christian community as a means of explaining the

pp. 95– 97; Kim, *The Origin of Paul's Gospel*, pp. 274–275; Beker, *Paul the Apostle*, pp. 184–186.

[127] ὁ γὰρ πᾶς νόμος ἐν ἑνὶ λόγῳ πεπλήρωται, ἐν τῷ ἀγαπήσεις τὸν πλησίον σου ὡς σεαυτόν (Gal 5:14). Admittedly, this reference to love (alone) as the fulfillment of the Law requires a drastic reinterpretation of it. However, under the thesis proposed, it is hard to see how any positive statement regarding the Law would have been in order. Likewise Paul's positive characterization of the Law as ἁγία καὶ δικαία καὶ ἀγαθή (Rom 7:12) would become inexplicable, or would suggest that Paul underwent a second reversal of views, given this proposed reconstruction. Contra Hübner, while Paul reinterprets the Law in Gal 5:14, it is nevertheless *the Law* which he employs as the basis of his appeal to love. It is unlikely that Paul uses the expression ὁ πᾶς νόμος merely as an ironic rejection of his opponents position, since, as Hübner notes, the wording here is different from Gal 5:3 (ὅλος ὁ νόμος). One would expect identical wording if a slogan were under attack. Such a degree of 'mirror-reading' is entirely questionable in any case. Moreover, the admonition of Gal 5:13, 14 clearly serves as a qualification to Paul's own statements regarding freedom. Hence it is hard to attribute the radically negative image of the Law to Paul which Hübner suggests. See, Hans Hübner, *The Law in Paul's Thought*, trans. James C. G. Greig (Edinburgh: T.&T. Clark, 1984), pp. 36–37.

[128] See the interpretive rendering of Deut 21:33 in 11Q Temple 64:10–12.

[129] See Tuckett's criticism of this thesis, above.

[130] Dunn's reconstruction of Paul's logic, viz. since God vindicated the cursed Jesus, he must also favor all those outside the covenant, clearly does not follow necessarily, 'A Light to the Gentiles,' pp. 264–265.

crucifixion of the Messiah. Paul's vision of Jesus therefore would have served as a confirmation of the claim that Jesus' death on the cross took place as a substitution for the guilt of the Jewish people. The attempt to reconcile Jesus' Messianic status and the pronouncement of *Torah* leads inevitably to the conclusion that the curse upon the crucified Jesus was not inherently his own, but was one borne for others: a common enough explanation for the suffering of the innocent.[131] It is unlikely that Paul reached such a conclusion by sheer deductive logic. But it is clear that the appearance of the risen Jesus would have been a strong impetus for Paul to adopt this understanding of Jesus' death, which was already current in the early Church.[132]

Such a conclusion does not fully deal with the effects of Paul's conversion on his view of *Torah* however, since the *meaning* of atonement traditions to Paul at the time of his conversion is not

---

[131] See the discussion by Kim, *The Origin of Paul's Gospel*, pp. 275–278.

[132] That traditions in which Jesus' death was regarded as a substitutionary atonement existed at a very early stage of the development of the Church is clear from the variety which they had attained by the time at which Paul took them up and repeated them in various formulaic expressions. E.g. 1 Cor 11:24; 15:3, 2 Cor 5:21; Rom 4:25. The finer points of the current debate over the origin of the interpretation of Jesus' death as an atonement are beyond the scope of this study. All that is essential is that Paul came into contact with the early Christian interpretation of Jesus' death as an atonement (whether Hellenistic Jewish or Palestinian in form) around the time of his conversion. Martin Hengel, in *The Atonement: A Study in the Origins of the Doctrine in the New Testament* (Philadelphia: Fortress, 1981), has sufficiently dealt with objections to an early Palestinian provenance for the idea. The thesis of Sam K. Williams, that, on the basis of the evidence of 4Macc, the idea of an atoning death was transmitted to Hellenistic Christianity via Hellenistic Judaism in Antioch is artificial and vulnerable on several fronts. See his *Jesus' Death as a Saving Event: The Background and Origin of a Concept*, HDR 2 (Missoula, Mont.: Scholars Press, 1975). As Hengel has repeatedly emphasized, Greek-speaking Jews probably formed a segment of the Church from the very beginning, making a strict division between Palestinian and Diasporic Judaism difficult to maintain. Furthermore, as we have seen in Chapter 2 and as Bernd Janowski has shown, ideas of representative expiation of sin were current in the Qumran community. See 'Sündenvergebung 'um Hiobs willen': Fürbitte und Vergebung in 11QtgJob 38:2f. und Hi 49:9f. LXX,' *ZNW* 73 (1982):251–280. Thus, Williams has not sufficiently addressed the possibility that the understanding of Jesus' death as a substitutionary atonement arose in Palestine. Williams also fails to make the case that ideas of vicarious expiation of sin are absent from such passages as Isa 53 and 2 Macc 7:37, 38. In the latter case he overlooks the fact that whether ἐν ἐμοὶ δὲ καὶ τοῖς ἀδελφοῖς μου is taken as instrumental or locative, the violent death of the brothers is to bring an end to the wrath which has come upon all (ἐπὶ τὸ σύμπαν ἡμῶν γένος), a result which, contra Williams, the following context (8:5) relates to the death of the brothers, through the reference to God's wrath turning to mercy. On this matter, see M. deJonge, 'Jesus' Death for Others and the Death of the Maccabean Martyrs,' in *Text and Testimony: Essays on New Testament and Apocryphal Literature in Honour of A.F.J.Klijn,*

yet clarified.[133] Paul later plainly employs traditions concerning Jesus' death in rejection of obligation to *Torah*.[134] But while ideas of Jesus' redemptive death are susceptible to this interpretation they do not necessarily lead to this result.[135] The reason for Paul's dichotomizing Christ and the Law, by which he distinguished

ed. T. Baarda, et al. (Kampen: J. H. Kok, 1988), pp. 142–151. The mention of two relevant qualifications to Hengel's view is in order. First, there is no apparent reason why ἀποθνῄσκειν ὑπέρ should bear any more once-and-for-all character than the more Semitic description δοῦναι τὴν ψυχὴν ὑπέρ when it is applied to the death of the Messiah. Both of these expressions are susceptible to less radical interpretations with regard to the Law. I.e., neither of these interpretations of Jesus' death *require* that *Torah* or even Temple sacrifices be diminished in importance, although they clearly leave room for such a conclusion. On the traditions of Jesus' death as atonement see, inter alia, H.Riesenfeld, 'ὑπέρ,' in *Theologisches Wörterbuch zum Neuen Testament*, ed. G. Kittel and G. Friedrich (Stuttgart: Kohlhammer, 1969), 8:510–516; Peter Stuhlmacher, 'Jesu Auferweckung und die Gerechtigkeitsanschauung der vorpaulinischen Missionsgemeinden,' in *Versöhnung, Gesetz, und Gerechtigkeit* (Göttingen: Vandenhoeck & Ruprecht, 1981), pp. 66–86; Hermann Ridderbos, 'The Earliest Confession of the Atonement in Paul,' in *Reconciliation and Hope*, ed. Robert Banks (Grand Rapids: Eerdmans, 1974), pp. 76–89; Pannenberg, *Grundzüge der Christologie*, pp. 251–288; E. Lohse, *Märtyrer und Gottesknecht: Untersuchungen zur urchristlichen Verkündigung vom Sühnetod Jesu Christi²*, FRLANT 64 (Göttingen: Vandenhoeck & Ruprecht, 1963); Wilckens, 'Christologie und Anthropologie,' pp. 67–72; Joachim Gnilka, 'Martyriums-paränese und Sühnetod in synoptischen und jüdischen Traditionen,' in *Die Kirche des Anfangs*, ed. R. Schnackenburg, J. Ernst, and J. Wanke (Freiburg: Herder, 1978), pp. 223–276. Bultmann, *Theologie*, pp. 48–50, 292–306; Käsemann, 'Die Heilsbedeutung des Todes Jesu bei Paulus,' in *Paulinische Perspektiven* (Tübingen: J.C.B. Mohr [Paul Siebeck], 1969), pp. 61–107.

[133] For this reason Wilckens' treatment of Paul's taking up atonement traditions is unsatisfactory. He fails to explore their significance for Paul in distinction to other Jewish Christians ('Christologie und Anthropologie,' pp. 69–72). On the understanding of the relation between atonement and justification in the early Christian community, see the discussion of Rom 3:24–26 in Chapter 4, Section II.B.

[134] Gal 1:4; 2:20, 21; 3:13.

[135] No intrinsic equation exists between ideas of redemption and deliverance and the conception of sin as an inescapable 'power.' That such is the case is clear from the use of these images in 4 Macc 6:28,29; 17:21, 22. It is also true that a number of Paul's own statements (e.g. Rom 4:25; 8:32), which may represent borrowed traditions, do not *in themselves* require a radical interpretation of 'sin.' *Pace* Stuhlmacher, who makes a good case that Rom 3:25, 26 reflect a critical stance toward the Law and Temple by Hellenistic Jewish believers ('Jesu Auferweckung und die Gerechtigkeitsanschauung,' pp. 80–84). At bare minimum, though, the interpretation of Jesus' death as an atoning sacrifice among early Jewish Christian believers presumes that the practice of Judaism, i.e. the observance of *Torah*, was deficient among the Jewish people. The crucified, cursed Messiah had borne *someone's* guilt on the cross, just as Eleazar and his family worked atonement for the nation in their death by torture recorded in 4 Maccabees. However, unlike the atoning death of Eleazar and his family, who died as virtuous defenders of the Law, Jesus' death was that of a transgressor: he both died by crucifixion and failed to establish the eschatological blessings which were expected of the Messiah (cf. 4 Ezra12, 13; 2 Bar 29-32; Pss. Sol 17, 18). In its proclamation of vindicated Jesus as Messiah, then, the early believing community assigned a role usually reserved for *Torah* to the atoning death of the crucified Jesus.

himself from many of his contemporaries, is to be found, most likely, in his radical pursuit of *Torah* prior to his conversion. The analysis of Phil 3:49 below will provide further clarification of how Paul's coming to interpret Jesus' death as an atonement for others led him to a radical rejection of the Law as a guarantee of salvation.

C. *Philippians 3:2–11*

1. Textual Analysis. The nature of the opponents whom Paul attacks in Phil 3 continues to be a matter of debate, as is the unity of the letter. The latter issue impinges on the present discussion only in so far as it affects the construal of Paul's adversaries. A considerable variety of opinions have been offered regarding their identity.[136] Despite the appeal of assorted 'unified front' theories (e.g. Judaizing Gnostics [Schmithals], Judaizers with Gnostic tendencies [Koester], or Judaizing *Weisheitslehrer* [Schenk]), it is probably better to interpret Paul as combating a two-fold danger to the Philippian congregation.[137] It is unlikely that a proselytizing movement which advocated observance of *Torah* would exhibit the features of moral laxity which Paul's admonition in 3:17–21 presumes.

Alternative readings of the latter portion of Phil 3 which postulate an attack on faults other than immorality fail to be convincing. Koester contends that the reference to κοιλία (3:19) has to do with maintenance of Jewish food-laws.[138] Schenk sees Paul making a derogatory play on the connection between καρδία and κοιλία in Wisdom literature.[139] Mearns discerns a reference to the male sexual organ (and hence to the demand for circumcision).[140] But despite the evidence which these exegetes adduce in favor of differing readings of κοιλία, the concept of self-indulgence still seems the most fitting given Pauline usage of the term.[141] Furthermore, the

---

[136] For a survey of recent views on Paul's Philippian adversaries see Chris Mearns, 'The Identity of Paul's Opponents at Philippi,' *NTS* 33 (1987):194–204; Wolfgang Schenk, 'Der Philipperbrief in der neueren Forschung,' in *ANRW* 25.4, ed. Wolfgang Haase (Berlin: deGruyter, 1987), pp. 3294–3299.
[137] See Robert Jewett, 'Conflicting Movements in the Early Church as Reflected in Philippians,' *NovT* 12 (1970):362–390.
[138] H. Koester, 'The Purpose of the Polemic of a Pauline Fragment (Phil3),' *NTS* 8 (1962):317–332.
[139] Wolfgang Schenk, *Die Philipperbriefe des Paulus* (Stuttgart: W.Kohlhammer, 1984), pp. 287–289.
[140] Mearns, 'Paul's Opponents at Philippi,' 198–200.
[141] Assuming that Rom 16 is a part of the original letter to Rome, neither the idea of food-laws, nor that of the male sexual organ (and circumcision) is likely in v.18. The latter view seems especially absurd as a reference to Judaizers: δου-

context clearly has to do with a judgment regarding the conduct of the πολλοί who present a threat to the Philippians.[142] It is difficult therefore to see a reference to mere false teaching as Schenk's theory of *Weisheitslehrer* would seem to imply. Moreover, Judaizing opponents would very likely have been just as strongly oriented toward an apocalyptic hope as Paul, making his contrasting allusion to the expectation of the *Parousia* ill-fitting if such teachers were envisioned as adversaries.[143]

The external occasion for the letter is the reception of the gift of the Philippian congregation, sent by the hand of Epaphroditus. That which moves Paul to write what he does is far more theological. It is fairly clear that the most basic problem at work in the mind of Paul is the possibility that he might not be able to visit the church in the near future, either through extension of his imprisonment or through death. While there are no outstanding theological differences between Paul and the Philippians, his prolonged or permanent absence presents certain dangers to the congregation. The loss of a leader like Paul opens the possibility that strife might arise within in the congregation (an instance of which Paul is aware of). Furthermore, the Philippians' obvious attachment to the person of Paul in itself presents the danger that his death might devastate the church. And the constant threat of Paul's opponents, whether Judaizers or libertines, endangers the future adherence of the church to Paul's Gospel.

In response, Paul offers the church a series of models and anti-models which describe what it means to share in the salvation promised by the Gospel. The fundamental pattern is found in Phil 2:5–13, where conformation to (and not merely imitation of) the incarnation, obedience and exaltation of Christ are set forth as constitutive of salvation. This model repeated in Phil 3:1–16. Here Paul expresses the transforming power of the Gospel in his own life. In both instances, the model contains a distinct apocalyptic thrust, which serves to ward off any attempts to foreshorten the full accomplishment of salvation at the Parousia, whether by licentiousness or legalism.

λεύουσιν τῇ ἑαυτῶν κοιλίᾳ! With regard to the former idea, the reference hardly fits the issue of food-laws, which Paul treats as an *adiaphoron*. In contrast, Rom 16:18 envisions opponents who promulgate practices which contradict the teaching the Roman church had received: τὰ σκάνδαλα παρὰ τὴν διδαχὴν ἣν ὑμεῖς ἐμάθετε ποιοῦντας (16:17). Furthermore, an implicit connection between gastronomical pleasures (κοιλία) and illicit sexual ones is inherent in Paul's repetition of the Corinthian slogan in 1 Cor 6:13. Hence the reading of Phil 3:19 as a reference to licentious behavior is not at all outside the Pauline range of meaning of κοιλία.

[142] Phil 3:17, 18.
[143] Phil 3:20, 21.

In contrast to Galatians, Paul presents virtually no defense of his apostolic status in Phil 3. His self-disclosing approach is probably the result of the failure of adversaries to gain a foothold in the Philippian congregation. Paul's authority was not questioned, hence there was no need for him to defend himself. Instead he simply presents himself as a paradigm for the believing community. Consequently, Paul's rehearsal of the radical change which accompanied his faith in Christ is given in an entirely personal and existential manner in Phil 3:2–11, rather than in a description of his actions and movements as in Galatians. In place of a turnabout in behavior, we find a reversal of values.

The significance of this personalizing of the Gospel should not be overlooked. At the time of Paul's writing Phil 3, he was able to articulate his Gospel in terms of his own self-understanding, not that of the status of his Gentile converts. The same is the case in Rom 7.

2. Historical Reconstruction. Paul's claim that he was κατὰ νόμον Φαρισαῖος (Phil 3:5) most likely serves to indicate that he adhered to a strict interpretation of *Torah*.[144] Otto Betz observes that:

> Das Selbstzeugnis des Paulus in Phil. 3, 5f. ist ... das einzige, das wir von einem Pharisäer besitzen, abgesehen von Flavius Josephus (vgl. Vita 12), die aber nicht als eine theologische Rechenschaftsablage eines Pharisäers verstanden sein will.[145]

This passage therefore provides important insight into the theology of first-century Pharisaism—a counterpoint to the earlier Psalms of Solomon.[146]

As we noted in the discussion of Bultmann's interpretation of Paul, this passage in Phil 3 provides no real support for the idea that prior to his conversion Paul regarded his observance of *Torah* as solely a self-effort to obtain righteousness.[147] The fleshly advantages of which Paul makes mention in Phil 3:5, 6 fall into two types: those mediated through his birth and upbringing (περιτομῇ ὀκταήμερος, ἐκ γένους Ἰσραήλ, φυλῆς Βενιαμίν, Ἑβραῖος ἐξ Ἑβραίων) and those which resulted from his own piety (κατὰ νόμον Φαρισαῖος, κατὰ ζῆλος διώκων τὴν ἐκκλησίαν). The final element of the chain, κατὰ δικαιοσύνην τὴν ἐν νόμῳ γενόμενος ἄμεμπτος, is most

---

[144] Cf. Josephus, *J.W.* 2.162–163; *Ant.* 13.297–298.
[145] Betz, 'Paulus als Pharisäer,' p. 54.
[146] On current research regarding the Pharisees, see Gary G. Porton, 'Diversity in Postbiblical Judaism,' in *Early Judaism and Its Modern Interpreters*, ed. R. Kraft and G. Nickelsburg (Atlanta: Scholars Press, 1986), pp. 69–72.
[147] See esp. Bultmann, *Theologie des Neuen Testaments*, p. 268.

likely a summary of all these benefits. Otherwise it would be fundamentally redundant, given the two preceding statements which clearly affirm his devotion to *Torah*.[148] Moreover, the basic issue at stake in Paul's conflict with Judaizers is circumcision.[149] It is likely then, that his final characterization of his Jewish background reaches back as a summary of all his κέρδη, including the first element of the series, which addresses the matter at hand (περιτομῇ ὀκταήμερος). Therefore Paul's 'blamelessness according to the righteousness in the Law' consisted not merely in his own obedience, but in the heritage into which he was born.[150] Consequently, when he refers back to 3:6, μὴ ἔχων ἐμὴν δικαιοσύνην (3:9), he does not imply that such a personal righteousness was entirely self-acquired.

Paul leaves no doubt however, that prior to his conversion he treasured his accomplishments in the faithful observance of *Torah*: ἅτινα ἦν μοι κέρδη (3:7). His claim to having been 'blameless according to the righteousness in the Law' represents his preconversion self-estimation, which his postconversion soteriology exposed as less than adequate. Given that Paul's first-person statements in Rom 7:7–13 are self-inclusive, his claim here is best understood not as an assertion of sinlessness, but of complete compliance with *Torah* interpreted in covenantal terms, through which forgiveness and cleansing were available.[151] Nevertheless, Paul was cognizant of the value of his 'blamelessness.' Whatever the various motivations he might have had for obedience to the Law, among them was the belief that his endeavors had soteriological significance, and that they would be recompensed by God. We have seen the same to be true in our examination of Gal 1:10–17. The preconversion Paul, like the Pss. Sol. and (within a predestinarian framework) 1QS, attached salvific value to obedience.[152]

---

[148] Joachim Gnilka rightly notes: 'Die Tadellosigkeit in der Stellung zum Gesetz war schon durch seine Anhängerschaft bei der Pharisäerpartei kundgetan,' *Der Philipperbrief*, HTKNT (Freiburg: Herder, 1968), p. 190.

[149] Phil 3:2, 3.

[150] Josephus also uses ἄμεμπτος in a sense which includes both behavioral and ritual purity, *Ant.* 3.278–279; 4.228– 230.

[151] Interestingly, Philo makes a sharp distinction between being ἄμεμπτος and three other qualities: εὐάρεστος (Gen17:1), καθαρὸς ἀπὸ ῥύπου (Job14:4), and δίκαιος (*de Mut. Nom.* 47–51). The former involves merely abstinence from sin, the latter three qualities indicate the positive exhibition of virtue. Cf. Goguel, 'Remarques sur un aspect de la conversion de Paul,' pp. 261–262; John M. Espy, 'Paul's 'Robust Conscience' Re-examined,' *NTS* 31 (1985):161-188; Thielman, *From Plight to Solution*,p. 110.

[152] To a certain extent, the postconversion Paul also retained these views. However, he placed them in a radically different constellation. See the excursus at the close of this chapter.

According to Paul, his earlier confidence in his blamelessness was replaced by his hope in a righteousness given solely through Christ:

καὶ εὑρεθῶ ἐν αὐτῷ, μὴ ἔχων ἐμὴν δικαιοσύνην τὴν ἐκ νόμου ἀλλὰ τὴν διὰ πίστεως Χριστοῦ, τὴν ἐκ θεοῦ δικαιοσύνην ἐπὶ τῇ πίστει (Phil 3:9).

The righteousness which Paul here anticipates at the Parousia (εὑρεθεῖν surely has an eschatological significance), was decidedly *not* his, that stood in contrast to the status which he, aided by God, had achieved ἐν νόμῳ. For this reason, he characterizes his former righteousness obtained through the Law not merely as worthless, but as a positive loss, ζημία (Phil 3:7). His earlier acts of obedience were loss precisely because they were gain to him. In his measuring his religious status by them, they had hindered his recognition of the crucified Jesus as Messiah.

The righteousness to which Paul refers in 3:9 is a status which brings vindication, not a behavioral righteousness. The context of eschatological expectation and the exhortation to live in light of this hope, which characterizes the whole of Phil 3, inclines one toward a forensic interpretation from the start.[153] Furthermore, the contrast which Paul draws here is not between a righteousness gained by his own efforts, and that which comes through God's gracious help. He rather says that he has embraced a righteousness which was altogether extrinsic in place of the righteousness which was the product of God's gifts and his obedience. He describes this new righteousness as ἐπὶ τῇ πίστει (3:9), '(given) on the basis of faith,' a phrase which bears an exclusive sense.[154] Paul's strong emphasis on his relationship to Christ further serves to underscore the external, 'christocentric' nature of Paul's hope, in contrast to his former life in which his own behavior was obviously of primary consideration.[155]

---

[153] Cf. Phil 3:12–16, 17–21.

[154] Both the πίστις Χριστοῦ of 3:9 and the γνῶσις Χριστοῦ of 3:8 are to be interpreted as objective genitives in light of the parallel constructions with which they are coupled. The γνῶσις Χριστοῦ is followed by a τοῦ γνῶναι αὐτὸν (3:10), which clearly shows the objective sense of the genitive. Likewise the δικαιοσύνη ἐπὶ τῇ πίστει, which presupposes the act of faith, with all probability reveals the sense of πίστις Χριστοῦ.

[155] It should be noted that the participatory language which takes up much of the rest of Phil 3 displays a decided chronological shift. I.e., while it is directed toward an apocalyptic hope, it has to do with a *present perspective* in virtue of such a hope. In contrast, the εὑρεθεῖν of 3:9 is absolutely eschatological in its orientation. Thus the familiar tension between the indicative as an eschatological pronouncement and the imperative as a present mandate reappears here (see esp. 3:12) J. A. Ziesler produces no convincing arguments to the contrary, *The Meaning of*

Following his vision of the risen Jesus, Paul must have radically reconsidered the value which he once assigned to his heritage and to his practice of Judaism. As we have seen in the discussion above, one theological effect of Paul's conversion was his adoption of the interpretation of Jesus' death as an atoning sacrifice. On this basis, the contrast which is drawn between Paul's pre- and postconversion motivations in Phil 3 may be assigned to the earliest period of Paul's faith in Jesus.

III. PAUL'S CONVERSION AND THE DEVELOPMENT OF HIS UNDERSTANDING OF 'JUSTIFICATION BY FAITH' IN LIGHT OF HIS SELF-REFERENCES

For much of the early believing community, faith in Jesus as Messiah was regarded as a necessary supplement to normal adherence to *Torah*, Jesus' death providing forgiveness for transgressions. Most did not develop a theology of abrogation of the Law. However, given that Paul adopted these traditions at the time of his conversion, they must have taken on more radical consequences for

---

Righteousness in Paul: A Linguistic and Theological Enquiry, SNTSMS20 (Cambridge: Cambridge University Press, 1972), pp. 148–151. Sanders suggests that 'the soteriology of the passage . . . could have been written without the term 'righteousness' at all.' (Sanders, *Paul and Palestinian Judaism*, p. 505). But the behavioral content of the chapter cannot be played off against the forensic, eschatological statement of 3:9. Both Ziesler and Sanders overlook the fact that the whole passage, not merely the part directed at Judaizing opponents, is shaped by Paul's rhetorical aims. As we have indicated above, it is likely that Paul is fighting a two-front battle here. Paul's references to his knowing, attaining, and pursuing (vv.10–14) are clearly introduced as exemplary appeals in the face of the danger presented by the unnamed πολλοί (3:15,17). Neither the forensic nor the dynamic and behavioral can be said to reveal Paul's true *thought* more than the other, since the conditions of the contingent *argument* largely determine the stress each receives in the passage. Moreover, the logical relation between the two manners of describing salvation remains unclear. It is not the case that the language involving righteousness appears in a purely subordinate mode. On the contrary, for the sake of his language concerning righteousness, Paul depersonalizes 'Christ': καὶ ἡγοῦμαι σκύβαλα ἵνα Χριστὸν κερδήσω (3:8). The κερδαίνω, which is transparently used in opposition to Paul's former κέρδη (3:7), can hardly be applied to 'Christ' considered as a person. Instead 'Christ' is here regarded as a salvific commodity, as in the following coordinate καὶ εὑρεθῶ ἐν αὐτῷ (3:9). *Hoc est Christum cognoscere, beneficia eius cognoscere* (Melancthon). The participial expression of 3:9 (μὴ ἔχων ἐμὴν δικαιοσύνην, κ.τ.λ.) therefore expresses the mode in which Paul contemplates the salvific state in Christ, viz., the hope of a eschatological verdict of acquittal on the basis of faith in Christ. Therefore, the knowledge of Christ is explicated in forensic terms in 3:8, 9, just as strongly as it is in terms of power and participation in the following verses (3:10, 11). Neither category supplants the other. *Both* categories, since they conceive of Christ as a salvific entity, interpret and qualify the alternative manner in which Paul speaks of Christ as a person to be obeyed (3:8a).

him. Paul knew himself to have been 'blameless.' When he interpreted the crucifixion of the Messiah as an atonement, he had to
accept it as divinely intended to resolve the problem of transgression and guilt, including his own.[156] It would have been possible
for Paul to assume the stance which other Jewish Christians took,
that the Messiah's death was a supplement to *Torah*, *if* he had been
willing to look upon his earlier zeal as somehow incomplete or
insufficient. Yet he apparently was not willing to pass this judgment on himself, or on the Pharisaic movement of which he had
been a part. So long as he interpreted his previous conformity to
the requirements of *Torah* as flawless, he was forced to regard the
atoning death of the Messiah as signaling the dissolution of the
guarantee of mercy and salvation he once found in the Law.

It is possible to describe the crisis which Paul faced in social
terms as well. As we noted above, the idea of a crucified Messiah
challenged the validity of the whole of apocalyptic Jewish piety.
Paul's investment in the structures of Pharisaism was so complete
that his acceptance of Jesus' messianic status demanded that he
regard them, and *Torah* which they embodied, as done away with.
The crucified Christ replaced the Law as guarantor of salvation.

Paul's understanding of sin as an overwhelming 'power' and his
linking of the Law and sin would have become possible through his
coming to interpret Jesus' death on the cross as a divine act of
atonement.[157] Following his encounter with the risen Jesus, Paul

---

[156] This guilt included, but would not have been limited to, Paul's persecution
of believers. Kim states the matter too strongly when he implies that Paul was
thereby led to the conclusion that the Law leads to sin (*The Origin of Paul's Gospel*,
pp. 280–281). Rather, it was Paul's mistaken interpretation of Jesus' death in the
light of the Law which was called into question by his encounter with Jesus. The
Law had not prevented him from this error—it had revealed its weakness, but it
was not concomitantly shown to be sinful (cf. Rom 7:7!). Grundmann formulates
the matter better when he states that the revelation of the risen Jesus showed Paul
that *seine Gesetzerfüllung* was his sin ('Paulus, aus dem Volke Israel,' p. 270).

[157] This is precisely the direction which a number of Paul's statements take,
when he interprets Christ's atoning death in terms of redemption, deliverance or
'justification' (e.g. Gal 1:4; Rom 3:24–26; 4:25; 5:6–8; 2 Cor 5:21). The significance of the theme of atonement for Paul continues to be a contested question in
current scholarship. Do Paul's references to Jesus' atoning death represent relics of
inherited traditions which Paul supplants with alternative conceptions of Jesus'
death? Or are the various interpretations of Jesus' death which appear in Paul's
letters developments of the idea that Jesus' death was an atoning sacrifice, and
essentially related to this concept? Both Bultmann and Käsemann, e.g., argue that
while Paul accepts notions of Jesus' death as an atoning sacrifice, such ideas
recede in Paul's thought. Instead, freedom from sin as a 'Power' stands in the
foreground. See Bultmann, *Theologie*, pp. 292–306 (33); Käsemann, 'Heilsbedeutung des Todes Jesu,' pp. 72–84. Likewise, Hübner, 'Paulusforschung seit 1945,'
pp. 2709–2721. The widespread acceptance of traditions in which Jesus' death
was interpreted as an atonement within the early Christian community means

in retrospect regarded his former life as having been subject to sin.[158] Despite his observance of its requirements, the Law had failed to guarantee salvation from the apocalyptic manifestation of God's final judgment. God had made atonement apart from the provisions of *Torah* in the crucifixion of the Messiah. Therefore, the relationship between Paul's preconversion experience of rebellion (cf. Rom 7:7–13), and his later interpretation of sin as a death-producing 'power' is understandable on the basis of this reconstruction of Paul's conversion.

Likewise, Paul's conclusion that righteousness is given solely through Christ would have been concomitant to his adoption of early Christian traditions of Jesus' death as an atonement. Because his acceptance of such traditions would have had quite specific and significant implications for him, the issue of forensic justification must have been inherent to the very nature of his conversion. What he once thought was necessary and sufficient preparation for the apocalyptic entrance of the kingdom, he came to regard as not only insufficient but unnecessary. In this manner he radically altered his soteriology and rejected the 'pattern of religion' which he once embraced. The righteousness which he, by God's gracious help, had formerly attained in the Law, he came to regard as an obstacle to the righteousness mediated through faith in Christ. While in his former pursuit of the Law, he could view the righteousness

---

that they would have been relatively uncontested. For this reason Paul rarely, if ever, stresses *merely* that Jesus' death was an atonement. Where he does employ such traditions, he assigns considerable importance to them (Rom 3:24–26; 1 Cor 15:3). Hence Paul's emphasis on the significance of Jesus' atoning death (rather than on the atonement itself), should not lead to the conclusion that the interpretation of Jesus' death as an atonement was unimportant to Paul. Moreover, it is not true, as is sometimes suggested, that the various modes of expressing the meaning of Jesus' death (vicarious sacrifice, redemption, deliverance) stand in opposition to the idea of a propitiatory sacrifice. Already in Hellenistic Judaism the images of cultic sacrifice, redemption, and deliverance could be combined (4 Macc 6:28, 29; 17:21, 22). The same is the case for Paul. For example, he can connect Christ's giving himself for sins (n.b. *plural*), to deliverance from this age in Gal 1:4. Here he moves from the idea of forgiveness of transgressions, stemming from the interpretation of Jesus' death in cultic terms, to that of deliverance from evil as a present 'power.' He likewise interprets Christ's bearing of the Law's curse as redemption (Gal 3:13, cf. Gal 4:5). Moreover, for Paul the notion of sin as a 'power' is related to acts of transgression. He corroborates his assertion that all are under sin in Rom 3:9 with a catena of Scriptural citations which include various iniquities (Rom 3:10–18). Likewise, he asserts that if God has not raised Christ, i.e. if he has not performed the act which secures freedom from the power of sin and death, the Corinthians are 'still in (their) sins' (1 Cor 15:7).

[158] Of course Paul most likely was not plagued by a struggle with guilt after his conversion, either. In a sense, one can affirm with Sanders that Paul reasoned from solution to plight (*Paul and Palestinian Judaism*, pp. 442–447).

which he attained as due to a combination of God's prevenient gifts and his own faithfulness, his encounter with the crucified and risen Jesus would have by its very nature have been understood as a salvific event in which Paul played no contributory role.[159] This is the manner in which Paul formulates his eschatological hope in Phil 3:9: he expects a righteousness solely ἐκ θεοῦ, to the exclusion of his cooperative efforts. Paul therefore came to a radical reformulation of the relationship between mercy and obedience as a result of his coming to faith in Jesus as Messiah. Our conclusion partially corroborates Stendahl's thesis and simultaneously overthrows it. It was not Paul's 'introspective conscience' which led him to a fresh understanding of righteousness. Rather it was Paul's very boldness of conscience regarding his earlier practice of Judaism which allowed him to come to a new understanding of righteousness.[160]

Just as the soteriology of 1QS and the Pss. Sol. reflect social structures, Paul's theological conversion had a social dimension. The narrow and definite boundaries drawn by the Qumran community between the righteous and the wicked reveal the sectarian nature of the group. The Pss. Sol. were composed as a result of Pharisaic struggles with other Jews, and were intended to foster allegiance to group norms. Paul, likewise, was conscious of the religious status which he derived from the Jewish society to which he belonged, and sought to preserve the structures which reinforced his piety in the face of a perceived threat from the believing community. His appropriation of traditions which interpreted Jesus' death on the cross as an atonement led him to his new understanding of righteousness as an unconditional gift. It was as a result of this shift in soteriology that Paul was able to embrace Gentiles as equal heirs to salvation, and to engage in a mission in which the distinction between Jew and Gentile was dismantled.

As we stated at the outset of this chapter, it is probably wrong to think that Paul's soteriology changed at the very instant of his vision of the resurrected Jesus. Such a massive reorientation is hardly likely in a momentary experience. But given the religious dilemma that the idea of a crucified Messiah would have presented, some resolution would have been necessary within a fairly short period of time. Therefore it is likely that Paul accepted traditions which interpreted Jesus' death as an atonement early in his life as a believer in Jesus. The crux of the matter has been

---

[159] Cf. 1 Cor 15:9, 10.
[160] Stendahl, 'The Apostle Paul and the Introspective Conscience of the West,' pp. 199–215.

argued above: the shift in Paul's soteriology was intrinsically connected to his conversion, and preceded his engagement in Law-free
mission to Gentiles.

Nevertheless, a difference must be recognized between the shift
in Paul's soteriology following his conversion, which can be described only in the most general language, and the arguments which
he later enunciates in Galatians, Phil 3 and Romans. The arguments regarding 'justification by faith apart from works of the Law'
constitute a development in Paul's thought, which was precipitated
by the struggle over the issue of Gentile circumcision and table-
fellowship between Jewish and Gentile believers. We have noted
already that Paul went through a period of uncertainty when first
confronted with a challenge from Judaizers. And it is scarcely
imaginable that Paul's companion in Gentile mission, Barnabas,
would have wavered at Antioch if earlier he had been exposed to
the full force of the polemic Paul employs in the letter to Galatia.[161]
Cephas' behavior at Antioch likewise suggests that at Jerusalem
relations between believing Jews and Gentiles had not yet been
fully discussed.[162] One must suppose that Paul operated on the
basis of his insight regarding God's gift of righteousness through
Christ prior to fully enunciating his position.[163] The development
of arguments and the elaboration of his views were distinct from his
own acceptance of a righteousness given through faith in Christ
alone. Our conclusions do not exclude development in Paul's
thought, which seems to have occurred in response to conflict over
the relationship of the Gentile mission to the Jewish believing
community.

We shall see, in fact, that Paul's insight into 'justification by
faith' underwent further development. Paul's use of 'justification'
to address the new situation which the church at Rome represented
will be the subject of Chapter 4.

EXCURSUS: OBEDIENCE AND GRACE
IN THE THEOLOGY OF PAUL'S LETTERS

The postconversion Paul expected that believers in Christ would be
rewarded (or punished) for their conduct on earth.[164] However, he

---

[161] Cf. Gal 2:13.

[162] Gal 2:11–14.

[163] As we have observed, 1 Thess may be counted as evidence of this situation,
as may Paul's interaction with the 'pillars' in Jerusalem, reported in Gal 2:1–10.
Luke's report of Paul's preaching in Pisidean Antioch is completely plausible
(Acts 13:38, 39).

[164] E.g. Rom 2:6–10; 14:10–12; 2 Cor 5:10.

also assigns an absolute priority to God's obedience-producing work within the believer.[165] In Phil 2:12, 13, the priority of the working of God (θεὸς γάρ ἐστιν ὁ ἐνεργῶν ἐν ὑμῖν καὶ τὸ θέλειν καὶ τὸ ἐνεργεῖν ὑπὲρ τῆς εὐδοκίας) stands over against the imperative, μετὰ φόβου καὶ τρόμου τὴν ἑαυτῶν σωτηρίαν κατεργάζεσθε. In the self-reference in 1 Cor 15:10, the structure of the paradox is altered, but the effect is nearly the same. Here the ἐγώ is fully excluded from the outset (χάριτι δὲ θεοῦ εἰμι ὅ εἰμι, καὶ χάρις αὐτοῦ ἡ εἰς ἐμὲ οὐ κενὴ ἐγενήθη), and appears in the latter portion of the verse as a purely passive vehicle for the grace of God: οὐκ ἐγὼ δὲ ἀλλὰ ἡ χάρις τοῦ θεοῦ [ἡ] σὺν ἐμοί. Paul's activity is interjected, but is qualified by the bracketing references to grace (περισσότερον αὐτῶν πάντων ἐκοπίασα). His statements on reward are best understood in this framework, since generally they are accompanied by references to the 'indicative' of gracious divine action in Christ.[166]

The Qumran materials, particularly 1QS, display the same sort of tension between divine sovereignty and human obedience. Both Paul and 1QS, because of their adherence to such predestinatory ideas, construe grace and obedience in a way which might anachronistically be designated 'Augustinian.'[167] But in contrast to the Qumran community, Paul never attaches an atoning value to the behavior of believers in Christ. Thus despite the proximity of Paul's understanding of grace to that of Qumran Essenism, it is unlikely that his preconversion thought was shaped in a fundamental manner by Essenes.[168] Josephus distinguishes between the Essenes and Pharisees precisely on the matter of human free will.[169] And there is no evidence of a deterministic stance outside the Qumran setting.[170] Gerhard Maier observes that the teaching on the two spirits (1QS 3:13–4:26), is given the heading, 'for the Instructor, to instruct and teach all the sons of light. . .,' most likely indicating that the predestinarian teaching which follows was regarded as a distinctive doctrine of the community.[171] The question of how Paul the Pharisee came to adopt a predestinatory stance would entail an investigation of its own.

---

[165] Phil 3:12; Phil 2:12, 13; 1 Cor 15:10.

[166] See, e.g., Rom 2:16; 14:7–9; 2 Cor 5:1–5.

[167] Cf. Augustine, *Epist.* 194.5.19: *cum Deus coronat merita nostra, nihil aliud coronat quam munera sua.*

[168] It is not impossible, of course, that Paul did encounter Essenes and was familiar with their thought.

[169] Ant. 13.171–173; 18.11–22.

[170] The Pss. Sol. differ from the Qumran materials in this regard, affirming human freedom, Pss. Sol. 9:4, 5.

[171] Maier, *Mensch und freier Wille*, pp. 222–233, 261.

CHAPTER FOUR

THE FUNCTION OF 'JUSTIFICATION BY FAITH'
IN THE LETTER TO ROME

I. INTRODUCTION

The decision to examine the function of Paul's arguments concerning 'justification by faith' in Romans hardly requires a defense. The theme of righteousness as a 'gift' clearly plays a significant role in the letter.[1] In Romans, moreover, it receives its fullest and final treatment by Paul.

We have found that Paul's conversion led to his interpreting Jesus' atoning death as the source of forensic justification. Conflicts with Judaizers subsequently forced him to develop arguments to defend his practice of Gentile mission which was facilitated by this understanding of the Gospel. We shall see that in his letter to Rome Paul employs 'justification by faith' to address fresh issues. Romans therefore provides evidence that a forensic conception of justification assumed a larger role in Paul's thought than merely that of a means by which the place of Gentiles within the Church could be maintained.

In our survey of interpreters of Paul in the first chapter of this study, we saw that efforts to describe Paul as a theologian have been hampered by the lack of reasonable criteria by which Paul's personal beliefs might be distinguished from the arguments which he employs solely for the sake of a contingent situation. We will attempt to overcome this difficulty by focussing our attention on Paul's aim in writing Romans. If Paul's purpose for this letter can be determined, the functions served by its arguments may be described. One may ask why 'justification by faith' appears as a topic in Paul's argument, how it is used, and what Paul hoped to

---

[1] The reasons for restricting the discussion of 'justification' to its forensic aspect in this study have been enunciated in the treatment of Käsemann's views in Chapter 1, Section V. This approach will be continued in the analysis of Paul's purpose in writing to Rome which follows, with some additional exegetical support being given for accepting a conceptual distinction between the forensic and behavioral aspects of the divine gift of righteousness.

achieve through it. In this manner, the text of the letter may be used to provide some control for theories about 'what Paul really thought' when he wrote.

This approach is clearly superior to the alternative method of playing off the structure of one letter against another, as for example Sanders does in his interaction with Bultmann.[2] The selection and order of arguments in a given letter are in large part determined by the situation addressed. One cannot know whether the argument of Galatians or that of Romans more closely represents Paul's reasoning, unless one knows what Paul was attempting to do in each letter, and why he wrote what he did. The logic of Paul's argument, taken by itself, does not necessarily provide a clue to his thinking. Paul's convictions, to the extent that they reveal themselves at particular points in time, are to be found in his aims in writing.[3]

The elucidation of Paul's purposes in writing also provides advantages over the use of the test of logical coherence as a means of evaluating the 'real' content of Paul's thought.[4] As we noted at the outset, the considerable historical distance between the interpreter and Paul and the fact that we possess only a few of Paul's occasional letters mean that gaps and breaks which appear to us as inconsistencies are to be expected. However, it may be presumed that Paul in the act of communication attempted to produce consistent and effective arguments. If the goal of the interpreter is to understand Paul (and not merely to examine his isolated statements), the task of determining *why and how Paul thought himself to be consistent* must be prior to that of determining where he might be inconsistent. The attempt to locate Paul's 'thought' by looking for logical consistencies or inconsistencies *alone* therefore illegitimately by-passes the necessary, intermediate step of analyzing Paul's aims in writing and how he attempted to effect them.

Our references to 'Paul's aims in writing' touch upon the notion of a 'rhetorical situation,' which through the renewed interest in rhetorical criticism has received increasing attention from Biblical scholars.[5] This concept provides an important additional step to

---

[2] Sanders, *Paul and Palestinian Judaism*, pp. 474–497.

[3] Even Paul's 'presuppositions' and the 'hermeneutical methods' which he employs in interpreting inherited traditions must be regarded as unreliable indicators of his thought, since these factors, too, are shaped by the argumentative situation.

[4] Cf. the discussion of Räisänen's views in Chapter 1, Section VIII.C.

[5] The dimensions of the rhetorical criticism are manifold, ranging from stylistics and epistolography, to the study of the theory and practice of rhetoric in antiquity, and further to the philosophical and hermeneutical fields of the 'new' rhetoric. See

the investigation of the historical situation of a text. Both approaches stress the importance of determining the intended audience and the aims of the author in writing. However, the idea of the 'rhetorical situation' is more precise:

> Rhetorical situation may be defined as a complex of persons, events, objects, and relations presenting an actual or potential exigence which can be completely or partially removed if discourse, introduced into the situation, can so constrain human decision or action as to bring about the significant modification of the exigence.[6]

The recognition that communication involves a prompting force demands that the interpreter of texts ask what perception of the audience and its attendant circumstances caused the author to write. Therefore, rather than allowing the historical situation and the author's purpose to remain only loosely correlated, the use of the concept of a 'rhetorical situation' requires the articulation of a specific reason for communication.[7]

This insight is particularly valuable for the interpretation of Paul's letter to Rome.[8] The letter was penned in a multi-faceted

---

the brief survey of the use of rhetorical criticism in Biblical studies by Wilhelm Wuellner, 'Where is Rhetorical Criticism Taking Us?' *CBQ* 49 (1987): 448–463. It is beyond the scope of this investigation to probe the historical and philosophical dimensions of rhetoric. Nevertheless, in so far as rhetorical theory is an attempt to describe the 'universal aspects of human communication,' some of its more patent insights may be justifiably employed as a means of better understanding Paul. See George A. Kennedy, *New Testament Interpretation through Rhetorical Criticism* (Chapel Hill: University of North Carolina Press, 1984), pp. 10–12. Even aside from the historical question of Paul's familiarity with rhetorical technique, there are good reasons for applying rhetorical theory to Paul's letters. As Franz Schnider and Werner Stenger note, New Testament letters are directed toward communication with specific groups and thus may be regarded as *Redeersatz* (Franz Schnider and Werner Stenger, *Studien zum neutestamentlichen Briefformular* NTTS 11 [Leiden: Brill, 1987], pp. 26–27). This observation is especially applicable to the letters of Paul, which serve as a means of mediating his apostolic presence. Cf. R. W. Funk, 'The Apostolic Parousia,' in *Christian History and Interpretation*, ed. W. R. Farmer, C. F. D. Moule, and R. R. Niebuhr (Cambridge: Cambridge University Press, 1967), pp. 249–268.

[6] Lloyd Bitzer, 'The Rhetorical Situation,' *Philosophy and Rhetoric* 1 (1968):6. I am grateful to Dr. Neil Elliott for calling to my attention the articles by Bitzer and Consigny.

[7] Scott Consigny's critique of Lloyd Bitzer's description of the rhetorical situation is an important correction in that it allows for the creativity of the rhetor, 'Rhetoric and Its Situations,' *Philosophy and Rhetoric* 7 (1974):175–186.

[8] Among the growing number of treatments of Romans in terms of rhetorical criticism, see: Wilhelm Wuellner, 'Paul's Rhetoric of Argumentation in Romans: An Alternative to the Donfried-Karris Debate Over Romans,' in *The Romans Debate*, ed. Karl P. Donfried (Minneapolis: Augsburg, 1977), pp. 152–174; Robert Jewett, 'Following the Argument of Romans,' *WW* 6 (1986):382–389; Kennedy, *New Testament Interpretation*, pp. 152–156; David E. Aune, *The New Testament in Its Literary Environment*, LEC 8 (Philadelphia: Westminster, 1987), pp. 219–221.

historical context. Paul writes in preparation to travel to Jerusalem with contributions from Gentile churches which he had established. He plans to proceed via Rome to Spain, where he will continue his mission to Gentiles. His letter to Rome, informing his readers of his plans, constitutes his first contact with the church there. The complexity of this situation allows interpreters considerable room for theorizing about the purpose of Romans. Yet the framework of the letter, Paul's expressions of intent, and his appeals to the church for behavioral responses are rarely used to provide a unified and comprehensive statement of his aim in writing.

This lack may be found, for example, even in Dunn's careful introduction to Romans.[9] Dunn does not ignore Paul's indications of his aim in writing, of course. But Paul's own remarks and Dunn's historical reconstruction are presented as equivalent considerations. Paul's request for prayer (Rom 15:30), which Dunn construes as an indication of Paul's purpose in writing, is immediately followed by the suggestion that at this crucial stage in his career Paul might have wanted to produce a summary of his thought—with the result that he penned Romans.[10] Shouldn't information Paul gives about himself in the text be kept distinct from the surmise of the interpreter, however valid it might be? I.e., isn't the reconstruction of the 'implied author' a separate task from that of describing the 'real author'? Even though there is no evidence to suggest that the two are radically divergent in this case, methodological clarity demands that they be distinguished. Moreover, despite the space he gives to the discussion of rhetorical criticism, Dunn fails to enunciate an overall function for the letter. As is frequently done in the interpretation of Romans, he is content to speak of Paul's 'purposes.' There is no doubt that there are multiple aspects to Paul's aim in writing to Rome. But is it impossible to formulate a coherent description of Paul's intent? If one does not attempt such a formulation, has one succeeded in discovering why Paul composed the massive theological argument which constitutes the body of the letter?

---

[9]   Dunn, *Romans*, pp. xxxix–lxxii. Dunn is hardly alone. The same problem may be found in the recent monograph by A. J. M. Wedderburn, *The Reasons for Romans* (Edinburgh: T. & T. Clark, 1988), pp. 6-7. See also the commentaries by Wilckens, Cranfield and others. Cf. however, the focussed discussions of Dieter Zeller, 'Der Zweck des Schreibens,' *Der Brief an die Römer*, RNT (Regensburg: Friedrich Pustet, 1985), pp. 15–19 and Heinrich Schlier, *Der Römerbrief*, HTKNT 6 (Freiburg: Herder, 1977), pp. 6–9.

[10]   Dunn, *Romans*, pp. liv–lviii.

In the discussion of the purpose of Romans which follows, it is presumed that the 'implied' Paul is coherent (though, of course, not coextensive) with the 'real' Paul. It is hardly illegitimate to do so: virtually all explanations for the letter assume this congruence, since there is little in Romans to suggest otherwise. This assumption has an important methodological ramification. We will not ignore the historical situation in which Paul wrote. But we will give primary consideration to Paul's indications of his aim with his audience.

The recognition that Paul's letters represent his attempts to persuade specific audiences of the value of certain beliefs and behavior leads the interpreter to view the structure of the letters not merely as epistolary conventions, but as contributing to the development of arguments. The framework of a letter then becomes something more than a dispensable formality. The prescript and thanksgiving which begin the letter function in a manner similar to the *exordium* of an argument: Paul here attempts to gain the sympathy of his audience for the ideas which he will subsequently lay before them. Likewise, the close of the letter, with its final exhortations, greetings, and *Gnadenwunsch* operates like the *peroratio*, where one would expect to find an enunciation of the desired effect Paul hoped to achieve. In the following consideration of the purpose of Romans, particular attention will be given, then, to clues which the framework of the letter might give regarding Paul's aim in writing.[11]

We shall see that Romans was not composed under direct pressure from adversaries in Rome or in Jerusalem. Rather, Paul wrote in order to gain support for his apostolic mission, and to implant his theology in a church which was already in fairly close agreement with him. The theme of forensic righteousness therefore functions as something more than a *mere* polemical doctrine in Romans. Paul's assertions concerning 'justification' reflect his own understanding of salvation and of the community of faith at the time of his writing the letter.

A significant corollary to this thesis arises from the ways Paul employs the theme of 'justification by faith' in Romans. We shall see that in Rom 5:1–11 and 9:30–10:21, Paul uses 'justification by faith' to address the Gentile members of his audience, and that in Rom 7:14–25 his argument presumes that righteousness given freely through Christ is relevant to Jewish believers at Rome. The

---

[11] See now L. Ann Jervis's valuable study, *The Purpose of Romans: A Comparative Letter Structure Investigation*, JSNTSup 55 (Sheffield: JSOT Press, 1991).

theme therefore receives a broadened application in Romans, extending its significance beyond the sphere of Jew-Gentile relations.

The unity of Rom 16:1–23 with the original letter to Rome is presumed throughout the investigation which follows. Because of its importance to our thesis, a defense of the originality of Rom 16 appears in an excursus at the close of the chapter.

II. THE PURPOSE OF THE LETTER TO ROME

A. Appeals and Disclosures of Intent

In nineteen instances in Romans, Paul makes statements of self-disclosure which directly convey concerns and intentions related to his audience.[12] Each of these deserves to be considered in formulating a description of his purpose in writing. Some of these statements have relevance primarily for their immediate context.[13] Others demand particular attention because of their location at strategic points in the discourse of the letter. We will focus our attention on these.

The three appeals which are introduced by παρακαλῶ (I encourage, urge) are of special significance.[14] Carl Bjerkelund has shown that these clauses indicate transitions to new sections.[15] One might expect them to express the intended effect of a preceding or following portion of the letter.[16] The location of the παρακαλῶ clauses in

---

[12] Rom 1:8, 9, 11, 13; 3:5; 6:19; 7:1; 9:1; 10:2; 11:13, 25; 12:1, 3; 15:15, 24, 30; 16:1, 17, 19.

[13] Paul's disclosures of intent in the central part of the body of the letter signal his concerns in context (Rom 3:5; 6:19; 7:1; 9:1; 10:2). We will not treat them in detail here.

[14] Rom 12:1; 15:30; 16:17. In two instances further appeals are related to the παρακαλα clauses, so that one may treat Rom 12:1–3 and 16:17–19 as units. Likewise Rom 15:30–33 must be considered as a whole.

[15] Carl J. Bjerkelund, *Parakalô: Form, Funktion und Sinn der parakalô-Sätze in den paulinischen Briefen* (Oslo: Universitetsforlaget, 1967), p. 189. Bjerkelund also argues that Paul's use of the word παρακαλῶ implies neither a command nor an entreaty, but a personal appeal. He suggests that Paul employs παρακαλῶ when the question of his apostolic authority is not in question. In such instances he can appeal to the congregation as fellow believers. But Bjerkelund draws a false dichotomy here. Paul can make a personal appeal with παρακαλαῶ where his authority is in question (2 Cor 10:1). And Paul's appeal through familial imagery (ἀδελφοί) would seem to serve rather than to displace the aim of obtaining recognition of his apostolic authority at Rome. It is better to say that Paul uses παρακαλῶ when he wants to create a *pathos* based on a common faith in Christ, than to presume as Bjerkelund does, that Paul's authority was not in question in letters in which he uses παρακαλῶ.

[16] In general, Paul's usage of παρακαλῶ clauses bears out this judgment. Paul's appeal to the Corinthian church for unity in 1 Cor 1:10 is clearly related to the following discussion of the impropriety of boasting, the foolishness of the cross, and the role of those who proclaim it. See also 1 Cor 4:16 at the close of the

Romans strongly suggests that they to some extent reveal Paul's purpose in writing. The first such clause at Rom 12:1, marks the shift from theological argument to parenesis. The second closes the parenetic material.[17] The final παρακαλῶ clause introduces the concluding greetings.[18] The appearance of these exhortations at nodal points of the letter conveys the impression that they express various aspects of Paul's aim.

1. Rom 1:1–15. The prescript of Romans, 1:1–7, differs from the usual prescripts to Paul's letters in providing a detailed definition of his apostolic authority.[19] Paul states that he has been called by Jesus Christ as apostle of the Gentiles, among whom those called as saints in Rome are included.[20] This apostolic calling is a commission to proclaim the Gospel (ἀφωρισμένος εἰς εὐαγγέλιον θεοῦ) which will secure the 'obedience of faith' among all the Gentiles, including those at Rome. This initial reference to apostolic authority over believers at Rome represents Paul's first direct contact with the church as a whole and provides an important indication of his aim in writing.

Correspondingly, Paul states a particular understanding of the Gospel, which is relevant to the letter. The Gospel has been announced by the prophets in the Scriptures. Its central focus is Jesus Christ, God's son, who, κατὰ σάρκα, became the son of David, and who was designated υἱὸς θεοῦ by resurrection from the dead.[21] The clear appeal to Jewish themes indicates from the start that Paul intends to impress upon the church at Rome that his Gospel represents the fulfillment of divine promise.[22]

Having defined the essential 'theological' parameters of the

---

same section. Cf. 1 Cor 16:15. Likewise 1 Thess 4:10 is transparently related to Paul's securing obedience to his teaching in Thessalonica. This verse leads directly to the following parenesis. The appeal to Euodia and Syntyche to agree with one another (Phil 4:2) may be readily related to Paul's earlier exhortation to unity and humility, Phil 3 being an intervening excursus.

[17] Rom 15:30–33.

[18] Rom 16:25–27 is probably not original.

[19] Cf. the brief introductions in 1 Cor 1:1; 2 Cor 1:1; Gal 1:1; Phil 1:1; 1 Thess 1:1. As in Phil 1:1, Paul introduces himself first as δοῦλος Χριστοῦ Ἰησοῦ. Wilckens plausibly suggests that Paul's placing of the title 'slave' before that of 'apostle' is due to his need to introduce himself as apostle to a church which he had not founded (*Der Brief an die Römer*, 1:61–62). See Jervis, *The Purpose of Romans*, pp. 72–73.

[20] Rom 1:1, 5–7.

[21] Rom 1:2–4. It is generally agreed, on the basis of unusual vocabulary and parallelism of style that Paul takes up an earlier confession here.

[22] This theme of fulfillment runs through the letter: e.g. Rom 3:21; 4:23–25; 9:30–33; 12:1, 2; 15:7–9.

relation between himself and the Roman community, Paul continues in the thanksgiving period and following narrative by indicating his emotional disposition within this relation, inviting reciprocation.[23] He is aware of them. They are objects of constant concern in his prayers. And he always prays for the opportunity to see them.[24] He wants to 'impart a spiritual gift' and to be 'encouraged by one another's faith' while among them.[25]

In his final statement about himself, he provides an explanation for the discrepancy between the concern he has expressed and his failure to visit them. He is obligated not only to those in Rome, but to 'the rest of the Gentiles.'[26] He acknowledges the status of Rome while offering an indirect apology, by dividing the Gentiles into the classes of Greek and barbarian, a distinction which is repeated in the descriptives 'wise' and 'without understanding.'[27] Although until now he has been constrained to evangelize the uneducated barbarians of the provinces, the cultured Greeks in Rome lie within his sphere of responsibility as well. Paul here anticipates his later explanation for not yet coming to Rome.[28]

Rom 1:15 has often been taken to reveal a fluctuation from Paul's stance in 1:11–12. Although he addresses them as αδελφοί, he now says, 'I have long been eager to preach the Gospel in Rome.' It would be wrong to conclude, however, that Paul here suddenly views his audience as missionary objects. Proclamation of the Gospel involves not merely initial evangelization, but Paul's continuing ministry to his churches. Or more properly put, Paul regards the whole of his task as proclamation of the Gospel.[29]

---

[23] See Schnider and Stenger, *Studien zum neutestamentlichen Briefformular*, pp. 44–68, who distinguish between the thanksgiving (1:8–12), which serves as a *captatio benevolentiae*, and a following self-recommendation (1:13–15), which provides an *ethos* appeal in preparation for the argument of the letter.

[24] Rom 1:9–10. Cf. Rom 15:30–33.

[25] Rom 1:11–12.

[26] Rom 1:13.

[27] Rom 1:14.

[28] Cf. Rom 15:17–24.

[29] See Gal 1:8, 9; 4:13, and especially 1 Cor 9:15–18. Probably 1 Cor 1:17 should be understood in this way. The resolution of this problem severely undercuts Schmithals's partitioning of Romans, cf. *Der Römerbrief als historisches Problem* (Gütersloh, Gerd Mohn, 1975), pp. 162–180. Peter Stuhlmacher has recently pointed to a different solution to this difficulty, 'Der Abfassungszweck des Römerbriefes,' *ZNW* 77 (1986):186–187. The translation of the verbless cause of 1:15 might be translated with past time. But it would be a bit odd for Paul to introduce the body of the letter with a statement about what he once wanted to do. And the statement of 1:13 clearly applies to his present (ἐκωλύθην ἄχρι τοῦ δεῦρο), as does the immediately preceding present tense clause. The verse is best translated with a perfective aspect.

Since his letter serves as a temporary substitute for his visit, this statement of intent sends a strong signal that Paul's purpose in writing is to proclaim the Gospel to the church at Rome. His well-known introduction to the body of the letter, 'for I am not ashamed of the Gospel' confirms this conclusion. And as we shall see, further disclosures which begin and conclude the parenetic material give it added support.[30]

2. *Rom 11:13, 25–27.* Although Paul's expressions of intent in 11:13, 25–27 are directly related only to Rom 9–11, and not the letter has a whole, they provide a clue for discerning the function of Paul's initial formulation of the Gospel in Jewish terms in 1:3, 4. There, as well as here and elsewhere in the letter, Paul is concerned that the Gentiles within the church recognize that the Gospel is the message of the gracious dealings of the one God of Israel.

Paul's address to Gentiles, which begins implicitly at Rom 9:1,[31] marks a return to his initial characterization of his audience in the opening of the letter. Much of the intervening material in Rom 1–8 has its primary relevance for the Jewish segment of the church, which must have been a small minority. Paul shifts his focus back to the Gentile majority in Rom 9–11 in order to clarify the meaning of God's dealings with Israel.

Paul makes it clear in 11:13 that in spite of his calling as apostle of the Gentiles, he has not abandoned his hope for his fellow Jews. God's purposes for Israel have not been exhausted with their failure to respond to the Gospel. In 11:25 Paul describes the current state of affairs as a 'mystery': the (partial) hardening of Israel is temporary ('until the fullness of the Gentiles has entered in') and comprehended within the divine plan. Paul makes this disclosure, he says, in order that his Gentile audience might not think themselves wise.

This statement indicates that Paul perceives a danger of hubris present for the Gentiles within the church. It is a verbatim anticipation of a later admonition, which is set in the midst of parenetic material clearly designed to preserve unity in the church.[32] And, as we shall see, it probably is related to the closing exhortation in 16:17–20.

3. *Rom 12:1–3.* The παρακαλῶ period in Rom 12:1, 2 represents a generalized 'imperative' which Paul derives from the 'indicative' of the Gospel. The consecutive particle οὖν *(παρακαλῶ οὖν ὑμᾶς)* and

---

[30] See also Jervis, *The Purpose of Romans*, pp. 108–109.
[31] See Section III.D., below.
[32] See Rom 12:16.

the instrumental phrase διὰ τῶν οἰκτιρμῶν τοῦ Θεοῦ, which supplies the basis for response, link the appeal to the preceding references to God's mercy in Rom 11:28–36.[33] Paul, continuing to speak to Gentiles here, alludes to the Gospel as the vehicle of divine mercy to them.[34] The content of 12:1, 2 likewise reflects Paul's earlier admonitions to yield the body and its members to God, exhortations which are grounded on God's saving act in Christ, just as God's mercy in the Gospel forms the basis of this appeal.[35]

The παρακαλῶ clause is also thematically related to the introduction to Romans through its expression of continuity with the purposes of the God of Israel.[36] Paul employs Jewish categories of worship in Rom 12:1,[37] but interprets them in Hellenistic terms. Christian obedience stands in the place of the Temple cult.[38] The will of God to which believers are to conform is expressed by Hellenistic ideals (τὸ ἀγαθὸν καὶ εὐάρεστον καὶ τέλειον).[39] This reinterpretation of the will of God on the basis of the Gospel corresponds to the opening of the letter, where Paul describes his

---

[33] Contra Bjerkelund, Parakalô, pp. 162–168, who takes the διά-phrase as an invocation, and Dunn, Romans, p. 709 who, following Furnish, takes similar instances of διά-phrases as signifying the instrument of Paul's locutionary act. Paul uses διά-phrases in παρακαλῶ clauses elsewhere (Rom 12:3; 15:30; 1 Cor 1:10 and probably 2 Cor 10:1; cf. 2 Cor 13:3, 4), not only to express his motivation, but also to appeal to his audience. Despite Paul's shift in word usage from ἐλεέω-ἔλεος (Rom 11:28–36) to οἰκτιρμός (Rom 12:1) the prepositional phrase, διὰ τῶν οἰκτιρμῶν τοῦ θεοῦ, here most likely refers back to the preceding summary of God's working of mercy as the basis upon which the audience is to respond. Οἰκτίρμων and ἐλεήμων are frequently paired in the LXX (reflecting רחם and חנן, e.g. LXX Pss 102:8; 110:4; 111:4; 144:8). And similar shifts in terminology between ἔλεος and οἰκτιρμῶν (LXX Ps 24:6) and ἐλεῶ and οἰκτιρμῶν appear (LXX Ps 50:3). See Käsemann, An die Römer, p. 314.

[34] Rom 11:28. The παρακαλῶ clause picks up the preceding address ἀδελφοί from 11:25, indicating that Paul continues his focus on Gentiles. As in the opening of the letter, he again acts as if the church consisted entirely of them. The content of 12:1, 2 and the exhortation to humility which follow likewise suggest a Gentile audience. Cf. Furnish, Theology and Ethics, pp. 98–106. Furnish errs, however, in too quickly equating the imperative with 'what it means to receive by faith the revealing of God's righteousness.' While the indicative and imperative must cohere in practice according to Paul, they are clearly logically distinct here, since the imperative inferentially follows the indicative. Furnish's statement is correct then, only if 'means' is understood as 'have as a consequence' (and not as 'refer to the same thing as').

[35] Cf. Rom 6:12–13, 19.

[36] Rom 1:1–7.

[37] Cf. Rom 1:9 (θεός) ᾧ λατρεύω ἐν τῷ πνεύματί μου ἐν τῷ εὐαγγελίῳ τοῦ υἱοῦ αὐτοῦ; 9:4 Ἰσραηλῖται, ὧν . . . ἡ λατρεία.

[38] Käsemann's reading of 12:1 as a devaluing of cultic observances in view of the sanctification of the way of life must be accepted in view of Paul's emphasis on τὰ σώματα (An die Römer, p. 315).

[39] Cf. Rom 12:1, λογικός, Furnish, Theology and Ethics, pp. 103–104; Zeller, Der Brief an die Römer, p. 207.

apostolic commission as one of bringing about the ὑπακοὴ πίστεως ('obedience which springs from faith') among the Gentiles, by means of the Gospel which is the fulfillment of divine promises to Israel.[40]

The manner in which the 'imperative' of Rom 12:1, 2 is concretized in the following command in Rom 12:3 is also suggestive of Paul's purpose in writing. The earlier allusion to the Gospel as the foundation for obedience has a counterpart here in Paul's appeal to his apostolic authority, which is likewise expressed in indirect language (διὰ τῆς χάριτος τῆς δοθείσης μοι).[41]

At the close of the parenetic material in 15:15, 16, Paul makes reference to his apostolic authority in identical wording (διὰ τῆς χάριτος τῆς δοθείσης μοι), and again describes his ministry of the Gospel in cultic terms. He is a priestly minister, who by his service with the Gospel renders the Gentiles an acceptable offering to God. A chiastic arrangement therefore emerges, which marks 12:1–15:16 as an *inclusio*.

This observation has considerable importance for assessing the purpose of the letter. Paul's appeal to his Gentile readers in 12:1, 2 to yield themselves as a sacrifice (n.b. singular) matches his description of his ministry of the Gospel as the preparation of the Gentiles as an offering in 15:16. By implication, therefore, Paul regards the theological argument of the letter in Rom 1–11 upon which 12:1, 2 is based as a 'priestly service of the Gospel.'

It is important to note the very generality of the exhortation in Rom 12:1, 2. As we suggested above, it is a comprehensive appeal, based on the Gospel. The absence of polemics at this crucial juncture indicates that it is unlikely that Paul attacks adversaries within the church at Rome in this letter.[42] If Paul's preceding arguments in Rom 1–8 and 9–11 had been directed toward opponents within the church, one would have expected to find here a polemical statement or enunciation of the specific issues at stake.[43]

---

[40] Rom 1:1–4, 1:5 ἐλάβομεν χάριν καὶ ἀποστολὴν εἰς ὑπακοὴν πίστεως ἐν πᾶσιν τοῖς ἔθνεσιν. In light of the further references to obedience in Romans, it is best to understand πίστεως as a genitive of source, not an epexegetic genitive, cf. 6:16; 15:18; 16:19.

[41] See Rom 1:5; 15:15.

[42] Wedderburn suggests that the exhortation of Rom 12:2 introduces the (theological) thrust of the following hortatory material, *The Reasons for Romans*, pp. 75–87. This may be the case. But the fact that Paul does not immediately address the conflict between the 'weak' and the 'strong' indicates that Jew-Gentile tensions were not the primary motivation for the letter. See our discussion of this issue in Section II.C. below.

[43] See Gal 5:1–6, where Paul explicitly states the problem toward which the preceding theological argument has been directed.

The seriousness with which Paul treats the issue of humble self-estimation and his call to unity in one body which is joined to this charge in 12:3 indicate that Paul perceived a potential threat of division. Here he expands his address to explicitly include the whole church ('I say to everyone who is among you'), anticipating the conflict between 'weak' and 'strong' in 14:1–15:7, and his warning against schismatics in 16:17–20.

4. Rom 15:15, 16. The ministry of the Gospel includes not only theological arguments of Rom 1–11, but the exhortations based on them. As Dunn recognizes, Paul's expression of aim τολμηρότερον δὲ ἔγραψα ὑμῖν ἀπὸ μέρους ('I have written to you, in part, most boldly') has to do with the parenetic material in 12:3–15:13.[44] This is clear not only from the limiting phrase ἀπὸ μέρους, but from the very repetition of apostolic mandate which serves to bracket the material extending back to 12:3, 'I have written . . . on account of the grace of God given to me.'[45]

The descriptive Paul chooses for his bold writing ὡς ἐπαναμιμνῄσκων ὑμᾶς ('as a reminder to you') is a repeated recognition of the validity of the traditions and faith of the Roman church.[46] His preceding expression of confidence in his addressees in 15:14 almost requires such language here.

5. Rom 15:23, 24. In Rom 15:23, 24 Paul declares his intention of visiting the believers at Rome, at which he has hinted in the opening of the letter.[47] His preceding narrative of his evangelization of the eastern Mediterranean also supplies an explicit reason for his delay. He has given priority to proclaiming Christ in places where others have not. Only now that his work in the East is completed is he free to come to Rome.[48] Even this stop in Rome is only transitory. Paul hopes that the church at Rome will help him carry out a further pioneer mission in Spain.[49]

As Paul's following description of the gift of 'Macedonia' and 'Achaia' for the poor in Jerusalem underscores, spiritual benefits should be reciprocated by a material response. When Paul arrives in Rome with the fullness of Christ's blessing (15:29), the church at Rome should be prepared to help him in his apostolic ministry.

---

[44] Dunn, *Romans*, pp. 858–859.
[45] Rom 15:16 corresponds to 12:1, 2.
[46] Cf. Rom 1:8, 12; 6:17.
[47] Rom 1:13.
[48] Rom 15:17–23.
[49] Rom 15:24.

Paul already looks forward to this request in the opening of the letter in his expectation of being encouraged by the faith of the Roman believers.[50] In effect, Paul's description of his obligation to 'barbarians,' in the opening of the letter decentralizes the church at Rome. It makes the Roman believers aware that the Gospel and the apostolic commission which Paul represents involve obligations extending far beyond them. Paul's extensive 'boasting' in 15:17–22 must be understood in this manner as well. It is an invitation to the church at Rome to accept Paul as apostle to *all* the Gentiles. If they do so, they will be prepared to give him material aid for further evangelization.

Some scholars have stressed Paul's proposed mission to Spain as the central motivation for the letter.[51] This claim falters, however, on the observation that the mission is not mentioned directly until the conclusion of the letter, and then in a minor key.[52] As we have seen, Paul's disclosure of intent in 15:15 ends an *inclusio* extending back to 12:1, in which Paul seeks to gain adherence to his Gospel and its demands. The reference to Spain is part of Paul's following description of his apostolic ministry (15:17–29), which is followed by an appeal to welcome Paul to Rome in 15:30–33. The two sections of the 'apostolic parousia' are independent, self-contained units, which by their very parallelism suggest that they stand in a coordinate, not subordinate relation. Furthermore, in the concluding appeal in 15:30–33, all mention of Spain drops out, shifting the focus entirely to Paul's stay in Rome.

6. Rom 15:30–33. The second παρακαλῶ clause of the letter in Rom 15:30 has provided the starting point for another influential interpretation of Paul's letter to Rome. In this exhortation Paul requests the Roman believers to pray on his behalf, that he might 'be delivered from the disobedient in Judea' and that his service in Jerusalem, i.e. the delivery of the collection from the churches in the East for the poor, 'might be acceptable to the saints.'[53] This concern about the upcoming journey to Jerusalem is thought to supply the occasion for Paul's letter. In view of his plans to travel to

---

[50] Rom 1:12.

[51] So, e.g., Dieter Zeller, *Juden und Heiden in der Mission des Paulus*, FB 8 (Stuttgart: Katholisches Bibelwerk, 1973), pp. 39–77; Robert Jewett, 'Romans as an Ambassadorial Letter,' *Int* 36 (1982):5–20.

[52] It should be remembered too, that Paul's depiction of his visit to Rome as a 'passing through on the way to Spain,' was necessary to his appearing consistent to his audience. If for years he had failed to come to Rome because of unevangelized areas in the East, how could he ignore pioneering work in the West?

[53] Rom 15: 26, 31, 32.

Rome after his visit to Jerusalem, Paul first sent this letter to the Roman Christians as an appeal for support for his cause. The letter, which is thought to reflect a variety of themes from earlier conflicts with Judaizers, was written, it is suggested, in preparation for a similar confrontation with the conservative Jewish-Christians in Jerusalem.[54]

A number of factors indicate that conflict between Paul and the Jerusalem church was not a primary concern in his writing Romans.[55] The petition certainly indicates a tension between Paul and Jerusalem, but it is important to separate historical reconstruction from Paul's intent in writing. If the focal point of the letter was a serious breach with the leaders of the Jerusalem church on the crucial issue of Gentile circumcision and the legitimacy of Paul's mission, one would expect to find some evidence of this in the letter, e.g., a request for prayer that the truth of the Gospel would be upheld, or an argument that circumcision should not be demanded of Gentile believers,[56] or a reference to the agreement with the Jerusalem leaders which had been reached earlier.[57] There may well have been continuing tensions with the Jerusalem church on the matter of Gentile circumcision. The petition that the offering would be well received indicates that some form of skepticism of Paul and his mission remained. But if a crisis with the Jerusalem leadership was Paul's central concern in Romans, one would expect more evidence of it.[58]

---

[54] Jacob Jervell argues that Romans may be regarded as a 'Letter to Jerusalem': it was penned in view of the Jerusalem visit, in *The Romans Debate*, ed. Karl P. Donfried (Minneapolis: Augsburg, 1977), pp. 61–74. M. J. Suggs similarly contends that the Roman epistle is a conciliatory letter in which Paul aims to gain the support of the Jerusalem believers, " 'The Word is Near You': Romans 10:6–10 within the Purpose of the Letter,' in *Christian History and Interpretation*, ed. W. R. Farmer, C. F. D. Moule, and R. R. Niebuhr (Cambridge: Cambridge University Press, 1967), pp. 289–313. Günther Bornkamm, who stresses the Roman address of the letter more than either Jervell or Suggs, suggests that Romans contains a reflective summary of Paul's thought, composed in light of anticipated conflict in Jerusalem, 'The Letter to the Romans as Paul's Last Will and Testament,' in *The Romans Debate*, ed. Karl P. Donfried (Minneapolis: Augsburg, 1977), pp. 17–31.

[55] Cf. Suggs, " 'The Word is Near You,' " p. 295; Jervell, 'The Letter to Jerusalem,' pp. 65–70.

[56] A number of Gentiles were accompanying Paul to Jerusalem: 2 Cor 8:16-24; Rom 16:21-23; cf. Acts 20:4.

[57] Cf., e.g., Gal 2:1-10.

[58] Cf. Zeller, *Der Brief an die Römer*, pp. 16–17. Jervell further argues that if the gift from the Gentile churches was rejected in Jerusalem, Paul's future missionary work, especially the contemplated visit to Spain, would be jeopardized, or indeed impossible, 'The Letter to Jerusalem,' p. 68. There is no denying that a break with Jerusalem would have been a serious blow to Paul, and would have likely produced problems in the churches of the eastern Mediterranean. But according to

Moreover, it is hard to imagine that Romans was intended to be a conciliatory letter as Jervell and Suggs suggest.[59] The letter contains the one locus in the Pauline correspondence in which the Jewish person receives direct rhetorical address. But Paul's tone here is bitingly critical.[60] The portion of the epistle which is most explicitly positive toward Jews is addressed not to Jewish Christians, but to the Gentiles in Paul's audience.[61] And if a Jerusalem address of the letter is assumed, it is hard to account for Rom 6:19, which is clearly directed to readers with a former pagan existence. In short, the claim that Paul writes Romans in a manner which would be positively viewed in Jerusalem, or that it represents an orderly exposition for a Jewish audience fails to be convincing.[62]

The Jerusalem theory also fails to explain why the letter was sent to Rome at all. Since Rom 16 was a part of the original letter, Paul clearly had Roman readers in mind when he wrote. It is difficult to agree with Jervell, that Roman representation was important to Paul as a symbol of a fulfilled Gentile mission.[63] The Gentile mission plainly was not fulfilled for Paul with this offering, since he still planned missionary activity in Spain. Moreover, he asks no Roman representatives to join him on his journey to Jerusalem. If Rome was to symbolize the Gentiles of the West, one could hardly expect less. The suggestion that the exposition of the letter was intended to win support from the Roman church is further undermined by the observation that Paul does not ask for any concrete support. He simply requests prayer. It is hard to believe that Paul sent a lengthy letter simply to request prayer from a congregation which as a whole was still unknown to him.[64]

---

the principle expressed in 15:20, Paul has consistently avoided previously missionized regions in the past. The journey to Spain undoubtedly represents the continuation of this practice (Rom 15:24, 28). In the case of a falling out in Jerusalem, it is highly unlikely that he would face opposition upon his arrival in Spain, which was rather remote from Jerusalem. Despite the recent difficulties Paul had experienced with the congregation in Corinth, in the Roman letter he seems to look upon his mission in the East as completed and stable (2 Cor 11–13 esp. 10:15, 16, cf. Rom 15:17–19). Any conjectures about what the outworkings of a failure in Jerusalem might have meant to Paul remain speculative.

[59] Jervell, 'The Letter to Jerusalem,' pp. 69–70; Suggs, "The Word is Near You," pp. 297–299.

[60] Rom 2:17–29.

[61] Rom 11:11–36, esp. 11:13.

[62] Cf. Wedderburn, *The Reasons for Romans*, pp. 20–21.

[63] ervell, 'The Letter to Jerusalem,' p. 74.

[64] Ulrich Wilckens's more nuanced reading of Romans falls under the same judgment. He views Rom 1–11 as prepared in view of the upcoming confrontation of Paul with skeptics in Jerusalem, yet penned for the purpose of helping resolve the strife among Gentile Christians over adherence to synagogue practices

The παρακαλῶ clause of 15:30 has more to do with Paul's anticipated visit to Rome than his mission in Jerusalem. The prayer he
requests for his διακονία in Jerusalem is intermediary to the final
telic statement of Rom 15:32. The church is asked to pray for
Paul's deliverance and for the success of his mission so that they
may welcome and support the apostle to the Gentiles: ἵνα . . .
συναναπαύσωμαι ὑμῖν. The completion of his service in Jerusalem
will allow him at last to come to Rome.[65] The appeal for prayer for
the διακονία in Jerusalem therefore represents an invitation to the
Roman believers to embrace Paul and his anticipated visit. They
are to pray that the last remaining hindrance to his travel to Rome
might be successfully completed, so that he might safely and quickly come to them.[66]

Rom 15:30–33 concludes the second section of the lengthy
'apostolic parousia.' The first part (15:14–16) concludes with
Paul's reason for his 'most bold' exhortations. In 15:17–29 Paul
describes in detail his apostolic activities: the pioneer mission in the
East, and the delivery of the collection for the saints in Jerusalem.
Just as 15:14–16 functions as an appeal for the church to accept his
preceding admonitions and theology, 15:30–33 urges them to support Paul's apostolate.

Comparison of this conclusion with the opening of the letter
reveals another chiasm. Paul's initial characterization of his apostolic calling (1:1–7) moves to an emphasis on his desire to proclaim
the Gospel in Rome (1:15). Correspondingly, Paul's description of
his calling as a ministry of the Gospel to the Gentiles (15:15, 16) is
followed by a narrative of his apostolic activities, for which he seeks
future assistance (15:30–33). These two complementary concerns
introduce and conclude the letter, and supply the purpose for
Paul's writing.

7. Rom 16:1. In 16:1 Paul commends Phoebe, a minister of the
church in Cenchreae to the believers at Rome. He bases his request

---

(Rom 14–15). See 'Über Abfassungszweck und Aufbau des Römerbriefs,' in
Rechtfertigung als Freiheit (Neukirchen/Vluyn: Neukirchner, 1974), pp. 110–170;
Der Brief an die Römer, pp. 33–46, 128–131. However, since (according to Wilckens) both of the Gentile parties involved in the conflict reject the practice of
circumcision, *both* distance themselves from full observance of *Torah*. The difference between them is therefore one of the degree to which other practices of the
synagogue should be maintained. But in this case, the earlier chapters do not
address the issue at stake between the two parties, since Paul, e.g. in Rom 2, 3,
goes about defining the nature and value of being a Jew—an issue foreign to the
groups Wilckens envisions. It is difficult to see then why Paul sends material
oriented toward the significance of being Jewish to a quite different situation.
  [65] Rom 15:23–24, 29. Cf. 1:8–12.
  [66] Rom 15:32.

for her support on her past service to others, and, significantly, to him. The Roman church, in receiving her, in some measure is receiving Paul and his authority. She almost certainly was the bearer of the letter to Rome.

8. Rom 16:17–20. The third παρακαλῶ clause, which introduces Rom 16:17–20, has rarely been taken into account in the reconstruction of Paul's aim in writing. In part, doubts about the origin of Rom 16 have kept interpreters from seeking to define its relation to the letter as a whole. Nevertheless, an increasing number of scholars have rightly concluded that Paul composed this chapter along with the rest of Romans.[67] Given the originality of Rom 16, the bearing of Rom 16:17–20 on the remainder of the letter must be taken into consideration. Like the preceding παρακαλῶ clauses, this exhortation falls at the conclusion of a well-defined section of the letter, the closing greetings. One would expect then that some facet of the exigence which prompted the letter would be reflected here, just as it is in the other παρακαλῶ clauses.

Although the warning contained in Rom 16:17-20 sometimes has been thought to be an insertion which interrupts the pattern of the closing greetings, that is not the case. Rather than constituting a closing parenesis, Rom 16:17–20 should be regarded as an expanded form of the 'curse/reminder' motif which sometimes forms part of the concluding formula of Paul's letters. The promise of divine subjugation of Satan coupled with Paul's customary, concluding Christological 'grace wish' (ἡ χάρις τοῦ κυρίου ἡμῶν Ἰησοῦ μεθ' ὑμῶν) causes 16:17–20 to conform to the closing pattern found in 1 Cor and Gal.[68] Although the greetings of Paul's companions and amanuensis (Rom 16:21–23) are displaced from their expected position following Rom 16:16, the presence of the 'grace wish' (16:20b) fits the form of Paul's personal greetings.[69] Moreover, given that Pauline closings tend to display unusual word–usage, the vocabulary of Rom 16:17–20 is not exceptional and does not necessarily indicate that the verses

---

[67] See the excursus at the end of this chapter.

[68] See 1 Cor 16:22, 23; Gal 6:16–18.

[69] The order of closing greetings varies in Paul's letters. In 1 Cor the expression of greetings precedes the greeting directive and is followed by Paul's greeting (16:19–21). In 2 Cor and Phil the greeting directive comes first and an explicit greeting of Paul is lacking (2 Cor 13:12, 13; Phil 4:21–23). Greetings fail altogether in Gal. See, Käsemann, *An die Römer*, p. 401; Wilckens, *Der Brief an die Römer*, 3:139–140; Dunn, *Romans*, pp. 901–902; Schnider and Stenger, *Studien zum neutestamentlichen Briefformular*, p. 108.

have been inserted.[70] The passage therefore should be regarded as integral to the remainder of the chapter.

The abrupt appearance of this polemical statement is not altogether surprising. As Wilckens notes, a final sharp exhortation is not uncharacteristic of Paul.[71]

Paul here warns the church to 'watch out' for opponents to the διδαχή which they had learned.[72] He explains his mention of this threat on the basis of a widespread knowledge of their obedience (ὑπακοή), recalling the effect of the Gospel among Gentiles (ὑπακοὴ πίστεως), and indicating that Paul here again is treating the church as Gentile in nature.[73]

The fact that Paul employs the definite article (τοὺς τὰς διχοστασίας . . . ποιοῦντας), that he speaks of the success of his opponents,[74] and that his warning is predicated upon the reputation of the Roman church,[75] indicates that he had specific types of people in mind.[76] Yet the generality of his language suggests that he is not thinking of a coherent movement, but of a variety of individuals.

It is likely that they were outsiders to the church at Rome. Above all else, the location of this exhortation at the very end of the letter, after matters internal to the congregation have been

---

[70] The *hapax legomena* of 16:17–20 include 16.17 σκοπεῖν (in a negative sense), χρηστολογία, ἀκάκος, συντρίβω, ἐν τάχει. Cf. e.g. 1 Cor 16:22 (μαρὰν ἀθά), Gal 6:16, 17 (κανόνι στοιχεῖν, Ἰσραὴλ τοῦ θεοῦ, κόπους παρέχειν, στίγματα).

[71] Wilckens, *Der Brief an die Römer*, 3:139. Cf. 1 Cor 16:22; Gal 6:12–17. Wilckens further attempts to explain the unexpectedness of Paul's warning here by suggesting that Paul received news of the arrival of his adversaries in Rome only after he had completed the body of the letter. But this thesis is artificial. And if such was the case, one would expect that he would explicitly refer to his unfolding of his Gospel in the earlier part of the letter, which, whether the opponents represented Judaizing or libertinistic views, would have served as an appropriate counter to a pressing threat. The very vagueness of the connection to the earlier portion of the letter suggests that the church was in no immediate danger (contra Käsemann, *And die Römer*, p. 401). The church may have encountered representatives of views opposed to the traditions which it had adopted, as Wilckens suggests, but it seems to have remained committed to its original position. Moreover, if Romans was written from Corinth in the early spring of 56 or 57 CE, as Wilckens accepts, one may not assume that Paul had received immediate news from Rome. The sea lanes of the Adriatic were unreliable in winter. Cf. F. F. Bruce, 'The Romans Debate—Continued,' *BJRL* 64 (1981/82):334–359; A. M. Ramsay, 'The Speed of the Roman Imperial Post,' *Journal of Roman Studies* 15 (1925):60–74.

[72] Cf. Rom 6:17, where Paul affirms the τύπος διδαχῆς which his audience had received.

[73] Rom 1:5; 15:18.

[74] Rom 16:18b.

[75] Rom 16:19a.

[76] Contra Wilckens, the use of the definite article reveals only Paul's familiarity with these opponents, not necessarily that of the church (*Der Brief an die Römer*, 3:140).

dealt with, indicates that the enemies are external. And despite the
sharpness of Paul's admonition, the tone of Paul's address to the
church corresponds with the positive expressions elsewhere in the
letter concerning the faith and obedience of the community.[77] He
praises the church for its obedience.[78] It is the adversaries from
without who are the object of his attack.

They present a two-fold danger to the church: they create dis-
sensions and offenses (σκάνδαλα) contrary to the teaching the
church had learned. The mention of potential division within the
church recalls the conflict between 'weak' and 'strong' which Paul
addresses in 14:1–15:13, as does Paul's reference to σκάνδαλα.[79]
This dispute, we shall see, had to do with relations between Jews
and Gentiles within the church.

Although it is difficult to determine the identity of these opponents, the exhortation seems to be directed against adversaries who
advocated immoral and idolatrous practices.[80] They profess belief
in Christ.[81] Paul's charge that they 'serve their own bellies' should
probably be understood as an accusation of greed.[82] They have
proven to be attractive to some in other churches which Paul had
founded.[83] While their views might have been appealing to some of
the Gentile majority, Jewish members of the church would react
strongly against them.

Unlike the dispute between the 'weak' and the 'strong,' however, they do not merely set Jew against Gentile, but act contrary
to the teaching which the church had received. Paul describes

---

[77] See Rom 1:8, 11–12; 6:17–18; 15:14. The absence of polemic against adversaries in Rome suggests that such comments represent Paul's real estimation of the
church. The thanksgiving which Paul offers for their obedience to a pattern of
teaching in common with his own in Rom 6, further confirms that the church was,
at bottom, in line with his theology.

[78] Rom 16:19a ἡ γὰρ ὑμῶν ὑπακοὴ εἰς πάντας ἀφίκετο·

[79] Rom 14:13.

[80] It is not clear that the opponents are Gnostics. Schmithals, who has made
the most forceful case for this view, rests much of his argument upon the questionable assumption that Paul's adversaries in Philippi, Corinth, and Galatia also
were Gnostics. But it is unlikely that only one group (i.e. 'Jewish-Christian
Gnostics') is under attack in Phil 3. See Walter Schmithals, 'Die Irrlehrer von
Rm 16:17–20,' *ST* 13 (1959):51–69. As Schmithals points out, most of the vocabulary of the passage is found elsewhere in Paul's letters. Only διὰ τῆς χρηστολο-
γίας καὶ εὐλογίας is unusual. Not much can be learned about the adversaries from
this phrase. Moreover, Paul attacks Jewish-Christian 'super-apostles' at Corinth
in 2 Cor 10–13, but is not clear that they were Gnostics, nor that they maintained
libertinistic views, contra, e.g., Käsemann, *An die Römer*, pp. 401–402.

[81] Rom 16:18a οἱ γὰρ τοιοῦτοι τῷ κυρίῳ ἡμῶν Χριστῷ οὐ δουλεύουσιν.

[82] See Chapter 3, Section II.C; Dunn, *Romans*, p. 903.

[83] Rom 16:17b. It should not be forgotten that Paul is writing from Corinth
where he had confronted such problems.

them as leading the naive into evil.[84] His language in Rom 16:19b ('I want you to be wise with respect to good, and pure with respect to evil'), and his reference to Satan in Rom 16:20 associates these opponents with the serpent of Gen 3.[85] They are further said to accomplish their aims through pleasant words and beautiful speech (or blessing?: εὐλογία), which is again reminiscent of the Genesis account.[86]

This final warning against agitators from outside the church has a dual function. First, it is meant to ensure the continued 'obedience' of a basically Gentile church. The term ὑπακοή implies the exclusive allegiance to the God of Israel effected by the Gospel, which Paul has repeatedly described in Jewish terms at crucial points in the letter. His earlier warnings against Gentile pride find practical expression in this exhortation, which connotes the avoidance of idolatrous practices.

Secondly, the faithfulness of the Gentiles to the teaching they had received would prevent further division. Paul closes with a promise of victory over Satan from the 'God of peace,' alluding to an end to the conflict between Jews and Gentiles in the church.[87]

B. Jew-Gentile Tensions within the Congregation

In Rom 14:1–15:6, Paul addresses conflicts between the 'weak in faith' (14:1: ὁ ἀσθενῶν τῇ πίστει, cf. 15:1) and the 'strong' (15:1: ἡμεῖς οἱ δυνατοί, cf. 14:22). We have seen above that Paul was aware of factions within the church. The length of his discussion of this issue has suggested to a number of scholars that strife between Jews and Gentiles within the circle of house-churches which formed the Roman believing community was the cause for Paul's writing the letter.[88] We shall find however, that it was one of

---

[84] Rom 6:18. Contra Wilckens, *Der Brief an die Römer*, 3:141–142, 143–145, and Zeller, *Der Brief an die Römer*, p. 249 it is unlikely that Paul has Judaizers in view.

[85] Cf. Gen 3:4, 5. The language here is also reminiscent of 2 Cor 11:12–15, where Paul describes his adversaries as 'ministers of Satan.'

[86] Rom 16:18b.

[87] Rom 15:13, 33.

[88] H. Preisker, e.g., accepting earlier work by W. Lütgert, regards the letter to have been directed against Gentile Christian enthusiasts, with libertinistic leanings, who were at odds with Jewish Christian nomists ('Das historische Problem des Römerbriefes,' *Wissenschaftliche Zeitschrift der Friedrich Schiller Universität Jena* 1 [1952/3]:25–30). G. Harder regards the letter as having been written in response to an appeal by Gentile Christians, who were battling nomists at Rome ('Der konkrete Anlaß des Römerbriefes,' *Theologia Viatorum* 6 [1958/59]:13– 24). Willi Marxsen proposes that proselytes who had later become Christians were weary of the chains which they had taken on, appealed to Paul for help, thus prompting the letter (*Einleitung in das Neue Testament⁴* [Gütersloh: Gerd Mohn, 1978], pp. 88– 96). Karl P. Donfried, regards the problem of returning Jewish-Christians to have

a number of applications of his desire to minister the Gospel in Rome.

It is probable that the tension between 'weak' and 'strong' is a reflection of some dimension of Jew-Gentile relations within the church. It would be a deviation from the normal pattern of his letters for him to give advice without first providing a theological basis for it.[89]

The church at Rome was composed predominantly of Gentile believers at the time of Paul's writing. That is apparent from both the manner in which he chooses to address the church, and the assumptions he makes about the nature of the congregation. As we have noted, he explicitly refers to the church as Gentile in composition.[90] And in expressing the reasons for his desire to see them, he assumes that the terms Ἕλληνες and σοφοί would be titles of honor.[91] He portrays them as leading a pagan existence prior to their conversion.[92] Furthermore, his discussion of the

---

again prompted 'the old Galatians 2/Acts 15 problem of Jewish-Gentile relationships.' See 'A Short Note on Romans 16,' in *The Romans Debate*, ed. Karl P. Donfried (Minneapolis: Augsburg, 1977), pp. 50–60. But as we have seen, the Gentiles were in the majority, the 'strong' group was dominant, and Paul's argument in Rom 1–11 is not directed against the imposition of the Law on Gentiles. Wolfgang Wiefel suggests that Jewish Christians who had been expelled from Rome by Claudius in 49 CE, upon their return at the beginning of Nero's reign, found a new church structure: Gentile house-churches (*collegia*) instead of the former synagogue fellowship. Paul wrote to Rome, in the face of the anti-Semitism present in the city, to assist Jews and Gentiles in living together as believers, 'The Jewish Community in Ancient Rome and the Origins of Roman Christianity,' in *The Romans Debate*, ed. Karl P. Donfried (Minneapolis: Augsburg, 1977), pp. 100–119. H.-W. Bartsch has furthered the suggestion that Paul wrote against anti-semitic and libertinistic Gentiles in Rome. See, 'Die antisemitische Gegner des Paulus im Römerbrief,' in *Antijudaismus im Neuen Testament*, ed. W. P. Eckert, et al. (München: Chr. Kaiser, 1967), pp. 27–43; 'Die historische Situation des Römerbriefes,' in *Studia Evangelica IV*, TU 102, ed. F. L. Cross (Berlin: Akademie, 1968), pp. 281–291; 'Die Empfänger des Römerbriefes,' *ST* 25 (1971):81–89. W. S. Campbell regards the letter to have been addressed to the 'liberal-minded Gentile majority (the strong in faith),' who 'were unwilling to have fellowship with the conservative Jewish Christian minority (the weak in faith).' See, 'Why Did Paul Write Romans?' *ExpT* 85 (1973–74):264–269. But the 'weak' and 'strong' do not represent strictly Jew and Gentile groups. And given Paul's positive statements about the congregation, and the nature of the parenesis in 12:1–15:33, it is unlikely that he is combating libertinism *within the church at Rome*. P. S. Minear visualizes five groups within the Roman congregations on the basis of 14:1–16:27, *The Obedience of Faith: The Purposes of Paul in the Epistle to the Romans*, SBT 19 (London: SCM, 1971). But his analysis is overly precise and artificial.

[89] See now Wedderburn, *The Reasons for Romans*, pp. 30–34.

[90] Rom 1:6: ἔθνοι . . . . ἐν οἷς ἐστε καὶ ὑμεῖς κλητοὶ Ἰησοῦ Χριστοῦ

[91] Rom 1:14, 15: Ἕλλησίν τε καὶ βαρβάροις, σοφοῖς τε καὶ ἀνοήτοις ὀφειλέτης εἰμί· οὕτως τὸ κατ' ἐμὲ πρόθυμον καὶ ὑμῖν τοῖς ἐν Ῥώμῃ εὐαγγελίσασθαι.

[92] Rom 6:19.

failure of Israel to receive the Gospel and his warning to Gentiles not to boast presuppose that Gentile converts outnumber Jews in the church.[93]

Nevertheless, Jewish believers were present in the church at Rome as well. His addresses to Jews in the letter suggest that this is Paul's understanding.[94] The list of greetings in Rom 16 shows that a number of Paul's acquaintances at Rome were Jewish.[95] It is likely, too, that the Christian movement in Rome was begun by Jewish believers, some of whom, no doubt were still within the circle of house-churches which constituted the Roman Christian community.

The fact that Paul writes to a basically Gentile church in Rome with the knowledge that they had already experienced some form of persecution provides evidence that Romans was written at a time when Christianity was emerging as an entity distinct from Judaism in Rome.[96] The severe difficulties which were to come under Nero less than ten years later, were preceded by the recognition of Christians as a distinct social group. Tacitus indicates that Nero's selection of Christians as scape-goats for the burning of Rome was aided by a wide-spread hatred of the group by the general population.[97] Paul's remarks indicate that this appearance

---

[93] See Rom 9:1–5, 30–33; 11:1–5, 12–24.

[94] Rom 3:5, 9; 4:1, and the rhetorical address of Rom 2:17–29, which most likely has Jewish Christians in view.

[95] Rom 16:3, 6, 7, 11.

[96] Rom 5:3; 8:17, 18, 31–39; 12:14–21.

[97] Tacitus, *Ann.* 15.44: quos per flagitas invisos vulgus Chrestianos appellabat.

[98] The shift of Roman Christianity from a Jewish to a Gentile base seems to have been accelerated by external forces. It is likely that considerable numbers of Jews were forced out of the city in 49 CE as reported by Suetonius and by Luke (*Claud.* 25.4, cf. Acts 18:2). The dating of this incident to 49 CE, derived from inscriptional evidence and the record of Acts, is confirmed by the fifth century Christian historian Orosius, who assigns it to the ninth year of Claudius' reign, but (apparently) falsely attributes his information to Josephus (*Ant.* 7.6.15). The conflicting report of Dio Cassius (late 2nd century, *Hist.* 60.6), that Claudius did not expel the Jews from Rome, was made in reference to the first year of Claudius' reign and in connection with Tiberius' expulsion of the Jews in 19 CE. It is most likely that Dio Cassius mentions an earlier act by which Claudius allowed Jews to continue their traditions, but as an attempt to prevent riots, prohibited them from 'gathering.' Claudius was already aware of serious disturbances in Alexandria between the Jewish and Gentile populations at the beginning of his reign. Tiberius' expulsion of the Jews from Rome in 19 CE occurred for similar reasons (Tacitus *Ann.* 2.85.4; Dio Cassius *Hist.* 57.18). Luke, Suetonius, and Orosius refer to a later removal of the Jews in the ninth year of Claudius' reign. This expulsion was the result of disturbances which already occurred within the Jewish community, perhaps through the introduction of Christianity (Suetonius *Claud.* 25.4 Iudaeos impulsore Chresto assidue Roma expulit. This reference to 'Chrestus' is

of a Christianity independent of the synagogue had already begun to take place.[98]

Given the changing character of the church at Rome, one might expect problems concerning religious observances to arise. One would also anticipate that such problems would involve differences between Jews and Gentiles.

The habits which Paul attributes to the 'weak in faith' do much to confirm this impression. This group restricted their diet to vegetables.[99] They fasted in conjunction with special days.[100] It may be that they also abstained from wine, although the absence of mention of wine in the first part of the chapter might indicate that Paul's readiness to do so is only rhetorically intended.[101]

The observance of special days distinguishes the 'weak' from Neo-Pythagoreans and Hellenistic ascetics.[102] It also shows that Rom 14–15 is directed to a situation different from that of 1 Cor 8–10, since the commemoration of certain days goes beyond the avoidance of idols.[103]

A number of sources provide attestation of Jews in a pagan environment restricting themselves to vegetables and refusing wine.[104] The restriction to vegetables may reflect the impossibility of obtaining meat that was ritually pure. Cranfield observes that the mention of clean-unclean distinctions provide clear parallels to טהור and טמא.[105]

Harry Leon notes that many Roman authors thought that Jews fasted on the Sabbath. He cites the historian Pompeius Trogus and a letter from Augustus to Tiberius to this effect.[106] It is quite

likely a confusion of 'Christus,' whom Suetonius mistakenly took to be in Rome on the basis of his sources). After the accession of Nero (54 CE), large numbers of Jews were free to return to the city, as the presence of Jewish names in Rom 16 shows. In the period between 49 and 54, when many of the original leaders of the Christian movement in Rome were absent, it is likely that a Gentile Christianity substantially independent of the synagogue developed. Cf. Stuhlmacher, 'Abfassungszweck,' pp. 184–185; F. F. Bruce, 'Christianity under Claudius,' *BJRL* 44 (1961–62):309–326.

[99] Rom 14:2.

[100] Rom 14:3.

[101] Rom 14:21. Cf. Rom 14:1–3. See Dio Cassius, *Hist.* 60.7 and similar references in Suetonius *Nero* 16, where it is said that Claudius and Nero, respectively, in an attempt to improve public morality, abolished taverns and prohibited the sale of boiled meat which was sold in them.

[102] Schmithals, *Römerbrief*, p. 99.

[103] Romans also lacks any mention of 'things offered to idols' (τὰ εἰδωλόθυτα).

[104] E.g. Dan 1:3–16; 2 Macc 5:27; Josephus, *Vita* 3.13. For additional references see Wilckens, *Der Brief an die Römer*, 3:114.

[105] C. E. B. Cranfield, 'Some Observations on the Interpretation of Romans 14,1–15, 13,' *Communio Viatorum* 17 (1974):197–200. Rom 14:14: οἶδα καὶ πέπεισμαι ἐν κυρίῳ Ἰησοῦ ὅτι οὐδὲν κοινὸν δι' ἑαυτοῦ; Rom 14:20: πάντα μὲν καθαρά.

plausible then that Jews in Rome fasted frequently, leading to this confusion of fast days with the Sabbath by Roman writers.

As both Schmithals and Cranfield rightly note, Paul's treatment of the 'weak' strongly suggests that the group was made up of Jewish Christians. It is unlikely that Paul would have tolerated a pagan practice.[107] Paul elsewhere meets the observance of special days by his Gentile converts with forceful objections.[108]

If the identity of the 'weak in faith' and the 'strong' remains at all in doubt on the basis of the contents of Rom 14, the connection of Rom 15:7 to 15:8, 9 makes it certain that the issues at stake involved the distinction between Jew and Gentile. Paul follows the statement of 15:7 which is directed to 'weak' and 'strong' by an explanatory γάρ in 15:8. The second person plural of 15:7 (Χριστὸς προσελάβετο ὑμᾶς) is therefore treated as equivalent to Jews and Gentiles in the expansion of Paul's thought in 15:8, 9: Christ became a minister to the circumcision and to the Gentiles.

The problem remains as to why Paul chooses the language of 'weak' and 'strong' if the conflict which he seeks to resolve in 14:1–15:13 has to do with Jew-Gentile relations. His use of these terms may be attributed to the fact that the division between 'weak' and 'strong' did not lie entirely along Jew-Gentile lines. Some Jews within the congregation very likely did not follow the practices of the 'weak.' Paul includes himself among the 'strong.'[109] No doubt some of his Jewish acquaintances in the church at Rome also had liberal views.[110] The segment of the church which maintained fast days and dietary restrictions therefore represented only the conservative Jewish Christian segment of the church, and not all Jewish Christians at Rome.

In this case, the tension between the 'weak' and the 'strong' was less a matter of struggle between ethnic groups than it was of differing theological positions. The categories of 'Jew' and 'Gentile' entered into the dissension between the groups only in so far as they impinged upon the self-understanding of the conservative Jewish Christians and Gentile Christians who looked down on

---

[106] Harry J. Leon, *The Jews of Ancient Rome* (Philadelphia: Jewish Publication Society of America, 1960), p. 13.

[107] Schmithals, *Römerbrief*, pp. 98–107. Cranfield, 'Observations,' pp. 193–204.

[108] Gal 4:8–10.

[109] Rom 15:1.

[110] One thinks in particular of Prisca and Aquila, who, according to Paul, had 'risked their neck' for Paul and the 'churches of the Gentiles' (Rom 16:3–5). Since they were leaders of a house-church, it is likely that they would have influenced other Jews to a more Pauline view of the Law. Others whom Paul names in Rom 16 were very likely in line with his stance.

one another. Paul's argument in Rom 1–11 is therefore of central importance to the strife between the 'weak' and the 'strong,' although the discussion of Jewish questions contained in these chapters do not indicate the actual groupings involved in the battle.

The conflict which Paul addresses should not be regarded as the primary occasion for the letter. Other concerns follow the theological portion of the letter, pushing this advice to the close of the parenesis. The appeal of Rom 12:1, 2 in particular, since it is directed to Gentiles and stated in very general terms indicates that Paul's interest is broader than that of conflict resolution.

Further qualifications may be given to this insight. The 'strong' are clearly in the ascendancy, since it is they who are first admonished to accept the 'weak in faith' and bear with their weakness.[111] The issue of the circumcision of Gentiles is never raised in the letter. It is unlikely then, that Paul wrote with the immediate concern of defending Gentile converts against pressure to conform to Jewish practices. The social situation was somewhat the reverse. Conservative Jewish Christians were in danger of being cut off from the main body of the church.

Nevertheless, Paul cannot be regarded simply as a defender of these outnumbered conservative Jewish Christians. His attack on those who prided themselves in being Jewish could not help but be offensive to such a group.[112] The solution to the conflict which he offers is in no way an attempt to defend the equality of those who retained practices of the synagogue. Theologically, he takes the ground out from underneath their position. They are, after all 'weak in faith.' Their practices are unnecessarily restrictive.[113] One can hardly say then, that Paul was concerned to assure the equal status of conservative Jewish Christians. He obviously is concerned to ensure that they remain united with the rest of the church. But his address to the situation is determined by his theological stance, not by egalitarian ideals. The manner in which Paul treats the conflict between the 'weak' and the 'strong' therefore confirms the interpretation of Paul's purpose derived already. He is not driven by the need to support any particular ethnic or social group within the church at Rome. His guiding principle in admonishing the two factions is theological: the uniting of the church under his Gospel.

---

[111] Rom 14:1; 15:1.
[112] Rom 2:17–29.
[113] Rom 14:14: οἶδα καὶ πέπεισμαι ἐν κυρίῳ Ἰησοῦ ὅτι οὐδὲν κοινὸν δι' ἑαυτοῦ·

C. Summary

We have found that Paul's crucial disclosures of intent in Rom 1:1–5; 12:1, 2 and 15:15, 16 reveal that his purpose in writing to Rome is to minister the Gospel to the church there. This conclusion clearly corresponds to the extensive argumentation of the letter. It represents a theological explication and defense of Paul's Gospel formulated on the basis of questions current to his day. Probably, as Ann Jervis has argued, Romans serves as a substitute for an immediate visit.[114] The letter is a proclamation of the Gospel in advance of Paul's arrival.

Paul's motivation for writing derives from his conception of his apostolic calling. He has been set apart for the Gospel, in order to effect the 'obedience of the Gentiles,' so that they may be brought, like an offering, to God himself.[115] Christ, who is the center of the Gospel message, is also the agent behind Paul's mission. He has called Paul as apostle, and has worked the obedience of the Gentiles in the East through him.[116] The completion of this mission, which will be marked by the presentation of the gift for Jerusalem, will allow Paul to come to the Roman believers by the will of God, since they too lie within his sphere of responsibility.[117] The letter temporarily replaces Paul's anticipated apostolic ministry.

It is clear that Paul expected his proclamation of the Gospel in Romans to have several results in his addressees. It was to warn Gentiles against the danger of pride, to unify the church by bringing together the warring factions, to win a welcome and support for Paul and his mission, and to prevent adversaries from gaining a foothold in the congregation. Yet, as very plurality of such expressions of intent as well as their location within the structure of the letter indicate, Paul regarded them as products of his ministering the Gospel, not as his primary aim.

This interpretation of Paul's purpose corresponds well with the historical situation in which the letter was written. One need not adopt Günter Klein's interpretation (viz., Paul's wanted to make the community at Rome a 'church' by an apostolic visit) to realize the powerful effect Paul's letter and subsequent stay in Rome might have had on the church there.[118] Since believers in Rome

---

[114] Jervis, *The Purpose of Romans*, pp. 161–164.
[115] Rom 1:1b, 5; 15:15, 16, 18.
[116] Rom 1:1a, 5; 15:17–21.
[117] Rom 1:6, 10; 15:22–24, 30–33.
[118] Günter Klein focuses attention on a tension between Rom 1:11–15 and 15:20 noted by R. A. Lipsius ('Paul's Purpose in Writing the Epistle to the Romans,' in *The Romans Debate*, ed. Karl P. Donfried [Minneapolis: Augsburg,

were gathered in various house-churches, which very likely had
been planted by more than one individual, a real danger existed
of the movement splintering.[119] Paul may well have hoped that his
personal presence mediated by the letter would help unify the
church in allegiance to his Gospel.[120]

1977], pp. 32–49). On the one hand, Paul makes known his readiness to proclaim
the Gospel in Rome, although he acknowledges the faith already present within
the congregation there (1:8, 15). Yet in the latter portion of the letter he affirms a
principle of non-interference, i.e. not to evangelize where Christ is already named
(15:20, cf. 2 Cor 10:12–18). How can these two statements be reconciled? Klein
explains this apparent conflict by suggesting that Paul abstained from mission
activity in areas in which the apostolic foundation of the believing community was
in place. Since the Roman church did not owe its existence to an apostolic
missionary effort, Paul wrote to Rome and planned his visit in order to provide
the apostolic stamp, thus qualifying Rome as a church. But Paul's understanding
of his apostolic calling becomes highly official if one accepts Klein's thesis. This
contradicts Klein's own observation that Paul regarded his calling as apostle to
consist in the proclamation of the Gospel. Klein's appeal to the absence of
reference to the Roman community as ἐκκλησία is unconvincing. It is a weak
argument given the lack of the word in the letter to the Philippian church, which
Paul had founded himself. And it fails entirely if Rom 16 was part of the original
letter (16:5 καὶ τὴν κατ᾽ οἶκον αὐτῶν ἐκκλησίαν). Klein's proposal cannot draw any
direct support from the tension between 1:11–15 and 15:20 either, since the lack of
an apostolic foundation remains an inference which Klein draws, and is hardly
intimated by the verses themselves. The problem which Klein has underscored
may be resolved. Paul describes his practice in 15:20: οὕτως δὲ φιλοτιμούμενον
εὐαγγελίζεσθαι οὐχ ὅπου ὠνομάσθη Χριστός, ἵνα μὴ ἐπ᾽ ἀλλότριον θεμέλιον
οἰκοδομῶ. The verses which follow indicate that Paul regarded his travel to Rome
to be in line with this practice. The principle of proclamation to those who have
not heard is used to explain his delay in coming to Rome. The aim to evangelize
Spain provides Paul with an 'excuse' for a long desired visit to Rome. Käsemann
rightly recognizes that this resolves at least part of the conflict between the texts
(An die Römer, pp. 14–18). We already have discussed Paul's understanding of
proclamation of the Gospel, which provides a solution to the remaining tension
between 1:8–12 and 1:13–15.
    [119] Cf. Rom 16:5.
    [120] Despite the difficulties which Paul had faced from the Galatian and Cor-
inthian congregations, he seems to have regarded matters settled in these churches, since he indicates in Rom 15:18–23 that his work in the eastern
Mediterranean is complete.
    [121] E.g. Käsemann, An die Römer, pp. 14–18, 372–374; Stuhlmacher 'Abfas-
sungszweck,' pp. 180–193. Schmithals views Paul as seeking to win converted
God-fearers from allegiance to the synagogue. He regards a first letter to Rome
(1:1–11:36 + 15:8–13) to have been addressed to Gentile believers who as God-
fearers had not yet separated themselves from the synagogue. Paul wrote to win
these Christians over to a Law-free understanding of the Gospel, and in doing so
to unite them in an ἐκκλησία outside the synagogue. But Paul's argument in
Rom 1–11 takes much of its orientation from the significance of the Jew, not
that of the God-fearer who had not become a full proselyte. Schmithals's thesis
further rests on two highly questionable premises. He refuses to allow that there
were Jewish Christians among the Gentile Christian majority in Rome, despite
the clear indications in the body and final greetings of the letter that some of the
believers in Rome were Jewish (cf. esp. 2:17–4:12; 16:3, 7, 11). He further regards
the Gentiles who made up the Roman congregation to represent converts from the

The alternative reading of Romans as a defensive letter, directed against opposition within the church, fails to be convincing.[121] Evidence that Paul wrote in response to adversaries at Rome is lacking. Paul's positive comments about the faith of the Roman church set him more in the role of spiritual adviser than antagonist.[122] His two brief references to enemies of his Gospel are not joined to arguments directed against specific opposition at Rome.[123] In view of Paul's strategy in the face of conflict elsewhere (e.g. Galatians, 1 and 2 Corinthians), it seems unlikely that he would retreat from controversy at Rome if he had been aware of it. Furthermore, if Paul was polemically engaged with Judaizers, it is inexplicable that he never treats the issue of Gentile circumcision in the letter.[124] If Paul was under attack from Judaizing opponents, how can it be that he never warns against the promulgation of Gentile circumcision or observance of the Law?[125]

Our construal of Paul's aim in Romans bears some significant implications for the task of describing the function of his arguments concerning righteousness given as a 'gift' to faith. First and fore-

---

churches of the East, who had been converted within the synagogue and were as yet unfamiliar with the Pauline Gospel. But one can hardly exclude the possibility that Gentiles converted through Pauline influence have made their way to Rome, as the number of Paul's acquaintances named in Rom 16 suggests was the case.

[122] See Rom 1:8, 12; 6:17; 15:14; 16:19. His reference to the conversion of his audience in Rom 6:17 is noteworthy, since Paul here implicitly affirms the Gospel to which the Roman believers had been introduced. Stanley Olson rightly sounds a note of caution regarding the use of Paul's expressions of confidence in his audience ('Pauline Expressions of Confidence in His Addressees,' *CBQ* 47 [1985]:282–295). It is undoubtedly true that such statements serve as appeals to his audience. Yet in Romans, the statements are diverse, and evidence that Paul is at odds with the believers in Rome is lacking. For this reason Käsemann's insistence that Paul felt himself threatened (*An die Römer*, pp. 16–17, with reference to 1:8–15) and that his positive comments about the church were mere *Schmeichelei* without substance (*An die Römer*, pp. 376–378, with reference to 15:14, 15) is not persuasive.

[123] Aside from Rom 16:17–20, only 3:8 mentions opponents. These 'certain ones' misrepresent Paul as proclaiming 'cheap grace': φασίν τινες ἡμᾶς λέγειν ὅτι ποιήσωμεν τὰ κακὰ ἵνα ἔλθῃ τὰ ἀγαθά. Whether Paul agrees with them that such a position is blasphemous or pronounces a condemnation on them (ὧν τὸ κρίμα ἔνδικόν ἐστιν)— interpretation here is difficult—he does not engage their views polemically. Paul is aware of some suspicion of his Gospel at Rome (probably from conservative Jewish Christians), yet he does not attack it.

[124] While Paul's address to 'the Jew' in Rom 2:17–29 clearly would have bearing for Jewish Christians at Rome, and might well be called 'polemical,' it is unlikely that Jewish Christians represented a serious threat to Paul's influence in the church. Hence it is unlikely that this address is directed against adversaries at Rome.

[125] Even Wedderburn, who argues that a 'Judaizing Christianity' existed in Rome at this time, admits that the evidence for this claim is weak. See, *Reasons for Romans*, pp. 50–65.

most among these is the observation that the argument of Romans
represents Paul's understanding of his Gospel at the time of his
writing the letter. That his theology had been shaped in conflict
with opposing positions, does not lessen the fact that in the writing
of Romans it was Paul's own.

This thesis is confirmed by Paul's identification of his apostolic
status with this Gospel. Either the church at Rome was going to
accept him, Gospel and all, or it was not going to accept him at all.
If he had merely wanted a warm reception and financial support,
there would have been less risky ways of going about it. Paul was
ready to jeopardize his further work by laying himself open theologically to a community with which he was personally unacquain-
ted. Doubts about whether the conclusions of Paul's arguments
represent his convictions therefore are absurd.[126] It is impossible
to make a distinction between a *Kampfeslehre* and Paul's 'real'
thought in the letter to Rome.

III. 'JUSTIFICATION BY FAITH' AND THE DISPOSITION OF PAUL'S ARGUMENT

Since Paul's arguments on 'justification by faith' are introduced as
an explanation of Paul's Gospel, their function is largely determined by his aim of winning adherence to his theology. Nevertheless, Paul's arguments on forensic justification do not constitute
the whole of his Gospel, or of his aim in writing. This is made clear
by Rom 12:1, where Paul expresses the behavioral result he desires
the preceding discussion to engender without any reference to
'righteousness,' forensic or otherwise. The concept of God's righteousness constitutes the 'primary' expression of the Gospel since
Paul initially defines his Gospel in these terms.[127] But the precise
function of the arguments concerning forensic justification within
the letter deserve further clarification.

In the light of the conclusions we have drawn already concerning the purpose of Romans, it is clear that when Paul introduces his
theological arguments with this theme in Romans, it is not because
he is polemically engaged with adversaries. Rather, it is because he
regarded a forensic justification by faith as integral to his Gospel.
The following discussion will strengthen this claim.

As we indicated at the beginning of this chapter, we will develop
a second thesis regarding Paul's use of the theme of 'justification by

---

[126] This is not to claim that the disposition of the letter represents Paul's logical
processes, but that he adhered to the positions for which he contends.
[127] Rom 1:16, 17.

faith' in Romans. In Rom 5 and in Rom 9:30–10:21, Paul employs the theme of righteousness given through Christ for purposes relevant to Gentiles in the church, who do not seem to have been troubled by the question of whether or not they ought to be circumcised. Furthermore, we shall see that Paul's argument in Rom 7:14–25 operates on the assumption that the 'gift' of righteousness remains essential to every believing human being, including Paul himself. These expansions of the field of forensic justification to questions broader than the status of uncircumcised Gentiles, both confirm the fundamental significance it had to Paul's thought, and indicate that Paul's theology of 'justification by faith' had undergone development.

At various points in our investigation, we have argued that the idea of a forensic righteousness by faith, conceptually independent of behavioral righteousness, may be attributed to Paul. In Chapter 2, we saw that a technical usage of the expression 'the righteousness of God' as 'God's salvation/obedience creating power,' is lacking in apocalyptic Judaism. Our discussion of 1QS in the same chapter further demonstrates that a distance existed between Paul and Qumran, since the gift of righteousness there was conceived of in terms of the practices of the community. We have also seen that it is improbable that Paul attaches the meaning 'salvation/obedience creating power' to the expression in Romans. Although our primary focus will be on the role the arguments concerning 'justification by faith' play in the letter, the following analysis will further support this thesis.

A. Romans 1:16, 17

Interpreters have long recognized that these verses express fundamental theses which in one way or another determine the content of all that follows. This is clear from the fact that Paul's confession, 'I am not ashamed of the Gospel,' is a culminating self-disclosure, preparing the audience for his theological argument in the body of the letter. As we have noted, in the prescript he defines his call as apostle as a 'being set apart for the Gospel.'[128] In the thanksgiving clause and following narration, he describes his attitude toward the church at Rome in terms of his resultant obligation to preach.[129] The initial clause of Rom 1:16 (οὐ γὰρ ἐπαισχύνομαι τὸ εὐαγγέλιον) therefore returns to the topic of the Gospel, upon which Paul's apostolic calling is predicated.

---

[128] Rom 1:1–5.
[129] Rom 1:8–15.

The phrase οὐκ ἐπαισχύνομαι is most likely a formulaic expression, indicating Paul's willingness to confess the Gospel and, as Richard Hays has suggested, echoing the faith of the Biblical psalms.[130] It should not be understood in purely psychological terms, although a subjective element can hardly be absent.[131] The shift in the characterization of humanity from Rom 1:14 (Ἕλληνες καὶ βαρβάροι, σοφοῖ καὶ ἀνοήτοι) to Rom 1:16 (Ἰουδαίος καὶ Ἕλλην) indicates that Paul's use of the expression οὐκ ἐπαισχύνομαι is directed toward asserting the comprehensive scope of the Gospel, not a toward particular situation in Rome which might have been cause for fear.

Paul bases his claim that the Gospel transcends all social and religious distinctions on the assertion that it meets a universal need for salvation: δύναμις γὰρ θεοῦ ἐστιν εἰς σωτηρίαν παντὶ τῷ πιστεύοντι, Ἰουδαίῳ τε πρῶτον καὶ Ἕλληνι. The apocalyptic framework of the statement is unmistakable.[132] Human need is here conceived in fundamentally Jewish terms: salvation is deliverance from the final wrath of God.[133] Nevertheless, the Jew is primary to the Gospel's work (Ἰουδαίῳ τε πρῶτον καὶ Ἕλληνι), implying the necessity of the Gospel and denying any salvific benefit to being Jewish. The qualifying θεοῦ attached to δύναμις marks out the exclusivity of the Gospel over against Torah, just as εἰς σωτηρίαν asserts its efficaciousness apart from Torah.

The Gospel as δύναμις θεοῦ εἰς σωτηρίαν, unlike δικαιοσύνη Θεοῦ in 1:17, includes the nova obedientia of believers, since it embraces the theology of the entire letter. Although Paul's statement in Rom 1:16 is formulated on the basis of a distinction between Jew and Gentile, and is followed by an assertion regarding righteousness by faith, v. 16 cannot be interpreted as having merely a forensic force. As Käsemann and others in his wake have argued, for Paul the gift of 'justification' is always accompanied by obedience. According to Paul, those righteous by faith will also exhibit righteous behavior and enjoy eschatological salvation.[134]

Paul's reference to τὸ εὐαγγέλιον without further explanation in Rom 1:16 indicates that he assumed that his audience shared his basic conception of this expression. In Rom 1:1–3, he stresses

---

[130] Richard B. Hays, *Echoes of Scripture in the Letters of Paul* (New Haven: Yale University Press, 1989), pp. 38–39.

[131] See Wilckens, *Der Brief an die Römer*, 1:82.

[132] See especially Rom 13:11; 1 Thess 5:8, 9. Cf. Cranfield, *Commentary on Romans*, 1:88–89.

[133] Cf. Rom 1:18.

[134] See e.g. Rom 2:12–16; 6:15–23.

(through the use of an early formula?) that the Gospel is the fulfillment of prophetic promise concerning the Son of God, born of the seed of David and designated as Son by his resurrection. Yet Paul does not spell out its saving message here. It is likely that he relies upon a common understanding of the Gospel as the proclamation of Jesus' death as atonement for sin, and his resurrection and exaltation as the promise of salvation at his impending *Parousia*. Other passages in Paul's letters attest that the passion and resurrection were interpreted in this manner in the early believing community, and that the proclamation of these themes was encapsulated in the expression $\epsilon \dot{v} a \gamma \gamma \dot{\epsilon} \lambda \iota o \nu$.[135] The omission of mention of atonement in 1:1–3 probably is due to the focus of the confession on the identity of the 'son of God,' not his work.[136]

Paul backs his thesis that the Gospel is necessary and sufficient for salvation to all, by asserting that $\delta \iota \kappa a \iota o \sigma \dot{v} \nu \eta$ $\Theta \epsilon o \hat{v}$ is revealed in the Gospel. It is sometimes presumed that this expression is a reflection of Paul's conflicts with Judaizers elsewhere. But this view cannot be substantiated. $\Delta \iota \kappa a \iota o \sigma \dot{v} \nu \eta$ $\Theta \epsilon o \hat{v}$ is noticeably lacking in Galatians, where Paul is clearly in heated debate. In Phil 3, where he is combating the danger of Judaizers he uses $\dot{\eta}$ $\dot{\epsilon} \kappa$ $\theta \epsilon o \hat{v}$ $\delta \iota \kappa a \iota o \sigma \dot{v} \nu \eta$, which bears the sense of 'righteousness from God,' from which the meaning of $\delta \iota \kappa a \iota o \sigma \dot{v} \nu \eta$ $\Theta \epsilon o \hat{v}$ in Rom 1:17 most likely differs. In 2 Cor 5:21, Paul is not battling Judaizing tendencies, but a challenge from opponents who adopted an over-realized eschatology.[137] On balance then, it is likely that 'righteousness of God' (in its various forms) represents Paul's selection of commonly understood language, not his resorting to a polemical slogan.

References to God's righteousness seldom appear in the New Testament apart from Paul's letters.[138] The sole occurrence of $\delta \iota \kappa a \iota o \sigma \dot{v} \nu \eta$ $\theta \epsilon o \hat{v}$ which may be reliably dated prior to Romans, is in 2 Cor 5:21, where it should be understood in a forensic manner.

---

[135] That the atoning nature of Jesus' death was a feature of the traditional understanding of $\epsilon \dot{v} a \gamma \gamma \dot{\epsilon} \lambda \iota o \nu$ is supported by 1 Cor 15:1–7, and the Lord's Supper traditions (1 Cor 11:23–26). On the currency of the term $\epsilon \dot{v} a \gamma \gamma \dot{\epsilon} \lambda \iota o \nu$ in the early Church see Gal 1:6–7; 1 Cor 9:14. Cf. Peter Stuhlmacher, 'Das paulinische Evangelium,' in *Das Evangelium und die Evangelien*, WUNT 28, ed. Peter Stuhlmacher (Tübingen: J. C. B. Mohr [Paul Siebeck], 1983), p. 166; *Versöhnung, Gesetz, Gerechtigkeit*, pp. 66–74; Georg Strecker, '$\epsilon \dot{v} a \gamma \gamma \dot{\epsilon} \lambda \iota o \nu$,' in *Exegetisches Wörterbuch zum Neuen Testament* 3 vols., ed. Horst Balz and Gerhard Schneider (Stuttgart: W. Kohlhammer, 1981), 2:177–178; 'Das Evangelium Jesu Christi,' in *Eschaton und Historie* (Göttingen: Vandenhoeck & Ruprecht, 1979), pp. 197–204.

[136] Cf. Phil 2:5–11.

[137] Cf. 2 Cor 5:6–13; 6:1.

[138] See Jas 1:20; Matt 6:33; 2 Pet 1:1.

Although the parallelism and christological focus of Paul's statement suggest that it represents a formula, one cannot be certain of its sense apart from its context. Clearly δικαιοσύνη Θεοῦ signifies a quality here, not a definite referent, since it lacks the article. The meaning of the purpose clause (ἵνα ἡμεῖς γενώμεθα δικαιοσύνη θεοῦ ἐν αὐτῷ) must be derived from the main clause (τὸν μὴ γνόντα ἁμαρτίαν ὑπὲρ ἡμῶν ἁμαρτίαν ἐποίησεν). God did not make Christ to *behave sinfully*, but to suffer the punitive measures reserved for the sinful. In this sense, Christ 'became' sin. Those 'in' Christ 'become' God's righteousness in a corresponding manner. The preceding call to be reconciled to God (5:20) indicates Paul's stress here. It is a call to the Corinthians to embrace the Gospel of the crucified Christ, and consequently Paul's ministry (6:1–10). The thrust of Paul's statement is directed not against licentious behavior, but against a false estimation of the cross, which Paul here stresses as working the acceptance of the Corinthians (and of the world) by God, and which therefore is not to be despised.

The infrequent use of the expression δικαιοσύνη Θεοῦ suggests that the phrase was not widely employed in early Christian tradition prior to Paul.[139] Given this condition, it is likely that Paul presumes that his audience was familiar with the usage of δικαιοσύνη from early Christian traditions, the synagogue, and from the Septuagint.[140] No doubt many of the Gentiles in the church had been God-fearers prior to adopting Christianity, giving them access to Hellenistic Jewish use of the term.

The immediate context of the expression δικαιοσύνη Θεοῦ in Rom 1:17 leaves only two basic options open to the interpreter.[141] Either the expression is to be taken as building upon apocalyptic Jewish conceptions of 'God's saving/obedience-producing power,' or as 'the righteousness which has its origin in God' (either as gift or as authoritative demand). The interpretation of δικαιοσύνη Θεοῦ as a reference to God's covenant faithfulness *alone* (not as a obedience-producing power), through an appeal to the Scriptures, is insufficient, since it fails to explain the clear anthropological moment,

---

[139] *Pace* Stuhlmacher, *Gerechtigkeit Gottes*, pp. 74–77. Rom 3:25–26a represents a early Christian tradition in which reference is made to God's righteousness in the sense of 'covenant faithfulness.'

[140] In the absence of a technical usage, one must, at the very least, include for consideration the range of meanings allowed to the word δικαιοσύνη, and not merely the phrase δικαιοσύνη θεοῦ.

[141] For discussions of the various interpretations of the expression see Käsemann, *An die Römer*, pp. 22–27; Cranfield, *Commentary on Romans*, pp. 91–97; Wilckens, *Der Brief an die Römer*, 1:223–233.

expressed by ὁ δὲ δίκαιος ἐκ πίστεως ζήσεται.[142] The δικαιοσύνη Θεοῦ here is the means by which the individual becomes δίκαιος. It is not merely a manifestation of salvation or forgiveness.

We already have offered arguments for rejecting the line of interpretation of Rom 1:17 represented by Käsemann.[143] Foremost among these is the observation that as in the case of εὐαγγέλιον, the manner in which Paul introduces δικαιοσύνη Θεοῦ indicates that he assumes that his audience is familiar with the expression.[144] It is unlikely in this case that he is thinking of an 'obedience producing power.' Rom 6 would hardly have been necessary if his audience was familiar with such a tradition. The redundancy in which such a reading results (the Gospel is God's power because it reveals God's power) further inclines one toward the alternative interpretation of δικαιοσύνη Θεοῦ either as a divine requirement or as a gift.[145]

The genitive, Θεοῦ, is somewhat ambiguous. Although the interpretive option here is frequently described as a choice between subjective and authorial genitive, the category 'subjective genitive' is not quite appropriate. True subjective (or objective) genitives express the subject (or respectively, object) of the verbal idea contained in a noun which denotes action (e.g. ἀγάπη θεοῦ).[146] But δικαιοσύνη is not derived directly from a verb: it denotes the abstract quality or state of being δίκαιος.[147] The true interpretive choice lies between genitive of possession or belonging and its more precise sub-category, genitive of origin. The former is represented by the reading 'God's covenant faithfulness' and Käsemann's line of interpretation ('God's own salvation creating power').[148] Since these readings seem unlikely here, one is inclined to read Θεοῦ as a genitive of origin.

---

[142] Contra C. H. Dodd, *The Epistle of Paul to the Romans* (London: Hodder and Stoughton, 1932), pp. 9–13; Williams, 'The 'Righteousness of God' in Romans,' pp. 260–263. Hence the sense of 'his' (i.e. God's) righteousness which appears in Rom 3:25–26a does not lie behind Paul's usage here.

[143] See Chapter 1, Section VII.

[144] So also Wilckens, *Der Brief an die Römer*, 1:86.

[145] While Williams comes to a different conclusion regarding the meaning of δικαιοσύνη Θεοῦ here, he affirms the points spelled out in this paragraph, 'The 'Righteousness of God' in Romans,' pp. 255–263.

[146] See H. W. Smyth, *Greek Grammar*, rev. G. M. Messing (Cambridge, Mass.: Harvard University Press, 1956), 1328.

[147] Smyth, *Greek Grammar*, 840. This is not to suggest that the abstract state δικαιοσύνη does not manifest itself in action. It is, of course, frequently used in this sense in the LXX as a reflection of צדקה. This Septuagintal usage is then a concretion of an abstract.

[148] Käsemann, of course, combines with this idea that of origin as well.

Even this category is somewhat broad. It allows either the idea of a quality concretized in a divine requirement, or a status conferred (which, by implication, includes a requirement). In Rom 10:3, Paul shifts between these two concepts. The concept of a divinely given status is to be preferred in 1:17, since as we have noted, the conclusion of the verse speaks of a human standing *coram Deo*.[149]

The interpretation of δικαιοσύνη as a status required for eschatological salvation and life is well-grounded in terms of Paul's word-usage and background.[150] Paul's opponents elsewhere had asserted that the righteousness of *Torah* was essential to salvation.[151] The fact that Paul's opposition employed such language shows that this meaning of δικαιοσύνη was current in the synagogue and some segments of the early church.[152] And Paul's use of the expression δικαιοσύνη Θεοῦ in 2 Cor 5:21 obviously bears soteriological overtones, as its following context shows.[153] Furthermore, Paul's own earlier consciousness of his acquisition of righteousness prior to his conversion links him to the type of thought found in the Pss. Sol., where being δίκαιος and having δικαιοσύνη are prerequisites for deliverance.[154]

Allusion to traditional concepts operates here at the level of the word-combination, 'the righteousness of God is revealed,' which brings into play the associations of other contexts. As many interpreters rightly have pointed out, Paul's language in Rom 1:16, 17 reflects that of several passages from Isaiah and the Biblical psalms, especially Psalm 97:2, 3 (LXX) and Isa 51:4–8 (LXX). Paul's wording recollects promises of God's saving covenant–faithfulness, *iustitia salutifera*, reinforcing Paul's emphasis on the universal scope of the Gospel.

---

[149] Cf. the early Luther on Rom 1:17, '*Justitia* qua tali salute dignum est *enim Dei* qua sola iusti sunt coram Deo.' *Vorlesung über den Römerbrief 1515/1516* 2 vols. (Weimar: Hermann Böhlaus, 1960), 1:40.

[150] Sanders, *Paul and Palestinian Judaism*, p. 494, wrongly attempts to play off the notion of a presently acquired righteousness against its forensic-eschatological significance. In 1QS, righteousness is linked to the life of the community in which salvation from eschatological wrath is available. And in the Pss. Sol., it is 'the righteous' who are guaranteed eschatological deliverance. Phil 3:6–9 shows that prior to his conversion Paul, too, looked upon his righteousness as the assurance of salvation. The idea continues in the language of Paul's letters, e.g. Rom 2:13; 3:22–24; 8:10; 10:5–10; Gal 2:21; Bultmann, *Theologie des Neuen Testaments*, pp. 271–275.

[151] E.g. Gal 2:21; 3:21; 5:5.

[152] Both Matt (5:20; 6:33) and Jas (1:20; 2:23) attest to an understanding of righteousness as a prerequisite for salvation in the early Christian community.

[153] 2 Cor 6:1, 2.

[154] See Chapter 3, Section III. Cf. Ps. Sol. 1:2, 3; 2:34, 35; 9:4, 5; 13:11. Righteousness was required for salvation according to the Qumran community as well, although this righteousness was embodied in the life of the community. See Chapter 2, Section II.E.

Yet, as Richard Hays has observed, the echoing of earlier tradition involves some measure of reinterpretation: old voices are heard differently in new settings.[155] In fact, Paul's 'recollection' of these Biblical texts does not involve a direct appropriation of the idea of saving covenant–faithfulness. The lack of article with δι-καιοσύνη Θεοῦ alerts us that Paul alludes only obliquely to these passages.

Moreover, there is a certain degree of ambiguity regarding divine righteousness in both Psalm 97:2, 3 (LXX) and Isa 51:4–8 (LXX). In the former, God's righteousness, while displayed to the nations, consists in his faithfulness to Israel and adumbrates his coming to judge the world 'in righteousness.' Likewise, in Isa 51:4–8 (LXX), while God announces the nearness of his righteousness and salvation, he also proclaims that 'those who dwell in the earth' shall perish, particularly the opponents of his people. Divine righteousness is not universally and unequivocally salvific in these texts. Most significantly, the words of these Biblical passages are repeated in other early Jewish writings in such a manner that the idea of a status necessary for salvation was implied, while the notion of divine covenant–faithfulness was retained.

ולפי קורבי קנאתי על כול פועלי
רשע ואנשי רמיה כי כול קרוביך
לא ימרו פיך וכול יודעיך לא
ישנו דבריך כי אתה צדיק ואמת
כול בחיריך וכול עולה]שע[
תשמיד לעד ונגלתה צדקתך
לעיני כול מעשיך

1QH 14:13b–16 And according to my drawing near (to you), I display my zeal against all who do wickedness and the deceitful. For all who draw near to you do not alter 'your mouth.' And all who know you do not change your words, for you are righteous and all that you have chosen is true. And all evil [and wicked]ness you will destroy forever. *And you will reveal your righteousness before the eyes of all your works.*[156]

Paul's 'echo' modifies the thrust of the Biblical text in the same direction as the Qumran references do, only he makes the concept of righteous status primary rather than secondary. The divine

---

[155] Hays, *Echoes of Scripture*, pp. 14–21.

[156] See also CD 20:18b–21a: God took note and listened to their words and a book of remembrances was written [before him] of the ones who fear God and honor his name (Mal 3:16) *until salvation and righteousness are revealed* for those who fear [God and] you again [see] the difference between the righteous and the wicked (Mal 3:18).

righteousness to which Paul refers in Rom 1:17 is that by which one becomes righteous.

This righteous status is mediated by faith. Paul's assertion in 1:16 that the Gospel works salvation for the one who believes is developed here through the phrase ἐκ πίστεως εἰς πίστιν. This expression should be understood in connection with ἀποκαλύπτεται.[157] If Paul had intended a direct association with δικαιοσύνη Θεοῦ, ἐκ πίστεως εἰς πίστιν most likely would have followed it immediately. And the pairing of ἐκ and εἰς is not simply intensifying. The use of a prepositional phrase followed by εἰς governing an identical object clearly denotes progress toward a goal or outcome.[158] Faith is the (mediate) source from which a righteous status conferred by God is revealed. The revelation of God's righteousness leads to the act of faith (εἰς πίστιν) which appropriates it (παντὶ τῷ πιστεύοντι). The righteousness conferred by God, revealed in the Gospel through faith, is given to faith. The dual prepositional usage is not merely stylistic then. The phrase εἰς πίστιν removes any misunderstanding regarding the means by which the δικαιοσύνη manifest in the Gospel is acquired. Since the righteousness which assures salvation is given to faith, Paul is able to use the Habbakuk citation (ὁ δὲ δίκαιος ἐκ πίστεως ζήσεται) as a summary of the whole.[159]

Πίστις is not merely a formal concept in this context. It quite clearly has the Gospel as its object, as Paul's initial assertion in Rom 1:16 shows.[160] This idea is continued in Rom 1:17, where the Gospel is the locus of the revelation of God's righteousness. Paul does not appeal here to the Gospel as a Lehrsatz, in which the necessity of faith is taught.[161] Rather, as we have observed already, he is operating here with the common understanding of Jesus' atoning death and vindicating resurrection which was current in the early Church. His assertion then is that in the message of Jesus' death and resurrection the divinely authoritative requirement for righteousness is revealed and met for the one who believes.

---

[157] Contra Cranfield, *Commentary on Romans*, 1:100.

[158] See 2 Cor 2:16; 3:18; 4:17. Cf. LXX Ps 83:6–8; Jer 9:2, 3; Wilckens, *Der Brief an die Römer*, 1:88–89.

[159] The ἐκ πίστεως here might modify either the subject (ὁ δίκαιος) or the verb (ζήσεται). But the reading offered above of δικαιοσύνη Θεοῦ as a status conferred by God somewhat favors taking the phrase with the verb. The sense would then cohere with the context of the Habbakuk passage of which Paul himself must have been aware, since the oracle given to the prophet calls for trust in God.

[160] τὸ εὐαγγέλιον, δύναμις . . . θεοῦ ἐστιν . . . παντὶ τῷ πιστεύοντι. See Wilckens's excellent discussion in which he distinguishes Paul's understanding of faith from Bultmann's interpretation, *Der Brief an die Römer*, 1:232.

[161] So, rightly, Adolf Schlatter, *Gottes Gerechtigkeit: Ein Kommentar zum Römerbrief* (Stuttgart: Calwer, 1935), pp. 42–43.

The function of the idea of righteousness by faith in relation to the purpose of the letter now may be fairly well described. Paul's aim of obtaining adherence to his Gospel in Rome has a specific theological aspect, expressed in the thesis statement of Rom 1:16: the Gospel is the necessary and sufficient means of salvation for all. It is the Gospel's universality and efficacy for salvation, which Paul wants his audience to embrace. He supports his assertion by a single statement: that the righteousness required for salvation is supplied by the Gospel. In making such a claim for the Gospel, he is adopting a specific understanding of the traditional formulation represented by the term. Paul interprets Jesus' death and resurrection as a divine offer of righteousness by faith alone.[162]

B. Romans 3:21–5:21

We have seen that Paul's claim for the relevance of the Gospel is predicated upon a universal need for salvation. Naturally, his supporting argument that the righteousness of God, the divinely determined means to salvation, is revealed in the Gospel is contingent upon the same consideration. Rom 1:18–3:20 subsequently serves to confirm that a universal need for salvation exists, and that salvation is available through the righteousness of God revealed in the Gospel.

In Rom 1:18–32 Paul describes the peril of the Gentile world before the wrath of God in a manner common to Jewish wisdom and apocalyptic literature.[163] His discussion then shifts to a dialogue with an imaginary Jewish partner in Rom 2:1– Rom 4:15. In the first portion of this conversation, he addresses the person who acts as moral judge of others, by implication attacking the Jew who condemns Gentiles (Rom 2:1–16). In Rom 2:17–2:29, he speaks to the Jew who lives irreligiously, endeavoring to show that the circumcised Jew and not merely the Gentile is subject to judgment.[164] He then derives from Scripture the charge that such a judgment results in a guilty verdict.[165] The argument therefore moves from the shared premise of an impending eschatological wrath against the disobedient, to the assertion that the Jew is a transgressor as well, subject to divine condemnation.

---

[162] On the distinctiveness of Paul's understanding of 'justification,' see Nils A. Dahl, 'The Doctrine of Justification: Its Social Function and Implications,' in *Studies in Paul* (Minneapolis: Augsburg, 1979), pp. 105– 109.

[163] See Wilckens, *Der Brief an die Römer*, 1:95–100.

[164] Paul's argument moves on to a paradox: the Jew has a great advantage (3:1, 2a Τί οὖν τὸ περισσὸν τοῦ Ἰουδαίου, ἢ τίς ἡ ὠφέλεια τῆς περιτομῆς; πολὺ κατὰ πάντα τρόπον) which does not profit (3:8 Τί οὖν προεχόμεθα; οὐ πάντως).

[165] Rom 3:4, 9–20.

This assertion regarding Jewish culpability subsequently plays an essential role in Paul's expanded explication of 'justification by faith' in Rom 3:21–26. Paul's fundamental assertion in this passage is that a 'righteousness of God' which is χωρὶς νόμου has been made manifest. The δικαιοσύνη Θεοῦ is mediated 'through faith in Jesus Christ to all who believe.'[166] These complementary assertions concerning the righteousness of God, χωρὶς νόμου, εἰς πάντας τοὺς πιστεύοντας, are defended in Paul's following statements. Negatively, Paul claims that universal sinfulness means that God makes no distinction on the basis of *Torah* observance in his dispensation of this gift. Positively, Paul appeals to the redemption which God accomplished through Christ's atoning death as the vehicle for forensic justification.

Paul's reference to redemption and atonement in Rom 3:25, 26 very likely represents his use of an early formula describing Jesus' death.[167] In this tradition, Jesus' atoning death is interpreted as a display of God's righteousness. It is widely recognized that the reference to God's righteousness here signifies his covenantal faithfulness. Usually this righteousness is interpreted as *iustitia salutifera*, God's saving righteousness, enacted on behalf of the covenantal people.[168] However, while the reference to God's covenantal faithfulness is clear, the assumption that a saving righteousness is in view is questionable. The interpretation of Jesus' death as an atonement (ὃν προέθετο ὁ θεὸς ἱλαστήριον διὰ [τῆς] πίστεως ἐν τῷ αὐτοῦ αἵματι), presupposes that it occurred in order to provide forgiveness of sin. This observation strongly inclines one to interpret πάρεσις as a temporary dismissal of sin, rather than as full

---

[166] The same interpretive options for δικαιοσύνη Θεοῦ are present here as in 1:17. One's choice is largely determined by the decision reached there. Most recent commentators (Dunn, Wilckens, Schlier, Zeller), following variations of Käsemann's line of thought, opt for the idea of a salvation-creating power in both contexts. Cranfield retains the interpretation of δικαιοσύνη Θεοῦ as a righteousness given as a gift, *Commentary on Romans*, 1:202. Despite the current debate over πίστις Ἰησοῦ Χριστοῦ, the stress on faith as the means by which righteousness is appropriated and the absence of the theme of Jesus' faithfulness strongly suggest that Ἰησοῦ Χριστοῦ is to be interpreted as an objective, not subjective genitive. Cf. Dunn, *Romans*, pp. 166–167.

[167] In view of the unusual vocabulary of 3:25, most commentators regard 3:25–3:26a as reflecting a pre-Pauline formula. Cranfield, (*Commentary on Romans*, p. 200 n. 1) and Schlier (*Der Römerbrief*, pp. 109–110) argue that the material stems from Paul, although it undoubtedly reflects traditional language. It has already been noted that τὸ εὐαγγέλιον in Rom 1:16 contains an implicit reference to Jesus' death, which would have been understood as an atonement. It is unlikely that Rom 3:24 belonged to the tradition, since the language here is Paul's own, contra Käsemann, *An die Römer*, pp. 89–90. See Dunn, *Romans*, pp. 163–164, Wilckens, *Der Brief an die Römer*, 1:183–184.

[168] E.g. Wilckens, *Der Brief an die Römer*, 1:194–199.

remission.[169] If sins prior to Christ's death (προγεγονότα ἁμαρτήματα) had already received forgiveness in God's covenantal faithfulness, Christ's death could scarcely be interpreted as an atonement. Paul's reference to God's restraint (ἐν τῇ ἀνοχῇ τοῦ θεοῦ) points in this direction as well, since Paul refers to it elsewhere in Romans as a divine forestalling of punishment which allows for repentance.[170] In this case, the reference to God's righteousness as his covenantal faithfulness signifies his determination to punish those who because of transgression are outside of his covenant. That God's righteousness could take this punitive sense in Jewish tradition is attested by Isaiah, the Psalms, Daniel, and both 1QS and the Pss. Sol.[171]

The traditional statement of which Paul makes use in Rom 3:25–26a therefore interpreted Jesus' death as an atonement, which displayed not only God's mercy, but his faithfulness to punish those disobedient to the covenant. It reflects the underlying assumption of the early Jewish believing community that the nation had broken with the covenant, and that repentance and faith in God's act in the Messiah was necessary for forgiveness.[172] Paul's more radical understanding of forensic justification as entailing eschatological vindication is not explicit here however.[173]

Paul's expansion of the tradition in Rom 3:26b is marked by an emphasis on the universal applicability of Jesus' death in individualistic terms.[174] He repeats the idea that Jesus' atoning death

---

[169] Contra Kümmel, 'Πάρεσις und ἔνδειξις: Ein Beitrag zum Verständnis der paulinischen Rechtfertigungslehre,' in *Heilsgeschehen und Geschichte*, MTS 3 (Marburg: N. G. Elwert, 1965), pp. 260–270. See Dunn, *Romans*, pp. 173–174, and especially Williams, *Jesus' Death as Saving Event*, pp. 19–34. Williams's suggestion that the phrase relates to Gentile sin is unlikely, however, since the tradition appeals to God's covenantal faithfulness.

[170] Rom 2:4. As Williams, *Jesus' Death as Saving Event* , p. 26 notes, Kümmel's insistence that ἐν τῇ ἀνοχῇ τοῦ θεοῦ refers to the time of God's patience finds insufficient support in the text.

[171] See LXX Isa 51:4–8 and LXX Isa 63:1–7, where God's righteousness saves his people, but brings destruction on Gentiles. Likewise in the Psalms, God's righteousness preserves his servants, but destroys their foes (Ps 5:5–11; Ps 7:7–18; Ps 50:6, 16–23). In the prayer of confession in Dan 9:4–19, God's righteous deeds (9:16) are his acts of judgment upon his people as transgressors of the covenant. Likewise, in 1QM 4:6 the elect, who go forth to destroy the Gentiles and the transgressors of the covenant (1QM 1:2), carry on their banners the words 'the righteousness of God,' as a rallying cry. In Ps. Sol. 9:4, 5, God in his righteousness visits the wicked with destruction.

[172] Cf. Stephen's speech in Acts 7.

[173] See Dahl, 'The Doctrine of Justification,' pp. 96–105.

represented a display of God's faithfulness to covenantal provisions
(πρὸς τὴν ἔνδειξιν τῆς δικαιοσύνης αὐτοῦ), while stressing that this
divine act constitutes the definitive and ultimate display of God's
righteousness (ἐν τῷ νῦν καιρῷ). By acting in this manner God has
remained faithful to his covenantal provisions (εἰς τὸ εἶναι αὐτὸν
δίκαιον), while justifying anyone, including Gentiles, on the basis
of faith alone (καὶ δικαιοῦντα τὸν ἐκ πίστεως Ἰησοῦ).[175]

'Justification by faith' therefore represents Paul's formulation of
the scope of the atonement, which is defined in both its breadth
and depth by the condemnation of all humanity. Paul's preceding
claim, that the Jew stands under divine judgment, is therefore the
linchpin of his argument in Rom 3:21–26. The repetition of this
idea in Rom 3:23 (πάντες γὰρ ἥμαρτον καὶ ὑστεροῦνται τῆς δόξης
τοῦ θεοῦ) is not superfluous, but central to the argument of this
section. Given that Paul here seeks to establish the universal
significance of the Gospel, the initial 'proof' of the thesis he
introduces in Rom 1:16 is complete already in Rom 3:21–26.
The sole ground which Paul gives for his assertion that the
Gospel is the power of God for salvation to all is that the divine
demand (and gift) of righteousness is revealed in it. That argument, in turn, is contingent solely upon his audience recognizing
the plight of *all* humanity (including the Jew), since they already
share his interpretation of Jesus' death. The remainder of the
letter represents corollaries and expansions of his thesis concerning the power of the Gospel and its supporting arguments, intended to gain adherence in both theory and practice to that
Gospel. But in terms of conceptual coherence, the support for
the thesis which Paul introduces with δικαιοσύνη Θεοῦ in
Rom 1:17 is concluded at Rom 3:26.[176]

The following material in Rom 3:27–5:21 is therefore best regarded as containing four rhetorical units which expand, support,
and apply 'justification by faith.' Despite the obvious broadening

---

[174] Contra Käsemann, *An die Römer*, p. 95, it is difficult to read this passage in
cosmic terms. Paul not only explicitly refers to the individual here (καὶ δικαιοῦντα
τὸν ἐκ πίστεως Ἰησοῦ), he also makes a distinction elsewhere in the letter, between
Christ's redemptive work for Jews (as covenantal faithfulness) and that toward
Gentiles (as mercy; Rom 15:7–9). Hence it is difficult to see his development of the
tradition as an *expansion* of covenantal faithfulness to faithfulness to creation. It is
more a setting aside of the covenant.

[175] See Dunn, *Romans*, p. 164.

[176] This observation should not be taken to imply that the rest of the letter is of
lesser importance for Paul's aim. It merely highlights the fact that persuasion is
served by a variety of arguments, and not merely the linear development of an
idea.

of the discussion in Rom 5, Paul's continuing use of the language of 'justification' makes it clear that he is still building upon the theme of forensic righteousness given as a gift to faith.[177]

The first conclusion which Paul draws in Rom 3:27-31 from his argument on 'justification by faith' underscores the Jewish orientation of his argument. Appealing to the quintessentially Jewish theme of the unity of the sovereign God, Paul claims that boasting is excluded and that God will justify the uncircumcised through faith. Any superiority of the Jew given through the gift of *Torah* is obliterated in the face of the assertion that God justifies by faith χωρὶς ἔργων νόμου.[178]

The example of Abraham (Rom 4:1-25) serves as an attestation to 'justification by faith' from the patriarch of the Jewish religion and the first to accept the sign of circumcision. In the prescript of Romans, Paul describes the Scriptures as containing the promise of the Gospel. He repeats this idea with reference to the concept of justification apart from Law in Rom 3:21. Rom 4 serves to confirm this claim by showing the continuity of Paul's message with the will of God revealed in Scripture.

Correspondingly, the discussion begins as a debate with a Jewish interlocutor concerning Jew-Gentile distinctions. In the course of Rom 4, however, Paul's rhetorical audience shifts from the Jewish partner, to his addressees at Rome.[179] When he takes up a fresh application of 'justification by faith' in Rom 5:1, he presumes that the message has implications for his predominantly Gentile audience, apart from any question of Jew-Gentile distinctions.

Rom 5:1-11 is hortatory, either implicitly or explicitly.[180] It is

---

[177] On Rom 5, see below. Cf. 5:1 δικαιωθέντες οὖν; 5:17 ἡ δωρεὰ τῆς δικαιοσύνης; 5:18 δικαίωσις ζωῆς; 5:19 δίκαιοι; 5:21 ἡ χάρις (βασιλεύειν) διὰ δικαιοσύνης.

[178] Paul's conclusion should not obscure the fact that his statements are directed toward an audience of Christian Jews and Gentiles. Only believers who accepted the premises upon which Paul's argument is based would be prepared to accept his reasoning.

[179] The change appears in 4:16 (οὐ τῷ ἐκ τοῦ νόμου μόνον ἀλλὰ καὶ τῷ ἐκ πίστεως Ἀβραάμ, ὅς ἐστιν πατὴρ πάντων ἡμῶν) and continues through the end of the chapter (cf. 4:24, 25).

[180] The text-critical question as to whether one should read εἰρήνην ἔχομεν πρὸς τὸν θεὸν or εἰρήνην ἔχωμεν κ.τ.λ. in 5:1 is very difficult. The latter clearly has better support in the manuscripts. But given the easy confusion of omicron and omega, and the tendency of scribes to create exhortations it is difficult to tell which was original. Cf. Dunn, *Romans*, p. 245. Εἰρήνη probably bears a subjective dimension here, just as it does in the prescripts of Paul's letters (Rom 1:7; 1 Cor 1:3; 2 Cor 1:2; Gal 1:3; Phil 1:2; 1 Thess 1:1), and in Rom 14:17, 19. It includes the human perception and acknowledgment of a new relationship with God, not merely an external, objective condition. Furthermore, Rom 5:3 (οὐ μόνον δέ, ἀλλὰ καὶ

intended to give assurance of God's love and of the hope of salvation in the face of present trial.[181] 'Justification' here becomes the
basis for present peace amid turmoil, and the guarantee of eschatological deliverance.[182] As Klaus Haacker observes concerning
Paul's shift to the language of 'peace' and 'reconciliation,'

> Der nur von alttestamentlich-jüdisch Voraussetzungen her verstän-
> dliche Gedanke der 'Rechtfertigung' wird damit in allgemeinspra-
> chlich-nachvollziehbare soziale Metaphern übersetzt.[183]

If forensic justification was accomplished by the death of Christ
for sinners and enemies of God, *a fortiori*, those reconciled to God
will be saved from the apocalyptic manifestation of God's wrath.
Hence those who believe have occasion to boast in God, whatever
they might suffer at present.

The very fact that Paul must argue here that 'justification'
assures final salvation suggests that he addresses Gentiles here.[184]
Earlier in the letter Paul presumes that Jews in his audience perceived that the possession of righteousness implies salvation from
God's apocalyptic wrath. For example, the compact theological
statement which he uses to introduce the letter in Rom 1:16, 17
is built upon the premise that the revelation of God's righteousness
is an adequate explanation for the claim that the Gospel provides
salvation. Likewise, when arguing against a distinction between
Jew and Gentile in Rom 2:13, Paul, without introduction, discus-
ses forensic justification in an eschatological framework, assuming

---

καυχώμεθα ἐν ταῖς θλίψεσιν, εἰδότες ὅτι ἡ θλῖψες ὑπομονὴν κατεργάζεται) must be
understood as an exhortation, whether καυχώμεθα is interpreted as an indicative
or as a hortatory subjunctive. The passage as a whole then bears a hortatory tone.

[181] Rom 5:3–5.

[182] Paul's assertion that 'we' (i.e. Paul and the whole of his audience, especially
the Gentile majority) boast in the hope of God's glory (Rom 5:2), and in present
reconciliation to him (Rom 5:11), would underscore the universalism of Paul's
Gospel to Jewish believers in the church. However, the bulk of the argument is
given to assuring the church that despite present tribulation, God's gift of righteousness in Christ guarantees eschatological salvation (Rom 5:3–10). Hence it is
difficult to read the material as an argument for 'Christian boasting' in place of
that of the Jew. The passage is anticipatory of Paul's summary of his Gospel in
Rom 8:31–39.

[183] Klaus Haacker, 'Der Römerbrief als Friedensmemorandum,' *NTS* 36
(1990):30.

[184] On δικαιοῦν interpreted as 'forgive,' see, e.g. LXX Isa 43:6; Micah 6:11.
However, the concept of righteousness as a 'gift' differs from 'justification' understood as 'forgiveness,' and bears eschatological implications in an apocalyptic
Jewish framework. In Rom 5:1, Paul's use of δικαιοῦν is determined by his preceding references to righteousness as a 'gift,' clearly signifying its eschatological
ramifications for Jewish Christian readers.

that Jewish Christians, to whom his argument is directed, knew that 'justification' had an eschatological point of reference. Furthermore, Paul's references to a future forensic justification in Rom 3:19–20, 30 take their orientation from the idea of God as final Judge, again showing that Paul assumed Jewish Christians were aware of the eschatological implications of 'justification by faith.' Therefore, when he turns to arguing for the connection between present forensic justification and future deliverance from God's wrath, one must assume that he does so for the sake of Gentile Christians, who were less familiar with the eschatological implications of the gift of righteousness.

The latter half of the chapter is a recapitulation of the universal significance of 'justification' in light of its individualistic development in Rom 5:1–11.[185] Paul's affirmation that present forensic justification will issue in deliverance from God's wrath allows him to draw a comparison between the condemnation and death which was the result of the sin of Adam and the justification and eschatological life which is the effect of Christ's act of obedience on the cross.[186] The congruence which Paul draws between the two figures is obviously the means by which he appeals to his audience. If Adam's sin resulted in many deaths, it is not unreasonable to claim that Christ's obedience will result in life for 'the many.' The argument in Rom 5:12–21 supports Paul's thesis in Rom 5:1–11, that faith (and hence forensic justification) brings the assurance of eschatological salvation. Here the universal dimension of Christ's act of obedience on the cross is stressed, which brings the discussion back to Jewish questions. Rom 5:12–21 serves as a summary of Paul's arguments for 'justification by faith.'[187]

The place of 'justification by faith' within the argument of the letter may be given further precision in the light of this analysis of Rom 3:21–5:21. As we have seen, it represents Paul's interpretation of the atonement as having universal saving value. Since his audience accepted his premise that Jesus' death was an atonement, Paul's thesis is dependent solely on his claim that all of humanity, including the Jew, is under divine judgment. This facet of Paul's argument is complete at Rom 3:20 so that Rom 3:21–26 may be regarded as completing Paul's primary

---

[185] See Käsemann's argument for the theological unity of the two halves of the chapter, *An die Römer*, pp. 132–133; also Wilckens, *Der Brief an die Römer*, 1:307.

[186] Rom 5:15, 18–19.

[187] Cf. Hans Weder, 'Gesetz und Sünde: Gedanken zu einem Qualitativen Sprung im Denken des Paulus,' *NTS* 31 (1985):357–376.

argument concerning 'justification by faith.'[188] The two following sections, Rom 3:27–31 and Rom 4:1–25, serve to bolster Paul's case in terms relevant to Jewish Christians. Rom 5:1–11 moves beyond this realm to apply Paul's understanding of justification specifically to the hopes of Paul's predominantly Gentile audience. For the first time in his letters, Paul develops ramifications of 'justification by faith' for the specific needs of Gentiles. This explication of Paul's conception of forensic justification by faith for Gentiles untroubled by the question of circumcision and adherence to the Law obviously reflects a crucial development in Paul's use of the theme.

C. Romans 7:14–25

In Rom 6–8 Paul's argument shifts away from the topic of forensic justification.[189] The introduction of the topics of death to sin (Rom 6), and to the Law (Rom 7), and the indwelling by the Spirit which brings the hope of a new creation (Rom 8) are best understood as Paul's continuing explication of his Gospel, which is broader than the topic of 'justification by faith.' This reading of Rom 6–8 as a series of expansions of Paul's Gospel is confirmed by the fact that Christ's death and resurrection, basic elements of the Gospel tradition, introduce and form the basis of Paul's argument in each of the chapters.[190]

It is therefore difficult to agree with Schweitzer or with E. P. Sanders, who is inclined to follow Schweitzer's reading of Romans, that Rom 6–8 is a repetition of the idea of 'the new righteousness which comes through faith in Christ's atoning death.'[191] The belief that faith in the Gospel was accompanied by the gift of the Spirit and a new life of obedience does not necessarily carry the universal dimensions of Paul's arguments on

---

[188] As suggested above, it is not clear that all of Paul's audience regarded Jesus' atoning death as having universal efficacy. The conflict between the 'weak' and the 'strong' most likely would have raised questions in Paul's mind as to the theological stance of the community. Furthermore, not being fully familiar with the church, he probably wanted to ensure their adherence to his views, in view of the danger his adversaries presented.

[189] The concept(s) of forensic justification or of righteousness by faith reappears only in Rom 6:7(?); 8:4, 10, 30, 33. The idea of behavioral righteousness is frequent in Rom 6 (Rom 6:13, 16, 18, 19, 20).

[190] See Rom 6:3–11; Rom 7:4–6; Rom 8:3–4, 10–11. Cf. Rom 1:3, 4.

[191] Schweitzer, *Mystik*, p. 221: 'Im Römerbriefe ereignet sich das Erstaunliche, daß, nachdem die neue Gerechtigkeit ausführlich als aus dem Glauben an das Sühnopfer Christi dargestellt ist (Rom 3:1–5:21), sie noch einmal, ohne jegliche Bezugnahme auf das bisher Ausgeführte, aus der Mystik des Sterbens und Auferstehens mit Christo begründet wird (Rom 6:1–8:1).' Cf. Sanders, *Paul and Palestinian Judaism*, pp. 485–497.

'justification by faith.'[192] Nor is death to sin, or death to the Law, precisely the same idea as being (forensically) justified by faith in Christ. Moreover, Rom 6 can hardly be said to be independent of the preceding arguments, since the rhetorical question with which Paul introduces the chapter is predicated upon the conclusion to his discussion of the gift of righteousness in Christ.[193] It is best to regard Rom 6–8 as a continuation of Paul's explication of his Gospel, in light of his argument that righteousness is given as a gift to faith, apart from the Law.

It is also wrong to read Rom 1–8 as a bipartite argument divided between forensic justification and obedience.[194] Paul's discussion in Rom 6 obviously is developed in the light of his arguments on 'justification,' indicating a continuity with the earlier portion of the letter.[195] There is considerable overlap between Rom 5:1–11 and Rom 8 regarding the topics of suffering and final salvation. Rom 7 cannot be counted as a continuation of the theme of obedience, but returns to the relationship of the believer to the Law, a question related to the concept of forensic justification developed in Rom 1–5. Despite the obvious break in topic between Rom 5 and Rom 6, Rom 6–8 continues Paul's proclamation of the Gospel in Rome by expanding upon themes introduced in Rom 3–5.

It is clear as well then, that Rom 7 does not have to do with a 'defense of the Law,' as Kümmel claims.[196] Rather, Paul here defends his Gospel against the potential Jewish objection that it compromises the holiness of *Torah*. He has asserted earlier in the letter that God gives righteousness χωρὶς νόμου in Christ. Rom 7:1–6 represents a return to this declaration. The immediate prompting for his treatment of the Law is his concluding statement in Rom 6:23, which, echoing his earlier argument, makes Christ the sole agent of God's saving grace (τὸ δὲ χάρισμα τοῦ θεοῦ ζωὴ αἰώνιος ἐν Χριστῷ Ἰησοῦ τῷ κυρίῳ ἡμῶν). In Rom 7, therefore, he is attempting to persuade his audience of the validity of this exclusion of the Law from God's saving purpose.

---

[192] Sanders, *Paul and Palestinian Judaism*, pp. 487–497, resolves this problem by arguing that Romans was composed in view of Paul's coming trip to Jerusalem, where he would face conflict from Jewish Christians. Hence the initial portion of the letter represents his attempt to respond to anticipated arguments. We have shown that this interpretation of the purpose of the letter is unsatisfactory.

[193] See Rom 5:20–6:1.

[194] Contra Cranfield, *Commentary on Romans*, 1:28–29; cf. Beker's excellent discussion of this issue, *Paul the Apostle*, pp. 66–69.

[195] See Rom 6:1, 7, 15.

[196] Kümmel, *Römer 7*, 9.

Paul first argues on the basis of analogy from marriage law, that the Law itself supports the freedom which he claims (7:1–4). Yet his appeal to the Law can be sustained only if it is allowed that believers have in fact died to the Law. At this point Paul employs an authoritative assertion (7:4, 'You also were made to die to the Law'), which he undergirds by an argument from necessity: life in the flesh and under the Law resulted in death, while freedom from the Law results in a new life of service to God (7:5, 6). His persuasiveness depends heavily on his readers' willingness to adopt the verdict he has pronounced, that their former relation to the Law 'bore fruit for death' (7:5).

In this light, Paul's adoption of the first person in 7:7–25 is understandable. He invites his audience to enter into the same self–judgment which he has made. In Rom 7:7–13, he representatively applies to himself the image of initial human encounter with the Law as a way of asking his readers to recognize themselves as transgressors who are under the sentence of death.[197] As we shall see, in Rom 7:14–25 this argument continues by relating this judgment to the present condition of believers. Only in this manner will Paul gain the adherence of his audience to his claim that the Gospel alone is God's power for salvation. Moreover, by ascribing radical evil to the human being, Paul relieves his Gospel of the charge that it betrays the goodness of the Law.

We already have discussed a number of the important issues regarding the interpretation of Rom 7:14–25, including Kümmel's thesis that the ἐγώ here is entirely fictive.[198] The difficulties associated with this text require that we examine various interpretations of the passage on our way to adopting a fresh reading.

Building upon the work of Kümmel, Rudolf Bultmann further developed the fictive reading of Rom 7, interpreting the plight of the ἐγώ as existential and 'transsubjective' rather than ethical and experiential.[199] According to this understanding, the object of the striving of the ἐγώ is not the Law itself, but 'life,' the good which is offered by the Law. This human propensity to seek to establish itself by its own acts brings about death, the loss of the authentic existence of the individual. The one who is enmeshed in this struggle is not aware of its outcome. It is only from the perspective of believing existence that one is able to recognize that life under the

---

[197] See Chapter 3, Section II.A.1.
[198] See Chapter 3, Section II.A.1.
[199] Rudolf Bultmann, 'Römer 7 und die Anthropologie des Paulus,' in *Exegetica*, ed. Erich Dinkler (Tübingen: J. C. B. Mohr [Paul Siebeck], 1967), pp. 198–209.

Law led to such an awful consequence. Paul here is a believer theologically examining his past.[200]

A series of insurmountable difficulties attends this interpretation. The failure of the ἐγώ in 7:7–13 involves disobedience to the Law, not the futile pursuit of it: 'Sin, taking opportunity through the commandment (which prohibits coveting), effected in me *all coveting*' (7:8). The deception accomplished by sin consists in an enticement to transgress, not to establish one's own righteousness (7:11). This problem of transgression is carried over into 7:14–25, in which the situation of the ἐγώ after the introduction of the Law is described. 'The good' to which the ἐγώ cannot attain is the good embodied in the Law itself, not the 'life' which the Law offers (7:13, 16b). Consequently, the statement in 7:15, ὃ γὰρ κατεργάζ-ομαι οὐ γινώσκω, should be read as the renunciation of deeds, not as an admission of perplexity.[201]

This construal of οὐ γινώσκω is strengthened considerably by the observation that the ἐγώ speaks in three distinct, yet connected modes in 7:14–17. First, the ἐγώ makes a confession in the penitential manner found elsewhere in Jewish writings (7:14). It then serves as narrator of its experience (7:15). Since both these forms of expression are contemporaneous and connected in the text (ὃ γὰρ κατεργάζομαι οὐ γινώσκω), it is difficult to suppose that the ἐγώ of 7:15 is in a state of confusion. Verse 15 explains the confession of 7:14 in which the ἐγώ is not confused, but aware of its fallen state ('I am fleshly, sold under sin'). Moreover, the introductory first-person plural confession (οἴδαμεν) supplies a present time framework, preventing one from supposing that the narrator Paul is projecting himself into his past. In 7:16–17 Paul goes on to conclude that the ἐγώ agrees that the Law is good, despite its disobedience. The reasoning here is 'transsubjective,' but only in a limited sense: it is rendered without reference to the subjective state of the narrated ἐγώ. The earlier connection between the *narrating* ἐγώ (7:15) and the confessing ἐγώ (7:14) establishes that the former is conscious of its failure and prohibits an overarching 'transsubjective' reading of the passage.

---

[200] *Inter alia*, Bornkamm and Käsemann (who, of course, speaks of 'existence in relationship to the world') follow Bultmann in interpreting Rom 7 in 'transsubjective' terms. However, they, like others, broaden their reading of the passage to include transgression of the Law alongside its misuse as part of the failure of the ἐγώ. See Günther Bornkamm, 'Sin, Law, and Death: An Exegetical Study of Romans 7,' in *Early Christian Experience*, trans. P.L. Hammer (New York: Harper & Row, 1969), pp. 87–104; Käsemann, *An die Römer*, pp. 184–204.

[201] For such a use of γινώσκω, see 1 Cor 8:3; Gal 2:9; 4:9.

The existential reading of Rom 7 further imposes an illegitimate conception of early Judaism on the text. The image of the pious Jew pursuing the Law solely from the motive of securing 'life' is misrepresentative of early Judaism and of Paul's self-references elsewhere. E. P. Sanders has rightly reminded Christian scholars that one may easily find examples from early Judaism which illustrate nobler motives for obedience to the Law.[202] And as we have seen, Paul himself does not match the portrait which this theory paints. The texts such as Phil 3:4–7 and Gal 2:13, 14, which frequently have been used to corroborate such a reading, provide no indication that Paul's motive for obedience to the Law was simply the attainment of 'life.' In fact, they provide indication that other factors such as a confident religious zeal were at work in Paul.

Dissatisfaction with the fictive and 'transsubjective' interpretations of Rom 7 has resulted in the continuation of the older understanding of the chapter as disclosing some aspect of Paul's life in Judaism. Paul, it is thought, holds up to his readers his own experience of the Law prior to faith in Christ.

This theory is attractive because it accounts for the elements of Rom 7:7–25 which point to the representative nature of Paul's first-person usage. Moreover, advocates of this interpretation have rightly underscored aspects of the passage which rule out reading of 7:14–25 as a description of Paul's Christian experience. Nevertheless, this approach also suffers deficiencies which render it unacceptable.

In the first place, those who read 7:14–25 as a depiction of Paul's past have not developed a satisfactory description of the shift to the present tense which appears in 7:14 and continues through the end of the chapter. The most commonly repeated reason for the tense change is that Paul moves from a narration of the entrance of the Law to a vivid description of the subsequent condition of the ἐγώ post peccatum.[203] This recognition that the introduction of the present tense has to do with a change in aspect has been corroborated by recent ground-breaking work on the function of the Greek tenses, to which we will return.[204] The claim that 7:14–25 represents past time nevertheless runs into a number of difficulties. Normal use of

---

[202] E. P. Sanders, *Paul and Palestinian Judaism: A Comparison of Patterns of Religion* (Philadelphia: Fortress, 1977), pp. 117–125.

[203] E.g. Bornkamm, 'Sin, Law and Death,' p. 95; Wilckens, *Der Brief an die Römer*, 2:85. Despite his assertions to the contrary, Theissen's suggestion falls into this category, *Psychologische Aspekte*, pp. 187–194.

[204] See Stanley E. Porter, *Verbal Aspect in the Greek of the New Testament, with Reference to Tense and Mood*, Studies in Biblical Greek 1 (New York: Peter Lang, 1989).

past-referring ('historical') present, to which this context, according to theory, must be regarded as analogous, occurs in brief statements in passages which are heavily marked as past-time narrative. It is not impossible that an extended use of the present tense like that in Rom 7:14–25 might be past-referring, but one would expect to find clear indication of past time in context. One finds instead indicators that Paul's utterances are set in present time. First, the confessions of the ἐγώ in 7:21–24, especially its recognition of its imprisonment by sin, would seem to reflect Paul's Christian perspective, not his pre-conversion views. Those who understand the passage as representing Paul's analysis of his former state must operate with the strained assumption that the ἐγώ who speaks in 7:15, 18b–19 represents Paul's past, while the remainder of the material expresses Paul's present perspective. Secondly, and decisively, the opening and closing of the passage contain implicit present–time markers. As we have noted above, the passage is introduced in 7:14 by a first person plural, οἴδαμεν, which links the narrative to the present which Paul shares with his readers. No indication of a shift to past time appears in the confession of Rom 7:14b (ἐγὼ δὲ σάρκινός εἰμι, πεπραμένος ὑπὸ τὴν ἁμαρτίαν). Likewise, the seemingly anticlimactic conclusion of the ἐγώ in 7:25b (ἄρα οὖν αὐτὸς ἐγὼ τῷ μὲν νοῒ δουλεύω νόμῳ θεοῦ, τῇ δὲ σαρκὶ νόμῳ ἁμαρτίας), which advocates of this view have long recognized as problematic, is marked as having present reference by the preceding exclamation of thanks to God through Christ.

Moreover, if one reads 7:14–25 as Paul's retrospective on his life in Judaism, one is thrust into a dilemma noted by Kümmel long ago. The frustration of the ἐγώ with its inability to accomplish the good embodied in the Law cannot be reconciled with Paul's self-references elsewhere, particularly Phil 3:6, where Paul appears to have been a confident and enthusiastic adherent of the Pharisees.[205] This objection to ascribing anxiety and doubt to Paul prior to his conversion has been forcefully restated in recent years by E. P. Sanders, who has rightly rejected the older Protestant misconception.[206] Theissen has come the closest to surmounting this obstacle, by arguing that Paul's conflict with the Law was subconscious. But his psychological analysis fails to deal adequately with the present–time orientation of the text.[207]

Although now in disfavor, the (later) Augustinian interpretation of Rom 7:14–25 as a description of Paul's Christian experience

---

[205] Kümmel, *Römer 7*, pp. 111–117.
[206] Sanders, *Paul and Palestinian Judaism*, pp. 33–59.
[207] Theissen, *Psychologische Aspekte*, pp. 232–235.

prevailed in the West through the period of Protestant Orthodoxy. It continues to attract a minority following. Along with the theory that 7:14–25 represents Paul's past, this reading rightly understands the first-person usage as typical. It holds an advantage over the former in that it is able to account for the present time of 7:14–25. And the ascription of 7:14–25 to Paul's Christian existence removes the conflict between this passage and what is known of the Judaism of Paul. However, along with other approaches to Rom 7 this description contains some fatal flaws.

The structure of Paul's argument in Rom 7, 8 indicates that Rom 7:14–25 has to do with the person apart from Christ. Rom 7:7–25 and 8:1–30 develop 7:5 and 7:6 respectively, where the state of believers prior to faith is set in contraposition to Christian existence: 'once (7:5) . . . but now (7:6).' The condition described in 7:7–25 corresponds to the state depicted in 7:5: existing 'in the flesh' (7:14, 18), sinful passions working in the members (7:8, 22), resultant death (7:10, 13, 24). Similarly, the thought of 7:6 is taken up in Rom 8: release from the Law (8:3) and service in newness of the Spirit (8:2, 5–11, 12–16). Consequently, it is difficult to suppose that the topic of 7:14–25 is the spiritual struggle of the believer.

Further considerations confirm this impression. As Theissen rightly observes, although there is a change in verb tense, the transition between 7:13 and 7:14 is too weakly marked to conclude that Paul intends the reader to perceive a shift to a discussion of the Christian.[208] More importantly, the ἐγώ of 7:14 is absolutely powerless, 'fleshly, sold under sin,' obviously standing in contrast to the believers described in Rom 8 ('You are not in the flesh, but in the Spirit,' 8:9a). Although careful exegetes who apply the text to the Christian, such as Cranfield and Dunn, argue that Paul describes only one aspect of Christian existence here, the absolute statement of 7:14 (ἐγὼ δὲ σάρκινός εἰμι, πεπραμένος ὑπὸ τὴν ἁμαρτίαν) seems to prohibit taking the passage as expressing a conflict within the believer between the two epochs of Adam and Christ.[209] And one does not find any positive evidence in 7:14–25 to support the view that Paul is describing the spiritual battle of the Christian.[210]

---

[208] Theissen, *Psychologische Aspekte*, pp. 186.

[209] See C. E. B. Cranfield, *A Critical and Exegetical Commentary on the Epistle to the Romans*, ICC (Edinburgh: T. & T. Clark, 1975), 1:355–370; Dunn, *Romans*, pp. 387–412.

[210] One need not attribute an oblique reference to the Spirit to Rom 7:18a. The restrictive explanation 'that is, in my flesh' most likely has to do with the immediate contrast between the mind and the members (7:22, 25). This connection does not land one in a dualistic anthropology.

While advocates of a typical or representative understanding of the ἐγώ in Rom 7 have rightly dismissed the fictive and 'transsubjective' interpretations of the chapter, they have tended to over-emphasize the autobiographical aspect of the material. In reaction to Kümmel's work, many exegetes have focussed on the fact that Paul and his experience are included in the ἐγώ, at the expense of asking in what manner they appear there. The usual question put to the text, whether it reflects the preconversion or postconversion Paul, misses the decisive element of Paul's use of the ἐγώ. He here portrays himself, according to a pattern found in early Jewish penitential prayer and confession, from the limited perspective of his intrinsic soteriological resources.

Two features of Paul's first-person usage in Rom 7:14–25 are of particular importance.[211] One significant aspect of the passage is the movement from first-person plural to first–person singular which appears in 7:14. The shift from an audience- inclusive 'we' to 'I' is elsewhere regularly associated with Paul's explanation of his views to his audience or his modelling theology and behavior which he wants his audience to adopt.[212] The latter type of argument is present here. Clearly the introductory οἴδαμεν ὅτι ὁ νόμος πνευματικός ἐστιν in 7:14 expresses a conviction shared by Paul's audience.[213] In 7:14b Paul continues his earlier attempt to persuade his audience of his seemingly contradictory assertion that the Law brings death although it is good. He does so by resuming the singular which he employed in 7:7–13, explaining his position by using himself as representative in 7:14–25.

Of greater interest is the change from augmented tenses to the present tense, since this feature of Rom 7:7–25 is integral to the

---

[211] Paul's first-person statements may be categorized along several formal lines in order to test for material differences between them. Naturally, dividing the material on the basis of temporal reference (past, present, future) is of interest, as is distinguishing between singular and plural usage. As Theissen suggests, it is probably best to regard conditionals as a special class, since they are more likely to be used fictively. And the passages where the emphatic ἐγώ appears may be considered as a group. In terms of content, Paul's numerous self-references to his acts of writing deserve attention.

[212] The following texts contain the first–person singular following the uses of an audience inclusive first–person plural, excluding instances of the first-person singular which refer to Paul's immediate literary activity (e.g. λέγω, γράφω) and of non-self-referring first–person singular (e.g. 1 Cor 12:13–16): Rom 7:7–12; 8:38; 14:14; 1 Cor 8:13; 13:11; Gal 2:18–21; Phil 3:4– 14. Rom 3:5–7 is an exception to this pattern, since here Paul uses the first–person singular to express the viewpoint of a member of his implied audience. The content of the utterance as well as Paul's explicit statement in context (κατὰ ἄνθρωπον λέγω) signal this for the reader.

[213] Cf. Rom 2:2; 3:19; 1 Cor 8:1, 4.

debate over the subject of 7:14–25. While in many instances the
introduction of the present tense in first-person narratives involves
a move to present time, this is not always the case.[214] The use of the
present tense does not necessarily indicate generalization, either,
contrary to what Theissen suggests.[215] In an important study on
the relation of Greek tense and aspect, Stanley Porter has shown
that the tense forms are not based primarily on time, but on
aspect.[216] Present forms grammaticalize imperfective aspect, aorist, perfective. The distinction between the two has been variously
described, with the contrast often made between narrative (perfective) and descriptive (imperfective) categories.[217] Therefore the
interpretation offered by a number of scholars that the change in
tense usage denotes a shift from narration of an event to description
of a condition now can be seen to have a sound grammatical
base.[218]

Nevertheless, in many cases the present tense is used in present
time contexts, where temporal markers, not the tense forms, signal
the present setting. Rom 7:14 contains no strong present–time
deixis such as the adverb νῦν which is found in 7:6 and 8:2. Yet,
as we have noted above, the opening first-person plural and the
summary following the exclamation of Christian praise provide
clear indication that Paul's description of the ἐγώ has a present
setting. Paul does not demarcate 7:14–25 as belonging solely to his
present, contrary to what those who read the text as belonging to
Paul's Christian experience suppose. But he does indicate that the
condition of the ἐγώ extends into his present, contrary to what
those who read the passage as a depiction of Paul's past argue.
The change to the present tense in 7:14–25 signals a change to
description, but in this instance it is accompanied by a change in
time.

Although Rom 7:14–25 has features which make it unique to
Paul, it finds its closest parallels in the penitential prayers and
confessions of the Hebrew Bible and early Judaism. Stuhlmacher

---

[214] See 1 Cor 2:1–8; 9:19–23; 2 Cor 2:9, 10; 11:24–29; 12:8–10, which indicate
habitual activities of Paul.
[215] Theissen, *Psychologische Aspekte*, pp. 198–201. See e.g. Rom 1:13–14; 15:22–
24; 1 Cor 9:19–23; 2 Cor 11:2–3. Past-referring statements may readily be used in
a generalizing manner, e.g. 1 Cor 13:11.
[216] Porter, *Verbal Aspect*, pp. 75–109.
[217] Porter, *Verbal Aspect*, pp. 105–107. According to Porter, the imperfect, while
imperfective in aspect (unlike the aorist form), is distinguished from the present
form in expressing remoteness, *Verbal Aspect*, pp. 198–208. It is therefore suited to
narrative contexts, where it is frequently used.
[218] See Wilckens, *Der Brief an die Römer*, 2:85.

has rightly pointed in this direction recently.[219] Like Rom 7, a
number of these prayers and confessions include not only a rehearsal of past transgressions, but a description of the resultant state of
the repentant in imperfective aspect and present time.[220] The
similarity between Rom 7:14–25 and confessions in the Qumran
Hodayoth is especially striking. They share with Rom 7:14–25 a
concentration on the condition of the individual not found elsewhere.[221] And it is possible for such confessions to appear outside
the context of prayer, like Paul's statements in Rom 7:14–25.[222]

An important similarity exists between such prayers and confessions and Paul's statements in Rom 7:14–25, which has not been
taken into account by interpreters of Paul. All such passages represent the penitent(s) from a limited perspective determined by
group or personal guilt, while acknowledging that a broader framework exists, which is dependent upon divine mercies. This dual
perspective is especially apparent in the Qumran materials.[223] A
number of these confessions have to do with the lack of intrinsic
resources of the individual, while they are predicated upon the
saving action of God, which the individual has received or hopes
to receive. For example, the Qumran psalmist gives thanks that he
was made to enter into the company of heaven, while confessing
that he is formed of clay and without value or strength.[224] Elsewhere a Qumran psalmist praises God for giving him understanding, although he in himself remains a wandering and perverted
spirit without understanding.[225] Likewise, Aseneth confesses that
she is not worthy to open her mouth to the Lord in the very midst
of her prayer to him.[226] And Manasseh affirms that although he is
unworthy, God will in mercy save him.[227] In such confessions, the
individual is described from the limited perspective of his or her
intrinsic soteriological resources. The recognition that Paul's por-

---

[219] Stuhlmacher, *Der Brief an die Römer*, pp. 100–101.
[220] See Isa 63:5–12; Jer 3:22b–25; Ezra 9:5–15; JosAsen 12:1–13:15; Tob 3:1–6;
LXX Esth 4:17l–z, LXX Dan 3:24–45; Pr Man 1–15; Bar 1:15–3:8.
[221] See 1QH 1:21–27; 3:19–29.
[222] See 1QS 11:9, 10.
[223] See Lichtenberger, *Studien zum Menschenbild*, pp. 218–227. Like Paul, the
Qumran community regarded the eschatological order as being present, although
not yet consummated within member of the community, e.g. 1QS 3:13–4:26.
[224] See 1QH 3:20–24.
[225] 1QH 1:21–23.
[226] JosAsen 12:4, 5.
[227] Pr Man 14. It is most likely not accidental that the closest parallels to Paul
are found in Qumran, with its *sola gratia* concept of salvation, and in the types of
the converting pagan (Aseneth) and repentant sinner (Manasseh), where the
unworthiness of the individual is stressed.

trayal of himself here is derived from Biblical and early Jewish tradition goes a long way toward explaining why, as Kümmel reports, the search for a category for Paul's language in Greco-Roman rhetoric came to be abandoned.[228]

Differences exist, of course, between Rom 7:14–25 and these examples of penitential prayer and confession. Much of Paul's language in this section is formulated in explicitly argumentative terms. Yet it would be improper to place penitential psalms and confessions in a completely different category, since they too serve as arguments, implicitly modelling behavior and ideas. Rom 7:14–25 therefore is distinguished from them not by the presence of, but by the type of argument which appears in its middle section. Here we encounter the sort of enthymemes which we see elsewhere in Paul's letters: conditional statements followed by inferential conclusions.[229] The reason for the stronger form of argument which Paul uses almost certainly lies in the lesser degree of commitment to Paul's authority by his audience in comparison with, for example, the allegiance of the Qumran community to its leader.

In 7:14–25 the argument of 7:7–13 continues.[230] Despite possession of the good revealed in the Law (7:13), the fallen human being is 'sold under sin,' and incapable of satisfying its demand. Paul's discussion thus far has not dealt with Jewish belief in the capacity of the human to overcome transgression and attain to life through the Law. In some early Jewish circles, knowledge of the Law was thought to bring the potential to obey it, if one persevered. This view of the Law is reflected in the rhetorical address to the Jew in Rom 2:17–20 and is readily found in early Jewish sources.[231] Without compromising his affirmation of the Law's goodness, Paul maintains that death to the Law through Christ remains absolutely necessary. He retains the traditional confession of the holiness of the Law by locating evil in the ἐγώ which acknowledges that it is a prisoner of sin and under divine condemnation. This inability of the ἐγώ corroborates the validity of Paul's preceding claim that the Law brings death.

Although he is a believer in Christ who has died to the Law (7:4), in 7:14–25 Paul portrays his present person as one in the flesh and under the Law in the same manner that other early Jewish confessions focus on the inherent capacities of the individual despite awareness of a broader context. The fundamental distinction between the

---

[228] Kümmel, *Römer 7*, pp. 120–121.
[229] E.g. Rom 3:25, 26; 5:17, 18; 7:2, 3; 8:11, 12.
[230] See Chapter 2, Section II.A.
[231] E.g. Philo, *Decal.* 17.176–178; Ps. Sol. 9:4–5; 4 Ezra 14:27–48.

believing Paul and the ἐγώ is not temporal, i.e. the ἐγώ is not what Paul once was: it is what he still is, intrinsically considered. The contrast which Paul draws here is between the soteriological resources of the fallen human being confronted with the Law and those given in God's saving act in Christ, which he anticipates in 7:25a and to which he returns in Rom 8 (8:2, ὁ γὰρ νόμος τοῦ πνεύματος τῆς ζωῆς ἐν Χριστῷ Ἰησοῦ ἠλευθέρωσέν σε).[232]

Paul's argument takes three forms in Rom 7:14–25. The first is based on Jewish penitential language, which as Stuhlmacher observes, invites the reader to the same confession.[233] Yet his invocation of this theme is insufficient to carry his argument, because his audience does not share his radical confession that the ἐγώ has been 'sold as a slave under sin.' Consequently, Paul's use of the ἐγώ takes a another form in 7:15, 19. Here he narrates his experience as an example, which is offered as a general rule applicable to the reader. Paul next turns to analysis of the narrative (7:16–17, 20), the results of which are ultimately taken up by the ἐγώ, and offered to the reader as a model in 7:21–25.

The passage should be seen as consisting in three sections, each beginning with a statement of self-knowledge, moving to a narration of behavior, and ending with a diagnosis of the ἐγώ confirming the confession which began the section. This structure may be discerned in the following outline:

Outline of Rom 7:14–25

7:14 οἴδαμεν γὰρ ὅτι ὁ νόμος πνευματικός ἐστιν· ἐγὼ δὲ σάρκινός εἰμι, πεπραμένος ὑπὸ τὴν ἁμαρτίαν.	7:18 οἶδα γὰρ ὅτι οὐκ οἰκεῖ ἐν ἐμοί, τοῦτ' ἔστιν ἐν τῇ σαρκί μου, ἀγαθόν·	7:21 εὑρίσκω ἄρα τὸν νόμον τῷ θέλοντι ἐμοὶ ποιεῖν τὸ καλὸν ὅτι ἐμοὶ τὸ κακὸν παράκειται·
7:15 ὃ γὰρ κατεργάζομαι οὐ γινώσκω·	τὸ γὰρ θέλειν παράκειταί μοι, τὸ δὲ κατεργάζεσθαι τὸ καλὸν οὔ·	

---

[232] The reading σε is to be preferred to με, as the *lectio difficilior*, and on the basis of its strong Western and Alexandrian attestation; Bruce M. Metzger, *A Textual Commentary on the Greek New Testament* (New York: United Bible Societies, 1971), p. 516.

[233] Stuhlmacher, *Der Brief an die Römer*, p. 101. Paul's reference to being 'sold under sin' displays particular resonance with the language of Isa 50:1; cf. Deut 28:68; Judith 7:25.

οὐ γὰρ ὃ θέλω τοῦτο πράσσω,	7:19 οὐ γὰρ ὃ θέλω ποιῶ ἀγαθόν,	7:22 συνήδομαι γὰρ τῷ νόμῳ τοῦ θεοῦ κατὰ τὸν ἔσω ἄνθρωπον,
ἀλλ’ ὃ μισῶ τοῦτο ποιῶ.	ἀλλὰ ὃ οὐ θέλω κακὸν τοῦτο πράσσω.	7:23 βλέπω δὲ ἕτερον νόμον ἐν τοῖς μέλεσίν μου ἀντιστρατευόμενον τῷ νόμῳ τοῦ νοός μου καὶ αἰχμαλωτίζοντά με ἐν τῷ νόμῳ τῆς ἁμαρτίας τῷ ὄντι ἐν τοῖς μέλεσίν μου.
7:16 εἰ δὲ ὃ οὐ θέλω τοῦτο ποιῶ,	7:20 εἰ δὲ ὃ οὐ θέλω [ἐγὼ] τοῦτο ποιῶ,	
σύμφημι τῷ νόμῳ ὅτι καλός.		
		7:24 ταλαίπωρος ἐγὼ ἄνθρωπος· τίς με ῥύσεται ἐκ τοῦ σώματος τοῦ θανάτου τούτου;
		7:25 χάρις δὲ τῷ θεῷ διὰ Ἰησοῦ Χριστοῦ τοῦ κυρίου ἡμῶν.
7:17 νυνὶ δὲ οὐκέτι ἐγὼ κατεργάζομαι αὐτὸ ἀλλὰ ἡ οἰκοῦσα ἐν ἐμοὶ ἁμαρτία.	οὐκέτι ἐγὼ κατεργάζομαι αὐτὸ ἀλλὰ ἡ οἰκοῦσα ἐν ἐμοὶ ἁμαρτία.	ἄρα οὖν αὐτὸς ἐγὼ τῷ μὲν νοῒ δουλεύω νόμῳ θεοῦ, τῇ δὲ σαρκὶ νόμῳ ἁμαρτίας.

The organization of the passage strongly suggests that Paul's use of the first person constitutes a carefully designed argument.[234] One is at once struck by its repetitive pattern, especially the first two sections which conclude with precisely the same utterance. This impression is confirmed by the explanatory transitions (γάρ, 7x) which provide the internal structure of the passage, and which shift to consequential statements in the third section (ἄρα, ἄρα οὖν). The coolly reflective summary of 7:25b following the emotional interjection of 7:24–25a highlights the rhetorical nature of the presentation. And the bulk of the text consists in

---

[234] Contra E. P. Sanders, *Paul, the Law, and the Jewish People* (Philadelphia: Fortress, 1983), pp. 76–81.

confession or inference, only a limited portion given to narration of experience (7:15, 18b–19, 22–23). It seems clear, then, that Paul employs the ἐγώ in order to bring his readers to a theological self-judgment.

Progress may be noticed within each section. Each begins with an acknowledgment of moral inability, followed by a confirming narrative, and a conclusion.[235] The first two sections end with the judgment, 'I no longer effect it (disobedience), but sin which indwells me.' As the summary section, 7:21–25, shows, this assessment is not an evasion of responsibility, but a repeated admission of impotence. In these first two sections then, an initial confession of inability is supported by a narrative and a subsequent analysis aimed at convincing the reader of the validity of that confession.

The passage as a whole develops in two ways. First, it builds upon the knowledge gained in the argumentative conclusions (7:16–17, 20). In 7:14–17, the fact that the ἐγώ performs the deeds it detests leads to the conclusion that the ἐγώ agrees that the Law is good (7:16).[236] This allows a second inference: indwelling sin has overpowered the ἐγώ (7:17).[237] The first conclusion is taken up in the second section by repetition of confession, narrative and analysis which incorporate the recognition by the ἐγώ that the Law is good (7:18b, 19; cf. 7:13). The second conclusion is employed in the contrasting affirmation that no good resides within the ἐγώ (7:18a, 18b–19).

The second section, 7:18–20, not only advances the first by making use of its insights, but by shifting emphasis from the Law to the ἐγώ. Paul's highly repetitive language indicates that his aim here is to reinforce the inference that the ἐγώ has been taken captive, with which he concludes the first section (7:20b, cf. 7:17). The juxtaposition of the spirituality of the Law with the sinfulness of the ἐγώ, which characterizes the confession and conclusions of the first section (7:14, 16–17), is missing here. We find instead only

---

[235] Each narrative is introduced by γάρ.

[236] (Tὸ) ἀγαθόν and τὸ καλόν (esp. 7:18, 21), which the ἐγώ desires to accomplish, is not a particular deed, but the moral perfection which is contained in the Law as a whole: ὁ μὲν νόμος ἅγιος, καὶ ἡ ἐντολὴ ἁγία καὶ δικαία καὶ ἀγαθή (7:13). The concretization of an abstract noun by means of the article is common in Greek, of course. Paul elsewhere uses τὸ ἀγαθόν and τὸ καλόν to signify 'the good' as an abstract quantity (Rom 2:10; 12:2, 9; 16:9; Gal 6:9, 10). For Jewish parallels to the widespread Hellenistic reference to τὸ ἀγαθόν and τὸ καλόν as abstract quantities, see LXX Job 34:2; Isa 7:16; Sir 33:14; 51:18, 19, and especially Deut 13:19, where obedience to the Law is described as ποιεῖν τὸ καλὸν καὶ τὸ ἀρεστὸν ἐναντίον κυρίου τοῦ θεοῦ σου.

[237] As noted above, this conclusion that the ἐγώ is captive is reached without reference to its subjective state.

the plight of the ἐγώ, in which no good dwells (7:18a). A generalized description of the predicament of the ἐγώ is now introduced into the narrative (τὸ γὰρ θέλειν παράκειταί μοι, τὸ δὲ κατεργάζεσθαι τὸ καλὸν οὔ· 7:18b).[238] And its subjugation to sin stands as the sole conclusion (7:20b).

In the third section, Paul brings the insights of the first two sections together in the person of the ἐγώ. The confessing ἐγώ is altered. It now appears as an ἐγώ which has gained perception through the preceding argument.[239] What was confessed has been found to be true.[240] The narrative becomes emotive here, because the argumentative conclusions of 7:16–17, 20 have been accepted by the ἐγώ, which now leaves its bare rehearsal and returns to metaphorical description of its plight as imprisonment (7:22–23; cf. 7:14). The generalization which the *narrator* applies to the ἐγώ in 7:18b is here recognized by the ἐγώ *itself* as a law which governs its behavior.[241]

In contrast with the earlier sections, anthropological description is added to the narrative in 7:22–23. The inner person, who delights in the Law, is captive to the sin indwelling the outward person.[242] This linking of the disobedience of the ἐγώ to ontology

---

[238] Contra Theissen, *Psychologische Aspekte*, pp. 213–223, Rom 7:14–25 cannot not be read as an example of the topic of *akrasia* in antiquity. The often repeated citation from Ovid's *Metamorphoses* 7.18 (video meliora proboque deteriora sequor), like the other instances of this *topos*, has to do with a tragic succumbing to passions in the face of better judgment. In contrast, the will of the ἐγώ in Rom 7:14–25 remains committed to the Law of God. Conflicting impulses of the will lie behind this passage (cf. 7:5, 8), but Paul does not enter into a discussion of them, and does not fit neatly into either the affective or cognitive camp, since for him sin works by an 'inevitable deception' (7:11). Moreover, the situation portrayed is not a single circumstance, but the entire existence of the ἐγώ, which brings on itself the judgment of God, not a particular calamity.

[239] Note the verbs of perception employed in this section, εὑρίσκω (7:21), βλέπω (7:23).

[240] Note the shift from οἶδα, οἴδαμεν to εὑρίσκω.

[241] The νόμος of 7:21, the ἕτερος νόμος ἐν τοῖς μέλεσίν μου (7:23a), and the νόμος τῆς ἁμαρτίας ὁ ὢν ἐν τοῖς μέλεσίν μου (7:23b) signify the rule or norm of action to which the ἐγώ is enslaved, not the Law of Moses. This is suggested above all else, by the fact that νόμος is the object of verbs of perception (εὑρίσκω, βλέπω). Paul plays upon the term νόμος here, as he does in Rom 3:27. See Kümmel, *Römer 7*, pp. 61–63.

[242] Paul obviously makes use of Hellenistic anthropological terms here. But despite the distinction he draws between the mind and the body, the human remains for Paul a unitary being with respect to salvation. Thus the whole person is fleshly (7:14), and enslaved to sin (7:23). The deliverance for which the ἐγώ longs is from the sinful body (τὸ σῶμα τοῦ θανάτου τούτου, 7:24), not from the body as such (8:11, 13, 23). As Wilckens has noted, the term 'members' places emphasis on the body as the locus of sinful acts, in contrast to the usual Hellenistic devaluation of the body (*Der Brief an die Römer*, 2:92–93). Paul's use of ontological categories therefore differs from Hellenistic parallels in that it conveys the idea

establishes that the condition of the ἐγώ is inherent to the ἐγώ as a fallen human being. Paul's further use of this distinction in his summary statement (7:25b) underscores its significance for his argument. The ἐγώ recognizes that it is divided in a fundamental manner. Despite its affirmation of the good Law, it remains a slave of sin. It is inescapably under the sentence of death ('the body of this death').

The interjection of 7:24–25a, far from being a reflexive outburst, is a careful expression of emotion and faith in response to the narrative description of 7:22–23. The existential anguish of the ἐγώ in 7:24 effectively draws the conclusion toward which Paul's argument is directed. Life in the sinful body brings the certain sentence of death. Devoid of soteriological resources, one is directed by faith to God's saving act in Christ alone (7:25a). The shout of praise in 7:25a anticipates the contrasting hope of salvation Paul will describe in Rom 8. The exclamations of 7:24–25a therefore represent Paul's use of *pathos* in order to drive home the point of the preceding narrative.

The contrasting sober conclusion (7:25b) reaffirms the basic truth which Paul wants his audience to adopt: even the human who affirms that the Law is spiritual remains a slave to sin under divine condemnation. The ἐγώ thus serves Paul as a model intended to persuade his first readers of the validity and necessity of the exclusion of the Law from God's saving purpose, as he has asserted in 7:5.

According to this reading of 7:14–25, Paul attributes existence in the flesh and its resultant condemnation to the believer (ἐγὼ δὲ σάρκινός εἰμι, πεπραμένος ὑπὸ τὴν ἁμαρτίαν, 7:14) even though it has been superseded in Christ (ὑμεῖς δὲ οὐκ ἐστὲ ἐν σαρκὶ ἀλλὰ ἐν πνεύματι, 8:9). Contrary to those who regard the overlap of the ages as *internal* to the believer and evidenced in moral struggle in Rom 7,[243] the absolute statements of 7:14, 18, 23–24 require that one understand Paul as depicting the believer as belonging entirely to the old order in 7:14–25, the new order being expressed in *extrinsic* terms in 7:25a. As the broader context shows, Paul portrays life under the Law in 7:14–25 in order to gain the confession of his audience that the Gospel brings freedom from the Law for believers, not in order to prevent them from abandoning faith in Christ in favor of the Law. His argument therefore does not have to do with a 'shattered moralism of the past' but with realities

---

of an inescapable predicament, rather than pointing to the way of escape (cf. Philo *Heres.* 267–283).

[243] E.g. Dunn, *Romans*, pp. 405–412.

current to his audience as fallen human beings, as the dual assertion of 7:25 indicates.

The same overlap of 'now' and 'then' is reflected in Paul's
description of life in the Spirit in Rom 8 also, so that one cannot
dismiss this interpretation by an appeal to 'salvation-historical'
progress from Rom 7 to Rom 8. Even in Rom 8 Paul envisions
sin as a continuing reality, inherent to life in the body of the fallen
human being. The new realities have overcome, but have not yet
eliminated the juridical and ontological conditions of the old order.
The body of the one who is in Christ is 'dead,' i.e. subject to death,
because of sin's presence (8:10). Likewise, the bodies of believers
are θνητὰ σώματα, 'mortal bodies' (8:11). Those who are led by the
Spirit 'continue to put to death the deeds of the body' (8:13).
There is an unending battle against sin until the 'redemption of
the body' (Rom 8:23). The salvation which Paul describes in
Rom 8 is extrinsic, building on the earlier argument. Deliverance
from 'the law of sin and death' is an act of God, external to the
believer (8:2).[244] 'The law of the Spirit of life' which frees the
believer is based on the resurrection of the incarnate Son whom
God sent to overcome sin (8:3). God will raise to life those who
belong to Christ, just as he raised Christ from the dead (8:11). The
plight of the fallen human being pictured in Rom 7:14–25 is now
countered by the act of God in Christ, as anticipated by 7:25a.

The purpose clause of 8:4 deserves some comment. Although it is
usually taken to mean that Paul expects believers to fulfill the Law,
a number of factors indicate that a passive sense is to be preferred.
The verbal form πληρωθῇ is passive, of course, suggesting a passive
interpretation from the start. Moreover, reading 8:4 as an active
fulfillment of the Law by Christians does not fit the statements in
Rom 8:10, 11, 13, 23 which we have noted above, in which Paul
presumes that believers will continue to sin so long as they remain in
this life. And the passive interpretation of the clause more closely
matches Paul's presentation of salvation as realized by an external
act by God in 8:2, 3, 11. The generally held view that Paul alludes
to an idealized conception of the Law such as the love command is
unlikely on account of the obliquity of the supposed allusion. A
much more plausible point of reference is found in Rom 5:16–19,
where the terms κατάκριμα and δικαίωμα cross, as they do in 8:1–4.
In 8:4 Paul takes up his earlier description of Christ's death as a
fulfillment of a righteous requirement of God (5:18b, οὕτως καὶ δι᾽

---

[244] Both references to νόμος in Rom 8:2 represent continuing wordplay, not 'the
Law.' Paul's use of the second-person singular here confirms the thesis that his
first–person statements are an invitation to the reader.

ἑνὸς δικαιώματος εἰς πάντας ἀνθρώπους εἰς δικαίωσιν ζωῆς·). By qualifying it as 'the righteous requirement of the Law' in 8:3, 4 (ὁ θεὸς τὸν ἑαυτοῦ υἱὸν πέμψας . . . κατέκρινεν τὴν ἁμαρτίαν ἐν τῇ σαρκί, ἵνα τὸ δικαίωμα τοῦ νόμου πληρωθῇ ἐν ἡμῖν), he gives it a covenantal nuance and contrasts it with the ἐγώ of Rom 7, who is impotent to fulfill the Law. The vicarious conception of Christ's death which this reading necessitates is manifest in 8:3, where Christ's divesting sin of its power ἐν τῇ σαρκί conveys the idea of corporate solidarity between Christ and fallen humanity.

The juxtaposition of a description of extrinsically accomplished salvation in Rom 8:1–4 with the intrinsic plight of the ἐγὼ described in 7:14–25 makes it clear that the argument of Rom 7, and of 7:14–25 in particular, is related to Paul's earlier explication of 'justification by faith alone' (Rom 1:16–5:21). The thrust of Paul's discussion itself strongly implies this, since his aim of defending his exclusion of the Law from God's saving purposes and attributing radical evil to the human being corresponds with his understanding of 'justification.' Yet the rhetorical situation of Rom 7 is different from Paul's initial presentation of forensic justification. While in Rom 1:16–5:21 Paul's argument is directed to Jewish believers as *Jews*, in Rom 7:14–25 it is directed toward Jewish believers as *believers*. Paul here seeks to gain assent to his assertion in Rom 7:1–6 that by virtue of God's act in Christ, the life of the believer, including its ethical dimension, is free from the Law.[245]

The significance of Paul's assumption of the role of a fallen human being should not be overlooked. His capacity to model himself in this way indicates that he regards the conditions of the past as still applicable to believers, even though they have been overcome. The believer is at once οὐκ ἐν σαρκὶ ἀλλὰ ἐν πνεύματι and yet σάρκινος, πεπραμένος ὑπὸ τὴν ἁμαρτίαν. In accepting his analysis, one is thrust into relying upon the extrinsic act of God in Christ, and hence the forensic aspect of Paul's Gospel to which

---

[245] Our interpretation of Rom 7:14–25 corresponds not only with Rom 8, but with Rom 6, and the remainder of Paul's writings. The 'already-not yet' tension which we have found here represents the paradoxical juxtaposition of 'indicative' and 'imperative' which we have discussed elsewhere in this study. See Chapter 1, Section III; Bultmann, 'Das Problem der Ethik bei Paulus,' pp. 179–199. The believer has died to sin (Rom 6:11), *therefore* she or he is not to allow sin to reign in the body (Rom 6:12). Despite his confidence that salvation has been effected in Christ, Paul acknowledges the present reality of sin. While the 'indicative' here and elsewhere indeed presupposes that believers will attain to perfection, Paul anticipates it only at the apocalyptic consummation of salvation. Cf. Phil 1:10; 2:16; 3:11–14, 21.

Paul directs his readers in Rom 8:1–4. Our interpretation of Rom 7:14–25 shows therefore that Paul regarded his understanding of justification by faith as relevant to the existence of individual believers, and not merely social relations between Jews and Gentiles. Furthermore, this reading of Rom 7:14–25 provides corroboration for our analysis of Paul's conversion in Chapter 3 of this study. The change which we found took place in Paul's self–understanding in conjunction with his coming to faith continues to evidence itself in his later theological argumentation.[246]

D. Romans 9:30–10:21

The manner in which one describes the function of the theme of forensic justification here, which Paul reintroduces after a considerable hiatus, depends on two critical questions. On the one hand, some explanation must be provided for Paul's treatment of the problem of Israel, which, whether it is viewed as the culmination of the preceding argument or the introduction of an entirely new topic, constitutes a decided shift in the argument of the letter. On the other hand, the role of 'justification by faith,' which reappears in a brief section of Rom 9–11 (Rom 9:30–10:21), must be described in relation to the function of the chapters as a whole.

The widespread tendency to limit a construal of the relationship between Rom 9–11 and 1–8 to theological terms, or to search for a unifying concept as a first step to understanding Rom 1–11 as a whole, is an interpretive error.[247] The same may be said for the occasional effort to ascribe Rom 9–11 to Paul's own psychological

---

[246] This continuity in Paul's interpretation of the Gospel suggests that in other instances in which he models the relevance of the Gospel for the individual (e.g. Gal 2:15–21) he is engaging in actual self-disclosure and not *ad hominem* argument.

[247] This sort of argument is frequent. E.g. Käsemann regards the material relation between salvation-history and Paul's teaching on 'justification' as an argument for the necessity of the discussion in Rom 9–11: 'In diesem Rahmen muß allerdings das Problem Israels erörtert werden, und zwar als Problem der Treue Gottes zu seinem ergangenen Wort (*An die Römer*, p. 244)'. Cf. also his, 'Paulus und Israel,' in *Exegetische Versuche und Besinnungen*[2], 2 vols. (Göttingen: Vandenhoeck & Ruprecht, 1965), 2:194–197, where the entire section is attributed to an exemplary use of Israel as an attack on the *homo religiosus*. Cranfield, too, argues for viewing Rom 9–11 as an integral part of the letter on the basis of logical necessity (*Commentary on Romans*, 2:445-446). Similar statements may be found in Wilckens, *Der Brief an die Römer*, 2:182–183; W. G. Kümmel, 'Die Probleme von Römer 9–11 in der gegenwärtigen Forschungslage,' in *Heilsgeschehen und Geschichte*, MTS 16, ed. E. Grässer and O. Merk (Marburg: N. G. Elwert, 1978), 2:252–255; and Otfried Hofius, 'Das Evangelium und Israel,' *ZThK* 83 (1986):299. Examples could be multiplied.

struggles.[248] Both theological and psychological approaches have their rightful place in attempting to understand Paul. But it is methodologically illegitimate to use them as the sole or primary means of interpreting the break in topic at Rom 9:1, which is in the first place an *epistolary* phenomenon. In other words, it is improper to assume that it was necessary for Paul to develop the logical consequences of his arguments fully. Romans, despite serving as a proclamation of the Gospel, is a letter written with persuasive aims, not a dogmatic treatise.

While the problem of Israel naturally would have relevance to the Jewish segment of the church, it is likely that Paul intends these chapters primarily for the Gentile majority of his audience. The letter provides little evidence that Paul's extensive treatment of the problem of Israel was necessary on account of the Jewish Christians. There is no solid evidence that Judaizers were present in the church. The conservative Jewish believers who constituted the 'weak' party would have represented only a part of the Jewish Christian minority. Moreover, they seem to have been an embattled group, not an ascendant one. It is therefore difficult to believe that Paul was forced to deal with the problem of Israel on account of pressure from them.

On the other hand, as we have seen in our examination of Paul's disclosures in Rom 11:13 and 11:25–27, there are a number of indications that Paul has the whole church, and hence primarily the Gentile majority in view in the bulk of Rom 9–11.[249] In contrast to his dialogue with the Jew in Rom 2–4, he here creates a rhetorical distinction between his implied audience and Israel, speaking of, e.g., '*my* (not our) brethren,' and '*their* (not our) salvation.'[250] When he refers to 'Isaac our father' in Rom 9:10, it is after he has asserted that it is the children of promise, like Isaac—*not* the children 'of the

---

[248] Sanders, *Paul, the Law, and the Jewish People*, p. 185. He suggests that Paul found himself in a logical dilemma as the result of the discrepancy between his Christian and Jewish convictions. On the one hand, God had elected and had promised to redeem Israel. Yet God also had appointed Jesus Christ, whom most Jews were rejecting, to be the Savior. The struggle to hold these two beliefs together runs throughout Rom 9–11, according to Sanders. But this appeal to a state of cognitive dissonance in the mind of Paul is less than satisfactory as a solution to Paul's purpose in writing Rom 9–11. In view of the allegory of Hagar and Sarah which Paul develops in Gal 4:21–31, and the forceful statements Paul makes about unbelieving Jews in 1 Thess 2:14–16, it is apparent that Paul had reflected on the fate of his people long before writing to the church at Rome. In addition, Paul attributes the anguish which he expresses in Rom 9 not to conflicting convictions, but to the need of his fellow Jews for salvation (Rom 9:1–5).

[249] See above, Section II.A.2.

[250] Cf. Rom 3:5a, 7, 9a.

flesh'—who are children of Abraham.[251] While Paul's use of the
term 'Israel' (Rom 9:6, 7) implies a reference to believing Jews,
his elaboration of his statements in Rom 9:8, 9 completely redefines
the people of God, so that both believing Jews and Gentiles are
included. This claim is verified by his following reference to his
audience and himself as '(those) whom (God) has called, not from
among Jews alone, but from among Gentiles.'[252] In Rom 9, 10
therefore, Paul addresses the church as a whole, especially the
Gentile majority.

As we have seen, when in Rom 11 Paul expresses the behavior
which he wishes his preceding arguments to engender, he explicitly
speaks to Gentile believers.[253] This shift in perspective, Paul's move
from regarding his audience as believers, to speaking to them as
Gentiles, is indicative of his aim in these chapters. Gentile believers
are the primary object of Paul's discussion of Israel. His initial
approach to them as *believers* represents a form of argumentative
appeal: they, too, are to regard themselves, above all else, as those
called by God to faith, through the proclamation of the Gospel.[254]
They are not *as Gentiles*, to become proud, but to continue in faith.[255]

In this case, the destiny of Israel described in Rom 9–11 serves as
a warning to Gentile believers to adhere to 'faith,' by which they
presently stand and by which they will continue in God's kindness.[256] They are in danger themselves of becoming proud and
boasting in a superiority over Israel, a boasting in their own wisdom.[257] Since he underscores the utter graciousness of God to the
Gentiles of his audience, Paul here implicitly extends the message
of justifying faith to the broader principle that any boasting in
human capacity to achieve salvation is illegitimate. The radical
mercy which God has shown to them is to lead them to continued
grateful submission to God's kindness, which has been expressed to
them in the Gospel.[258] Clearly at this point in the letter, Paul's
reference to the Gospel in 11:28 must be understood as *his* Gospel,
which includes his understanding of 'justification by faith.'[259]

Paul's use of Israel as an example runs along two tracks, which

---

[251] Rom 9:8.

[252] Rom 9:24.

[253] Rom 11:13a: 'Υμῖν δὲ λέγω τοῖς ἔθνεσιν. See Rom 11:13–24, 28–31.

[254] Rom 9:24.

[255] Rom 11:20.

[256] Rom 11:18–24.

[257] Rom 11:18, 19, 25. As Rom 12:3–7, 14:1–15:13, and 16:17–20 show, Paul
perceived a threat of disunity to the church stemming from Gentile pride.

[258] Rom 11:22, 28.

[259] It is only this interpretation of the Gospel which allows Paul to say that
unbelieving Jews are enemies of God on *account of the Gentiles*.

might seem mutually exclusive. On the one hand, in Rom 9:30–10:21 Israel's failure is attributed to its unwillingness to submit to the Gospel.[260] Israel's faithlessness is an admonition to Gentiles not to do the same.[261]

On the other hand, Israel's failure is presented as an outworking of God's mode of operation in the past, and a part of the sovereign plan which guides his dispensing of salvation in history.[262] This theme, although seemingly conflicting with the first, serves the same purpose. Gentile believers have no occasion to boast, since God according to his own plan made them to be 'vessels of mercy.'[263] Likewise, God will fulfill his promises concerning Israel's salvation at the *Parousia*.[264] The mercy shown to the Gentiles is therefore 'a mere interim' in God's plan for Israel. All the more reason to be grateful for this opportunity for salvation: if they as Gentiles should fall from God's kindness, they have no guarantee of final restoration.[265]

The theme of 'justification by faith,' which reappears in Rom 9:30–10:21, is reintroduced as the fulfillment of the promises of Scripture. Paul here charges Israel with a failure to respond to the revelation of God's will, once promised and now decisively made known through the proclamation of Christ. Despite its fervor for the Law, Israel did not attain to righteousness, because it did not heed the promise of righteousness through faith in Christ. This is undoubtedly the sense of Rom 9:31 (Ἰσραὴλ δὲ διώκων νόμον δικαιοσύνης εἰς νόμον οὐκ ἔφθασεν) which is followed by a reference to the promise of eschatological justification by faith (ὁ πιστεύων ἐπ' αὐτῷ οὐ καταισχυνθήσεται). For them, Christ is a stumbling

---

[260] 'Faith' in this passage signifies acceptance of the message of Christ, as Rom 10:17 shows. See Rom 9:32; 10:3, 16, 21.

[261] Cf. Rom 11:21: εἰ γὰρ ὁ θεὸς τῶν κατὰ φύσιν κλάδων οὐκ ἐφείσατο, [μή πως] οὐδὲ σοῦ φείσεται. While a number of particularities of Käsemann's, 'Paulus und Israel,' pp. 194–197, differ from the interpretation offered here, his primary point that the chapters are exemplary is correct. Yet his overemphasis on the theological coherence of these chapters with Paul's understanding of justification by faith tends to obscure the fact that Rom 9–11 represent a significant interpretive act on Paul's part: he here, at a particular stage in the life of the church at Rome, expands the relevance of 'justification by faith' to human religious pride in general and not merely that of the Jew.

[262] Rom 9:6–29, 11:28–36.

[263] Rom 9:22–26.

[264] Rom 11:25–27.

[265] Rom 11:22–24. Paul, quite understandably, brings his own attitudes and actions into the argument of Rom 9–11 as a model. Since the proclamation of the message of 'justification' is corroborated by Scripture, Paul merely acts in obedience to revelation (Rom 10:4–21). He himself has no illusions regarding his superiority, but longs and prays for the salvation of his people (Rom 9:1–5; 10:1–3).

block, as written in Isaiah.[266] Paul's explanatory statement in
Rom 10:4, τέλος νόμου Χριστὸς, which has been the subject of
considerable dispute, is best interpreted as an assertion that Christ
is the culmination of the Law, implying that he is both goal and
end. The sense of disjunction and termination derives not from
τέλος, but from the reference to 'Christ' as a saving entity, which
is antithetical to Law.[267] In the Law one finds not only Moses'
enunciation of the Law's demand. One is also directly and personally addressed by 'the righteousness of faith' which speaks of God's
gracious saving action independent of human effort.[268] The Scripture likewise promises that everyone, Jew and Gentile alike, who
believes will not be ashamed, and that all who 'call on the name of
the Lord' will be saved.[269]

   This passage plays a significant role in Paul's argument toward
Gentile believers in Rome. Israel's failure to respond to the Gospel
is presented as disobedience to the righteousness by faith promised
in Scripture. This affirmation first serves as a warning to Gentiles
against religious arrogance. If God did not spare unbelieving Jews,
'the natural branches' of the 'olive tree' which represents the
people of God, neither will he spare the 'ingrafted' Gentiles.[270]
Unless they, by faith, continue in God's kindness, they too will
be cut off.[271] Secondly, the fact that the gift of righteousness in
Christ (along with Israel's failure) was anticipated in Scripture,
shows that God, as ever, remains in control of human history.
Hence the entrance of believing Gentiles into the people of God
is not an occasion for their boasting in their wisdom.[272] Their
acceptance is part of the divine unfolding of salvation-history,
which includes the eschatological salvation of Israel.[273]

   In Rom 9–11, therefore, as in Rom 5:1–11, Paul applies his
understanding of 'justification by faith' to an issue other than that

---

[266] Rom 9:32, 33.
[267] E.g. Rom 3:21, 22; 7:4. Contra Robert Badenas, *Christ the End of the Law:
Romans 10:4 in Pauline Perspective*, JSNTSup 10 (Sheffield: JSOT, 1985). Cf. Dunn,
Romans, pp. 589–591.
[268] Rom 10:6–8. See Mark A. Seifrid, 'Paul's Approach to the Old Testament
in Rom 10:6–8,' *TrinJ* 6 (1985):6–10.
[269] Rom 10:11–12
[270] Rom 11:21
[271] Rom 11:19–24 Πίστις here carries with it the full force of Paul's understanding of justification by faith, which excludes human contribution to salvation.
Cf. Rom 10:6–8, 17.
[272] Paul's drawing of an antithesis between faith (in the Gospel) and boasting
in human capacities, which is reminiscent of his address to Jewish questions in
Rom 2–4 (Rom 2:17, 23; 3:27; 4:2), shows that his discussion here is informed by
his understanding of justification by faith.
[273] Rom 11:25–27.

of Gentile adherence to the Law. Here he takes it up in order to warn Gentile believers against boasting. This development in Paul's thinking could have taken place only under the conditions which were present in Rome, where the Gentile majority of the church was untroubled by the question of circumcision. Paul's ability to employ his message in a new way underscores the fact that the concept was not merely a polemical doctrine for Paul, but a fundamental element of his understanding of the Gospel.

IV. SUMMARY

We have seen that in several respects the function which 'justification' serves in Romans precludes relegating it to the status of a mere polemical doctrine. In the first place, the very purpose of the letter, a proclamation of Paul's Gospel, not an attack upon adversaries, renders illegitimate the description of this 'doctrine' as a mere *Kampfeslehre*. At the time of writing Romans, Paul quite clearly owned the theology of his Gospel.

Moreover, it is apparent from the letter that Paul had reflected theologically on the idea of 'justification by faith alone.' No longer is the theme of forensic justification by faith used solely in regard to Jew-Gentile relations. As we have seen above, in Rom 5:1–11 it has become the means for assuring Gentile readers of deliverance from the apocalyptic manifestation of God's wrath. In Rom 9–11, through Israel's example, it has become the reason for excluding boasting in any religious pride. This expansion and broadened application of the idea provides a clear indication of Paul's theological commitment to 'justification by faith alone.'

And perhaps most significantly, Paul's argument in Rom 7:14–25 indicates that he perceived a continuing relevance of 'justification by faith' to the existence of the believer. Beyond the immediate issues within the church at Rome, Paul construed his Gospel in relation to the individual, as the proclamation of an act of God in Christ which brings freedom from the Law.

EXCURSUS: THE UNITY OF CHAPTER 16
WITH THE BODY OF THE LETTER

In its purest form, the view that Romans was originally intended to be a circular letter has been represented by only a few scholars.[274]

---

[274] Anton Fridrichsen, 'The Apostle and His Message,' *UUÅ* 3 (1947):1–23; John Knox, 'A Note on the Text of Romans,' *NTS* 2 (1955–56):191; T. W. Manson, 'St. Paul's Letter to the Romans—and Others,' in *The Romans Debate*, ed. Karl P. Donfried (Minneapolis: Augsburg, 1977), pp. 1–16 = *BJRL* 31 (1948):224–245.

While this theory has not found broad support, it has been widely accepted that Rom 16, representing a letter fragment, letter fragments, or a letter of recommendation in its entirety, was originally directed to Ephesus.[275] This view is essential only to the proposal that Romans ought to be regarded as a circular letter (or 'manifesto,' as Manson expresses it). However, it bears some weight for any reconstruction of Paul's basic purpose in the letter: if Rom 16, containing greetings with twenty-six individual names, was a part of the letter to Rome as it was first composed by Paul, it lends support to the thesis that the text was directed to the Christian community in Rome. The question as to whether or not Rom 16 belongs to the original composition, therefore not only decides the fate of a thesis such as Manson's, but also determines to some extent the relative probabilities of a whole range of proposals as to the purpose of Romans.

As the following discussion will show, despite the broad appeal of the various forms of the Ephesian hypothesis, it is best to regard Rom 16, or at least vv. 1–23, as having been composed by Paul along with the remainder of the letter.[276] Since a decision on the relation of Rom 16 to the rest of the letter depends partially on a text-critical judgment, the studies by Harry Gamble (1977), Kurt Aland (1979), and Peter Lampe (1985), which focus on explaining the transmission of the text, offer substantial contributions to the discussion.[277] Harry Gamble's work is particularly valuable since he combines text-critical work with an investigation of Hellenistic and Pauline epistolary form.

---

[275] E.g. Käsemann, *An die Römer*, pp. 396–403; Bornkamm, 'Paul's Last Will and Testament,' pp. 23–25; Marxsen, *Einleitung*, pp. 109–118. A detailed enunciation of a representative form of the Ephesian hypothesis may be found in Schmithals's *Der Römerbrief als historisches Problem*. According to Schmithals, 16:1–20 was originally a letter of recommendation of Phoebe to the church in Ephesus. Verses 21–23 belong to a second letter to the church at Rome. Verses 25–27 were added by a compiler of the Pauline Corpus. Helpful reviews of arguments for this type of position are found in Harry A. Gamble, *The Textual History of the Letter to the Romans: A Study in Textual and Literary Criticism*, SD 42 (Grand Rapids: Eerdmans, 1977), pp. 36–55 and in Wolf-Henning Ollrog, 'Die Abfassungsverhältnisse von Rom 16,' in *Kirche: Festschrift für Günther Bornkamm zum 75. Geburtstag*, ed. D. Lührmann and Georg Strecker (Tübingen: J. C. B. Mohr [Paul Siebeck], 1980), pp. 221–244.

[276] Many recent commentators accept the originality of Rom 16. See Schlier, *Der Römerbrief*, pp. 439–440; Wilckens, *Der Brief an die Römer*, 1:24–27; Dunn, *Romans*, pp. 884–885, Wedderburn, *The Reasons for Romans*, p. 12–18.

[277] Gamble, *Textual History*; Peter Lampe 'Zur Textgeschichte des Römerbriefes,' *NovT* 27 (1985):273–277; Kurt Aland, 'Der Schluß und die ürsprungliche Gestalt des Römerbriefes,' in *Neutestamentliche Entwürfe*, ed. Kurt Aland (München: Chr. Kaiser, 1979), pp. 284–301.

Frequently it is contended that the numerous, and in a number of instances, quite personal greetings to individuals in Rom 16 are inconsistent with the remainder of the letter, since Paul writes to a congregation which he has not yet visited.[278] It is more likely, so it is reasoned, that Rom 16 represents all or part of a letter addressed to Ephesus, a congregation with which Paul was familiar. But, as Gamble observes, this *a priori* judgment is contradicted by the evidence of the Pauline epistles. In no letter to the churches which Paul founded do we find greetings to individuals.[279] It is reasonable that Paul would avoid singling out particular individuals for personal greetings, as though to play favorites, within letters to those congregations with which he was acquainted. On the other hand, the sending of greetings to numerous persons with whom Paul had enjoyed positive relations in the not-too-distant past, persons who may be assumed to have had a good standing among the Roman believers, could only serve to commend Paul and further his relationship with the circle of house-churches in Rome. The extensive individual greetings then not only do not support the Ephesian hypothesis, but actually strengthen the case for viewing Rom 16 as the authentic closing to the letter.

Against the objection that it is unlikely that so many of Paul's former acquaintances would have made their way to Rome, two points may be noted. The mere mention of a name need not imply direct acquaintance with the person. Naturally, some of the addresses clearly indicate familiarity (e.g. 'Rufus, a choice man in the Lord, and his mother and mine' 16:13), but even so explicit a greeting as, 'Greet Maria, who has labored much for you,' (16:6) may reflect indirect report, rather than personal knowledge.[280] One need not assume then, that Paul had personally encountered all the individuals named in the greetings. Secondly, there was a fairly constant movement of foreign groups from the East into Rome in this period, due to emigration and the importation of slaves.[281] In view of this, it is not surprising that Paul was able to name so many within the Roman church. The internal evidence of the greetings themselves therefore does not contradict a Roman setting for Rom 16, and in some respects commends it.

---

[278] Cf. Rom 1:10-15.

[279] Gamble, *Textual History*, p. 48. In fact, as B. N. Kaye notes, only in Colossians does one find a greeting directed to an individual: Col 4:15, Nympha and the church in her house. B. N. Kaye, "To the Romans and Others' Revisited,' *NovT* 18 (1976):39–40.

[280] Gamble, *Textual History*, pp. 47–48.

[281] See the widely cited study of George LaPiana, 'Foreign Groups in Rome During the First Centuries of the Empire,' *HTR* 20 (1927):183–403, esp. 188–224.

A second objection to a Roman destination for Rom 16 is the sharp warning against false teachers found in 16:17–20. It is thought that the harsh warning, which presupposes a serious conflict, can hardly fit the remainder of the letter, the tone of which is relatively mild. But as we have observed above, the admonition in this passage reads as if the false teaching is not present within the Roman churches. It is rather an anticipated danger.

The evidence brought by the Chester Beatty (II) papyrus, P[46], the oldest manuscript of the Pauline corpus, is more weighty. In this important manuscript, the doxology now found at Rom 16:25–27, is placed after Rom 15, thus providing an early attestation for a fifteen chapter form of Romans. It was the discovery of this papyrus which stimulated the widely influential article by Manson.

While P[46] provides evidence for the early existence of a fifteen chapter form of Romans, it also presents severe problems both for Manson's view that Rom 16 was appended to the letter by Paul, and for other scholars who maintain that the redactor of the *Corpus Paulinum* (thought to be working in Ephesus) attached the chapter. The problem lies in explaining the origin of P[46], in which 15:33 is followed by the doxology (16:25-27) and then by 16:1-23. To adopt P[46] as evidence for an original fifteen chapter form, to which Paul added Rom 16 before sending it on to Ephesus, Manson must postulate a process by which the posited Roman form (1:1-15:33) interacted with a fourteen chapter form which included the doxology (1:1– 14:23 + 16:25–27).[282] This proposal must result in a stemma which requires three unattested forms.[283]

Moreover, the hypothetical intermediate form 1:1–15:33 + 16:25–27, which according to this stemma is derived from a fifteen chapter form, is very difficult to explain, since Rom 15:30- 33 forms a satisfactory conclusion of its own.[284] The doxology is in this case superfluous.

On the other hand, if the motive behind both the fourteen chapter and fifteen chapter editions is the universalizing of the Roman letter, as Gamble argues, the derivation of this intermediate form is

---

[282] This form is usually taken to be the result of an abbreviation of the text by Marcion, but see Gamble, *Textual History*, pp. 101–107, who casts doubt on the testimony of Origen's commentary and quite plausibly suggests that both the 14 and 15 chapter forms of Romans arose through early attempts at universalizing the letter.

[283] Aland, 'Schluß,' pp. 295–297.

[284] Or at least at first sight it seems to.

readily explained as resulting from the interaction of fourteen and sixteen chapter forms containing the doxology.[285]

In brief, the form which P[46] represents is explicable given the priority of a sixteen chapter form, but the motives behind its development are difficult to understand given the priority of a fifteen chapter form. In this respect P[46] favors the priority of the sixteen chapter form.

Likewise, P[46] cannot be readily used as evidence for the hypothesis that Rom 16 came into circulation when it was appended to the letter by the editor of the *Corpus Paulinum*. The existence of Romans 1:1–16:23, according to this theory, is the beginning of the transmission process of forms containing Rom 16. In this case, if P[46] is to be explained without recourse to an independently distributed Rom 16, it is of no evidential value for this hypothesis. And if P[46] is taken to indicate that Rom 16 underwent some degree of distribution, which allowed a manuscript like P[46] to come into existence, it is not likely that the editing of the *Corpus Paulinum* was the occasion for the addition of Rom 16, since it is not very plausible that an Ephesian redactor would in this situation produce the form represented by P[46], in which 16:25–27 is inserted at the close of Rom 15.

A final judgment on the original text requires attention to Pauline epistolary form. Gamble's monograph makes a substantial contribution here. He casts doubt on the suggestion that comparable Hellenistic letters of recommendation favor viewing Rom 16 as a formerly self-contained letter: letters of recommendation are themselves often found within the conclusions of lengthier letters.[286] He also addresses the important question of the nature of the 'closing' in 15:33. If this verse represents a Pauline conclusion, then it provides good evidence that the letter as it was composed by Paul ended here, and the appended material, i.e. Rom 16, creates a doubling of the basic Pauline ending. But both Gamble and Ollrog have persuasively argued that 15:33 does not represent a usual Pauline ending. They both observe that 15:33 is a 'wish of peace' (*Friedenswunsch*), which rather than being final in the Pauline letters, is penultimate.[287] The closing, which consists of a

---

[285] Because of the plausibility of this motive, Gamble's reconstruction of the textual history of Romans has much to commend it over against the stemma developed by Aland and Lampe. See Gamble, *Textual History*, pp. 96–125; Aland, 'Schluß,' pp. 284–301; Lampe, 'Zur Textgeschichte,' pp. 273–277.

[286] Gamble, *Textual History*, pp. 84–87.

[287] 1 Thess 5:23; Gal 6:16; 2 Cor 13:11. Gamble, *Textual History*, pp. 67–73, 82–83; Ollrog, 'Abfassungsverhältnisse,' p. 226.

'benediction' (*Gnadenwunsch*) generally follows intervening greetings and/or a closing admonition.[288] In this case, the thesis that
Rom 16 belongs to the letter as a whole receives strong support,
since Rom 16 then provides a proper ending to the letter and the
fifteen chapter hypothesis—if it is to be sustained at all—must
postulate a lost original ending to the letter.

In summary then, the stylistic considerations just mentioned as
well as the list of greetings in Rom 16 support the thesis that
Rom 16 is original. The evidence of P[46] makes Manson's theory
of the addition of Rom 16 from the hand of Paul himself unlikely,
and provides no support to the Ephesian hypothesis of redaction.
Likewise, the warning against false teachers does not militate
against a Roman address for Rom 16.

---

[288] 1 Thess 5:28; 1 Cor 16:23; 2 Cor 13:13; Gal 6:18; Phil 4:23; Phlm 25 cf.
Rom 16:20b; 16:24. Ollrog, 'Abfassungsverhältnisse,' p. 226; Gamble, *Textual
History*, pp. 65–67, 82–83.

CHAPTER FIVE

JUSTIFICATION BY FAITH:
A CENTRAL PAULINE THEME

I. SUMMARY OF THE INVESTIGATION

We have seen that Paul's understanding of 'justification' underwent at least three phases of development. The initial stage involved his coming to recognize Jesus' death (and vindicating resurrection) as a divine offer of righteousness apart from the Law. A second stage was initiated by his interaction with Judaizing opponents. It was in this period that arguments for 'justification by faith apart from Law' such as those found in Galatians were formed. A third stage was reached with Paul's use of forensic justification in relation to Gentile believers, as is evidenced by his letter to Rome. Paul developed the application of the idea beyond its original sphere of significance and used it to address entirely new problems.

Each of these phases clearly indicates that Paul regarded this interpretation of the message of Christ's death and resurrection as indispensable to his Gospel. Paul consistently reflected upon and applied to various concrete situations his belief that deliverance from impending divine wrath was supplied on the basis of God's act in Christ alone.

His conviction had its origin in his conversion. Paul's setting aside the righteousness which he once had attained through the Law entailed a change in his understanding of salvation. He no longer viewed God as cooperating with human effort within the framework of the covenant with Israel. Now for Paul, God's act in Christ effected salvation in itself. In the period following his conversion, he began his Law-free mission to Gentiles on the basis of this insight into the righteousness provided through faith in Christ. His understanding of the Gospel allowed him to proclaim salvation from eschatological wrath through faith in Christ to Gentiles, without making any demands upon them for obedience to the Law. Therefore the social dimensions of Paul's Gospel, which placed Jew and Gentile on equal standing before God, were the result of a change in his soteriology.

Resistance to Paul's Law-free mission, which arose first in Antioch and later in Galatia, forced Paul to articulate a defense for the understanding of the Gospel which he had already adopted in practice. A number of the arguments Paul offers in the letter to Galatia were undoubtedly derived from Paul's own wrestling with such questions as a Jewish Christian. His unwillingness to compromise on the issue of Gentile circumcision indicates that he regarded the theological position which he had embraced concerning a forensic justification by faith as necessary to his Gospel.

It is clear, nevertheless, that Paul's thought underwent development. The *Kampfeslehre* of Galatians represents theological continuity on Paul's part, since he here seeks to prevent his previously adopted understanding of the Gospel from being eroded. But the advancing of arguments was a *novum*, intended to further the existence of congregations of Gentile believers in Jesus as Christ who did not adhere to the Law. Innovation was necessary for the preservation of 'the truth of the Gospel.'

Paul's letter to Rome provides further evidence of his fundamental commitment to 'justification by faith.' This attempt to implant his understanding of the Gospel in a church which was not under attack, and which was to a large extent in agreement with him already, shows that he regarded 'justification by faith' as inseparable from his calling as apostle to the Gentiles.

Paul's use of the idea of a present forensic justification as an assurance of eschatological salvation for Gentile believers in Romans is a natural extension of his earlier practices. Since he had already proclaimed a Gospel which offered Gentile believers the promise of salvation through faith (e.g. 1 Thess), it is not at all surprising that he should develop his discussion of 'justification by faith' in this manner in Rom 5:1–11. Nevertheless, the theological move which Paul makes here is significant, since he here attempts to make the concept of 'righteousness as a gift' relevant to Gentiles apart from the question of circumcision.

The same is true in an even more important sense for Rom 9–11, in which 'justification by faith' is presented as a fulfillment of divine promise (Rom 9:30–10:21). Since God's mercy is dispensed to faith—obedient submission to the Gospel as the revelation of God's will (Rom 10:3, 16)—and not to the wisdom of the hearer, Gentiles have no cause for boasting.[1] Through Israel's example, Paul uses his message of 'justification by faith' to warn the Gentile majority at Rome against religious pride. Faith in the Gospel,

---

[1] Rom 11:19–22.

which initially signified to Paul the disqualification of Jewish boasting in *Torah*, now becomes a standard against which Gentile feelings of religious superiority must be judged.[2]

The expanded use to which the theme of justification by faith is put in this instance again shows Paul's concern to maintain theological continuity under the demands of a new situation. The circumstances in the church at Rome were different from those which Paul had faced elsewhere. If 'justification by faith' had served him merely as the means of ensuring Gentile acceptance by Jewish Christians, he need not have made 'faith' the criterion by which this predominantly Gentile church would stand or fall.[3] Paul's rejection of Gentile boasting, undergirded as it is by his call to faith, represents a consistent application of his understanding of righteousness as a 'gift' to faith. His refusal to allow any legitimacy to Gentile pride is coherent with his rejection of obedience to *Torah* as contributing to salvation.

Furthermore, the obverse side of Paul's Gospel, i.e. the plight of the human being condemned by the Law, which Paul applies to believers in Rom 7:14–25, indicates that he regarded forensic justification as having a continuing relevance to the individual. Although Luther incorrectly regarded Rom 7:14–25 as a depiction of the Christian, he rightly grasped the paradoxical condition of the believer which Paul's argument entails: *simul iustus et peccator*.

Paul therefore came to understand the implications of forensic justification as transcending Jew-Gentile relations. It primarily appears in contexts where Paul's intent is to attack religious pride based on the presumed benefits of being Jewish. But Paul was prepared to extend the topic to Gentile boasting as well, so that Käsemann's judgment has some basis:

> Wen repräsentiert der jüdische Nomismus, gegen den Paulus sich wandte? . . . Er vertritt jene Gemeinschaft frommer Menschen, welche Gottes Verheißungen zu ihrem Privileg . . . machen.[4]

And Paul perceived the justification of sinners accomplished through the death of Christ as having relevance beyond the demolition of hubris: for the community in tribulation it offers hope.

II. TOWARD A SYNTHESIS OF PAUL'S THOUGHT

As we saw in Chapter 1, until recently much of the discussion of the place of 'justification by faith' in Paul's thought has been carried

---

[2] Rom 11:20.
[3] Rom 11:20.
[4] Ernst Käsemann, 'Rechtfertigung und Heilsgeschichte im Römerbrief,' in *Paulinische Perspektiven* (Tübingen: J. C. B. Mohr [Paul Siebeck], 1969), pp. 125–126.

out by asking whether or not it is a 'center' from which the remainder of Paul's thought may be developed logically. Despite his assertion of a minimal 'center' to Paul's thought ('Christ is Savior of all'), Sanders marks the change which current discussion of Paul has undergone.[5] Most scholars now recognize that no single concept drawn from Paul's letters provides the interpreter with a *theologoumenon* sufficient to explain all of Paul's arguments.

This widespread conclusion, which has prevailed especially in North America, has not led to agreement on an appropriate means by which to characterize Paul's thought. The Pauline Theology Group of the Society of Biblical Literature has explored various avenues for synthesizing the theology of Paul over the past several years without reaching a consensus on either the proper categories by which to proceed, or the nature of 'Paul's theology' itself: is it his theological activity, his resultant letters, or the effect of those letters?

Much of the disparity which exists between interpreters is the result of a failure to reach agreement on the qualities appropriate to a 'theology of Paul' and to a synthesis of it. In what follows, we will attempt to describe some characteristics which seem requisite to this goal. These requirements lead to a certain understanding of what ought to be included in such a 'theology,' and determine to some extent how one goes about the task of description. Richard Hays has observed that any attempt at synthesis is an 'act of imagination on the part of the interpreter.'[6] The same may be said for the effort to delineate the categories essential to a 'good reading' of Paul.[7] Yet one is not free to use an unbridled imagination in this endeavor. There are at least a few commonly accepted insights regarding the nature of Paul's thought. And a recommendation to others on what a description of 'Paul's thought' ought to contain must be accompanied by reasons.

There is considerable agreement in theory, if not in practice, that a description of Paul's theology must aim at comprehensiveness. The more a synthesis allows one to explain and relate all of Paul's extant letters in their theological aspect, the more desirable it is. The current broad consensus on the inadequacy of a single *Mitte* to summarize Paul's thought is based on this judgment and obviously makes sense: one cannot fully (nor perhaps properly) understand a part of Paul's theology unless one relates it to the whole.

---

[5] See the discussion of Sanders's views in Chapter 1, Section VI.
[6] Hays, 'Crucified with Christ,' p. 321.
[7] Hays, 'Crucified with Christ,' p. 321.

Some of the ramifications of this insight have not been appreciated in recent discussion. Jouette Bassler, for example, has suggested that 'Paul's theology' should be understood as his theological activity, i.e. the convictions by which Paul modifies received tradition and with which he addresses the situations he encounters.[8] Implicit in this proposal is the assumption that 'Paul's theology' should be understood as 'the theology distinctive to Paul.' Clearly the task which Bassler envisages is a necessary part of describing the theology found in Paul's letters. But it is difficult to see why 'Paul's theology' should be limited to that which is unique to him, especially since he sometimes applies received tradition directly to situations.[9] Such an approach runs into the danger inherent to the use of the criterion of dissimilarity to describe the historical Jesus: one might end up with what is peculiar to Paul without finding what was characteristic of him.

Although the aim of being 'complete' should not be confused with the accomplishment of this elusive end, it should be possible to produce refined syntheses of Paul's thought which approach the whole as a mathematical function approaches a limit. One has no guarantee that the attempt to include all the material of Paul's letters in a synthesis will result in an accurate historical description of his thought. Everything that appears in the letters we possess is the result of Paul's selections of arguments from a broader range of possibilities, the extent of which we will never fully know. But the development of a comprehensive description of the letters should result in the mapping of a fairly complete semantic field against which any particular choice of argument on Paul's part might be measured. Likewise, as Steven Kraftchick rightly observes, it is impossible to fully capture the poetic impact which Paul intended his many metaphors to have upon his readers.[10] But it should be possible to describe substantially the theological relevance of such poetic force.

The need for a synthesis to be as comprehensive as possible is related to another desideratum, specificity. As Beker and Furnish

---

[8] Jouette M. Bassler, 'Paul's Theology: Whence and Whither? A Synthesis (of sorts) of the Theology of Philemon, 1 Thessalonians, Philippians, Galatians, and 1 Corinthians,' in *Society of Biblical Literature 1989 Seminar Papers*, ed. David J. Lull (Atlanta, Ga.: Scholars Press, 1989), pp. 417–418. Steven Kraftchick (rightly) recognizes a distinction between personal conviction and theological argument and contends that to understand Paul's 'theologizing,' one must go beyond this to ask how and why Paul employs the 'warrants' and 'backings' he does, 'A Response to 'Paul's Theology: Whence and Whither?," unpublished paper presented to the Pauline Theology Group at the Society of Biblical Literature Annual Meeting 1989, p. 19.

[9] E.g. 1 Cor 15:1–12.

[10] Kraftchick, 'A Response,' pp. 25–27.

among others have insisted, any representation of Paul's thought must bear a demonstrable relation to the text of his letters in order to guard against the imposition of the assumptions of the interpreter on Paul.[11] The metaphors, 'behind the text' or 'beneath the text,' which are frequently employed to describe the task of synthesizing the material in Paul's letters, are unfortunately ambiguous. On the one hand, they may signify the derivation of abstract theological categories (e.g. the 'indicative'), which is necessary to any comprehensive description of Paul. Yet the same language may be used to articulate a completely different approach to understanding Paul, such as focussing on his intuition,[12] his 'experiential awareness' of standing at the turning point of the ages,[13] or a system of purported unconscious 'convictions.'[14] All such shifts in paradigm, which sacrifice inclusion of Paul's conscious theological endeavors, create the risk that Paul might become merely a vehicle for furthering the interpreter's agenda.[15] Psychological, social and inter-textual insights have a role to play in adding depth and persuasiveness to a summary of Paul's thought. But it is hard to see why one should jeopardize specificity in a description of Paul in favor of non-theological methods of characterization.[16]

In order to guard against the accidental intrusion of ideas foreign to Paul, a synthesis must, in so far as it is possible, retain Paul's theological categories. The aim of creating a synthesis which is

---

[11] See J. Christiaan Beker, 'Paul the Theologian: Major Motifs in Pauline Theology,' *Int* 43 (1989):353–354; Victor Paul Furnish, 'Theology in 1 Corinthians: Initial Soundings,' in *Society of Biblical Literature 1989 Seminar Papers*, ed. David J. Lull (Atlanta, Ga.: Scholars Press, 1989), pp. 247–248.

[12] Räisänen, *Paul and the Law*, pp. 266–269.

[13] Colin Hickling, 'Centre and Periphery in the Thought of Paul,' in *Studia Biblica 1978*, JSNTSup 3, ed. E. A. Livingstone (Sheffield: JSOT, 1980), pp. 119–214.

[14] Daniel Patte, *Paul's Faith and the Power of the Gospel: A Structural Introduction to the Pauline Letters* (Philadelphia: Fortress, 1983). Patte distinguishes between Paul's theological argumentation (his 'ideas') and the assumptions which underlie Paul's arguments (his 'convictions'). If one searches Paul's argumentative logic for its basic assumptions, the system of Paul's unconscious 'convictions' should (to some extent) reveal itself. Patte fails to recognize that arguments are not based on the speaker/writer's personal 'convictions,' but on the ideas which she/he assumes are shared by her/his audience. Cf. Hübner's criticism of Patte in 'Methodologie und Theologie: Zu neuen methodischen Ansätzen in der Paulusforschung,' *KuD* 33 (1987):151–161.

[15] Bassler's proposal is subject to the same danger if one understands 'Paul's theological activity' as a mentalistic phenomenon.

[16] The claim has been made, of course, that Paul's letters contain inconsistencies which render his thought incoherent. But all such assertions are hard to sustain since the occasional nature of Paul's letters makes inconsistency just as difficult to demonstrate as consistency. And, as we have noted, even if one should find that Paul contradicts himself, one still has the task of explaining how he could have thought himself to have been consistent.

specific to Paul counterbalances, in one respect, that of being comprehensive. It is important to minimize the level of abstraction in a synthesis so that the result is a representation of Paul's thought and not that of anyone else. One cannot merely repeat the text of his letters, but a 'good reading' of Paul, while attempting exhaustive coverage of his writings, will employ his concepts to the fullest extent possible. Sometimes an overly-abstract summary of Paul's thought threatens to modernize Paul, as in Hendrikus Boers's argument that Paul's thought is based on a contradiction between existential and social 'micro-universes.'[17] In other instances, the terms employed in syntheses seem incapable of expressing what is distinctive to Paul over against his contemporaries, or even his adversaries. This is especially the case for those summaries which suggest that 'Christ' is the center of Paul's theology.[18] It is also true of Edgar Krentz's suggestion that the 'model out of which Paul works' is the concept of 'good news, gospel,' i.e. the message of Jesus Christ as Lord, through whom people are brought to know God 'in action to rescue humanity.'[19] Without further elaboration it would be difficult to distinguish between Paul and any other New Testament author using this description.

The criterion of specificity leads directly to recognition of the theological backdrop provided by the historical matrix in which Paul wrote. An important part of this task involves the analysis of early Jewish and early Christian traditions which Paul adopted, adapted, or corrected. As Beker has noted, Paul was not a systematic theologian, organizing his ideas on the basis of abstract categories, but an interpreter of the Gospel.[20]

Another aspect of the background to Paul's thought often has been curiously omitted in recent discussions of Paul's theology. Paul's theological activity in writing letters to churches was an extension of his missionary activity, which he understood as an apostolic commission. In most cases, the congregations which Paul addresses are the products of his own proclamation of the Gospel. He understands his role in relation to them as something more than the formulation of theological responses to their problems. It is his

---

[17] Hendrikus Boers, 'The Foundations of Paul's Thought: A Methodological Investigation—The Problem of the Coherent Center of Paul's Thought,' *ST* 42 (1988):55–68.

[18] See Joseph Plevnik's survey of Catholic scholars in, 'The Center of Pauline Theology,' *CBQ* 51 (1989):462–463.

[19] Edgar Krentz, 'Tracking the Elusive Center: On Integrating Paul's Theology,' unpublished paper presented at the Society of Biblical Literature Annual Meeting 1990.

[20] Beker, 'Paul the Theologian,' p. 353.

intent that his congregations embrace the truths he teaches, no matter how often he must bring his life and witness to bear on them. The pattern of his teaching is to become theirs as well, in both word and deed. Behind all his labor is his confidence that the Gospel which he proclaims and teaches has the power to transform the lives of his addressees. He often uses metaphors to describe his work which reflect this integration of life, labor, and theology: he is a farmer working a field, an architect constructing a building; he acts as an ambassador, wages war, betroths for marriage to Christ, renders priestly service to God, suffers birth-pangs. In contrast, many of the paradigms for interpreting Paul's thought, both past and present, are one-sidedly intellectual: he operates from a 'central idea,' thinks in terms of a foundational 'story,' interprets the Gospel.[21]

The recognition that Paul views the theology of his letters as a part of his broader work should lead to the treatment of Paul's letters to churches as theological acts in a series of actions which are theologically-based. The various recent attempts to dissociate Paul's conversion from his mission to Gentiles, which we examined in Chapter 1, implicitly acknowledge the connection between the theological aspect of Paul's activity and his theological writing.[22] Likewise, our approach to the theme of 'justification' has been built on the assumption that Paul's ceasing to persecute believers and beginning to evangelize Gentiles reflects some form of theological change. Paul's own understanding of his epistolary efforts demands this sort of reconstruction of his missionary work, in so far as it is possible.

Although summaries of Paul's thought have sometimes failed to capture the framework of mission in which it was formed, the concern to treat the theology of each of Paul's letters within their historical settings has not been lacking.[23] It is generally agreed that a synthesis of Paul's thought ought to have the capacity not only to comprehend all the material, but to allow for differences in theology and emphasis between letters, and to account for development in Paul's thought (although here there is some dissent). No theological pattern may be imposed *a priori* for the integration of the thought of diverse letters. The rhetorical situations

---

[21] Even Beker opts to describe Paul as an exegete rather than as a missionary. See J. Christiaan Beker, *The Triumph of God: The Essence of Paul's Thought* (Philadelphia: Fortress, 1990), p. 15.

[22] See Chapter 1, Section VI.C.

[23] The entire format of the Pauline Theology Group of the Society of Biblical Literature has been organized around the principle that the theology of each of the letters is to be assessed individually.

of the arguments themselves must serve as the means of organization.

Obviously, the repetition of an idea in varying contexts, which we have seen is the case with the theme of forensic justification, commends it as being of theological importance to Paul. And conversely, if a concept appears to be entirely situationally dependent, one is led to suspect that it represents an *ad hominem* formulation, particularly if it does not recur. Yet since no single theme is sufficiently comprehensive and specific to characterize Paul's thought, one cannot rely solely upon the appearance of certain phrases or expressions. One must take the risk of selection and abstraction, and endeavor to explain why in a given passage an idea is explicit, implicit, or absent on the basis of the context. The ideal condensation of Paul's thought should employ expressions and concepts which are always explicit when appropriate to Paul's argument. When such summary terms are not expressed in Paul's letters, one should be able to provide some evidence that they are assumed, and their implicit status should be explicable on the basis of the situation addressed.

Naturally, the structure of Paul's arguments, their presuppositions, inferences, conclusions, and the like, shed light on the nature of his thought to the extent that they reveal his rhetorical intent and method. And as we have argued is the case in Romans, an analysis of epistolary features is important to an assessment of the theological aims of a letter. Nor should the differences between Paul's letters blind the interpreter to the similarities in theology and argument which exist. Patterns of ideas, such as the consistent relationship between the 'indicative' and the 'imperative' may be traced through diverse situations. Consistent positions, such as the rejection of boasting in human achievement are expressed in varying terms.[24]

There is an additional reason for seeking to discover a logical consistency to Paul's thought. Paul manifests no consciousness of having undergone radical changes in theology from the beginning of his ministry to Gentiles (which he reports) through the period in which he wrote the letters we now possess. Moreover, he expressly demands faithfulness to his message of the Gospel.[25] And he understands this Gospel to place him under the obligation of being

---

[24] For example, compare Paul's reference to the 'calling' of the Corinthian Christians with his statement of the consequences of forensic justification: 1 Cor 1:26–31; Rom 3:27–31.
[25] Gal 1:6–9.

consistent in his dealings with his congregations.[26] As J. Paul
Sampley has observed, this commitment to integrity clearly went
beyond Paul's self-perception, since Paul was able to use his associates to impart his teaching and practices to his churches.[27]
Even if one concludes that Paul was inconsistent, it is necessary
to explain the coherence which he and at least some of those
around him thought that he maintained.

Despite the specificity to Paul of the concept of forensic justification by faith and the consistency of Paul's life and thought in
his development of arguments in support of his view, this theme,
like all other individual themes, is not adequate to comprehend
all the theology of Paul's letters. The problem with using forensic
justification as an organizing principle lies not so much in explaining the relation between 'being declared' and 'being made'
righteous. Even though Käsemann's suggested Jewish apocalyptic
tradition of God's 'obedience producing power' is absent, the two
ideas are obviously inseparable for Paul. The background of
thought which allowed Paul to link the two may yet be obscure, but the fact that for him faith in Christ necessarily issues
in the new obedience is indisputable. The primary difficulty arises
instead from the observation that for Paul forensic justification
itself presumes a broader framework based on the expectation of
a close to history, a final tribunal, and a divine triumph over evil.
This theme, as important as it is to Paul, is an anthropological
(and christological) moment of a theocentric understanding of the
world.

To say this is to acknowledge that even the (too) general theme
'the Gospel' is an insufficient condensation of Paul's theology,
unless it is understood to include both his retrospective affirmation
that the proclamation of Christ is κατὰ τὰς γραφάς, and his prospective expectation of divine victory in the resurrection of the
dead. Paul, in an important context, describes his Gospel in this
manner.[28] And it is significant that he does so when appealing to
the traditional base which he may be thought elsewhere to assume
as common ground. The free acts of the sovereign God, who
brought his promises to fulfillment in an unexpected manner in
Christ, and who presently—despite appearances to the contrary—speeds his saving ends toward their goal, are integral to Paul's

---

[26] 2 Cor 1:12–22.
[27] 1 Cor 4:17; J. Paul Sampley, 'Overcoming Traditional Methods by Synthesizing the Theology of Individual Letters,' in *Society of Biblical Literature 1986
Seminar Papers*, ed. Kent Harold Richards (Atlanta, Ga.: Scholars Press, 1986),
pp. 604–605.
[28] See 1 Cor 15:1–4.

Gospel.[29] As a result, it cannot be reduced to anthropology, especially not a human decision.

In making the preceding assertions, we are obviously embracing a central feature of the interpretation of Paul by which Käsemann entered into controversy with his teacher Bultmann in the early 1960's.[30] It is beyond our purpose to engage in a defense of this reading here, the basic validity of which has been widely acknowledged. Instead, in light of the questions we have raised regarding Käsemann's subsuming the whole of Paul's theology under the rubric of 'justification,' it is worthwhile to consider another recommendation for summarizing Paul's thought which was stimulated by Käsemann's work.

J. Christiaan Beker has put forward the claim that an 'apocalyptic structure of language' should be regarded as the 'center' of Paul's thought. This 'coherence' issues in a variety of contingent expressions as Paul addresses concrete situations in the churches to which he writes.[31] Two concerns shape Beker's thesis. He first wants to affirm, with perhaps even more emphasis than Käsemann, that certain ideas having their origin in Jewish apocalyptic thought form the framework for Paul's theology. A second, related idea arises from this proposal. None of the individual concepts which Paul employs in his letters, especially the soteriological metaphors, constitute the 'center' of Paul's thinking. They represent audience-related interpretations of the 'coherent center.'

Although Beker's simple appeal to 'apocalyptic thought' leaves considerable room for historical definition and substantiation (even when his recent elaborations are taken into account), the crucial aspects of his view seem beyond doubt.[32] The link which he perceives between Paul and apocalyptic Judaism consists of ideas arising from the problem of evil considered in relation to God's covenant with Israel:

(1) the faithfulness and vindication of God, (2) the universal salvation of the world [i.e. of creation and of nations without distinction],

---

[29] Rom 11:28–36.

[30] See Chapter 1, Section V.

[31] See Beker, *Paul the Apostle*, p. 16: It is in this sense that I speak about the coherent center of Paul's gospel as a symbolic structure: it is a Christian apocalyptic structure of thought—derived from a constitutive primordial experience (Beker is thinking here of Paul's call as apostle to the Gentiles) and delineating the Christ-event in its meaning for the apocalyptic consummation of history, that is, in its meaning for the triumph of God.

[32] See Beker, *The Triumph of God*, pp. 19–36; 61–65. He offers two basic reasons for his claim: 1. Paul the Pharisee inherited this world-view; 2. it therefore is the filter for all his utterances.

(3) the dualistic structure of the world [i.e. history], and (4) the imminent coming of God in glory.[33]

A series of issues remain unanswered here. One might legitimately ask to what extent Paul the Pharisee participated in such ideas, and (conversely) the degree to which they became his as a Christian (under the influence of the early believing community). Jewish apocalyptic thought manifested other motifs, (e.g. cosmological speculation), and presented them in literary forms (e.g. narration of visions) not found in Paul's letters. It is fair to inquire if Paul prior to faith in Christ might not have been influenced by them, and, if so, why such themes and forms are absent from his letters. Moreover, it not does not seem appropriate to describe Paul either before or after his conversion as embracing an undefined 'universalism.' And it is questionable as to how appropriate the unqualified adjective 'imminent' is to apocalyptic eschatology.[34]

Nevertheless, if universalism is limited to its cosmic aspect and 'imminence' is understood as anticipation of a sudden arrival of final events, the combination of the concepts to which Beker has pointed may be understood as a distinctive feature of early Jewish and Christian apocalyptic writings. In Paul's letters they appear in close association with traditions derived from the early Palestinian believing community, giving considerable weight to Beker's thesis.[35]

The more difficult problem, to which Beker does not fully respond, is that of explaining why and how a christologically modified apocalyptic eschatology may be said to constitute a 'coherent center' which is distinctive to Paul. Beker himself considers that his thesis might be jeopardized by Paul's letter to Galatians, because a hope in an 'imminent' cosmic triumph of God is pushed to the periphery of this letter.[36] But such a concession runs counter to Beker's own stress upon Paul's ability to interact with contingent situations. It is more appropriate to ask if apocalyptic eschatology

---

[33] Beker, *The Triumph of God*, p. 21.

[34] See, e.g. 4 Ezra 4:33–52. Harnisch, *Verhängnis und Verheissung*, p. 319, rightly comments on the eschatology of 4 Ezra: 'Die Naheschatologie wird zwar nicht preisgegeben, sondern grundsätzlich als, 'locus de novissimus' beibehalten; faktisch ist sie jedoch erweicht bzw. durch das Theorem der 'necessitas temporum' entschärft und gefahrlos gemacht.' Beker himself regards Paul's coming to faith in Christ as having intensified his expectation of an imminent end to history, *The Triumph of God*, p. 33.

[35] E.g. 1 Cor 11:26; 16:22 (which is to be read eschatologically).

[36] Beker, *Paul the Apostle*, p. 58. Boers, 'The Foundations of Paul's Thought,' p. 59, picks up on this point and uses it to argue that an 'apocalyptic symbolic structure' does not provide a sufficient means by which to interpret Paul's thought.

is presumed in Galatians (and it is, e.g. Gal 1:4; 6:15), and to show how the situation which Paul addresses results in the lack of explicit mention of apocalyptic motifs in much of the letter. One might further undertake to demonstrate how apocalyptic eschatology, when it does not serve as the subject matter itself, consistently constitutes the presuppositional substratum of all Paul's letters.

Even here one has not touched upon the real difficulty, which lies in Beker's description of Paul's apocalyptic eschatology as 'christologically modified.' Beker rightly calls attention to the eschatological orientation of all Paul's soteriological statements.[37] If this claim can be sustained (as seems likely), the various soteriological metaphors may be subsumed under an apocalyptic eschatology. The presence of such an eschatology in Paul's letters may be seen to arise from Paul's understanding of his mission.[38] It therefore is to be preferred to any particular soteriological metaphor in a description of Paul's thought. Yet the relationship between the triumph of God and the defeat of the foes of the human being remains undefined in Beker's proposal. Paul's apocalyptic eschatology and his soteriology are clearly linked for Beker: the 'coherent center' is that of 'Paul's gospel,' in which soteriological symbols are linked like the rings of the Olympic logo.[39] But Beker dispenses with 'concepts' or 'ideas' in describing the 'center' of Paul's thought. For Beker, the unifying center consists in 'a symbolic structure,' 'language,' 'metaphors,' in and through which, the Christ-event (which includes Paul's call as apostle) comes to expression.

This lack of clarification is intentional. Beker is attempting to explain the nature of Paul's argumentation in the letters generally accepted as authentic, which does not rely upon a body of tradition in the same manner as the Pastoral Epistles. He explicitly rejects the idea that Paul's thought contains 'a closed, rigid doctrinal system.'[40] While Beker's observation is highly significant, one wonders if he has not drawn an inappropriate dichotomy. Paul obviously does draw upon traditional confessional materials, which he regarded as containing 'inflexible doctrinal concepts.'[41] With time, the body of confessions current in the early Church developed, resulting in different forms and types of argument.

---

[37] Beker, *The Triumph of God*, p. xii, where he appeals to Wrede.
[38] E.g. 1 Cor 4:4, 5; 7:7, 29–31; 2 Cor 11:2; 1 Thess 19–20.
[39] Beker, *The Triumph of God* p. 62–63.
[40] Beker, *The Triumph of God*, p. 63.
[41] See 1 Cor 11:23–34, cf. Beker, *The Triumph of God*, p. xii.

Beker's prescinding from elaboration of the 'coherent center' in conceptual terms also allows him an umbrella under which he may claim comprehensive coverage of the theology of Paul's letters.[42] And this deliberate blocking out of the question of logical coherence has the advantage of allowing a historically descriptive account of Paul's letters, without requiring the interpreter to engage in a theological demonstration of Paul's consistency or inconsistency.[43]

One nevertheless must point to a deficiency here. A fundamental 'reality' is postulated as lying behind a variety of 'symbols,' without the admission that Paul's language expresses various concepts, which must in some manner be related to one another, if the claim that Paul works from a coherent 'reality' is to be maintained. In practice, Beker cannot avoid appealing to certain concepts as part of the 'coherent center' which he proposes for interpreting Paul. While an 'apocalyptic structure of thought' generally serves Paul as a hermeneutical grid or theological criterion, in 1 Cor 15 it comes into central focus as an object of theological contention between Paul and the Corinthian congregation. According to Beker, 1 Cor 15 shows that:

> Paul does not compromise—for the sake of missionary success—the central conviction of his gospel, i.e., the inseparable relation between the resurrection of Christ and the future resurrection of the dead.[44]

Likewise Paul's coherence in Romans is shown in that: Paul insists on the one church in the one gospel under the one triumphant God.[45]

In view of the preceding considerations, it is clear that further definition of the relationship between Paul's apocalyptic eschatology and his soteriology is required if one is to retain a form of Beker's proposal. One approach which might supply a framework for this task is that of Richard Hays, for whom 'the ground of coherence in Paul's thought is to be found not in a system of theological propositions' but in a 'kerygmatic story of God's action through Jesus Christ.'[46] Hays's preliminary sketch must be expanded if it is to be comprehensive: rather than beginning with God's promises to form and save a people, the 'story' to which

---

[42] See Beker, *The Triumph of God*, p. 114: Paul's evangelical 'center' should not be identified with one of its soteriological metaphors, for instance, 'the righteousness of God,' 'justification,' 'redemption,' 'reconciliation,' or 'being in Christ.'
[43] Beker, 'Paul's Theology: Consistent or Inconsistent?' *NTS* 34 (1988):368.
[44] Beker, 'Paul the Theologian," pp. 360–361.
[45] Beker, 'Paul's Theology,' p. 376.
[46] Hays, 'Crucified with Christ,' p. 324.

Paul refers extends back to creation itself.[47] Yet the pattern Hays proposes allows for a comprehensiveness to which few syntheses can attain. Not only does the paradigm of 'story' admit the narrative of God's words and deeds found in Scripture, which shaped Paul's views and to which he appealed in argument, but it incorporates the temporal, eschatological dimension by which Paul 'located' himself and his addressees.

Some of Hays's elaborations of Paul's thought are in danger of being inordinately 'ecclesiocentric,' like similar proposals which interpret Paul in terms of *Heilsgeschichte*. Hays recognizes that Paul regards two events, the death/resurrection of Christ and the day of the Lord, as the pivotal events in God's dealing with the world.[48] But his proposal does not explain why Paul focusses upon these two elements of the 'story.' Consequently, there is a danger of misinterpreting the 'drama' by failing to appreciate how the climactic points provide the meaning for the whole.

Although it is not immediately apparent, Hays's proposal is related to that of Beker, and may be provided with a necessary supplement from apocalyptic thought. Whatever differences exist between Paul's use of Scripture and that of other early Jewish apocalyptic groups—and there are some important distinctions which must be taken into account[49]—they manifest a common perspective in regarding themselves as the possessors of the definitive interpretation of the Scripture. This view is based on their likewise shared judgment that they possess the knowledge of the end and goal of the story of Scripture and of history.[50] Hays's treatment of 'echoes' of Scripture in Paul's letters goes beyond Paul's conscious appropriation of the text in arguments in helpful and important ways.[51] Nevertheless, Paul's theological intent and perspective cannot be forgotten in a summary of his thought. It is here, in connecting Paul's use of Scripture with that of other apocalyptically-oriented Jewish groups, that useful work could be done to further refine Hays's proposal theologically, and to give it

---

[47] See e.g. 1 Cor 15:45–49.

[48] Hays, 'Crucified with Christ,' p. 326.

[49] See Leonard Goppelt, 'Apokalyptik und Typologie bei Paulus,' in *Typos: Die typologische Deutung des Alten Testaments im Neuen* (Darmstadt: Wissenschaftliche Buchgesellschaft, 1966), pp. 259–299.

[50] See the classic reference in 1QH 7:1–8; cf. Ernst Käsemann, 'Die Anfänge christlicher Theologie,' in *Exegetische Versuche und Besinnungen*[2] (Göttingen: Vandenhoeck & Ruprecht, 1966), 2:95: Umgekehrt gilt, daß erst die Apokalyptik im Bereich des Christentums historisches Denken ermöglichte. . . . Der Weissagungsbeweis und die Typologie sind die ältesten Zeugnisse dieses in der Apokalyptik verwurzelt Erzählens (of the Gospels) . . . .

[51] See Hays, *Echoes of Scripture*, pp. 14–33.

the historical definition which is required if Paul is to be distinguished from a modern literary theorist.

It is beyond our scope to detail further a description of Paul's thought. We can only point in the direction in which the preceding considerations lead. The aim to be both comprehensive and specific in a synthesis leads beyond the use of a single soteriological metaphor, no matter how general it might be. In some fashion apocalyptic thought, especially eschatology, must serve as the backbone to a synthesis. This skeleton must be fleshed out by the assorted and specific christologically and soteriologically oriented arguments which can be shown to drive Paul's mission and his letters. The arrangement of this matter would be most properly carried out, it would seem, by noting similarities and differences in the argumentative situations in which it is employed. And one must not ignore the fact that Paul's perception of his task motivates his arguments: it is necessary to take into account the paradigmatic effect which Paul's apocalyptically-oriented understanding of Scripture had on his view of the world and his mission. Only knowledge of the extent of the semantic field from which Paul draws informs us of the significance of his individual choices.

III. CONCLUSION

An outline of Paul's thought of the type we have recommended should take account of his two—fold use of 'justification' not only to destroy hubris but to offer hope. It is appropriate, however, to search for a single metaphor by which this soteriological 'part' may be related to the apocalyptic-eschatological 'whole.' Terms such as 'integral,' 'fundamental,' 'essential,' and 'basic' might carry the false implication that all other themes are logically built upon or connected to forensic justification. It is better to use the expression 'central' to describe the place of 'justification' in Paul's thought, since it conveys the importance of the theme to Paul in his historical context, without suggesting that it is the logical starting point of all Paul's reflections.

'Justification by faith' derives from Paul's interpretation of the cross and is dependent on his apocalyptic eschatology. Historically, it was essential to his mission to Gentiles. Paul himself theologically developed its application to Gentile believers. It therefore may be said to have been an indispensable aspect of his Gospel, which was linked to his understanding of the 'story' of God's promises and covenant-faithfulness. It is a central Pauline theme.

SELECTED BIBLIOGRAPHY

Aland, Kurt. 'Der Schluß und die ürsprungliche Gestalt des Römerbriefes.' In *Neutestamentliche Entwürfe*, pp. 284–301. Ed. Kurt Aland. München: Chr. Kaiser, 1979.

Alexander, Philip. 'Rabbinic Judaism and the New Testament.' *ZNW* 74 (1983):235–245.

Aune, David E. *The New Testament in Its Literary Environment.* LEC 8. Philadelphia: Westminster, 1987.

Badenas, Robert. *Christ the End of the Law: Romans 10:4 in Pauline Perspective.* JSNTSup 10. Sheffield: JSOT, 1985.

Bammel, Ernst. 'Galater 1,23.' *ZNW* 59 (1969):108–112.

Banks, Robert. 'Rom7:25A: An Eschatological Thanksgiving?' *AusBR* 26 (1978):34–42.

Barr, James. *The Semantics of Biblical Language.* Oxford: Oxford University Press, 1961.

Barrett, C. K. 'Paulus als Missionar und Theologe.' *ZThK* 86 (1989):18–32.

Barth, Markus. 'Die Stellung des Paulus zu Gesetz und Ordnung.' *EvT* 33 (1973):496–526.

Bartsch, H.-W. 'Die historische Situation des Römerbriefes. In *Studia Evangelica IV*, pp. 281–291. TU 102. Ed. F.L.Cross. Berlin: Akademie, 1968.

Bartsch, H.-W. 'Die anti-semitische Gegner des Paulus im Römerbrief.' In *Anti-judaismus im Neuen Testament*, pp. 27–43. Ed. W. P. Eckert, et al. München: Chr.Kaiser, 1967.

Bartsch, H.-W. 'Die Empfänger des Römerbriefes.' *ST* 25 (1971):81–89.

Bassler, Jouette M. 'Paul's Theology: Whence and Whither? A Synthesis (of sorts) of the Theology of Philemon, 1 Thessalonians, Philippians, Galatians, and 1 Corinthians.' In *Society of Biblical Literature 1989 Seminar Papers*, pp. 412–423. Ed. David J. Lull. Atlanta, Ga., Scholars Press, 1989.

Baur, Ferdinand Christian. *Paulus der Apostel Jesu Christi*[2]. Part2. Leipzig: Fues's (L.W. Reisland), 1867.

Becker, Jürgen. *Das Heil Gottes: Heils- und Sündenbegriffe in den Qumrantexten und im Neuen Testament.* SUNT 3. Göttingen, Vandenhoeck & Ruprecht, 1964.

Beker, J. Christiaan 'Paul's Theology: Consistent or Inconsistent?' *NTS* 34 (1988):364–377.

Beker, J. Christiaan. 'Paul the Theologian: Major Motifs in Pauline Theology.' *Int* 43 (1989):352–365.

Beker, J. Christiaan. *Paul the Apostle: The Triumph of God in Life and Thought.* Paperback ed. Philadelphia: Fortress, 1984.

Beker, J.Christiaan. 'Review of *Paul and Palestinian Judaism* by E.P. Sanders.' *TToday* 35 (1978):108–111.

Berger, Klaus. 'Neues Material zur 'Gerechtigkeit Gottes'.' *ZThK* 68 (1977):266–276.

Bertram, Georg. 'κρεμάννυμι.' In *Theologisches Wörterbuch zum Neuen Testament*, 3:915–920. Ed. G. Kittel Stuttgart: Kohlhammer, 1938.

Betz, Hans Dieter. *Galatians*. Philadelphia: Fortress, 1979.

Betz, Otto. 'Paulus als Pharisäer nach dem Gesetz: Phil. 3.56 als Beitrag zur Frage des frühen Pharisäismus.' In *Treue zur Thora: Festschrift für Günther Harder*, pp. 54–64. Ed. Peter von der Osten Sacken. Berlin: Institut für Kirche und Judentum, 1977.

Betz, Otto. 'Rechtfertigung und Heiligung.' In *Rechtfertigung, Realismus, Universalimus in biblischer Sicht*, pp. 30–44. Ed.G. Müller. Darmstadt: Wissenschaftliche Buchgesellschaft, 1978.

Bitzer, Lloyd. 'The Rhetorical Situation.' *Philosophy and Rhetoric* 1(1974):1–14.

Bjerkelund, Carl J. *Parakalô: Form, Funktion und Sinn der parakalô-Sätze in den paulinischen Briefen*. Oslo: Universitetsforlaget, 1967.

Blass, F., Debrunner, A., and Rehkopf, F. *Grammatik des neutestamentlichen Griechisch*[15]. Göttingen: Vandenhoeck & Ruprecht, 1979.

Boers, Hendrikus. 'The Foundations of Paul's Thought: A Methodological Investigation—The Problem of the Coherent Center of Paul's Thought.' *ST* 42 (1988):55–68.

Bornkamm, Günther. 'The Letter to the Romans as Paul's Last Will and Testament.' In *The Romans Debate*, pp. 17–31. Ed. Karl P. Donfried. Minneapolis: Augsburg, 1977.

Bornkamm, Günther. 'The Revelation of Christ to Paul on the Damascus Road and Paul's Doctrine of Justification.' In *Reconciliation and Hope*, pp. 90–103. Ed. Robert Banks. Grand Rapids: Eerdmans, 1974.

Bornkamm, Günther. *Paulus*[3]. Stuttgart: Kohlhammer, 1977.

Bornkamm, Günther. 'The Letter to the Romans as Paul's Last Will and Testament.' In *The Romans Debate*, pp. 17–31. Ed. Karl P. Donfried. Minneapolis: Augsburg, 1977.

Bousset, Wilhelm. 'Paulus.' In *Religion in der Geschichte und Gegenwart*, 4:1275–1310. Ed. Friedrich Michael Schiele and Leopold Zscharnack. Tübingen: J. C. B. Mohr (Paul Siebeck), 1913.

Bousset, Wilhelm. *Die Religion des Judentums im Neutestamentlichen Zeitalter*. Berlin: ReutherundReichard, 1903, 1906[2.]

Bousset, Wilhelm. *Kyrios Christos: Geschichte des Christusglaubens von den Anfängen des Christentums bis Irenaeus*. FRLANT 21. Göttingen: Vandenhoeck & Ruprecht, 1913.

Bouttier, Michel. 'La Mystique de l'Apôtre Paul: Rétrospective et Prospective.' *RHPR* 56 (1976):54–67.

Braun, Herbert. 'Vom Erbarmen Gottes über den Gerechten: Zur Theologie der Psalmen Salomos.' In *Gesammelte Studien zum Neuen Testament und seiner Umwelt*[2], pp. 865. Tübingen: J. C. B. Mohr (Paul Siebeck),1967 = *ZNW* 43 (1950/1):1–54.

Braun, Herbert. *Spätjüdischhäretischer und frühchristlicher Radikalismus*. 2 vols. BHT 24. Tübingen: J. C. B. Mohr (Paul Siebeck), 1969.

Brock, Sebastian. 'The Psalms of Solomon.' In *The Apocryphal Old Testament*, pp. 649–682. Ed. H. F. D. Sparks. Oxford: Clarendon, 1984.

Bruce, F. F. 'Christianity under Claudius.' *BJRL* 44 (1961–62):309–326.

Bruce, F. F. *The Epistle to the Galatians*. New International Greek Testament Commentary. Grand Rapids: Eerdmans, 1982.

Bruce, F.F. 'The Romans Debate—Continued.' *BJRL* 64 (1981/82):334–359.

Büchler, Adolf. *Types of Jewish-Palestinian Piety from 70B.C.E. to 70C.E.* London: Oxford University Press, 1922.

Bultmann, Rudolf. 'Review of J.G. Machen's *The Origin of Paul's Religion*.'

TLZ 49(1924):13–14.

Bultmann, Rudolf. 'Christus des Gesetzes Ende.' In *Gesammelte Aufsäzte* II, pp. 33–58. Tübingen: J. C. B. Mohr (Paul Siebeck), 1952.

Bultmann, Rudolf. 'Das Problem der Ethik bei Paulus.' In *Das Paulusbild in der neueren deutschen Forschung*, pp. 179–199. WdF 24. Ed. K. H. Rengstorf. Darmstadt: Wissenschaftliche Buchgesellschaft, 1982.

Bultmann, Rudolf. 'Die Bedeutung der Eschatologie für die Religion des Neuen Testaments.' *ZThK* 27 (1917):76–87.

Bultmann, Rudolf. 'Die neutestamentliche Forschung 1905–1907.' *Monatsschrift für Pastoraltheologie* 5 (19081909):124–132, 154–164.

Bultmann, Rudolf. 'Die Schriften des Neuen Testaments und der Hellenismus.' *Christliche Welt* 25 (1911):589–593.

Bultmann, Rudolf. '*ΔΙΚΑΙΟΣΥΝΗ ΘΕΟΥ*.' *JBL* 83 (1964):12–16.

Bultmann, Rudolf. 'Ethische und mystische Religion im Urchristentum.' *Christliche Welt* 34 (1920):725–731, 738–743.

Bultmann, Rudolf. 'Geschichte der Paulus-Forschung.' In *Das Paulusbild in der neueren deutschen Forschung*. WdF 24. Ed. K. H. Rengstorf. Darmstadt: Wissenschaftliche Buchgesellschaft, 1982.

Bultmann, Rudolf. 'Karl Barths 'Römerbrief' in zweiter Auflage.' *Christliche Welt* 36 (1922):320–323, 330–334, 358–361, 369–373.

Bultmann, Rudolf. 'Paulus.' In *Die Religion in der Geschichte und Gegenwart*[2]. Ed. Hermann Gunkel and Leopold Zscharnack. Tübingen: J. C. B. Mohr (Paul Siebeck), 1930.

Bultmann, Rudolf. 'Römer 7 und die Anthropologie des Paulus.' In *Exegetica*, pp. 198–209. Ed. Erich Dinkler. Tübingen: J. C. B. Mohr (Paul Siebeck), 1967.

Bultmann, Rudolf. *Das Urchristentum*. Zürich: Artemis Verlag,1949.

Bultmann, Rudolf. *Exegetica: Aufsätze zur Erforschung des Neuen Testaments*. Ed. E. Dinkler. Tübingen: J. C. B. Mohr (Paul Siebeck), 1967.

Bultmann, Rudolf. *Theologie des Neuen Testaments*[9]. Tübingen, J. C. B. Mohr (Paul Siebeck), 1984.

Caird, G. B. 'Review of *Paul and Palestinian Judaism: a Comparison of Patterns of Religion*, by E. P. Sanders.' *JTS* 29 (1978):541–542.

Campbell, W. S. 'Why Did Paul Write Romans?' *ExpT* 85 (197374):264–269.

Caquot, André. 'Les Hasmonéens, les Romains, et Hérode: Observations sur Ps.Sal. 17.' In *Hellenica et Judaica*, pp. 213–218. Ed. A. Caquot, M. Hadas-Lebel, and J. Riaud. Leuven: Peeters, 1986.

Carson, D. A. *Divine Sovereignty and Human Responsibility: Biblical Perspectives in Tension*. Atlanta: John Knox, 1981.

Charlesworth, J. H. 'Les Odes de Salomon et les Manuscrits de la Mer Morte.' *RB* 77 (1970):522–549.

Charlesworth, J. H. 'Review of *Die Psalmen Salomos* by Joachim Schüpphaus.' *JAAR* 50(1982):292–293.

Charlesworth, J. H. 'A Critical Comparison of the Dualism in 1QS III.13-IV,26 and the "Dualism" in the Fourth Gospel.' *NTS* 15 (1972):389–418.

Consigny, Scott. 'Rhetoric and Its Situations.' *Philosophy and Rhetoric* 7(1974):175–186.

Conzelmann, Hans. 'Die Rechtfertigungslehre des Paulus: Theologie oder Anthropologie?' *EvT* 28 (1968):389–404.

Cooper, Karl T.'Paul and Rabbinic Soteriology: A Review Article.' *WTJ* 44 (1982):123–139.

Cranfield, C. E. B. *A Critical and Exegetical Commentary on the Epistle to the Romans*. 2 vols. ICC. Edinburgh: T.& T. Clark, 1975.

Cranfield, C. E. B. 'Some Observations on the Interpretation of Romans 14, 1–15, 13.' *Communio Viatorum* 17 (1974):193–204.

Cross, Frank Moore, Jr. 'The Development of the Jewish Scripts.' In *The Bible and the Ancient Near East*, pp. 133–202. Ed. G.E.Wright. Garden City, NY: Doubleday, 1961.

Dahl, Nils A. 'The One God of Jews and Gentiles.' In *Studies in Paul*, pp.178–191. Minneapolis: Augsburg, 1977.

Dahl, Nils A. 'The Doctrine of Justification: Its Social Function and Implications.' In *Studies in Paul*, pp. 95–120. Minneapolis: Augsburg, 1979.

Davies, W. D. *Paul and Rabbinic Judaism: Some Rabbinic Elements in Pauline Theology*. New York: Harper & Row, 1967.

Davies, W. D. *Torah in the Messianic Age And/Or the Age to Come*. JBL Monograph Series VII. Philadelphia: Society of Biblical Literature, 1952.

Deissmann, Gustav Adolf. *Paulus: Eine kultur- und religionsgeschichtliche Skizze²*. Tübingen: J. C. B. Mohr (Paul Siebeck), 1925.

Delcor, M. 'Psaumes de Salomon.' In *Dictionnaire de la Bible: Supplément*, 9:214–245. Ed. H. Cazelles and A. Feuillet. Paris: Letouzey and Ané, 1979.

Delcor, M. 'Qumrân. Règle de Communauté.' In *Dictionnaire de la Bible: Supplément*, 9:851–859. Ed. H. Cazelles and A. Feuillet. Paris: Letouzey and Ané, 1979.

Delling, Gerhard. 'Zum neueren Paulusverständnis.' *NovT* 4 (1960):95–121.

Dietzfelbinger, Christian. *Die Berufung des Paulus als Ursprung seiner Theologie*. WMANT 58. Neukirchen-Vluyn: Neukirchener, 1985.

Dimant, Devorah. 'Qumran Sectarian Literature.' In *Jewish Writings of the Second Temple Period*. CRINT 2, pp. 497–502. Ed. Michael E. Stone. Philadelphia: Fortress, 1984.

Dodd, C. H. *The Epistle of Paul to the Romans*. London: Hodder and Stoughton, 1932.

Donaldson, Terence L. 'Zealot and Convert: The Origin of Paul's Christ-Torah Antithesis.' *CBQ* 51 (1989):655–682.

Donfried, Karl P. 'A Short Note on Romans 16.' In *The Romans Debate*, pp. 50–60. Ed. Karl P. Donfried. Minneapolis: Augsburg, 1977.

Dunn, James D. G. 'The New Perspective on Paul.' *BJRL* 65 (1983):95–122.

Dunn, James D. G. 'Works of the Law and the Curse of the Law.' *NTS* 31 (1985):523–542.

Dunn, James D. G. 'Rom 7:14–25 in the Theology of Paul.' *TZBas* 31 (1975).

Dunn, James D. G. *Romans*. WBC 38. Dallas, Tx: Word, 1988.

Dunn, James D. G. '"A Light to the Gentiles": the Significance of the Damascus Road Christophany for Paul.' In *The Glory of Christ in the New Testament*, pp. 251–266. Ed. L. Hurst and N. T. Wright. Oxford: Clarendon, 1987.

Dupont, Jacques. 'La conversion de Paul et son influence sur sa conception du salut par la foi.' In *Foi et Salut Selon S. Paul*, pp.77–100. AnBib 42. Rome: Pontifical Biblical Institute, 1970.

Espy, John M. 'Paul's 'Robust Conscience' Re-examined.' *NTS* 31 (1985):161–188.

Evang, Martin. *Rudolf Bultmann in seiner Frühzeit*. BHT 74. Tübingen: J. C. B. Mohr (Paul Siebeck), 1988.

Fahlgren, K. Hj. 'Die Gegensätze von sedaqa im Alten Testament.' In *Um das Prinzip der Vergeltung in Religion und Recht des Alten Testaments*, pp. 87–129.

WdF 125. Ed. Klaus Koch. Darmstadt: Wissenschaftlichebuchgesellschaft, 1972.

Franklyn, P.N. 'The Cultic and Pious Climax of Eschatology in the Psalms of Solomon.' *JSJ* 18 (1987):1–17.

Fredriksen, Paula. 'Paul and Augustine: Conversion Narratives, Orthodox Traditions, and the Retrospective Self.' *JTS* 37n.s. (1986):3–34.

Fridrichsen, Anton. 'The Apostle and His Message.' *UUÅ* 3 (1947):1–23.

Funk, R. W. 'The Apostolic Parousia.' In *Christian History and Interpretation*, pp. 249–268. Ed. W. R. Farmer, C. F. D. Moule, and R. R. Niebuhr. Cambridge: Cambridge University Press, 1967.

Furnish, Victor Paul. *Theology and Ethics in Paul*. Nashville: Abingdon, 1963.

Furnish, Victor Paul. 'Theology in 1 Corinthians: Initial Soundings.' In *Society of Biblical Literature 1989 Seminar Papers*, pp. 246–264. Ed. David J. Lull. Atlanta, Ga., Scholars Press, 1989.

Gager, J. G. 'Some Notes on Paul's Conversion.' *JBL* 27 (1981):697–704.

Gamble, Harry A. *The Textual History of the Letter to the Romans: A Study in Textual and Literary Criticism*. SD 42. Grand Rapids: Eerdmans, 1977.

Garnet, Paul. *Salvation and Atonement in the Qumran Scrolls*. WUNT² 3. Tübingen: J. C. B. Mohr (Paul Siebeck), 1977.

Gärtner, Bertil. *The Temple and Community in Qumran and the New Testament*. SNTSMS 1. Cambridge: Cambridge University Press, 1965.

Gaston, Lloyd. *Paul and the Torah*. Vancouver: University of British Columbia, 1987.

Gaventa, B. R. 'Galatians 1 and 2: Autobiography as Paradigm.' *NovT* 28 (1986):309–326.

Gaventa, B. R. *From Darkness to Light: Aspects of Conversion in the New Testament*. Philadelphia: Fortress, 1986.

Gnilka, Joachim. *Der Philipperbrief*. HTKNT. Freiburg: Herder, 1968.

Gnilka, Joachim. 'Martyriumsparänese und Sühnetod in synoptischen und jüdischen Traditionen.' In *Die Kirche des Anfangs*, pp. 223–276. Ed. R. Schnackenburg, J. Ernst, and J. Wanke. Freiburg: Herder, 1978.

Goguel, Maurice. 'Remarques sur un aspect de la conversion de Paul.' *JBL* 53 (1934):257–267.

Goppelt, Leonard. 'Apokalyptik und Typologie bei Paulus.' In *Typos: Die typologische Deutung des Alten Testaments im Neuen*, pp. 259–299. Darmstadt: Wissenschaftliche Buchgesellschaft, 1966.

Gray, G. B. 'The Psalms of Solomon.' In *The Apocrypha and Pseudepigrapha of the Old Testament*,1:625–652. Ed. R. H. Charles. Oxford: Clarendon, 1913.

Grundmann, W. 'Paulus aus dem Volke Israel. Apostel der Völker.' *NovT* 4 (1960):267–291.

Gubler, M. L. *Die Früheste Deutungen des Todes Jesu*. OBO 15. Freiburg, Switzerland: Universitätsverlag, 1977.

Güttgemanns, Erhardt. "Gottesgerechtigkeit' und strukturale Semantik: Linguistische Analyse zu δικαιοσύνη θεοῦ.' In *Studia Linguistica Neotestamentica*, pp. 59–98. BEvT 60. München: Chr.Kaiser, 1971.

Haacker, Klaus. 'Die Berufung des Verfolgers und die Rechtfertigung des Gottlosen.' *Theologische Beiträge* 6 (1975):1–19.

Haacker, Klaus. 'Der Römerbrief als Friedensmemorandum.' *NTS* 36 (1990):25–41.

Haacker, Klaus. 'War Paulus Hillelit?' In *Das Institutum Judaicum der Universität Tübingen 1971–1972*, pp. 106–120. Tübingen: Institutum Judaicum, 1973.

Hagner, Donald A. 'Paul in Modern Jewish Thought.' In *Pauline Studies: Essays Presented to Professor F. F. Bruce on his 70th Birthday*, pp. 143–165. Ed. D. A. Hagner and M. J. Harris. Grand Rapids, Eerdmans, 1980.

Hahn, Ferdinand. *Das Verständnis der Mission im Neuen Testament.*WMANT 13. Neukirchen: Neukirchener,1963.

Hann, Robert R. *The Manuscript History of the Psalms of Solomon.* SBLSCS 13. Chico, CA: Scholars Press, 1982.

Hann, Robert R. 'The Community of the Pious: the Social Setting of the Psalms of Solomon.' *SR* 17 (1988):169–189.

Harder, G. 'Der konkrete Anlaß des Römerbriefes.' *Theologia Viatorum* 6 (1958/59):13–24.

Harnisch, Wolfgang. *Verhängnis and Verheißung der Geschichte. Untersuchungen zum Zeit- und Geschichtsverständnis im 4.Buch Esra und in der syr. Baruchapokalypse.* FRLANT 97. Göttingen: Vandenhoeck & Ruprecht, 1969.

Hays, Richard Bevan. 'Crucified with Christ: A Synthesis of 1 and 2 Thessalonians, Philemon, Philippians, and Galatians.' In *Society of Biblical Literature 1988 Seminar Papers*, pp. 318–335. Ed. David J. Lull. Atlanta, Ga.: Scholars Press, 1988.

Hays, Richard B. *Echoes of Scripture in the Letters of Paul.* New Haven: Yale University Press, 1989.

Hays, Richard B. 'Psalm143 and the Logic of Romans 3.' *JBL* 99 (1980):107–115.

Heitmüller, Wilhelm. 'Die Bekehrung des Paulus.' *ZThK* 27 (1917):136–153.

Heitmüller, Wilhelm. *Taufe und Abendmahl bei Paulus: Darstellung und religionsgeschichtliche Beleuchtung.* Göttingen: Vandenhoeck & Ruprecht, 1903.

Hengel, Martin. *The Atonement: A Study in the Origins of the Doctrine in the New Testament.* Philadelphia: Fortress, 1981.

Hengel, Martin. *Between Jesus and Paul.* Philadelphia: Fortress, 1983.

Hengel, Martin. *Judentum und Hellenismus: Studien zu ihrer Begegnungen unter besonderer Berücksichtigung Palästina bis zur Mitte des 2.Jh. v. Chr.* WUNT 10. Tübingen: J. C. B. Mohr (Paul Siebeck), 1969.

Hengel, Martin. 'Mors turpissima crucis: Die Kreuzigung in der antiken Welt und die 'Torheit' des 'Wortes vom Kreuz'.' In *Rechtfertigung: Festschrift für Ernst Käsemann*,pp.124–184. Ed. J. Friedrich, W.Pöhlmann, P. Stuhlmacher. Tübingen: J. C. B. Mohr (Paul Siebeck), 1976.

Hengel, Martin. Trans. John Bowden. *The Pre-Christian Paul.* Philadelphia: Trinity Press International, 1991.

Hengel, Martin. *Die Zeloten: Untersuchungen zur Jüdischen Freiheitsbewegung in der Zeit von Herodes I. bis 70 n.Chr.2.* AGJU 1. Leiden: E. J. Brill, 1976.

Hickling, Colin. 'Centre and Periphery in the Thought of Paul.' In *Studia Biblica 1978*, pp. 119–214. JSNTSup 3. Ed. E. A. Livingstone. Sheffield: JSOT, 1980.

Hill, David. *Greek Words and Hebrew Meanings: Studies in the Semantics of Soteriological Terms.* Cambridge: Cambridge University Press, 1967.

Hofius, Otfried. 'Das Evangelium und Israel.' *ZThK* 83 (1986):297–324.

Holm-Nielsen, Svend. 'Die Psalmen Salomos.' In *Poetische Schriften*, pp. 51–112. JSHRZ 4. Ed. W. G. Kümmel. Gütersloh: Gerd Mohn, 1977.

Holm-Nielsen, Svend. 'Erwägungen zu dem Verhältnis zwischen den Hodajot und den Psalmen Salomos.' In *Bibel und Qumran*, pp. 112–131. Ed. Siegfried Wagner. Berlin: Evangelische Haupt-Bibelgesellschaft, 1968.

Holm-Nielsen, Svend. 'The Importance of Late Jewish Psalmody for the Understanding of Old Testament Psalmodic Tradition.' *ST* 14 (1960):1–53.

Holtzmann, H. J. *Lehrbuch der neutestamentlichen Theologie.* 2 vols. Freiburg i. B. and

Leipzig: J. C. B. Mohr (Paul Siebeck), 1897.

Hooker, Morna. 'Paul and Covenantal Nomism.' In *Paul and Paulinism: Essays in Honor of C. K. Barrett*, pp. 47–56. Ed. M. D. Hooker and S. G. Wilson. London: SPCK, 1982.

Hübner, Hans. 'Gal 3.10 und die Herkunft des Paulus.' *KuD* 19 (1973):215–231.

Hübner, Hans. 'Methodologie und Theologie: Zu neuen methodischen Ansätzen in der Paulusforschung.' *KuD* 33 (1987):150–175, 303–329.

Hübner, Hans. 'Paulusforschung seit 1945. Ein kritischer Literaturbericht.' In *Aufstieg und Niedergang der römischen Welt*. 25.4, pp. 2649–2840. Ed. W. Haase. Berlin, deGruyter, 1987.

Hübner, Hans. *The Law in Paul's Thought*. Trans. James C. G. Greig. Edinburgh: T. & T. Clark, 1984.

Hübner, Hans. 'Pauli Theologiae Proprium.' *NTS* 26 (1980):445–473.

Hultgren, Arland J. 'Paul's Pre-Christian Persecutions of the Church: Their Purpose, Locale, and Nature.' *JBL* 95 (1976):97–111.

Huppenbauer, H.W. *Der Mensch zwischen zwei Welten*. ATANT 34. Zürich: Zwingli, 1959.

Ilg, Norbert. 'Überlegungen zum Verständnis von ברית in den Qumrantexten.' In *Qumrân: Sa piété, sa théologie et son mileau*, pp. 257–263. Ed. M. Delcor. Paris-Gembloux: Duculot, 1978.

Janowski, Bernd and Lichtenberger, Hermann. 'Enderwartung und Reinheitsidee: Zur eschatologischen Deutung von Reinheit und Sühne in der Qumrangemeinde.' *JJS* 34 (1983):31–62.

Janowski, Bernd. 'Sündenvergebung 'um Hiobs willen' Fürbitte und Vergebung in 11QtgJob 38:2f. und Hi 42:9f. LXX.' *ZNW* 73 (1982):251–280.

Janowski, Bernd. *Sühne als Heilsgeschehen: Studien zur Sühnetheologie der Priesterschrift und zur Wurzel KPR im Alten Orient und im Alten Testament*. WMANT 55. Neukirchen-Vluyn: Neukirchner, 1982.

Jansen, H. Ludin. *Die Spätjüdische Psalmendichtung ihr Entstehungskreis und ihr 'Sitz im Leben'*. Skrifter utgitt av Det Norske Videnskaps-Akademi i Oslo II. Hist.-Filos. Klasse 3. Oslo: Jacob Dybwad, 1937.

Jaubert, Annie. *La notion d'Alliance dans le Judasme aux abords de l'ère chrétienne*. Patristica Sorbonensia 6. Paris: Seuil, 1963.

Jeremias, Gert. *Der Lehrer der Gerechtigkeit*. SUNT 2. Göttingen: Vandenhoeck & Ruprecht, 1963.

Jervell, Jacob. 'The Letter to Jerusalem.' In *The Romans Debate*, pp. 61–74. Ed. Karl P. Donfried. Minneapolis: Augsburg, 1977.

Jervis, L. Ann. *The Purpose of Romans: A Comparative Letter Structure Investigation*. JSNTSup 55. Sheffield: JSOT, 1991.

Jewett, Robert. 'Conflicting Movements in the Early Church as Reflected in Philippians.' *NovT* 12 (1970):362–390.

Jewett, Robert. 'Following the Argument of Romans.' *WW* 6 (1986):382–389.

Jewett, Robert. 'Romans as an Ambassadorial Letter.' *Int* 36 (1982):5–20.

Jewett, Robert. 'The Agitators and the Galatian Congregation.' *NTS* 17 (1971):198–212.

Johnson, Roger A. *The Origins of Demythologizing: Philosophy and Historiography in the Theology of Rudolf Bultmann*. SHT 28. Leiden: Brill, 1974.

Jonge, M. de. 'Jesus' Death for Others and the Death of the Maccabean Martyrs.' In *Text and Testimony: Essays on New Testament and Apocryphal Literature in Honour of A.F.J.Klijn*, pp. 142–51. Ed. T. Baarda, et al. Kampen: J. H. Kok, 1988.

Jonge, M. de. *The Testaments of the Twelve Patriarchs: A Critical Edition of the Greek Text.* PVTG 1. Leiden: E. J. Brill, 1978.

Käsemann, Ernst. 'Die Heilsbedeutung des Todes Jesu bei Paulus.' In *Paulinische Perspektiven*, pp. 61–107. Tübingen: J. C. B. Mohr (Paul Siebeck),1969.

Käsemann, Ernst. 'Gottesgerechtigkeit bei Paulus.' In *Exegetische Versuche und Besinnungen*[2], 2:181–193. Göttingen: Vandenhoeck & Ruprecht, 1965.

Käsemann, Ernst. 'Paulus und Israel.' In *Exegetische Versuche und Besinnungen*[2], 2:194–197. Göttingen: Vandenhoeck& Ruprecht, 1965.

Käsemann, Ernst. 'Rechtfertigung und Heilsgeschichte im Römerbrief.' In *Paulinische Perspektiven*, pp. 108–139.Tübingen:J. C. B. Mohr (Paul Siebeck), 1969.

Käsemann, Ernst. *An die Römer*[3]. HNT 8a. Tübingen, J. C. B. Mohr (Paul Siebeck), 1974.

Kautsch, E. *Gesenius' Hebrew Grammar.* Trans. and rev. A. E. Cowley. Oxford: Clarendon, 1980.

Kaye, B. N. '"To the Romans and Others" Revisited.' *NovT* 18 (1976):33–77.

Kennedy, George A. *New Testament Interpretation through Rhetorical Criticism.* Chapel Hill: University of North Carolina Press, 1984.

Kertelge, Karl. 'δικαιοσύνη, δικαιόω.' In *Exegetisches Wörterbuch zum Neuen Testament*, 1:784–807. Ed. H. Balz and G. Schneider. Stuttgart: W. Kohlhammer, 1980.

Kertelge, Karl. *Rechtfertigung bei Paulus: Studien zur Struktur und zum Bedeutungsgehalt des paulinischen Rechtfertigungsbegriffs.* Münster: Aschendorff, 1967.

Kim, Seyoon. *The Origin of Paul's Gospel.* Grand Rapids: Eerdmans, 1982.

Kittel, G. 'Die Psalmen Salomos.' In *Die Apokryphen und Pseudepigraphen des Alten Testaments*, 2:127–148. Ed. E. Kautzsch. Tübingen: J. C. B. Mohr (Paul Siebeck), 1900.

Klein, Günter. 'Paul's Purpose in Writing the Epistle to the Romans.' In *The Romans Debate*, pp. 32–49. Ed. Karl P. Donfried. Minneapolis: Augsburg, 1977.

Klein, Günter. 'Righteousness in the NT.' In *Interpreter's Dictionary of the Bible*, pp. 750–752. Supplement. Nashville: Abingdon, 1975.

Klinzing, Georg. *Die Umdeutung des Kultus in der Qumrangemeinde und im Neuen Testament.* SUNT 7. Göttingen: Vandenhoeck & Ruprecht, 1971.

Knibb, Michael A. *The Qumran Community.* CCWJCW 2. Cambridge: Cambridge University Press, 1987.

Knox, John. 'A Note on the Text of Romans.' *NTS* 2 (1955–56):191.

Koch, Klaus. 'Die drei Gerechtigkeiten: Die Umformung einer hebräischen Idee im aramäischen Denken nach dem Jesajatargum.' In *Rechtfertigung: Festschrift für Ernst Käsemann zum 70. Geburtstag*, pp. 245–267. Ed. Johannes Friedrich, Wolfgang Pöhlmann, and Peter Stuhlmacher. Tübingen: J. C. B. Mohr (Paul Siebeck), 1976.

Koch, Klaus. 'צדק.' In *Theologisches Handwörterbuch zum Alten Testament*, 2:507–530. Ed. Ernst Jenni and Claus Westermann. München: Chr. Kaiser, 1976.

Koester, H. 'The Purpose of the Polemic of a Pauline Fragment (Phil 3).' *NTS* 8 (1962):317–332.

Kraftchick, Steven. 'A Response to "Paul's Theology: Whence and Whither?"' Unpublished paper presented to the Pauline Theology Group at the Society of Biblical Literature Annual Meeting 1989.

Krentz, Edgar. 'Tracking the Elusive Center: On Integrating Paul's Theology.' Unpublished paper presented at the Society of Biblical Literature Annual Meeting 1990.

Kuhn, Heinz Wolfgang. 'Die Kreuzesstrafe während der frühen Kaiserzeit: Ihre

Wirklichkeit und Wertung in der Umwelt des Urchristentums.' In *Aufstieg und niedergang der römischen Welt*. 25.1, pp. 648–793. Ed. H. Temporini and W. Haase. Berlin: de Gruyter, 1982.

Kuhn, Heinz Wolfgang. 'Jesus als Gekreuzigter in der frühchristlichen Verkündigung bis zur Mitte des 2. Jahrhunderts.' *ZThK* 72 (1975):1–46.

Kümmel W. G. 'Die 'konsequente Eschatologie' Albert Schweitzers im Urteil der Zeitgenossen.' In *Heilsgeschehen und Geschichte*, 1:328–339. MTS 3. Ed. E. Grässer, O. Merk, A. Fritz. Marburg: N. G. Elwert, 1965.

Kümmel, W. G. 'Πάρεσις und ἔνδειξις: Ein Beitrag zum Verständnis der paulinischen Rechtfertigungslehre.' In *Heilsgeschehen und Geschichte*, pp. 260–270. MTS 3. Marburg: N. G. Elwert, 1965.

Kümmel, W. G. 'Rudolf Bultmann als Paulusforscher.' In *Rudolf Bultmanns Werk und Wirkung*, pp. 174–193. Ed. B. Jaspert. Darmstadt: Wissenschaftlichebuchgesellschaft, 1984.

Kümmel, W. G. *Introduction to the New Testament*. Trans. H. C. Kee. Nashville: Abingdon, 1975.

Kümmel, W. G. *Römer 7 und die Bekehrung des Paulus*. Leipzig: J. G. Hinrichs'sche Buchhandlung, 1929. Reprint ed., *Römer 7 und das Bild des Menschen im Neuen Testament*. München: Chr. Kaiser, 1974.

Kümmel, W. G. 'Albert Schweitzer als Paulusforscher.' In *Rechtfertigung: Festschrift für Ernst Käsemann*, pp. 269–289. Ed. J. Friedrich, W. Pöhlmann, P. Stuhlmacher. Tübingen: J. C. B. Mohr (Paul Siebeck), 1976.

Kümmel, W. G. 'Die Probleme von Römer 9–11 in der gegenwärtigen Forschungslage.' In *Heilsgeschehen und Geschichte*, pp. 245–260. MTS 16. Ed. E. Grässer and O. Merk. Marburg: N. G. Elwert, 1978.

Kümmel, W. G. *Das Neue Testament: Geschichte der Erforschung seiner Probleme*. Freiburg/München: Karl Alber, 1958.

Kuss, Otto. *Paulus: die Rolle des Apostels in der theologischen Entwicklung der Urkirche*. Auslegung und Verkündigung 3. Regensburg: Friedrich Pustet, 1971.

Lampe, Peter. 'Zur Textgeschichte des Römerbriefes.' *NovT* 27 (1985):273–277.

Lang. 'כפר' In *Theologisches Wörterbuch zum Alten Testament*, 4:303–318. Ed. G. Botterweck, H. Ringgren, H. J. Fabry. Stuttgart: Kohlhammer, 1984.

LaPiana, George. 'Foreign Groups in Rome During the First Centuries of the Empire.' *HTR* 20 (1927):183–403.

Larsson, Edvin. 'Die Hellenisten und die Urgemeinde.' *NTS* 33 (1987):205–225.

Leaney, A. R. C. *The Rule of Qumran and Its Meaning*. London: SCM, 1966.

Leon, Harry J. *The Jews of Ancient Rome*. Philadelphia: Jewish Publication Society of America, 1960.

Lichtenberger, Hermann. 'Atonement and Sacrifice in the Qumran Community.' In *Approaches to Ancient Judaism: Volume II*, pp. 159–171. BJS 9. Ed. W. S. Green. Chico, Ca: Scholars, 1980.

Lichtenberger, Hermann. *Studien zum Menschenbild in Texten der Qumrangemeinde*. SUNT 15. Göttingen: Vandenhoeck & Ruprecht, 1980.

Liddell, H.G., Scott, R., and Jones, H. S. *A Greek-English Lexicon*[9]. Oxford: Oxford University Press, 1968.

Lohse, Eduard. 'Gerechtigkeit Gottes in der paulinischen Theologie.' In *Die Einheit des Neuen Testaments: Exegetische Studien zur Theologie des Neuen Testaments*, pp. 209–227. Göttingen: Vandenhoeck & Ruprecht, 1973.

Lohse, Eduard. *Märtyrer und Gottesknecht: Untersuchungen zur urchristlichen Verkündigung vom Sühnetod Jesu Christi*. FRLANT 64 Göttingen: Vandenhoeck & Ruprecht, 1955.

Longenecker, Bruce W. *Eschatology and the Covenant: A Comparison of 4 Ezra and Romans 1–11.* JSNTSup 57. Sheffield: JSOT Press, 1991.

Longenecker, Richard N. *Galatians.* WBC 41. Dallas, Tx: Word, 1990.

Longenecker, R. N. *Paul Apostle of Liberty.* New York: Harper & Row, 1964.

Luck, Ulrich. 'Die Bekehrung des Paulus und das Paulinische Evangelium.' *ZNW* 76 (1985):187–208.

Lüdemann, Gerd. *Paulus der Heidenapostel: Band I, Studien zur Chronologie.* FRLANT123. Göttingen: Vandenhoeck & Ruprecht, 1980.

Lüdemann, Gerd. *Paulus und das Judentum.* Theologische Existenz heute 215. München: Chr. Kaiser, 1983.

Lührmann, Dieter. 'Paul and the Pharisaic Tradition.' *JSNT* 36 (1989):75–94.

Luther, Martin. *Vorlesung über den Römerbrief 1515/1516.* 2 vols. Weimar: Hermann Böhlaus, 1960.

Lyons, George. *Pauline Autobiography: Toward a New Understanding.* SBLDS 73. Atlanta, GA: Scholars Press, 1985.

Maier, Gerhard. *Mensch und freier Wille: Nach den jüdischen Religionsparteien zwischen Ben Sira und Paulus.* WUNT 12. Tübingen: J. C. B. Mohr (Paul Siebeck), 1971.

Manson, T. W. 'St. Paul's Letter to the Romans—and Others.' In *The Romans Debate*, pp. 116. Ed. K. P. Donfried. Minneapolis: Augsburg, 1977.

Martin, Ralph P. *Reconciliation: A Study of Paul's Theology.* Atlanta: John Knox, 1980.

Martyn, J. Louis. 'Apocalyptic Antinomies in Paul's Letter to the Galatians.' *NTS* 31 (1985):410–424.

Marx, A. 'Y-a-t-il une prédestination Qumrân?' *RevQ* 6 (1967-9):163–181.

Marxsen, Willi. *Einleitung in das Neue Testament⁴.* Gütersloh: Gerd Mohn, 1978.

McGrath, Alister. *Iustitia Dei: A History of the Christian Doctrine of Justification.* 2 vols. Cambridge: Cambridge University Press, 1986.

McKnight, Scot. *A Light Among the Gentiles: Jewish Missionary Activity in the Second Temple Period.* Minneapolis: Fortress, 1991.

Mearns, Chris. 'The Identity of Paul's Opponents at Philippi.' *NTS* 33 (1987):194–204.

Meeks, Wayne. 'Toward a Social Description of Pauline Christianity.' In *Approaches to Ancient Judaism²*, pp. 27–41. Ed. William S. Green. Chico, CA: Scholars Press, 1980.

Meeks, Wayne. *The First Urban Christians: The Social World of the Apostle Paul.* New Haven: Yale University Press, 1983.

Menoud, Philippe. 'Le sens du verbe πορθεῖν.' In *Apophoreta: Festschrift für Ernst Haenchen*, pp. 178–186. BZNW 30. Ed. W. Eltester and F. H. Kettler. Berlin: Töpelmann, 1964.

Menoud, Philippe. 'Revelation and Tradition: the Influence of Paul's Conversion on His Theology.' *Int* 7 (1953):131–141.

Merrill, E. H. *Qumran and Predestination: A Theological Study of the Thanksgiving Hymns.* STDJ 8. Leiden: Brill, 1975.

Meyer, Rudolf. 'σάρξ.' In *Theologisches Wörterbuch zum Neuen Testament*, 7:109–118. Ed. G. Kittel and G. Friedrich. Stuttgart: Kohlhammer, 1964.

Minear, P. S. *The Obedience of Faith: The Purposes of Paul in the Epistle to the Romans.* SBT 19. London: SCM, 1971.

Montefiore C. G. *Judaism and St. Paul: Two Essays.* London: M. Goschen, 1914. Reprint ed., New York: Arno Press, 1973.

Moo, Douglas J. '"Law", "Works of the Law," and Legalism in Paul.' *WTJ* 45 (1983):73–100.

Moo, Douglas J. 'Israel and Paul in Rom 7.7–12.' *NTS* 32 (1986):122–135.

Moore, G. F. 'Christian Writers on Judaism.' *HTR* 14 (1921):197–254.
Munck, Johannes. *Paul and the Salvation of Mankind*. Richmond, Virginia: John Knox, 1959.
Murphy O'Connor, J. 'La Genèse Littéraire de la Règle de la Communauté.' *RB* 76(1969):528–549.
Neudorfer, Heinz-Werner. *Der Stephanuskreis in der Forschungsgeschichte seit F. C. Baur*. Giessen/Basel: Brunnen,1983.
Neugebauer, Fritz. 'Die hermeneutischen Voraussetzungen Rudolf Bultmanns in ihrem Verhältnis zur Paulinischen Theologie.' *KuD* 5 (1959):289–305.
Neusner, Jacob. 'The Use of the Later Rabbinic Evidence for the Study of Paul.' In *Approaches to Ancient Judaism*[2], pp. 43–59. Ed. William S. Green. Chico, CA: Scholars Press, 1980.
Neusner, Jacob. *The Idea of Purity in Ancient Judaism*. SJLA 1. Leiden: Brill, 1973.
Newton, Michael. *The Concept of Purity at Qumran and in the Letters of Paul*. SNTSMS 53. Cambridge: Cambridge University Press, 1985.
Nickelsburg, George W. *Jewish Literature Between the Bible and the Mishna*. Philadelphia: Fortress, 1981.
O'Dell, Jerry. 'The Religious Background of the Psalms of Solomon.' *RevQ* 3 (196162):241–257.
Oepke, Albrecht. 'Probleme der Vorchristlichen Zeit des Paulus.' In *Das Paulusbild in der neueren deutschen Forschung*, pp. 410–446. WdF 24. Ed. K. H. Rengstorf. Darmstadt: Wissenschaftliche Buchgesellschaft, 1982.
Ollrog, Wolf-Henning. 'Die Abfassungsverhältnisse von Rom 16.' In *Kirche: Festschrift für Günther Bornkamm zum 75. Geburtstag*, pp. 221–244. Ed. D. Lührmann and Georg Strecker. Tübingen: J. C. B. Mohr (Paul Siebeck), 1980.
Olson, Stanley. 'Pauline Expressions of Confidence in His Addressees.' *CBQ* 47 (1985):282–295.
Osten-Sacken, Peter, von der. *Gott und Belial: traditionsgeschichtliche Untersuchungen zum Dualismus in den Texten aus Qumran*. SUNT 6. Göttingen: Vandenhoeck & Ruprecht, 1969.
Packer, J. I. 'The 'Wretched Man' in Romans 7.' In *Studia Evangelica II*. TU 87, pp. 621–627. Ed. F. L. Cross. Berlin: Akademie, 1964.
Pannenberg, Wolfhart. *Grundzüge der Christologie*. Gütersloh: Gerd Mohn, 1964.
Paschen, Wilfried. *Rein und Unrein: Untersuchung zur biblischen Wortgeschichte*. SANT 24. München: Kösel, 1970.
Patte, Daniel. *Paul's Faith and the Power of the Gospel: A Structural Introduction to the Pauline Letters*. Philadelphia: Fortress, 1983.
Piper, John. *The Justification of God: An Exegetical and Theological Study of Romans 9:1–23*. Grand Rapids: Baker, 1983.
Plevnik, Joseph. 'The Center of Pauline Theology.' *CBQ* 51 (1989):461–478.
Porter, Frank C. 'Judaism in New Testament Times.' *Journal of Religion* 8(1928):30–62.
Porter, Stanley E. *Verbal Aspect in the Greek of the New Testament, with Reference to Tense and Mood*. Studies in Biblical Greek 1. New York: Peter Lang, 1989.
Porton, Gary G. 'Diversity in Postbiblical Judaism.' In *Early Judaism and Its Modern Interpreters*, pp. 57–80. Ed. R. Kraft and G. Nickelsburg. Atlanta: Scholars Press, 1986.
Pouilly, J. *La Règle de la Communaté de Qumrân: Son Evolution Littéraire*. CahRB 17 Paris: Gabalde et Cie, 1976.
Preisker, H. 'Das historische Problem des Römerbriefes.' *Wissenschaftliche Zeits-*

chrift der Friedrich Schiller Universität Jena 1 (1952/3):25–30.

Przybylski, B. *Righteousness in Matthew and His World of Thought*. SNTSMS 41. Cambridge: Cambridge University Press, 1980.

Qimron, Elisha. *The Hebrew of the Dead Sea Scrolls*. HSS 29. Atlanta: Scholars Press, 1986.

Qimron, Elisha and Strugnell, John. 'An Unpublished Halakhic Letter from Qumran.' *IEJ* 4 (1985):9–12.

Räisänen, Heikki. 'Legalism and Salvation by the Law.' In *The Torah and Christ: Essays in German and English on the Problem of the Law in Early Christianity*, pp. 25–54. Publications of the Finnish Exegetical Society 45. Helsinki: Finnish Exegetical Society, 1986.

Räisänen, Heikki. 'Paul's Call Experience and His Later View of the Law.' In *The Torah and Christ: Essays in German and English on the Problem of the Law in Early Christianity*, pp. 55–92. Publications of the Finnish Exegetical Society 45. Helsinki: Finnish Exegetical Society, 1986.

Räisänen, Heikki. 'Paul's Conversion and the Development of his View of the Law.' *NTS* 33 (1987):404–419.

Räisänen, Heikki. *Paul and the Law*. Philadelphia: Fortress, 1986.

Ramsay, A. M. 'The Speed of the Roman Imperial Post.' *Journal of Roman Studies* 15 (1925):60–74.

Reumann, John. *Righteousness in the New Testament*. Philadelphia: Fortress, 1982.

Ridderbos, Hermann. 'The Earliest Confession of the Atonement in Paul.' In *Reconciliation and Hope*, pp. 76–89. Ed. Robert Banks. Grand Rapids: Eerdmans, 1974.

Ridderbos, Hermann. *Paul: An Outline of His Theology*. Trans. John R. deWitt. Grand Rapids: Eerdmans, 1975.

Riesenfeld, H. 'ὑπέρ.' In *Theologisches Wörterbuch zum Neuen Testament*, 8:510–516. Ed. G. Kittel and G. Friedrich. Stuttgart: Kohlhammer, 1969.

Ringgren, H. *The Faith of Qumran*. Trans. E. Sander. Philadelphia: Fortress, 1963.

Ritschl, Albrecht. *Die christliche Lehre von der Rechtfertigung und Versöhnung*[4]. 2 vols. Bonn: A. Marcus und E. Weber, 1900.

Ryle, H. E. and James, M. R. Ψαλμοὶ Σολομῶντος *Psalms of the Pharisees, Commonly Called the Psalms of Solomon*. Cambridge: Cambridge University Press, 1891.

Safrai, S. and Stern, M., eds. *The Jewish People in the First Century*. 2 vols. CRINT 1. Philadelphia: Fortress, 1976.

Sampley, J. Paul. 'Overcoming Traditional Methods by Synthesizing the Theology of Individual Letters.' In *Society of Biblical Literature 1986 Seminar Papers*, pp. 603–613. Ed. Kent Harold Richards. Atlanta, Ga., Scholars Press, 1986.

Sanders, E. P. 'Jesus, Paul, and Judaism.' In *Aufstieg und niedergang der römischen Welt*. 25.1, pp. 390–450. Ed. W.Haase. Berlin: de Gruyter, 1982.

Sanders, E. P. 'Puzzling Out Rabbinic Judaism.' In *Approaches to Ancient Judaism* 2, pp. 65–79. Ed. William S. Green. Chico, CA: Scholars Press, 1980.

Sanders, E. P. 'On the Question of Fulfilling the Law in Paul and Rabbinic Judaism.' In *Donum Genticilium: New Testament Studies in Honour of David Daube*, pp. 103–126. Ed. E. Bammel, et al. Oxford: Clarendon, 1978.

Sanders, E. P. 'Patterns of Religion in Paul and Rabbinic Judaism: A Holistic Method of Comparison.' *HTR* 66 (1973):455–478.

Sanders, E. P. 'Paul's Attitude Toward the Jewish People.' *USQR* 33 (1978):175–187.

Sanders, E. P. 'The Covenant as a Soteriological Category and the Nature of Salvation in Palestinian and Hellenistic Judaism.' In *Jews, Greeks, and Chris-*

tians: Religious Cultures in Late Antiquity, pp. 11–44. Ed. Robert Hamerton Kelly and Robin Scroggs. Leiden: E. J. Brill, 1976.

Sanders, E. P. *Paul and Palestinian Judaism: A Comparison of Patterns of Religion.* Philadelphia: Fortress, 1977.

Sanders, E. P. *Paul, the Law, and the Jewish People.* Philadelphia: Fortress, 1983.

Sanders, Jack T. 'Paul's "Autobiographical" Statements in Galatians 1–2.' *JBL* 85 (1966):335–343.

Schäfer, Peter. 'Die Tora der messianischen Zeit.' In *Studien zur Geschichte und Theologie des rabbinischen Judentums*, pp. 198–213. AGJU 15. Leiden: E. J. Brill, 1978.

Schenk, Wolfgang. 'Der Philipperbrief in der neueren Forschung.' In *Aufstieg und niedergang der römischen Welt*. 25.4, pp. 3280–3313. Ed. Wolfgang Haase. Berlin: de Gruyter, 1987.

Schenk, Wolfgang. *Die Philipperbriefe des Paulus.* Stuttgart: W. Kohlhammer, 1984.

Schiffmann, Lawrence H. *Sectarian Law in the Dead Sea Scrolls Courts, Testimony and the Penal Code.* BJS 33. Chico, Ca.: Scholars Press, 1983.

Schlatter, Adolf. *Gottes Gerechtigkeit: Ein Kommentar zum Römerbrief.* Stuttgart: Calwer, 1935.

Schlier, Heinrich. *Der Brief an die Galater⁴.* KEK 7. Göttingen: Vandenhoeck & Ruprecht, 1965.

Schlier, Heinrich. *Der Römerbrief.* HTKNT 6. Freiburg: Herder, 1977.

Schmithals, Walter. 'Die Irrlehrer von Rm 16:17–20.' *ST* 13 (1959):51–69.

Schmithals, Walter. *Der Römerbrief als historisches Problem.* Gütersloh, Gerd Mohn, 1975.

Schnelle, Udo. *Gerechtigkeit und Christusgegenwart: Vorpaulinische und paulinische Tauftheologie.* GTA 24. Göttingen, Vandenhoeck & Ruprecht, 1983.

Schnider, Franz and Stenger, Werner. *Studien zum neutestamentlichen Briefformular.* NTTS 11. Leiden: Brill, 1987.

Schoeps, Hans-Joachim. *Paulus: Die Theologie des Apostels im Lichte der jüdischen Religionsgeschichte.* Tübingen: J. C. B.Mohr (Paul Siebeck), 1959.

Schrage, Wolfgang. "Ekklesia' und 'Synagoge': Zum Ursprung des urchristlichen Kirchenbegriffs.' *ZThK* 60 (1963):178–202.

Schrage, Wolfgang. *Ethik des Neuen Testaments.* Grundrisse zum Neuen Testament 4. Göttingen: Vandenhoeck & Ruprecht, 1982.

Schulz, Siegfried. 'Zur Rechtfertigung aus Gnaden in Qumran und bei Paulus.' *ZThK* 56 (1959):155–185.

Schüpphaus, Joachim. *Die Psalmen Salomos: Ein Zeugnis Jerusalemer Theologie und Frömmigkeit in der Mitte des Vorchristlichen Jahrhunderts.* ALGHJ 7. Leiden: Brill, 1977.

Schürer, Emil. *The History of the Jewish People in the Age of Jesus Christ.* Rev. and ed. Geza Vermes, Fergus Millar, Matthew Black. 3 vols. Edinburgh: T.&T. Clark, 1979–1986.

Schweitzer, Albert. *Die Mystik des Apostels Paulus.* Tübingen, J. C. B. Mohr (Paul Siebeck), 1930.

Schweitzer, Albert. *Geschichte der Paulinischen Forschung von der Reformation bis auf die Gegenwart.* Tübingen: J. C. B. Mohr (Paul Siebeck), 1911.

Segal, Alan F. *Paul the Convert: The Apostolate and Apostasy of Saul the Pharisee.* New Haven: Yale University Press, 1990.

Seifrid, Mark A. 'Paul's Approach to the Old Testament in Rom 10:68.' *TrinJ* 6 (1985):3–37.

Silva, Moisés. *Biblical Words and Their Meanings: An Introduction to Lexical Semantics.* GrandRapids: Zondervan, 1983.

Sjöberg, Erik. *Gott und die Sünder im Palästinischen Judentum.* BWANT 49. Stuttgart: W. Kohlhammer,1938.

Slingerland, H. Dixon. *The Testaments of the Twelve Patriarchs: A Critical History of Research.* SBLMS 21 Missoula, Mont.: Scholars Press, 1977.

Smyth, H. W. *Greek Grammar.* rev. G. M. Messing. Cambridge, Mass.: Harvard University Press, 1956.

Stählin, Gustav. 'σκάνδαλον.' In *Theologisches Wörterbuch zum Neuen Testament,* 7:338–358. Ed. G. Kittel and G. Friedrich. Stuttgart: Kohlhammer, 1964.

Stendahl, Krister. 'The Apostle Paul and the Introspective Conscience of the West.' *HTR* 56 (1963):199–215.

Stendahl, Krister. *Paul Among Jews and Gentiles.* Philadelphia: Fortress, 1976.

Strecker, Georg. 'Befreiung und Rechtfertigung: Zur Stellung der Rechtfertigungslehre in der Theologie des Paulus.' In *Rechtfertigung: Festschrift für Ernst Käsemann,* pp. 479–508. Ed. J. Friedrich, W. Pöhlmann, P. Stuhlmacher. Tübingen: J. C. B. Mohr (Paul Siebeck),1976.

Strecker, Georg. 'Das Evangelium Jesu Christi.' In *Eschaton und Historie,* pp. 183–228. Göttingen: Vandenhoeck & Ruprecht, 1979.

Strecker, Georg. 'εὐαγγέλιον.' In *Exegetisches Wörterbuch zum Neuen Testament,* 2:176–186. Ed. Horst Balz and Gerhard Schneider. Stuttgart: W. Kohlhammer, 1981.

Strecker, Georg. 'Indicative and Imperative According to Paul.' *AusBR* 35 (1987):60–72.

Stuhlmacher, Peter. '"Das Ende des Gesetzes": Über Ursprung und Ansatz der paulinischen Theologie.' *ZThK* 67 (1970):14–39.

Stuhlmacher, Peter. 'Achtzehnthesen Thesen zur paulinischen Kreuzestheologie.' In *Rechtfertigung: Festschrift für Ernst Käsemann,* pp. 509–525. Ed. J.Friedrich, W. Pöhlmann, and P. Stuhlmacher. Tübingen: J. C. B. Mohr (Paul Siebeck), 1976.

Stuhlmacher, Peter. 'Das paulinische Evangelium.' In *Das Evangelium und die Evangelien,* pp. 157–182. WUNT 28. Ed. Peter Stuhlmacher. Tübingen: J. C. B. Mohr (Paul Siebeck), 1983.

Stuhlmacher, Peter. 'Der Abfassungszweck des Römerbriefes.' *ZNW* 77 (1986):180–193.

Stuhlmacher, Peter. 'Jesu Auferweckung und die Gerechtigkeitsanschauung der vorpaulinischen Missionsgemeinden.' In *Versöhnung, Gesetz, und Gerechtigkeit,* pp. 66–86. Göttingen: Vandenhoeck & Ruprecht, 1981.

Stuhlmacher, Peter. 'Zur neueren Exegese von Röm 3.24–26.' In *Jesus und Paulus,* pp. 315–333. Ed. E. Earle Ellis and Erich Gräßer. Göttingen: Vandenhoeck & Ruprecht, 1975.

Stuhlmacher, Peter. *Das paulinische Evangelium.* Göttingen: Vandenhoeck & Ruprecht, 1968.

Stuhlmacher, Peter. *Gerechtigkeit Gottes bei Paulus.* FRLANT 87 Göttingen: Vandenhoeck & Ruprecht, 1965.

Suggs, M. J. '"The Word is Near You': Romans 10:6–10 within the Purpose of the Letter.' In *Christian History and Interpretation,* pp. 289–313. Ed. W. R. Farmer, C. F. D. Moule, and R. R. Niebuhr. Cambridge: Cambridge University Press, 1967.

Suhl, Alfred. 'Der Galaterbrief—Situation und Argumentation.' In *Aufstieg und niedergang der römischen Welte.* 25.4, pp. 3067–3134. Ed. H. Temporini and W. Haase. Berlin: de Gruyter, 1987.

Theissen, Gerd. *Psychologische Aspekte paulinischer Theologie.* Göttingen: Vandenhoeck & Ruprecht,1983.

Thielman, Frank. *From Plight to Solution: A Jewish Framework for Understanding Paul's View of the Law in Galatians and Romans.* NovTSup 61. Leiden: Brill, 1989.

Thompson, Alden. *Responsibility for Evil in the Theodicy of IV Ezra.* SBLDS 29. Missoula Mont.: Scholars Press, 1977.

Thyen, Hartwig. *Studien zur Sündenvergebung im Neuen Testament und seinen alttestamentlichen und jüdischen Voraussetzungen.* FRLANT 96. Göttingen: Vandenhoeck & Ruprecht, 1970.

Tomson, Peter J. *Paul and the Jewish Law: Halakha in the Letters of the Apostle to the Gentiles.* CRINT 3.1. Minneapolis: Fortress, 1990.

Trafton, Joseph L. 'The Psalms of Solomon: New Light from the Syriac Version?' *JBL* 105 (1986):227–237.

Trafton, Joseph L. *The Syriac Version of the Psalms of Solomon.* SBLSCS 11. Atlanta, GA: Scholars Press, 1985.

Tuckett, C. M. 'Deuteronomy 21.23 and Paul's Conversion.' In *L'Apôtre Paul: Personalité, Style, et Conception du Ministère,* pp. 345–350. BETL 73. Ed. A. Vanhoye. Leuven: Leuven University, 1986.

Viteau, J. *Les Psaumes de Salomon.* Documents pour l'etude de la Bible 4. Paris: Letouzey et Ané, 1911.

Watson, Francis. *Paul, Judaism and the Gentiles: A Sociological Approach.* Cambridge: Cambridge University Press, 1986.

Weder, Hans. 'Gesetz und Sünde: Gedanken zu einem Qualitativen Sprung im Denken des Paulus.' *NTS* 31 (1985):357–376.

Wedderburn, A. J. M. *The Reasons for Romans.* Edinburgh: T.&T. Clark, 1988.

Weizsäcker, Carl. *Das apostolische Zeitalter der Christlichen Kirche³.* Tübingen: J. C. B. Mohr (Paul Siebeck), 1902.

Wellhausen, J. *Die Pharisäer und die Sadducäer: Eine Untersuchung zur inneren jüdischen Geschichte.* Greifswald: Bamberg, 1874.

Wendland, Hans Dietrich. *Die Mitte der paulinischen Botschaft: Die Rechtfertigungslehre des Paulus im Zusammenhange seiner Theologie.* Göttingen: Vandenhoeck & Ruprecht, 1935.

Wengst, Klaus. *Christologische Formeln und Lieder des Urchristentums.* SNT 7. Gütersloh: Gerd Mohn, 1972.

Wernberg-Møller, P. *The Manual of Discipline.* STDJ 1. Leiden: Brill, 1957.

Wernle, Paul. *Der Christ und die Sünde.* Freiburg i.B./Leipzig: J. C. B. Mohr (Paul Siebeck), 1897.

Westerholm, Stephen. *Israel's Law and the Church's Faith: Paul and His Recent Interpreters.* Grand Rapids: Eerdmans, 1988.

Wiefel, Wolfgang. 'The Jewish Community in Ancient Rome and the Origins of Roman Christianity.' In *The Romans Debate,* pp. 100–119. Ed. Karl P. Donfried. Minneapolis: Augsburg, 1977.

Wilckens, Ulrich. 'Christologie und Anthropologie im Zusammenhang der paulinischen Rechtfertigungslehre.' *ZNW* 67 (1976):64–82.

Wilckens, Ulrich. 'Die Bekehrung des Paulus als religiongeschichtliches Problem.' In *Rechtfertigung als Freiheit: Paulusstudien,* pp. 11–32. Neukirchen: Neukirchener, 1974.

Wilckens, Ulrich. 'Über Abfassungszweck und Aufbau des Römerbriefs.' In *Rechtfertigung als Freiheit,* pp. 110–170. Neukirchen/Vluyn: Neukirchner, 1974.

Wilckens, Ulrich. 'Was heißt bei Paulus: "Aus Werken des Gesetzes wird kein Mensch gerecht"?' In *Evangelisch-Katholischer Kommentar zum Neuen Testament: Vorarbeiten,* 1:51–77. Neukirchen: Neukirchener, 1969.

Wilckens, Ulrich. *Der Brief an die Römer.* 3 vols. EKKNTV I. Zürich: Benziger, 1980.

Wilcox, Max. "Upon the Tree'—Deut 21:22–23 in the New Testament.' *JBL* 96 (1977):85–99.

Williams, Sam K. *Jesus' Death as a Saving Event: The Background and Origin of a Concept.* HDR 2. Missoula Mont.: Scholars Press, 1975.

Williams, Sam K. 'The 'Righteousness of God' in Romans.' *JBL* 99 (1980):241–290.

Wood, H. G. 'The Conversion of St Paul: its Nature. Antecedents and Consequences.' *NTS* 4(1955):276–282.

Wrede, William. 'Paulus.' In *Das Paulusbild in der neueren deutschen Forschung*, pp. 1–97. WdF 24. Ed. K. H. Rengstorf. Darmstadt: Wissenschaftliche Buchgesellschaft, 1982.

Wrede, William. 'The Task and Methods of "New Testament Theology."' In *The Nature of New Testament Theology.* SBT Second Series 25. Ed. and trans. Robert Morgan. Naperville, IL: Allenson, 1973.

Wright, R. 'The Psalms of Solomon, the Pharisees, and the Essenes.' In *The 1972 Proceedings of the International Organization for Septuagint and Cognate Studies*, pp. 136–147. SBLSCS 2. Ed. Robert A. Kraft. Los Angeles, CA: Scholars Press, 1972.

Wright, R. 'Psalms of Solomon.' In *The Old Testament Pseudepigrapha*, 2:639–670. Ed. J. H. Charlesworth. Garden City, NY: Doubleday, 1985.

Wuellner, Wilhelm. 'Paul's Rhetoric of Argumentation in Romans: An Alternative to the Donfried-Karris Debate Over Romans.' In *The Romans Debate*, pp. 152–174. Ed. Karl P. Donfried. Minneapolis: Augsburg, 1977.

Wuellner, Wilhelm. 'Where is Rhetorical Criticism Taking Us?' *CBQ* 49 (1987):448–463.

Yadin, Yigael. 'Pesher Nahum (4Q pNahum) Reconsidered.' *IEJ* 21 (1971):1–11.

Yadin, Yigael. *The Temple Scroll.* 3 vols. Jerusalem: Israel Exploration Society, 1983.

Zeller, Dieter. *Der Brief an die Römer.* RNT. Regensburg: Friedrich Pustet, 1985.

Zeller, Dieter. *Juden und Heiden in der Mission des Paulus.* FB 8. Stuttgart: Katholisches Bibelwerk, 1973.

Ziesler, J. A. *Pauline Christianity.* Oxford: Oxford University Press, 1983.

Ziesler, J. A. *The Meaning of Righteousness in Paul: A Linguistic and Theological Enquiry.* SNTSMS 20 Cambridge: Cambridge University Press, 1972.

INDEX OF AUTHORS

INDEX OF PASSAGES CITED
FROM ANCIENT LITERATURE

SUPPLEMENTS TO NOVUM TESTAMENTUM

ISSN 0167-9732

2. STROBEL, A. *Untersuchungen zum eschatologischen Verzögerungsproblem auf Grund der spätjüdische-urchristlichen Geschichte von Habakuk 2,2 ff.* 1961. ISBN 90 04 01582 5

6. *Neotestamentica et Patristica.* Eine Freundesgabe Herrn Professor Dr. Oscar Cullmann zu seinem 60. Geburtstag überreicht. 1962. ISBN 90 04 01586 8

8. DE MARCO, A.A. *The Tomb of Saint Peter.* A Representative and Annotated Bibliography of the Excavations. 1964. ISBN 90 04 01588 4

10. BORGEN, P. *Bread from Heaven.* An Exegetical Study of the Concept of Manna in the Gospel of John and the Writings of Philo. Photomech. Reprint of the first (1965) edition. 1981. ISBN 90 04 06419 2

13. MOORE, A.L. *The Parousia in the New Testament.* 1966. ISBN 90 04 01593 0

15. QUISPEL, G. *Makarius, das Thomasevangelium und das Lied von der Perle.* 1967. ISBN 90 04 01595 7

16. PFITZNER, V.C. *Paul and the Agon Motif.* 1967. ISBN 90 04 01596 5

17. BELLINZONI, A. *The Sayings of Jesus in the Writings of Justin Martyr.* 1967. ISBN 90 04 01597 3

18. GUNDRY, R.H. *The Use of the Old Testament in St. Matthew's Gospel.* With Special Reference to the Messianic Hope. Reprint of the first (1967) edition. 1975. ISBN 90 04 04278 4

19. SEVENSTER, J.N. *Do You Know Greek?* How Much Greek Could the First Jewish Christians Have Known? 1968. ISBN 90 04 03090 5

20. BUCHANAN, G.W. *The Consequences of the Covenant.* 1970. ISBN 90 04 01600 7

21. KLIJN, A.F.J. *A Survey of the Researches into the Western Text of the Gospels and Acts.* Part 2: 1949-1969. 1969. ISBN 90 04 01601 5

22. GABOURY, A. *La structure des Évangiles synoptiques.* La structure-type à l'origine des synoptiques. 1970. ISBN 90 04 01602 3

23. GASTON, L. *No Stone on Another.* Studies in the Significance of the Fall of Jerusalem in the Synoptic Gospels. 1970. ISBN 90 04 01603 1

24. *Studies in John.* Presented to Professor Dr. J.N. Sevenster on the Occasion of His Seventieth Birthday. 1970. ISBN 90 04 03091 3

25. STORY, C.I.K. *The Nature of Truth in 'The Gospel of Truth', and in the Writings of Justin Martyr.* A Study of the Pattern of Orthodoxy in the Middle of the Second Christian Century. 1970. ISBN 90 04 01605 8

26. GIBBS, J.G. *Creation and Redemption.* A Study in Pauline Theology. 1971. ISBN 90 04 01606 6

27. MUSSIES, G. *The Morphology of Koine Greek As Used in the Apocalypse of St. John.* A Study in Bilingualism. 1971. ISBN 90 04 02656 8

28. AUNE, D.E. *The Cultic Setting of Realized Eschatology in Early Christianity.* 1972. ISBN 90 04 03341 6

29. UNNIK, W.C. VAN. *Sparsa Collecta.* The Collected Essays of W.C. van Unnik Part 1. Evangelia, Paulina, Acta. 1973. ISBN 90 04 03660 1

30. UNNIK, W.C. VAN. *Sparsa Collecta.* The Collected Essays of W.C. van Unnik Part 2. I Peter, Canon, Corpus Hellenisticum, Generalia. 1980. ISBN 90 04 06261 0

31. UNNIK, W.C. VAN. *Sparsa Collecta.* The Collected Essays of W.C. van Unnik Part 3. Patristica, Gnostica, Liturgica. 1983. ISBN 90 04 06262 9

33. AUNE, D.E. (ed.) *Studies in New Testament and Early Christian Literature*. Essays in Honor of Allen P. Wikgren. 1972. ISBN 90 04 03504 4
34. HAGNER, D.A. *The Use of the Old and New Testaments in Clement of Rome*. 1973. ISBN 90 04 03636 9
35. GUNTHER, J.J. *St. Paul's Opponents and Their Background*. A Study of Apocalyptic and Jewish Sectarian Teachings. 1973. ISBN 90 04 03738 1
36. KLIJN, A.F.J. & G.J. REININK (eds.) *Patristic Evidence for Jewish-Christian Sects*. 1973. ISBN 90 04 03763 2
37. REILING, J. *Hermas and Christian Prophecy*. A Study of The Eleventh Mandate. 1973. ISBN 90 04 03771 3
38. DONFRIED, K.P. *The Setting of Second Clement in Early Christianity*. 1974. ISBN 90 04 03895 7
39. ROON, A. VAN. *The Authenticity of Ephesians*. 1974. ISBN 90 04 03971 6
40. KEMMLER, D.W. *Faith and Human Reason*. A Study of Paul's Method of Preaching as Illustrated by 1-2 Thessalonians and Acts 17, 2-4. 1975. ISBN 90 04 04209 1
42. PANCARO, S. *The Law in the Fourth Gospel*. The Torah and the Gospel, Moses and Jesus, Judaism and Christianity According to John. 1975. ISBN 90 04 04309 8
43. CLAVIER, H. *Les variétés de la pensée biblique et le problème de son unité*. Esquisse d'une théologie de la Bible sur les textes originaux et dans leur contexte historique. 1976. ISBN 90 04 04465 5
44. ELLIOTT, J.K.E. (ed.) *Studies in New Testament Language and Text*. Essays in Honour of George D. Kilpatrick on the Occasion of His Sixty-Fifth Birthday. 1976. ISBN 90 04 04386 1
45. PANAGOPOULOS, J. (ed.) *Prophetic Vocation in the New Testament and Today*. 1977. ISBN 90 04 04923 1
46. KLIJN, A.F.J. *Seth in Jewish, Christian and Gnostic Literature*. 1977. ISBN 90 04 05245 3
47. BAARDA, T., A.F.J. KLIJN & W.C. VAN UNNIK (eds.) *Miscellanea Neotestamentica*. I. Studia ad Novum Testamentum Praesertim Pertinentia a Sociis Sodalicii Batavi c.n. Studiosorum Novi Testamenti Conventus Anno MCMLXXVI Quintum Lustrum Feliciter Complentis Suscepta. 1978. ISBN 90 04 05685 8
48. BAARDA, T., A.F.J. KLIJN & W.C. VAN UNNIK (eds.) *Miscellanea Neotestamentica*. II. 1978. ISBN 90 04 05686 6
49. O'BRIEN, P.T. *Introductory Thanksgivings in the Letters of Paul*. 1977. ISBN 90 04 05265 8
50. BOUSSET, D.W. *Religionsgeschichtliche Studien*. Aufsätze zur Religionsgeschichte des hellenistischen Zeitalters. Hrsg. von A.F. Verheule. 1979. ISBN 90 04 05845 1
51. COOK, M.J. *Mark's Treatment of the Jewish Leaders*. 1978. ISBN 90 04 05785 4
52. GARLAND, D.E. *The Intention of Matthew 23*. 1979. ISBN 90 04 05912 1
53. MOXNES, H. *Theology in Conflict*. Studies in Paul's Understanding of God in Romans. 1980. ISBN 90 04 06140 1
55. MENKEN, M.J.J. *Numerical Litarary Techniques in John*. The Fourth Evangelist's Use of Numbers of Words and Syllables. 1985. ISBN 90 04 07427 9
56. SKARSAUNE, O. *The Proof From Prophecy*. A Study in Justin Martyr's Proof-Text Tradition: Text-type, Provenance, Theological Profile. 1987. ISBN 90 04 07468 6
59. WILKINS, M.J. *The Concept of Disciple in Matthew's Gospel, as Reflected in the Use of the Term "Mathetes"*. 1988. ISBN 90 04 08689 7
60. MILLER, E.L. *Salvation-History in the Prologue of John*. The Significance of John 1:3-4. 1989. ISBN 90 04 08692 7
61. THIELMAN, F. *From Plight to Solution*. A Jewish Framework for Understanding Paul's View of the Law in Galatians and Romans. 1989. ISBN 90 04 09176 9

64. STERLING, G.E. *Historiography and Self-Definition*. Josephos, Luke-Acts and Apologetic Historiography. 1992. ISBN 90 04 09501 2

65. BOTHA, J.E. *Jesus and the Samaritan Woman*. A Speech Act Reading of John 4:1-42. 1991. ISBN 90 04 09505 5

66. KUCK, D.W. *Judgment and Community Conflict*. Paul's Use of Apocalyptic Judgment Language in 1 Corinthians 3:5-4:5. 1992. ISBN 90 04 09510 1

67. SCHNEIDER, G. *Jesusüberlieferung und Christologie*. Neutestamentliche Aufsätze 1970-1990. 1992. ISBN 90 04 09555 1

68. SEIFRID, M.A. *Justification by Faith*. The Origin and Development of a Central Pauline Theme. 1992. ISBN 90 04 09521 7

69. NEWMAN, C.C. *Paul's Glory-Christology*. Tradition and Rhetoric. 1992. ISBN 90 04 09463 6